RISK AND RESILIENCE
IN CHILDHOOD

RISK AND RESILIENCE IN CHILDHOOD

AN ECOLOGICAL PERSPECTIVE

Mark W. Fraser, Editor

NASW PRESS

National Association of Social Workers
Washington, DC

Jay J. Cayner, ACSW, LISW, *President*
Josephine Nieves, MSW, PhD, *Executive Director*

Linda Beebe, *Executive Editor*
Nancy Winchester, *Director of Editorial Services*
Marcia D. Roman, *Production Editor*
Donna Daniels Verdier, *Copy Editor*
Patti Borthwick, Beth Gyorgy, *Proofreaders*
Bob Elwood, *Indexer*

First impression March 1997
Second impression February 1998

Library of Congress Cataloging-in-Publication Data
Risk and resilience in childhood: an ecological perspective / Mark W.
   Fraser, editor.
         p.   cm.
   Includes bibliographical references and index.
   ISBN 0-87101-274-X (alk. paper)
   1. Problem children—United States.   2.   Social work with children—
United States.   I.   Fraser, Mark W., 1946–
Hv741.R565   1997
362.74—dc21   96-6538
                                                                 CIP

Printed in the United States of America

CONTENTS

6

SCHOOL FAILURE: AN ECOLOGICAL–INTERACTIONAL–DEVELOPMENTAL PERSPECTIVE   95

Jack M. Richman and Gary L. Bowen

7

RISK AND PROTECTIVE FACTORS FOR ALCOHOL AND OTHER DRUG USE IN CHILDHOOD AND ADOLESCENCE   117

Jeffrey M. Jenson

8

RISK AND PROTECTIVE FACTORS IN THE DEVELOPMENT OF DELINQUENCY AND CONDUCT DISORDER   140

James Herbert Williams, Charles D. Ayers, and Michael W. Arthur

9

PREVENTING SEXUALLY TRANSMITTED INFECTIONS AMONG ADOLESCENTS   171

Kathleen A. Rounds

10

ADOLESCENT PREGNANCY: MULTISYSTEMIC RISK AND PROTECTIVE FACTORS   195

Cynthia Franklin, Jacqueline Corcoran, and Susan Ayers-Lopez

11

CHILDHOOD DEPRESSION: A RISK FACTOR PERSPECTIVE   220

M. Carlean Gilbert

12

PROMOTING THE DEVELOPMENT OF YOUNG CHILDREN WITH DISABILITIES   244

Irene Nathan Zipper and Rune J. Simeonsson

13

LIST OF TABLES
AND FIGURES

TABLES

FIGURES

ACKNOWLEDGMENTS

I am in debt to my many colleagues and friends who so greatly contributed to this book and who withstood with humor and grace my comments on preliminary manuscripts. Their dedication and scholarship have given our coverage of risk and resilience an unexpected breadth and depth. Maeda Galinsky, Kenan Professor at the School of Social Work, University of North Carolina, Chapel Hill, has been a constant source of inspiration and support. She assisted in editing manuscripts and cowrote the final chapter. Special thanks to her. Finally, very special thanks to Mary, who supports my propensity to hide out when I shouldn't, and to Alex and Katy, who keep me involved in the real world of bugs, fishing, and street chalk.

1

THE ECOLOGY OF CHILDHOOD: A MULTISYSTEMS PERSPECTIVE

Mark W. Fraser

I n spite of impressive improvements in public health, social services, and education during the 20th century, the social record of America is clouded by steep declines in the quality of life for children in the 1980s and 1990s. Beginning in the last quarter of the century, both the relative and official rates of childhood poverty climbed (Haveman & Wolfe, 1994). In big cities, in little towns, and in the open expanses of cattle, farm, and tribal lands, children are at increased risk in America. Between 1985 and 1993, the percentage of babies born weighing less than 5.5 pounds—an indicator of poor prenatal care and of developmental problems—rose 6 percent. During the same period, the violent death rate for teenagers increased 10 percent, the birth rate for teenagers increased 23 percent, and the violent crime arrest rate for juveniles increased 66 percent (Annie E. Casey Foundation, 1996).

Although these changes affect all children, they are particularly pronounced for children of color, who disproportionately bear the burden of poverty. Across the country, slightly more than one child in five now lives in poverty, but rates are far higher for African American, Hispanic, and American Indian children (Hernandez, 1993). The poverty rate for white children is approximately 15 percent. For African American children it is 54 percent, and for Latino children it is 44 percent (National Center for Children in Poverty, 1995). Moreover, close to two of three children in households in which the best-educated parent did not finish high school are poor. Similarly, some 58 percent of children in single-parent households—about 26 percent of all households with children—live below the poverty line (Larner & Collins, 1996).

For all poor children, the effects of poverty are both direct and indirect (Sherman, 1994). Poverty affects children directly by reducing the quality of food, shelter, health care, education, and transportation that a family can afford. Poor children live in less safe and more hostile physical environments. Poverty affects children indirectly by "bringing out the worst in parents who struggle to manage in often impossible circumstances" (Larner & Collins, 1996, p. 72). When they are exhausted from low-paying jobs and enervated by the sheer demands of coping with inadequate resources, parents simply find it harder to be consistent in discipline, to be responsive to children's needs, and to provide a range of socially and educationally stimulating experiences (Duncan, Brooks-Gunn, & Klebanov, 1994; Hart & Risley, 1995; Klebanov, Brooks-Gunn, & Duncan, 1994).

No one knows why the health and well-being of American children have changed so markedly. Some scholars argue that the U.S. labor market has changed. Not only have family farms ceased to exist, but, in what amounts to a second labor-related revolution in the 20th century, the smokestack industries—such as steel mills

where many former farmers and their children worked in the first half of the century—
have gone out of business. Low-paying service and high-paying technology-related
employment have come to characterize the U.S. labor market in the latter part of the
century. But high-technology jobs require higher education and so, for many displaced
workers and young adults trying to enter the labor force, service-related work has been
the only option. Work alienation and joblessness rose in the 1980s and 1990s, and real
wages for those who could find work stagnated. In fact, real wages for young adults and
poorly educated workers actually fell during this period (Haveman & Wolfe, 1994). In
1970, for example, a young male worker with a full-time job earned about $17.50 per
hour. In 1986, however, that same worker earned only $14.20 per hour, after adjustment
for inflation (Duncan, 1991). Thus, it could be said that earnings declined precisely for
the population of workers most likely to be having children. It was possible to work
and still be poor. Inadequate earnings, together with increased joblessness, produced a
lower quality of life for millions of American children.

But the labor market argument is complicated by significant changes in the
social landscape of America. Wage stagnation covaried with large increases in the divorce
rate and the percentage of single-parent households; more permissive norms regarding
sexual activity for men and women; declining public support of social, education, and
health programs; the growth of illicit drug markets in urban areas; and decreases in the
traditional authority of schools, religious organizations, and community agencies.
Whether the decline in the 1980s and 1990s in the status of children is attributable to
corrections in the labor market or to broader social and technological changes in society
is hotly debated. It is clear, however, that the ecology of childhood was dramatically
altered in the latter part of the 20th century.

An Ecological Perspective

Social workers and other professionals are confronted daily with the effects of these
changes. If anything, the work of social workers in child welfare agencies, hospitals,
mental health centers, neighborhood storefronts, residential treatment and correctional
facilities, schools, and youth service organizations has intensified. More children are
failing in school, getting in trouble with the courts, using illicit drugs, engaging in
unprotected sex, joining gangs, getting shot, and attempting and committing suicide.
More parents are at their wits' end. Voters are increasingly concerned about crime and
public safety. Frustrated employers challenge schools to produce graduates who have
more market-ready skills (see, for example, Slavin, Karweit, & Madden, 1988). And
legislators, leery of the costs of social and health services, demand evidence of
effectiveness. For health and human services workers, it is a pressure cooker.

How are we to respond? Without major social structural reforms that
significantly affect rates of poverty, there are few good answers. However, recent research
on risk and resilience in childhood offers important new guidance on the design and
delivery of social and health programs. Clearly, services can and must better address the
individual (both biological and psychological), family, neighborhood, and broader
contextual conditions that produce childhood problems. Two familiar perspectives—
ecological and systems theories—offer useful frameworks for understanding the risks
faced by children and their families. Coupled with these theories, the epidemiological

methods used in the field of public health provide a foundation both for developing more comprehensive case assessments and for designing more effective services. The purpose of this book is to describe this emerging perspective on risk and resilience.

DEFINITION OF RISK

Each chapter in the book employs the term "risk factor." By that, we mean any influence that increases the probability of onset, digression to a more serious state, or the maintenance of a problem condition (Coie et al., 1993). In the social and health sciences, risk factors are used to predict future outcomes, and they are usually expressed as probabilities. Of course, one can never predict with certainty, but the combination of several risk factors may lead to the conclusion that a child is at "high" risk for a certain outcome, such as alcohol abuse or mental illness. Conversely, the absence of risk factors may lead to the conclusion that a child is at "low" risk for a certain outcome. For exactly the same risk factor, the probability of the occurrence of a future problem may vary by the race or ethnicity, gender, and age of a child. The fact that we are beginning to understand these race or ethnicity, gender, and age differences is a most promising development. But, as with any discussion of human behavior, the concept of risk factors is complicated. Understanding risk factors and their relative effects is the subject of a rapidly growing body of research, which we will try to summarize throughout this book.

Although there is some evidence that childhood problems are highly interrelated and stem from one risk pattern (Jessor, 1987, 1993), there is stronger evidence that childhood problems have both common and unique risk structures (Mrazek & Haggerty, 1994). In other words, over and above a set of what might be called crosscutting or generic risk factors for all childhood problems, different individual, family, school, neighborhood, and contextual conditions produce different kinds of problems. Chapter 2 reviews the generic or common risk factors thought to underlie many childhood problems. Building on this common risk factor model, each subsequent chapter uses the same risk-centered terminology and introduces risk factors for different childhood problems.

SUCCESS AGAINST THE ODDS: RESILIENCE AND PROTECTIVE FACTORS

Many texts examine risk factors, but few examine the puzzling problem of why some children prevail over great adversity. Although poverty is a risk factor for poor academic achievement, not all poor children fail in school (see, for example, Duncan et al., 1994). What protects some poor children from school failure? And although exposure to violence is a risk factor for violence, not all children exposed to violence develop aggressive and coercive interpersonal styles. What protects these children from delinquency? Something operates to mitigate the risks for these children. These children appear to be "resilient" in the face of risk.

This book begins to define and deal with the idea of *resilience*, which arises from the strengths that are usually incumbent in the environments of high-risk children. Conceptually, we call these strengths "protective factors." *Protective factors* are those internal and external forces that help children resist or ameliorate risk. Like risk factors, protective factors include dispositional, familial, and extrafamilial characteristics. In aggregate, they are the positive forces that contribute to adaptive outcomes in the presence of risk (Garmezy, 1993). Chapter 2 further describes and discusses protective factors and resilience.

HIGH-RISK BEHAVIOR VERSUS HIGH-RISK ENVIRONMENTS: NEED FOR AN INCLUSIVE FRAMEWORK

In common parlance, risk is often defined after the fact; that is, a child is viewed as at risk because he or she already has gotten into trouble, been victimized, or failed in some way. There are two problems with this reasoning. First, it begs the question of predictability because the behavior has already occurred. True, prior behavior is one of the best predictors of subsequent behavior, but to plan early intervention services we need to rely on risk factors that exist before the outcome. Second, a definition of risk that relies only on engagement in "risky" behavior ignores the other conditions—the family, school, peer, and neighborhood environments that predispose children to certain kinds of problems (Resnick & Burt, 1996). All of these factors are useful in thinking about the problems of children. Thus, to give some order to the growing body of research on risk and resilience, we need a conceptual frame of reference that incorporates both individual and contextual conditions affecting the probability of a problem.

ECOLOGICAL THEORY: A MULTISYSTEMS PERSPECTIVE

Ecological theory has this inclusive characteristic and is fully compatible with a risk and resilience perspective. Ecological theory focuses both on the individual and on the context. As an early proponent of ecological theory, Bronfenbrenner (1979, 1986) argued that children's development is strongly influenced by the family, school, peer, neighborhood, and community contexts in which they live. Based on the interplay among genetic predisposition, physiological influences (neurochemical imbalances or exposure to a disease, for example), and often conflicting forces in the social environment, human behavior is thought to be transactional and subject to the dynamics of social exchange. In the context of biological influences, the theory posits that children develop and adapt through interactions with parents, siblings, peers, teachers, coaches, religious leaders, and a variety of others who, sometimes for better and sometimes for worse, people their lives. This person-in-environment perspective lies at the heart of social work and other helping professions (see, for example, Germain, 1991).

From this perspective, the social ecology of childhood can be conceptualized as consisting of interdependent and often nested parts or "systems." A child usually lives in a family. A family lives in a neighborhood. As they grow up, children in a family are involved with the school system, and later teenage children may work in the community. Each is a system, an "organized collection of activities and resources that exists within definable social and physical boundaries" (Berger, McBreen, & Rifkin, 1996, p. 42). And each exerts an influence on children. Systems such as the family and school have purposes and usually regulate social exchange. Whether open or closed, they have rules, roles, and power that determine activities and the use of resources.

This book employs the concept of multiple systems of influence; moreover, the authors argue that the central systems in children's lives make up an "ecology of childhood." However, we do not fully invoke the typology of general systems theory. Whereas Bronfenbrenner and others have proposed a layering nomenclature for various types of systems (microsystems, mesosystems, macrosystems, and exosystems), we adopt a simpler "multisystems" perspective. At some level above the family, it becomes quite difficult to identify higher- and lower-order systems. What constitutes the school system? Is it the local elementary or middle school that a particular child attends? Or is it the entire school district? How does the school system relate to the neighborhood? to the community? Which is superordinate? Instead of positing a nested structure of contextual influences, we simply identify risk and protective conditions that affect children across three systems-related domains. Introduced in chapter 2 and used throughout the text, these include individual psychosocial and biological characteristics; family, school, and neighborhood conditions; and broad environmental conditions.

RISK AND CAUSATION: A MULTISYSTEMS VIEW

The multisystems perspective has one further characteristic that makes it attractive. Patterns in systems are thought to arise from reciprocated causation. In Henggeler and Borduin's words (1990), "Behaviors are viewed as interdependent components of a spiral of recursive feedback loops. The behavior of person A influences the behavior of person B, which influences the behavior of person A, and so forth" (p. 14).

In sorting out the relative influences of biological factors, learned patterns (for example, cognitive schemata and heuristics), social interactions, and various contextual conditions, it may never be possible to fully identify causes and their effects. In the face of such complexity, causal order—at least in its traditional linear sense—may not exist. In any event, because the uncertainty is so great and our capacity to measure is so limited, a perspective that does not require notions of direct causation is desirable.

The multisystems ecological perspective admits to reciprocated causation; in so doing, it permits risk and protective factors to operate without the attendant baggage of being thought of as causes. Some risk and protective factors may truly be causes, of course, and the identification of causes is important in the context of developing scientific theories. But other risk factors may simply be markers that covary with true, but latent, causes. They are useful because they often mark the changing status of problems and signify the need for intervention. On balance, when we invoke an ecological and multisystems paradigm, we do not assume that all risk and protective factors operate as direct causes of child behavior or health.

STRUCTURE OF THE BOOK

Each chapter in the book builds on an ecological and multisystems perspective by introducing and reviewing risk and protective factors for various problems and disorders in childhood. Each chapter follows a similar outline:

- *Description of the Problem:* Delineating of national trends for the topic of the chapter. Presentation of incidence and prevalence data on differences by age, race or ethnicity, gender, and socioeconomic status, if available.

- *Description of Risk and Protective Factors:* Building on the common risk and protective factors discussed in chapter 2, a review of risk and protective factors specific to the topic of the chapter.
- *Description of Differences in Risk and Protective Factors by Age, Gender, and Race or Ethnicity:* Exploration of differences in risk and protective factors by child age, gender, and race or ethnicity.
- *Methods for Assessing Risk and Protective Factors:* Brief review of measurement instruments that may be useful in assessing risk and protective factors. In some chapters, a detailed exploration of methodological issues in measurement and case assessment.
- *Implications for Prevention, Early Intervention, or Treatment:* Based on a risk and resilience perspective, discussion of implications for the design of prevention, early intervention, or treatment services.

This book contains 13 chapters. Chapter topics were chosen because they represent common conditions, disorders, and social or health problems encountered by practitioners who work with children and their families. In selecting topics, we could not be exhaustive. For example, we included a chapter on depression, but we did not include a separate chapter on the closely linked topic of suicide. And even though they may be heritable or have developmental markers in early childhood, important problems that arise frequently in young adulthood or in marital relationships—including schizophrenia and family violence—are not addressed in the text. Similarly, problems that are quite serious but affect a comparatively small number of children—for example, Asperger's and Rett's disorders—are not included. The chapters are designed to be exemplars of the application of a risk and resilience perspective, and readers are encouraged to apply the methods described in the book to other problems occurring in childhood.

In chapter 2, Laura Kirby and Mark Fraser explore the concepts of risk, protection, and resilience. They define terms, describe types of risks, review the concept of resilience, and develop a model for common risk and protective factors thought to underpin many childhood problems. This chapter lays the foundation for other chapters in the book.

In chapter 3, James Nash and Mark Fraser outline methodological issues in measuring and comparing risk and protective factors. This chapter contains many examples of the estimation of odds, odds ratios, and relative risks, the central ways that risk and protective factors are compared in the social and health sciences. The chapter also introduces life tables and survival analysis, advanced methods of analysis that are used increasingly by social workers and others who study risk and resilience.

In chapter 4, Barbara Thomlison discusses risk factors both for child maltreatment and for recovery from child maltreatment. Reports of child abuse and neglect have soared in recent years (Curtis, Boyd, Liepold, & Petit, 1995; U.S. Department of Health and Human Services, 1996) and longitudinal studies indicate that child maltreatment is a risk factor for a variety of adjustment disorders (see, for example, Widom, 1989a, 1989b, 1989c). Thomlison discusses methods to assess risk of maltreatment, and she explores the elements of service that may be essential to promote recovery from victimization.

In chapter 5, S. Rachel Dedmon addresses attention-deficit hyperactivity disorder (ADHD), a common problem among young children and an increasingly recognized problem in adults. Dedmon reviews recent data on the incidence and prevalence of ADHD. She then conducts a comprehensive exploration of the risk and protective factors associated with the problem. For parents and teachers as well as social workers, counselors, and other human services professionals, her chapter is rich in practice wisdom and informative in its outline of treatment strategies, including the use of medications.

In chapter 6, Jack Richman and Gary Bowen investigate research on academic achievement, truancy, and school dropout. Their chapter might well be entitled "School Success," because they focus on factors that promote academic achievement, a factor that protects many children who are exposed to high risk. Sharing new data, Richman and Bowen review their "School Success Profile," a comprehensive and promising instrument for assessing the needs of youths in middle school and high school.

In chapter 7, Jeffrey Jenson explores alcohol and drug abuse, a problem that has mushroomed in importance in the last quarter of the 20th century. The growth of international cartels devoted exclusively to the sale of illicit drugs has resulted in extensive law enforcement efforts and programs for federal interdiction and foreign eradication of drugs. Jenson argues that demand-side strategies designed to prevent alcohol and drug abuse show great promise. He discusses risk and protective factors for the use of psychoactive substances. He then outlines risk-focused principles for the design of more effective programs for prevention and early intervention.

In chapter 8, James Herbert Williams, Charles Ayers, and Michael Arthur discuss recent studies of risk factors for delinquency and conduct disorder. Rich in theory and implications for practice, their chapter builds on the work of David Hawkins and Rico Catalano of the Seattle Social Development Group, School of Social Work, University of Washington (see, for example, Catalano & Hawkins, 1996). They outline the individual, family, school, and community conditions that promote antisocial, aggressive behavior. From the perspective of social development, they then explore issues related to the prevention of delinquency and conduct disorder.

No health problem has more serious consequences for children than AIDS. Children who are born with AIDS or who develop it through sexual contact are at enormous risk. In chapter 9, Kathleen Rounds discusses AIDS and sexually transmitted infections (STIs) from a public health perspective. She reviews recent data on the incidence and prevalence of major STIs, including AIDS. Then she explores our growing knowledge about the behaviors, beliefs, and conditions that increase the odds of contracting a STI. Finally, she discusses research findings from promising prevention and early intervention programs.

In chapter 10, Cynthia Franklin, Jacqueline Corcoran, and Susan Ayers-Lopez address the growing problem of adolescent pregnancy. Although teenage births dropped in the mid-1990s, the 1994 rate was still higher than that for any year between 1974 and 1989 (National Center for Health Statistics, 1996). For many young women (and men), pregnancy is a career-shaping event. Franklin and her colleagues review the risk and protective factors for adolescent pregnancy. Next they discuss the effect of adolescent pregnancy on educational achievement, economic security, maternal and child health, and social relations. After reviewing several case-assessment instruments that they have used in practice with adolescent parents, they explore a range of services that might both prevent pregnancy and help young mothers and fathers respond responsibly to the tasks of childrearing.

In chapter 11, Carlean Gilbert reviews the literature on the problem of childhood depression. Arguing persuasively that mental illness is best conceptualized as arising from the interaction between biological predisposition and environmental risk, Gilbert discusses the historical controversy over childhood depression. She outlines the findings from recent research and describes case-assessment instruments for measuring levels of depression.

Each year thousands of children are born with serious developmental disabilities, including autism. Whether caused by genetic risk, maternal substance abuse, environmental contaminants (lead, for example), or other factors, the birth of a child with a developmental disorder poses special challenges in parenting, child care, and education. In chapter 12, Irene Nathan Zipper and Rune Simeonsson discuss the challenge of creating means for children of all abilities to participate fully in community activities. Using a risk factor perspective, they review recent legislation, emerging concepts of inclusion, and barriers to more effective services.

Finally, in chapter 13, Mark Fraser and Maeda Galinsky revisit the central concepts of risk and resilience. With an emphasis on principles and guidelines emerging from the risk and resilience perspective, they explore the concepts of resilience-based practice, community involvement, "keystone" risks, empowerment, and strengths-based intervention.

REFERENCES

Annie E. Casey Foundation. (1996). *Kids count data book*. Baltimore: Author.

Berger, R. L., McBreen, J. T., & Rifkin, M. J. (1996). *Human behavior: A perspective for the helping professions*. White Plains, NY: Longman.

Bronfenbrenner, U. (1979). *The ecology of human development: Experiments by nature and design*. Cambridge, MA: Harvard University Press.

Bronfenbrenner, U. (1986). Ecology of the family as a context to human development: Research perspectives. *Development Psychology, 22*, 723–742.

Catalano, R. F., & Hawkins, J. D. (1996). The social development model: A theory of antisocial behavior. In J. D. Hawkins (Ed.), *Delinquency and crime: Current theories*. New York: Cambridge University Press.

Coie, J. D., Watt, N. F., West, S. G., Hawkins, J. D., Asarnow, J. R., Markman, H. J., Ramey, S. L., Shure, M. B., & Long, B. (1993). The science of prevention: A conceptual framework and some directions for a national research program. *American Psychologist, 48*, 1013–1022.

Curtis, P. A., Boyd, J. D., Liepold, M., & Petit, M. (1995). *Child abuse and neglect: A look at the states*. Washington, DC: Child Welfare League of America.

Duncan, G. J. (1991). The economic environment of childhood. In A. C. Huston (Ed.), *Children in poverty: Child development and public policy* (pp. 23–50). New York: Cambridge University Press.

Duncan, G. J., Brooks-Gunn, J., & Klebanov, P. K. (1994). Economic deprivation and early childhood development. *Child Development, 65*, 296–318.

Garmezy, N. (1993). Vulnerability and resilience. In D. C. Funder, R. D. Parke, C. Tomlinson-Keasey, & K. Widaman (Eds.), *Studying lives through time* (pp. 377–398). Washington, DC: American Psychological Association.

Germain, C. B. (1991). *Human behavior in the social environment: An ecological view*. New York: Columbia University Press.

Hart, B., & Risley, T. R. (1995). *Meaning differences in the everyday experience of young American children*. Baltimore: Paul H. Brookes.

Haveman, R., & Wolfe, B. (1994). *Succeeding generations: On the effects of investments in children*. New York: Russell Sage Foundation.

Henggeler, S. W., & Borduin, C. M. (1990). *Family therapy and beyond: A multisystemic approach to treating the behavior problems of children and adolescents*. Pacific Grove, CA: Brooks/Cole.

Hernandez, D. J. (1993). *America's children: Resources from family, government, and the economy*. New York: Russell Sage Foundation.

Jessor, R. (1987). Risky driving and adolescent problem behavior: An extension of problem behavior theory. *Alcohol, Drugs, and Driving, 3*, 1–11.

Jessor, R. (1993). Successful adolescent development among youth in high-risk settings. *American Psychologist, 48*, 117–126.

Klebanov, P. K., Brooks-Gunn, J., & Duncan, G. J. (1994). Does neighborhood and family poverty affect mothers' parenting, mental health, and social support? *Journal of Marriage and the Family, 56*, 441–455.

Larner, M., & Collins, A. (1996). Poverty in the lives of young children. In E. J. Erwin (Ed.), *Putting children first* (pp. 55–75). Baltimore: Paul H. Brookes.

Mrazek, P. J., & Haggerty, R. J. (Eds.) (1994). *Reducing risks for mental disorders: Frontiers for preventive intervention research*. Washington, DC: National Academy Press.

National Center for Children in Poverty. (1995). *Young children in poverty: A statistical update*. New York: Author.

National Center for Health Statistics. (1996). *Teenage births drop for third straight year*. Hyattsville, MD: Author.

Resnick, G., & Burt, M. R. (1996). Youth at risk: Definitions and implications for service delivery. *American Journal of Orthopsychiatry, 66*, 172–188.

Sherman, A. (1994). *Wasting America's future: The Children's Defense Fund report on the costs of child poverty*. Washington, DC: Children's Defense Fund.

Slavin, R. E., Karweit, N. L., & Madden, N. A. (1988*). Effective programs for students at risk*. Boston: Allyn & Bacon.

U.S. Department of Health and Human Services. (1996). *Child maltreatment 1994: Reports from the states to the National Center on Child Abuse and Neglect*. Washington, DC: U.S. Government Printing Office.

Widom, C. S. (1989a). Child abuse, neglect, and violent criminal behavior. *Criminology, 27*, 251–271.

Widom, C. S. (1989b). Does violence beget violence? A critical examination of the literature. *Psychological Bulletin, 106*, 3–28.

Widom, C. S. (1989c). The cycle of violence. *Science, 244*, 160–166.

2

RISK AND RESILIENCE IN CHILDHOOD

Laura D. Kirby and Mark W. Fraser

Early developmental theorists recognized the importance of studying both atypical and normative development to gain a more complete understanding of human functioning and adaptation (Cicchetti, 1990). In other words, they believed that knowledge about the etiology of problem behavior could inform efforts to promote or enhance adaptive functioning. Similarly, in an effort to influence health and illness in general, the emerging field of epidemiology explored factors related to the presence or absence of disease across populations (Lilienfield & Lilienfield, 1980). You may recall the story of John Snow and the town pump. When Snow removed the handle from the Broad Street water pump in 19th century London, he stopped the spread of cholera (Lilienfield & Lilienfield, 1980). With little understanding of how the disease was spread, Snow based his action on observed differences in the behavior of individuals with and without the disease. He succeeded in slowing the spread of cholera by identifying and then interrupting the route of transmission of the disease.

As a discipline, epidemiology developed from studying abnormal developmental pathways, and the search for factors that increase risks for diverse problem conditions grew out of that tradition (Garmezy, 1985). Risk factors, also called vulnerability factors, may include genetic, biological, behavioral, sociocultural, and demographic conditions, characteristics, or attributes. Risk or vulnerability represents a heightened probability of negative outcome based on the presence of one or more such factors.

Some risk factors are causally related to negative outcomes, whereas others simply represent correlates, sometimes called markers, of potential negative outcomes. Being male, for example, is often identified as a risk factor for various types of psychiatric and behavioral disorders, including conduct disorder (Mrazek & Haggerty, 1994). However, there is little evidence that a singular gender difference explains the heightened vulnerability of boys for conduct disorder. More likely, gender represents a marker for one or more other risk factors—some of which may be physiological but some of which may relate to socialization—that increase the probability of developing a behavior problem. It is often difficult to disaggregate causes from correlates, particularly in developmental risk models where child behavior may be influenced by different factors at different points during maturation.

RISK FACTORS

The chapters in this book use the concept of developmental risk and, in so doing, rely on a broad definition of risk factors. Based on work by Coie and others (see, for example, Coie et al., 1993), we define *risk factors* as any influences that increase the probability of onset, digression to a more serious state, or maintenance of a problem condition. Risk factors range from prenatal biological to broad environmental conditions that affect children. For example, there is growing evidence that perinatal trauma functions as an early biological risk factor for later academic difficulties (O'Dougherty & Wright, 1990). School failure in turn represents a risk factor for delinquency, and association with peers who are delinquent may lead to the maintenance of antisocial, aggressive behavior (Office of Juvenile Justice and Delinquency Prevention, 1995). This definition of risk factors thus encompasses individual (both biological and dispositional characteristics) and contextual conditions that elevate the probability of negative future outcomes for children. These conditions, described below, include risk traits, contextual effects, stressful events, and cumulative stress; also described are the concepts of risk processes and risk chains.

RISK TRAITS

A *risk trait* refers to an individual predisposition toward developing a specific problem condition (Pellegrini, 1990). Genetic markers are often thought of as risk traits. For example, children born to parents with schizophrenia are more likely than other children to develop symptoms of schizophrenia (Rende & Plomin, 1993). Although genetic research has provided strong evidence for the existence of specific genes that increase the probability of developing some mental and medical disorders (including schizophrenia and major depressive disorders), it also supports a multifactorial model of risk (Rende & Plomin, 1993); that is, environmental factors are believed to play a key, sometimes triggering, role in determining outcomes for individuals at genetic risk.

In practice, the term "risk trait" is often used to describe a wide range of risk conditions. In addition to genetic markers, risk traits may include characteristics of individuals, such as low IQ, or the presence of a specific disorder, such as attention-deficit hyperactivity disorder, which may function as markers of risk for a subsequent problem or disorder. Moreover, contextual variables such as poverty constitute a separate kind of risk trait. Contextual or environmental risk conditions must always be considered in assessments of an individual's predisposition toward negative outcomes. From individual through environmental influences, risk traits thus constitute the broadest category of risk factors.

CONTEXTUAL EFFECTS

Contextual effects are environmental conditions that have both direct and indirect effects on overall risk. For example, poverty directly affects children by lowering the quality of their food and shelter. It has indirect effects on children by placing parents under such constant strain that they find it difficult to respond consistently to a child's needs. Contextual effects often appear to be mediated by variables at the family and individual levels. For example, results from the Pittsburgh Youth Study, a study of 506 boys in public school, indicate that neighborhood effects on delinquency are largely mediated by such variables as hyperactivity and quality of parental supervision (Peoples & Loeber, 1994). Contextual effects appear to be like other risk factors in that they may exert strong effects in some settings and at some times and weak effects in other settings and times. For example, in the trauma of war, contextual effects may exert strong influences, causing soldiers to develop behaviors that disappear in the absence of the threat, chaos, and horror of battle. The identification and assessment of contextual effects present special challenges to practitioners, researchers, and scholars.

STRESSFUL OR CRITICAL LIFE EVENTS

One approach to studying risk has been to assess the impact of a single, significant stressful life event such as becoming pregnant or getting arrested. A second and often competing approach has been to consider small events or chronic stresses that occur within the context of everyday living. Teasing out causal relationships in this research is difficult. For example, failing a grade may represent a singularly stressful event for a child, but it may also represent the culmination of chronic minor stressors within the child's school and home environment. Both kinds of stress appear to be related to childhood problems. Many of the chapters in this book are organized around critical life events such as being the victim of child maltreatment, failing in school, or developing a mental disorder.

CUMULATIVE EFFECTS OF STRESS

There is growing evidence that the cumulation of stress has a major effect on child development and related problems (Coie et al., 1993; Garmezy, 1993a; Seifer, Sameroff, Baldwin, & Baldwin, 1992). One oft-heard hypothesis regarding stress is that prolonged exposure to a risk factor increases the likelihood of negative outcomes (Stouthamer-Loeber et al., 1993). School failure, for example, may not be associated with aggressive, antisocial behavior in early grades, but it may become associated with behavior problems as failures are repeated over time (see Farrington et al., 1993).

Highly interrelated risk factors often occur together or cluster to produce heightened vulnerability (Pellegrini, 1990). Children who lose a parent to death or divorce, for example, often suffer economic strains and a decline in social status as a consequence (Crook & Eliot, 1980). In the same vein, there is evidence that adolescent drug abuse clusters with other adolescent problems—delinquency, pregnancy, school misbehavior, and dropout (Hawkins, Catalano, & Miller, 1992). Furthermore, some broad contextual variables such as poverty often represent a latent clustering of risk factors, including, for example, low maternal education, low-status parental occupation, large family size, and the absence of one parent (Luthar, 1991).

As the number of risk factors increases, the cumulation exerts an increasingly strong influence on children. Rutter (1979) found that the presence of a single family stressor had a negligible effect on the rate of psychiatric disorder among children. The presence of two or more risk factors, however, multiplicatively increased the rate of disorder among children. Similarly, Sterling, Cowen, Weissberg, Lotyczewske, and Boike (1985) observed school adjustment problems associated with a stressful life event—the death of a parent, change in home residence, or birth of a new sibling, for example—worsened when another stressful event or circumstance arose concurrently. Thus, the effect of exposure to several risk factors may not be simply additive. Although the effect of a single stressor may be negligible, the effect of three stressors may be far greater than a threefold increase in risk.

Risk Processes

Risk factors that occur or exist at one moment in time, such as a stressful life event, may be useful in determining the risk status of children, but they provide little information about how or why a child came to be at risk. *Risk processes* refer to the mechanisms whereby a risk factor contributes over time to heightened vulnerability. For example, poor parenting practices, such as inadequate supervision of children, inconsistent responses to children's behavior, and constant nagging, may increase the risk that a child will be noncompliant in home, school, and other settings (Patterson, 1982). No single event produces a negative outcome. Rather, interactional processes shape behaviors and problems over time. The separation of risk processes from risk traits remains a major challenge for practitioners and researchers who work with troubled children and who seek to design more effective social programs.

Risk Chains

At least in principle if not practice, the health and social sciences have relied on causal chains or models to establish a logical foundation on which to base prevention and other intervention efforts (Simeonsson, 1994). Relationships among risk factors, child development, and social problems are complex, however, and unconfounded causal chains are difficult to identify and often the subject of heated debate. It may not be possible to specify causal models that both explain a high proportion of behavioral outcomes in children and are widely applicable.

Nevertheless, the causal modeling concept can be modified to identify sequential, though not necessarily causal, risk chains (Mrazek & Haggerty, 1994; Simeonsson, 1994). In a social development model of antisocial behavior proposed by O'Donnell, Hawkins, and Abbot (1995), for example, risk chains represent linkages of conceptually distinct risk factors or processes. Sequenced or chained risk factors for antisocial behavior include perceived opportunities for antisocial interactions, interaction with antisocial others, and perceived rewards for antisocial behavior. Linked together, they represent one of many logical, sequential pathways that lead children to antisocial behavior. Risk chains of this nature are testable and can be the basis of prevention, early intervention, or treatment.

The concept of risk is continually being refined. Clearly different types of risk exist, including risk traits, contextual risks, and stressful life events. Understanding risk is further complicated by related concepts such as cumulative risk, risk chains, and risk processes. What is clear is that risk is probabilistic, meaning that children exposed to risk factors are more likely to experience negative outcomes. Equally certain is that some children who are exposed to a high level of risk manage to overcome the odds (Werner & Smith, 1992). They are resilient.

Concept of Resilience

The study of resilience emerged as a byproduct of the search for risk factors. Curiously, researchers consistently found that some children who faced stressful, high-risk situations fared well in life (Garmezy, 1985; Rutter, 1987; Werner, 1984; Werner & Smith, 1977,

1982, 1992). For example, research showed that some children who were born prematurely and at low birthweights succeeded in school as well as in social settings. Other children who were victims of abuse or neglect were found to be quite successful in developing positive, productive, and intimate relationships with others later in life. On balance, data suggest that only about one-third of any population of "at-risk" children experiences a negative outcome (Wolin & Wolin, 1995). Two-thirds appear to survive risk experiences without major developmental disruptions. The term "resilience" has come to be used to describe children who achieve positive outcomes in the face of risk.

INVULNERABILITY VERSUS RESILIENCE

Anthony (1987) labeled resilient children "psychologically invulnerable" based on their apparent ability to maintain emotional competence despite severe or prolonged adversity. But the concept of invulnerability is controversial. There is little evidence to support the implication that some children are simply not vulnerable to the effects of risk factors (Fisher, Kokes, Cole, Perkins, & Wynne, 1987; Pellegrini, 1990). More recently, the term invulnerable has been superseded by the broader concept of resilience. Whereas invulnerability suggests that some children are unaffected by a risk factor that affects most children, resilience is defined by the presence of risk factors in combination with positive forces that contribute to adaptive outcomes (Garmezy, 1993b).

Within that framework, three types of resilience have been described (Masten, Best, & Garmezy, 1990). The first, commonly referred to as "overcoming the odds," is defined by the attainment of positive outcomes despite high-risk status. For example, a preterm infant is considered high risk by virtue of the correlation between prematurity and negative health outcomes. A preterm infant who does not experience negative outcomes may thus be described as overcoming the odds. This notion of resilience grew most directly out of the risk literature described above.

The second concept of resilience, grounded in the literature on stress and coping, refers to "sustained competence under stress." In families where conflict is high, for example, resilient children will display an ability to cope with chronic environmental and interpersonal stress. Coping in this sense refers to a child's efforts, including both thought and action, to restore or maintain internal or external equilibrium (Masten et al., 1990).

The third concept of resilience refers to "recovery from trauma." This type of resilience is evident in children who function well after an intensely stressful event such as sexual abuse or exposure to street violence. Many child survivors of German concentration camps have been recognized as resilient in this way. Resilience is thus best defined not as the absence of risk or dysfunction but as "successful adaptation despite adversity" (Begun, 1993; Benard, 1993; Cowan, Wyman, Work, & Parker, 1990; Masten, 1994; Werner & Smith, 1992).

RESILIENCE AND POSITIVE OUTCOMES

Various approaches to reaching positive outcomes have been used in resilience research. We often describe resilient children as competent. *Competence* may be most broadly defined as effectively adapting to the environment to further the process of development (Garmezy & Masten, 1991). In their sample of abused and neglected children, for example, Farber and Egeland (1987) used the successful resolution of critical developmental tasks as a criterion by which to assess competence.

Broad definitions of resilience, however, often obscure variation across different developmental domains of functioning. Defining resilience as competence implies that children survive without pain or anxiety, but this is rarely the case. Significant psychological distress has been observed in children who were behaviorally competent (Farber & Egeland, 1987; Luthar, 1991). Narrow definitions based on a single functional domain may also be problematic, because competence in any one area represents only a small part of what may be considered successful coping (Luthar, Doernberger, & Zigler, 1993). This book focuses on the wide range of risk conditions that affect children. Moreover, the book conceptualizes positive outcomes in terms of normative social functioning, where children reach developmental milestones at age-appropriate times and in appropriate sequences without experiencing serious childhood social problems.

RESILIENCE, RISK, AND CULTURE

In relying on normative functioning to define resilience, we must recognize that culturally determined behavior is a potential source of variation in outcomes. In other words, behavior considered adaptive and normative in one culture may not be similarly adaptive and normative in other cultures (Coie et al., 1993). Consider the example of "difficult" temperament. In some cultures, assertiveness is not highly valued and may be viewed as improper, if not dysfunctional, behavior. But in other cultures, an assertive and demanding temperament may be adaptive and perhaps even required for survival (Masten et al., 1990).

Similarly, some risk factors may be unique to specific populations. For example, in the Hopi Indian culture, significant social stigma used to be attached to traditionally disapproved marriages, such as marriage across tribes, mesas, and clans of disparate social status. Levy and Kunitz (1987) observed that children of parents who entered into such marriages were at increased risk of suicide (Mrazek & Haggerty, 1994). For Hopi children, then, cross-mesa marriage constituted a risk factor; for children from other backgrounds, it was less important.

RESILIENCE AND DEVELOPMENT

Developmental processes represent another potential source of variation in childhood resilience. Although risk is ubiquitous in the lives of most children, children respond differently to risk over time. Vulnerability or resistance to stressful experiences appears to shift as a function of developmental or maturational changes. The fluctuating nature of resilience may result from the interaction of individual and environmental conditions that change as children enter school, develop friendship networks, explore sexuality, and so on. Developmentally, constitutional or individual factors appear more important during infancy and childhood, and interpersonal factors appear more important during adolescence (Grizenko & Fisher, 1992).

In a longitudinal study on the Hawaiian island of Kauai, Werner and Smith (1977, 1982, 1992) traced the development of 698 children from birth to early adulthood. Children were variably exposed to a number of risk factors, including perinatal stress, chronic poverty, family discord, and parental psychopathology. About one-third of the total group (n = 201) was identified as high risk. Somewhat fewer than one-third of the high-risk children (n = 72) grew into competent, confident, and caring young adults and were classified as resilient. Clusters of protective factors were identified for these resilient children, including both individual characteristics (such as having a positive social orientation and being affectionate, active, and good-natured) and environmental characteristics (such as the presence of a warm, supportive home environment). However, Werner (1992) observed that most of the high-risk youths who developed serious coping problems in adolescence could be described as resilient by the time they reached their early 30s. On the basis of these and other similar data, it appears that resilience is not a fixed attribute, but rather a dynamic characteristic that may emerge even after poor interim outcomes.

CONCEPT OF PROTECTION

In the face of growing dissatisfaction with pathology-focused intervention strategies, professionals from mental health and other fields have joined public health practitioners in the search for factors that might promote resilience in children. Because they are conceptualized as protecting children from risk, these "protective" factors occupy an increasingly important position in developing our understanding of psychopathology and other social problems. Notwithstanding, the term "protective factor" has not been clearly or consistently defined. Some scholars distinguish between "resilience factors" as those that are internal to a child and "protective factors" as those that are external (Seifer et al., 1992). Others have adopted a broader definition in which individual protective factors are differentiated from environmental protective factors. Still others have argued that protective factors can be defined only in concert with risk factors because of their interrelatedness (Rutter, 1979). Here, we will define *protective factors* as both the internal and external forces that help children resist or ameliorate risk.

Norman Garmezy (1985), a leader in the emerging field of risk and resilience, identified three broad categories of protective variables that promote resilience in childhood. The first refers to dispositional attributes, including temperamental factors, social orientation and responsiveness to change, cognitive abilities, and coping skills. The second general category of protective factors is the family milieu. A positive relationship with at least one parent or a parental figure serves an important protective function. Other important family variables include cohesion, warmth, harmony, and absence of neglect. The third category of protective influences in childhood encompasses attributes of the extrafamilial social environment. These include the availability of external resources and extended social supports as well as the individual's use of those resources.

PROTECTIVE PROCESSES

The concept of protection, like that of risk, may be more useful for designing services when the focus turns to processes or mechanisms. Although many different kinds of protective processes may exist, four have been consistently cited in the risk and resilience literature (Rutter, 1987). The first, reduction of risk impact, includes processes that alter exposure to a risk condition. For example, consistent parental supervision and regulation of children's activities outside the home probably reduce the risk of drug abuse for children raised in high-risk environments (Hawkins et al., 1992).

A second protective process is the reduction of negative chain reactions that contribute to the long-term effects of exposure to a stressor or other risk. For example, support from one parent following the death of another parent may protect a child from vulnerability to a chain of stressors, which often follow the loss of a parent. A third protective process appears to operate through the development of self-esteem. Self-esteem may be enhanced through secure relationships with parents, for example, or through task accomplishment such as school successes. Self-esteem incorporates the concept of self-efficacy, or a belief in one's effectiveness. Across settings, a sense of self-efficacy may protect children by promoting adaptive behavior in the face of risk.

The opening of opportunities through social structural reforms constitutes a fourth protective mechanism. This mechanism usually operates at a societal level, but it can have individual effects. For example, changes in school policies may boost graduations from high school, which expands opportunities for graduates who might not have completed high school under earlier policies.

CUMULATIVE EFFECTS

Like risk factors, protective factors probably have cumulative effects. In a study of 243 premature, low-birthweight children living in poverty, Bradley et al. (1994) found that the presence of three or more protective family factors, including parental warmth, acceptance, organization, and infant stimulation, differentiated resilient children from nonresilient children. Although support for the view that protective factors exert a nonlinear effect on child outcomes is mixed, these data suggest that there are at least cumulative, additive effects across protective conditions.

INTERACTIONS BETWEEN RISK AND PROTECTIVE FACTORS

It is widely believed that resilience results in some way from the interplay between risk and protective factors, but the nature of the interactions that produce resilience are poorly understood and usually inconsistently described in the literature. Nevertheless, two basic models of interaction are consistently described, although the terminology varies. They are the additive and interactive models.

ADDITIVE MODELS

Additive models, in which protective factors are said to exhibit main effects, direct effects, or compensatory effects, posit that the presence of a risk factor directly increases the likelihood of a particular negative outcome and the presence of a protective factor directly increases the likelihood of a positive outcome (Luthar, 1991; Masten, 1987; Pellegrini, 1990). Risk and protection are usually seen as polar opposites. Along a continuum, for example, high family conflict is seen as a risk factor whereas low family conflict is considered a protective factor. According to this perspective, competence always declines as stress increases. A person with a high level of a protective attribute consistently functions better than a person with a low level of that attribute (Masten, 1987). To continue with the example of family conflict, children in families where conflict is high will be at increased risk for social problems relative to children in families where conflict is low. Thus, risk and protection are thought to counterbalance each other.

INTERACTIVE MODELS

Rutter (1979, 1983) used a different conceptualization. He employed the term interactive to describe risk and protective dynamics, pointing out that "interaction" better describes the relationship between risk and protective factors. In interactive models, protective factors have effect only in combination with risk factors. In other words, protective factors are thought to exert little effect when stress is low, but their effect emerges when stress is high (Masten, 1987). Immunization against disease provides a useful analogy for this process: Immunization does not directly promote positive physical health; rather, it provides protection from disease following exposure to a pathogen.

Within an interaction framework, protective factors have been conceptualized in three ways. First, they may buffer risk factors, serving as a cushion against the negative effects of risk factors. Social support is thought to operate in this way. For example, the nurturing and supportive parenting provided to girls participating in "Project Competence," a Minneapolis project for school-age children, appeared to moderate the extent to which exposure to high risk was linked to disruptive social behavior in school (Masten, 1987). Second, a protective factor may interrupt the risk chain through which risk factors operate. Interventions that aim to reduce family conflict, for example, may interrupt a chain of risks connecting family environment with peer affiliations and drug use. In other words, reducing family conflict may prevent early experimentation with drugs, which is a risk factor for greater and more persistent use of psychoactive substances (Hawkins et al., 1992). Third, protective factors may operate to prevent the initial occurrence of a risk factor. Positive temperamental characteristics, such as being easy to soothe, affectionate, and good-natured, may protect children from abuse or neglect, for example, by enabling them to elicit positive responses from caregivers (Morriset, 1993).

Research on these interactive protective pathways is inconclusive. Interaction effects can be tested with multiple regression analyses, wherein an equation with only main effects is compared to an equation that includes both main and interaction effects (Cohen & Cohen, 1983). Although few studies have done these analyses, interaction effects have generally been found to be statistically significant. However, the increase in variance accounted for by interactions is generally small (see, for example, Felix-Ortiz & Newcomb, 1992; Luthar, 1991; Moran & Eckenrode, 1992; Myers, Taylor, Alvy, Arrington, & Richardson, 1992). For example, in a study of adolescent drug use, Felix-Ortiz and Newcomb found that the interaction between a risk factor index and a protective factor index explained only 4.2 percent of the variance in alcohol use. Given such findings, some authors have suggested that direct additive effects should be the focus of resilience research (Loeber & Stouthamer-Loeber, 1996; Luthar & Zigler, 1991). Nevertheless, the existing data indicate that protective factors do indeed interact with risk factors, making it clear that processes whereby risk and protective factors lead to resilience are complex and, at least in part, nonlinear.

SYSTEMS OF INFLUENCE

Interactions among risk and protective factors are further complicated by the fact that both types of influence exist at many different levels in the ecology. Risk and protective factors have been identified within the individual, in the immediate family or school environment, and in the broader social context (Garmezy, 1985; Rutter, 1987; Werner & Smith, 1982, 1992). In the ecology of human behavior (Bronfenbrenner, 1979), resilience can be conceptualized as resulting from interactions among risk and protective factors. It also results from the relative balance of factors across multiple system levels (O'Keefe, 1994).

Risk researchers debate which of the system levels has the greater effect on resilience (Seifer & Sameroff, 1987). However, it is widely believed that "distal factors," or those that are situated farther away from the child, are less influential than "proximal factors," which impinge directly on the child (Baldwin, Baldwin, & Cole, 1990; Garbarino, Kostelny, & Dubrown 1991; Myers et al., 1992). Poverty, for example, is often considered a distal variable that limits opportunities and indirectly places children at risk. Through risk chains, however, poverty may lead to other more proximal risks. For example, a single mother's irritability and exhaustion caused by full-time work at a low-paying job may directly affect the parent–child relationship. An ecological framework that simultaneously considers a broad range of variables in individual, family, school, and neighborhood systems can help organize attempts to identify all the factors that may affect a child's life (Luthar & Zigler, 1991; Seifer & Sameroff, 1987). This book uses an ecological, multisystems perspective throughout.

A MODEL FOR COMMON RISK AND PROTECTIVE FACTORS

Not much is known about the ways that risk and protective factors interact to produce resilience, but a general model of resilience is emerging from research. On balance, evidence supports the presence of both additive and interactive effects, perhaps with additive effects playing the more important role. To account for the presence of effects at multiple system levels, risk and protective factors must be understood within an ecological framework. Moreover, a developmental framework must be used both to allow for changes in resilience in individuals at different points in time and to explain the cumulative effects of risk.

Dozens of studies exploring risk and resilience have found some risk and protective factors to be common to many childhood problems (Coie et al., 1993; Luthar & Zigler, 1991; Mrazek & Haggerty, 1994). This set of crosscutting risk and protective factors is shown in Table 2-1 and discussed briefly in the next section. Risk and protective factors are shown in the table at the system level where they occur, either as psychosocial and biological characteristics of individual children or as contextual factors in the family, school, neighborhood, and larger settings. Consistent with ecological theory, the classification schema reflects that risk and protective factors often occur simultaneously at multiple system levels. This multisystems perspective is rooted in the idea that a child's social ecology consists of many different systems, each of which has the capacity to influence developmental trajectories.

Identifying the common factors that produce risk and resilience in children is a first step both in conducting an ecologically based assessment and in designing ecologically focused services. Setting aside, for the moment, problem-specific risk and protective factors (these are reviewed in later chapters in the book), Table 2-1 attempts to lay a foundation by focusing on those common factors that place children at risk and appear to protect children in the context of high risk.

**Table 2-1. Common Risk and Protective Factors for
Serious Childhood Social Problems: An Ecological and
Multisystems Perspective**

SYSTEM LEVEL	RISK FACTORS	PROTECTIVE FACTORS
Broad Environmental Conditions	Few opportunities for education and employment Racial discrimination and injustice Poverty/low SES	Many opportunities for education, employment, growth, and achievement
Family, School, and Neighborhood Conditions	Child maltreatment Interparental conflict Parental psychopathology Poor parenting	Social support Presence of caring/supportive adult Positive parent–child relationship Effective parenting
Individual Psychosocial and Biological Characteristics	Gender Biomedical problems	"Easy" temperament as an infant Self-esteem and self-efficacy Competence in normative roles High intelligence

COMMON RISK FACTORS

BROAD ENVIRONMENTAL RISK FACTORS

Few Opportunities for Education or Employment

The environment is the context for child development. It provides children with opportunities to learn. It exposes them to adults who make meaningful contributions to their communities and who serve as role models and mentors. It provides incentives and disincentives for behaviors. And it is a source of social and economic support for families. When the environment is impoverished, children suffer.

The hypothesis that limited or "blocked" opportunities in work, school, and other environmental settings place children at risk is derived, in part, from theories in sociology about strain and structural opportunity (see, for example, Agnew, 1993; Farrington et al., 1993). Based on a large body of research, these theories posit that nearly all children develop high expectations for social, educational, and economic success. But as a result of unfavorable neighborhood and school conditions, some children learn that the odds against their success are high. The discrepancy between what a child hopes to achieve and what he or she actually expects to achieve through legitimate means is thought to be the source of frustration and anger. And at the end of the risk chain, according to strain and opportunity theory, frustration and anger cause high rates of alienation, delinquency, drug abuse, school failure, teen pregnancy, and other social problems.

Racial Discrimination and Injustice

As a result of a long history of racial discrimination, African American and other people of color bear a disproportionate share of the burden of poverty and unemployment in the United States (Nettles & Pleck, 1994; Taylor, 1994). Thus, these children experience increased vulnerability to the effects of low income and low socioeconomic status (SES). Moreover, significant noneconomic aspects of racism further place many children of color at risk (Kreiger, Rowley, Herman, Avery, & Phillips, 1993). These include differential opportunities for employment and education, plus the psychosocial effects of facing discriminatory behavior from individuals and institutions daily. For many children, the experience of repeated rejection and hostility inhibits their self-esteem and contributes to high levels of frustration and anger.

Poverty

Poverty has been identified as a risk factor for a range of poor outcomes, including child abuse and neglect (Vondra, 1990), delinquency (Hawkins et al., 1992), externalizing behavior disorders (Velez, Johnson, & Cohen, 1989), and socioemotional and educational maladjustment (Felner et al., 1995). The definition of socioeconomic status (SES), which is a complex measure of economic, educational, and occupational station, differs slightly from that of poverty or low income. However, the two indicators—poverty and low SES—operate similarly to place children at risk.

The significance of poverty as a risk factor is thought to lie in the presence of multiple stressors associated with inadequate resources (Bradley et al., 1994; McLoyd, 1990; Schteingart, Molnar, Klein, Lowe, & Hartman, 1995). Children living in poverty are more frequently exposed to such risks as medical illnesses, family stress, inadequate social support, and parental depression (Parker, Greer, & Zuckerman, 1988). Because poverty is a condition that rarely changes quickly, the cumulation of stressors over time may magnify risk (Garmezy, 1993a, 1993b).

At least three mechanisms are thought to operate in making poverty a common risk factor (Bradley et al., 1994). First, poverty circumscribes a family's resources; that is, the most direct effect of poverty is that it increases the potential that a child will lack adequate food, clothing, shelter, and other basic necessities. Second, poverty limits the access of many children to adequate health services. Poor children often do not receive preventive care, and when they need health services, they tend to use the most expensive form of care—emergency room treatment. Finally, poverty is thought to act as a risk factor through its association with unsupportive, unstimulating, and chaotic home environments (Hart & Risley, 1995). Studies have shown that economic hardship is correlated both with parental psychological distress and poor family management practices (Duncan, 1991; Larner & Collins, 1996; McLoyd, 1990).

Many experts agree that the effects of poverty and other sociocultural risk factors are mediated, at least in part, through risk chains (Bradley et al., 1994; Felner et al., 1995; McLoyd, 1990). Low SES, for example, may increase family stress, which can lead to inconsistent parenting, which in turn places children at risk of behavioral difficulties (see, for example, Duncan, Brooks-Gunn, & Klebanov,

1994). Thus, in conceptualizing the effect of poverty on childhood, one must usually think in terms of linkages between and across individual, family, school, and neighborhood risk factors.

FAMILY, SCHOOL, AND NEIGHBORHOOD RISK FACTORS

Child Maltreatment

All forms of child maltreatment—neglect, physical abuse, sexual abuse, and psychological abuse—place children at risk. Recent data strongly suggest that abused and neglected children are more likely than children who have not been victimized to engage in antisocial, aggressive acts, including delinquency (Office of Juvenile Justice and Delinquency Prevention, 1995; Widom, 1989). Overall, too, they are at greater risk for a variety of psychosocial and mental disorders (Mrazek & Haggerty, 1994; Youngblade & Belsky, 1990).

Two different mechanisms, both with theoretical underpinnings, appear to explain how maltreatment increases vulnerability in children. The first explanation is derived from attachment theory. It suggests that problems in infant–caregiver attachment prevent the successful adaptation of children (Youngblade & Belsky, 1990); that is, maltreatment by a parent inhibits bonding between the infant and parent, and adequate bonding is viewed as necessary for healthy child development.

The second mechanism is derived from social learning and cognitive theories in psychology. This hypothesis argues that children develop maladaptive cognitive schemas as a result of abuse. Abused children learn to be suspicious of and hostile toward other children and adults, particularly strangers. They develop negative self-images and low self-esteem (Rutter, 1994; Widom, 1989; Youngblade & Belsky, 1990). Moreover, there is modest evidence that the experience of abuse leads children to evaluate aggressive behavior as an effective interpersonal tool in achieving personal goals (Dodge, Bates, & Pettit, 1990). Thus, many abused and neglected children view the world as hostile and, because they lack role models of competent social problem solving, they develop aggressive interpersonal styles that place them at risk of school failure, delinquency, and other social problems (Fraser, 1996).

Interparental Conflict

There is a great deal of evidence suggesting that high levels of conflict between parents are linked with psychological difficulties and antisocial behavior in children (Emery & Forehand, 1994; Farrington et al., 1993; Hawkins et al., 1992; Office of Juvenile Justice and Delinquency Prevention, 1995; O'Keefe, 1994; Rae-Grant, Thomas, Offord, & Boyle, 1989). It is thought that frequent interparental hostility and fighting both desensitizes children to conflict and provides models of poor problem solving (Emery & Forehand, 1994). More generally, interparental conflict may act as a barrier to effective parenting, thereby leaving children vulnerable to environmental conditions and negative peer influences (Emery & Forehand, 1994).

Parental Psychopathology

Various forms of parental psychopathology, including mental illness, depression, and substance abuse, also appear to place children at risk of psychosocial problems (Sameroff & Seifer, 1990; Velez et al., 1989; Werner & Smith, 1982). Parental psychopathology cannot be relegated to any one risk chain, however. The mechanisms by which parental psychopathology may influence child development range from genetic transmission of heritable attributes to parental modeling of inappropriate, learned behaviors (Factor & Wolfe, 1990). Because of the symptoms of their illnesses, parents with severe mental disorders may have difficulty providing consistent care and appropriate discipline (Masten et al., 1990). In the absence of support and treatment, parental psychopathology may also increase risk by exerting a negative effect on marital relationships and overall family functioning (Factor & Wolfe, 1990).

Poor Parenting

Poor parenting is a common risk factor for antisocial behaviors, including both delinquency and substance abuse (Hawkins et al., 1992; O'Donnell et al., 1995). Poor parenting itself is a multidimensional construct consisting of poor communication, problem-solving, and monitoring skills. Central to the construct of poor parenting is the use of poor and inconsistent family management practices, which forms the basis for Patterson's (1982) theory of coercive family process. Based on social learning theory, the coercion model of poor family management posits that parents, by responding to children's behavior inconsistently and noncontingently, teach children to use aversive behavior to meet social goals in the family, at school, and in other settings. Although poor family management practices may not cause childhood problems that have biological origins, they can exacerbate them.

INDIVIDUAL PSYCHOSOCIAL AND BIOLOGICAL RISK FACTORS

Biomedical Problems

Biomedical problems affect children in at least two ways (O'Dougherty & Wright, 1990). First, some infants and children have serious medical disorders that significantly impair cognitive abilities or increase emotional lability (Masten et al., 1990). Lacking supportive family and educational environments, these children often experience developmental delays.

Second, some children experience prenatal, perinatal, neonatal, or early developmental events that insult the developing central nervous system and increase risk for future disorders. Compared to children not experiencing birth-related problems, for example, low birthweight or premature infants appear to be more vulnerable to life stressors (Grizenko & Pawliuk, 1994; Mrazek & Haggerty, 1994; Office of Juvenile Justice and Delinquency Prevention, 1995; Werner & Smith, 1992). For both categories of biomedical risk, research suggests that outcomes are largely determined by the interplay of biological and environmental factors (Mrazek & Haggerty, 1994; Werner, 1992;

Werner & Smith, 1982). That is, biomedical risk is usually mediated by individual, family, and other contextual factors.

Gender

Gender clearly affects risk chains. In response to a variety of stressors, including family discord, divorce, and out-of-home day care, boys often show more severe and prolonged disturbances than do girls (Luthar & Zigler, 1991; Morisset, 1993). Boys are also more likely to engage in aggressive, antisocial behavior (Compas, Hinden, & Gerhardt, 1995; Patterson, Reid, & Dishion, 1992). However, Werner and Smith (1982) reported that adolescent girls often have relatively more difficulties in school, and girls have a higher risk for some mental health disorders.

Gender may be a marker for certain conditions, but it is not clear whether it is a cause. As the social expectations and opportunities for boys and girls have changed over the past century, so have the comparative rates of social and health problems. Different risk chains may operate for boys and girls; moreover, the risk and protective factors that compose these chains appear to have changed over the years. Thus, gender differences may reflect both fundamental biological differences between boys and girls and changing beliefs, values, and norms. These differences are critically important. Where the research is sufficiently strong, gender effects are discussed in subsequent chapters.

COMMON PROTECTIVE FACTORS

BROAD ENVIRONMENTAL PROTECTIVE FACTORS: OPPORTUNITIES

Adolescents who have many opportunities for education, employment, growth, and achievement are less likely than those without such opportunities to reject prosocial values out of frustration and anger. They are more likely to expect to achieve their hopes and aspirations. Moreover, through involvement and commitment to school and community, youths develop attachments to other youths who share similar values and beliefs. When risk chains begin with opportunity and family support, children may be motivated to work harder in school, to resist negative peer influences, to delay childbearing, and to engage in other prosocial behaviors.

FAMILY, SCHOOL, AND NEIGHBORHOOD PROTECTIVE FACTORS

Social Support

In an early review of resilience, Garmezy (1985) identified the existence and use of social supports as one of three broad categories of protective factors for children at risk. The growing body of evidence since then suggests that social support has both direct and indirect effects on child behavior. Feeling supported and having the resources that derive from caring social relationships have been found to promote child development for both normal-term and preterm infants (Crnic, Greenberg, Ragozin, Robinson, & Basham, 1983), for children of depressed parents (Pellegrini et al., 1986), and for children experiencing other types of environmental stress (McLoyd, 1990; Seifer et al., 1992; Werner & Smith, 1992). In addition, a large body of literature indicates that intervention programs offering supporting services to high-risk children and their families promote positive outcomes, which strongly suggests that social support serves a protective function (Luthar & Zigler, 1991).

Positive interpersonal relationships and social support may mitigate the effect of stressful life events for children in much the same way that they do for adults (Morisset, 1993). That is, supportive relationships may serve as a buffer against life stressors. Supportive families may also protect children by providing models of and reinforcement for skills that improve problem solving, motivation, academic achievement, and later socioeconomic opportunities (Masten et al., 1990). And at the community level, schools, churches, and other organizations may serve a protective function by providing settings for supportive relationships (Masten, 1994).

Presence of a Caring, Supportive Adult

The presence of a caring, supportive adult has been consistently identified as a protective factor for children across a variety of risk conditions. For example, following the death of a parent or in the face of chronic family discord, the presence of a caring, supportive adult is widely acknowledged as helping children respond positively to and recover from loss, trauma, and stress (Brooks, 1994; Grizenko & Pawliuk, 1994; Rutter, 1987; Werner, 1993). The caregiver need not be a parent, but may be a grandparent or other extended relative, a teacher, a mentor, a human services worker, or a volunteer from community groups and agencies. Mechanisms whereby these adults protect children appear to include modeling prosocial skills and behavior, helping the child to build self-esteem, providing information and access to knowledge, and providing guidance and offering a source of protection against environmental stressors (Masten, 1994).

Positive Parent–Child Relationship

A good relationship with at least one parent has been shown to diminish the effects of interparental conflict (Emery & Forehand, 1994; Neighbors, Forehand, & McVicar, 1993; O'Keefe, 1994; Rutter, 1979). It also appears to function protectively against more generalized life stressors, such as economic hardship or stressful life events (Radke-Yarrow & Sherman, 1990; Werner & Smith, 1982). Positive parent–child relationships help children feel secure and they promote more consistent supervision and discipline. Moreover, they contribute to cognitive and social development both through direct instructional activities, such as helping with homework, and through the indirect processes associated with mentoring, caring, and nurturing (Neighbors et al., 1993).

Effective Parenting

Werner (1993) concluded that the effects of several risk conditions, including poor birth outcomes such as low birthweight, were almost totally mediated by the quality of child-rearing conditions. For very young children, effective parenting may promote self-efficacy and self-worth through the development of secure infant–caregiver attachments, providing a basis for subsequent cognitive development and social adaptation (Masten et al., 1990; Morisset, 1993). Furthermore, effective parents provide children with a model for effective action, provide opportunities for children to experience mastery, and may persuade children of their own effectiveness, thereby increasing feelings of self-efficacy (Bandura, 1982).

INDIVIDUAL PSYCHOSOCIAL AND BIOLOGICAL PROTECTIVE FACTORS

Easy Temperament

One of the most frequently cited protective factors in infants is a positive or "easy" temperament (Cowan et al., 1990; Grizenko & Pawliuk, 1994; O'Keefe, 1994; Werner, 1993). Temperament refers to such attributes as activity level, feeding patterns, adaptability, intensity of reactions to stimuli, and reflectiveness in meeting new situations. Temperament may operate directly as a protective factor by influencing a child's perception of and reaction to a stressor, or it may operate indirectly by enabling children to elicit positive responses from caretakers (Morisset, 1993; Rutter, 1987).

Competence in Normative Roles: Self-Efficacy

Bandura (1977, 1982) conceptualized a process by which competence serves a protective function for children through the development of self-efficacy (a belief in one's personal effectiveness). He argued that success in one developmental setting increases a child's view of himself or herself as effective, in turn enhancing the motivation to act positively in other developmental settings. In one sense, then, self-efficacy is thought to promote adaptation, coping, and achievement across systems. Empirical evidence supports the idea that experiences of success lead to increased self-efficacy (Brooks, 1994; Morisset, 1993; Rae-Grant et al., 1989; Rutter, 1985; Wills, Baccara, & McNamara, 1992). Although it is not clear whether self-efficacy mediates academic, social, or athletic success in school, it is clear that success in school protects children against delinquency, substance abuse, teen parenting, and other social and health problems (Carnahan, 1994; O'Donnell et al., 1995; Scott-Jones, 1991).

Self-Esteem

Self-esteem has been cited as a major protective factor for recovery from child maltreatment (Moran & Eckenrode, 1992) and a variety of other social and health problems (Garmezy, 1985; Masten et al., 1990 ; Rutter, 1979; Werner & Smith, 1992). According to Brooks (1994), "Self-esteem may be understood as including the feelings and thoughts that individuals have about their competence and worth, about their abilities to make a difference, to confront rather than retreat from challenges, to learn from both success and failure, and to treat themselves and others with respect" (p. 547). So defined, self-esteem incorporates the elements of self-efficacy. Enhancement of self-esteem may represent the protective mechanism through which many commonly cited protective factors—participation in hobbies (Grizenko & Pawliuk, 1994), responsibility for regular household chores (Werner & Smith, 1992), or good performance in school (Carnahan, 1994)—operate.

Intelligence

Finally, as measured by IQ and other tests, intelligence appears to be moderately negatively associated with some social and health problems. Controlling for race or ethnicity and SES, low intelligence is often correlated with aggressive, antisocial behavior, including various forms of delinquency (Farrington et al., 1993). In turn, high intelligence is often cited as a protective factor against antisocial behavior (Masten, 1994). Studies have also demonstrated the protective effects of high intelligence against generalized life stress (Radke-Yarrow & Sherman, 1990). In pondering such findings, Rutter (1979, 1985) speculated that high intelligence operates as a protective factor through two pathways. First, he suggested that high intelligence may lead to academic success, which in turn leads to higher self-esteem and self-efficacy. Second, he argued that more capable children may develop more sophisticated problem-solving skills, which give rise, in turn, to comparatively more effective responses to stressful situations.

CONCLUSION

This chapter has defined the basic concepts of risk, resilience, and protection that characterize a new way to understand human behavior and the ecology of childhood. Employing both ecological and multisystems perspectives, it discussed risk traits, stressful life events, cumulative risk, and risk chains. The interplay of risk and protective factors was then explored from the viewpoint of resilience. Finally, the chapter addressed risk and protective factors that appear to be common to many childhood disorders and problems. This model of common risk and protective factors serves as the basic reference for the chapters that follow.

REFERENCES

Agnew, R. A. (1993). Why do they do it? An examination of the intervening mechanisms between "social control" variables and delinquency. *Journal of Research in Crime and Delinquency, 30*, 245–266.

Anthony, E. J. (1987). Risk, vulnerability, and resilience: An overview. In E. J. Anthony & B. J. Cohler (Eds.), *The invulnerable child* (pp. 3–48). New York: Guilford Press.

Baldwin, A. L., Baldwin, C., & Cole, R. E. (1990). Stress-resistant families and stress-resistant children. In J. Rolf, A. Masten, D. Cicchetti, K. H. Nuechterlein, & S. Weintraub (Eds.), *Risk and protective factors in the development of psychopathology* (pp. 257–280). New York: Cambridge University Press.

Bandura, A. (1977). Self-efficacy: Toward a unifying theory of behavioral change. *Psychological Review, 84*, 191–215.

Bandura, A. (1982). Self-efficacy mechanisms in human agency. *American Psychologist, 37*, 122–147.

Begun, A. L. (1993). Human behavior and the social environment: The vulnerability, risk, and resilience model. *Journal of Social Work Education, 29*, 26–35.

Benard, B. (1993). Fostering resiliency in kids. *Educational Leadership, 51*(3), 44–49.

Bradley, R. H., Whiteside, L., Mundfrom, D. J., Casey, P. H., Kelleher, K. J., & Pope, S. K. (1994). Early indications of resilience and their relation to experiences in the home environments of low birthweight, premature children living in poverty. *Child Development, 65*, 346–360.

Bronfenbrenner, U. (1979). *The ecology of human development: Experiments by nature and design.* Cambridge, MA: Harvard University Press.

Brooks, R. B. (1994). Children at risk: Fostering resilience and hope. *American Journal of Orthopsychiatry, 64*, 545–553.

Carnahan, S. (1994). Preventing school failure and dropout. In R. J. Simeonsson (Ed.), *Risk, resilience, and prevention: Promoting the well-being of all children* (pp. 103–124). Baltimore: Paul H. Brookes.

Cicchetti, D. (1990). A historical perspective on the discipline of developmental psychopathology. In J. Rolf, A. Masten, D. Cicchetti, K. H. Nuechterlein, & S. Weintraub (Eds.), *Risk and protective factors in the development of psychopathology* (pp. 2–28). New York: Cambridge University Press.

Cohen, J., & Cohen, P. (1983). *Applied multiple regression/correlation analysis for the behavioral sciences* (2nd ed.). Hillsdale, NJ: Lawrence Erlbaum.

Coie, J. D., Watt, N. F., West, S. G., Hawkins, J. D., Asarnow, J. R., Markman, H. J., Ramey, S. L., Shure, M. B., & Long, B. (1993). The science of prevention: A conceptual framework and some directions for a national research program. *American Psychologist, 48*, 1013–1022.

Compas, B. E., Hinden, B. R., & Gerhardt, C. A. (1995). Adolescent development: Pathways and processes of risk and resilience. *Annual Reviews in Psychology, 46*, 265–293.

Cowan, E. L., Wyman, P. A., Work, W. C., & Parker, G. R. (1990). The Rochester Child Resilience Project: Overview and summary of first year findings. *Development and Psychopathology, 2*, 193–212.

Crook, T., & Eliot, J. (1980). Parental death during childhood and adult depression: A critical review of the literature. *Psychological Bulletin, 87*, 252–259.

Crnic, K. A., Greenberg, M. T., Ragozin, A. S., Robinson, N. M., & Basham, R. B. (1983). Effects of stress and social support on mothers and premature and full-term infants. *Child Development, 54*, 209–217.

Dodge, K. A., Bates, J. E., & Pettit, G. S. (1990). Mechanisms in the cycle of violence. *Science, 250*, 1678–1683.

Duncan, G. J. (1991). The economic environment of childhood. In A. C. Huston (Ed.), *Children in poverty: Child development and public policy* (pp. 23–50). New York: Cambridge University Press.

Duncan, G. J., Brooks-Gunn, J., & Klebanov, P. K. (1994). Economic deprivation and early childhood development. *Child Development, 65*, 296–318.

Emery, R. E., & Forehand, R. (1994). Parental divorce and children's well-being: A focus on resilience. In R. J. Haggerty, L. R. Sherrod, N. Garmezy, & M. Rutter (Eds.), *Stress, risk and resilience in children and adolescents: Processes, mechanisms and interventions* (pp. 64–99). New York: Cambridge University Press.

Factor, D. C., & Wolfe, D. A. (1990). Parental psychopathology and high-risk children. In R. T. Ammerman & M. Hersen (Eds.), *Children at risk: An evaluation of factors contributing to child abuse and neglect* (pp. 171–198). New York: Plenum Press.

Farber, E. A., & Egeland, B. (1987). Invulnerability among abused and neglected children. In E. J. Anthony & B. J. Cohler (Eds.), *The invulnerable child* (pp. 253–288). New York: Guilford Press.

Farrington, D. P., Loeber, R., Elliott, D. S., Hawkins, J. D., Kandel, D. B., Klein, M. W., McCord, J., Rowe, D. C., & Tremblay, R. E. (1993). Advancing knowledge about the onset of delinquency and crime. In B. B. Lahey & A. E. Kazdin (Eds.), *Advances in clinical child psychology* (Vol. 13, pp. 283–342). New York: Plenum Press.

Felix-Ortiz, M., & Newcomb, M. D. (1992). Risk and protective factors for drug use among Latino and white adolescents. *Hispanic Journal of Behavioral Sciences, 14*, 291–309.

Felner, R. D., Brand, S., Dubois, D. L., Adan, A. M., Mulhall, P. F., & Evans, E. (1995). Socioeconomic disadvantage, proximal environmental experiences, and socioemotional and academic adjustment in early adolescence: Investigation of a mediated effects model. *Child Development, 66*, 774–792.

Fisher, L., Kokes, R. F., Cole, R. E., Perkins, P. M., & Wynne, L. C. (1987). Competent children at risk: A study of well-functioning offspring of disturbed parents. In E. J. Anthony & B. J. Cohler (Eds.), *The invulnerable child* (pp. 211–228). New York: Guilford Press.

Fraser, M. W. (1996). Cognitive problem-solving and aggressive behavior among children. *Families in Society, 77*, 19–32.

Garbarino, J., Kostelny, K., & Dubrown, N. (1991). What children can tell us about living in danger. *American Psychologist, 46*, 376–383.

Garmezy, N. (1985). Stress-resistant children: The search for protective factors. In J. E. Stevenson (Ed.), *Recent research in developmental psychopathology* (pp. 213–233). Tarrytown, NY: Pergamon Press.

Garmezy, N. (1993a). Children in poverty: Resilience despite risk. *Psychiatry, 56*, 127–36.

Garmezy, N. (1993b). Vulnerability and resilience. In D. C. Funder, R. D. Parke, C. Tomlinson-Keasey, & K. Widaman (Eds.), *Studying lives through time* (pp. 377–398). Washington, DC: American Psychological Association.

Garmezy, N., & Masten, A. (1991). The protective role of competence indicators in children at risk. In E. M. Cummings (Ed.), *Life span developmental psychology: Perspectives on stress and coping* (pp. 151–176). Hillsdale, NJ: Lawrence Erlbaum.

Grizenko, N., & Fisher, C. (1992). Risk and protective factors for psychopathology in children. *Canadian Journal of Psychiatry, 37*, 711–721.

Grizenko, N., & Pawliuk, N. (1994). Risk and protective factors for disruptive behavior disorders in children. *American Journal of Orthopsychiatry, 64*, 534–544.

Hart, B., & Risley, T. R. (1995). *Meaning differences in the everyday experience of young American children*. Baltimore: Paul H. Brookes.

Hawkins, J. D., Catalano, R. F., & Miller, J. Y. (1992). Risk and protective factors for alcohol and other drug problems in adolescence and early adulthood: Implications for substance abuse prevention. *Psychological Bulletin, 112*, 64–105.

Kreiger, N., Rowley, D. L., Herman, A. A., Avery, B., & Phillips, M. T. (1993). Racism, sexism, and social class: Implications for studies of health, disease, and well-being. *American Journal of Preventive Medicine, 9*(6)(Suppl.), 82–122.

Larner, M., & Collins, A. (1996). Poverty in the lives of young children. In E. J. Erwin (Ed.), *Putting children first* (pp. 55–75). Baltimore: Paul H. Brookes.

Levy, J. E., & Kunitz, S. J. (1987). A suicide prevention program for Hopi youth. *Social Science and Medicine, 25*, 931–940.

Lilienfield, A. M., & Lilienfield, D. E. (1980). *Foundations of epidemiology* (2nd ed.). New York: Oxford University Press.

Loeber, R., & Stouthamer-Loeber, M. (1996). The development of offending. *Criminal Justice and Behavior, 23*(1), 12–24.

Luthar, S. S. (1991). Vulnerability and resilience: A study of high-risk adolescents. *Child Development, 62*, 600–616.

Luthar, S. S., Doernberger, C. H., & Zigler, E. (1993). Resilience is not a unidimensional construct: Insights from a prospective study of inner-city adolescents. *Development and Psychopathology, 5*, 703–717.

Luthar, S. S., & Zigler, E. (1991). Vulnerability and competence: A review of research on resilience in childhood. *American Journal of Orthopsychiatry, 61*, 6–22.

Masten, A. (1987). Resilience in development: Implications of the study of successful adaptation for developmental psychopathology. In D. Cicchetti (Ed.), *The emergence of a discipline: Rochester symposium on developmental psychopathology* (pp. 261–294). Hillsdale, NJ: Lawrence Erlbaum.

Masten, A. (1994). Resilience in individual development: Successful adaptation despite risk and adversity. In M. C. Wang & E. W. Gordon (Eds.), *Educational resilience in inner-city America: Challenges and prospects* (pp. 3–26). Hillsdale, NJ: Lawrence Erlbaum.

Masten, A., Best, K. M., & Garmezy, N. (1990). Resilience and development: Contributions from the study of children who overcome adversity. *Development and Psychopathology, 2*, 425–444.

McLoyd, V. C. (1990). The impact of economic hardship on black families and children: Psychological distress, parenting, and socioemotional development. *Child Development, 61*, 335–343.

Moran, P. B., & Eckenrode, J. (1992). Protective personality characteristics among adolescent victims of maltreatment. *Child Abuse & Neglect, 16*, 743–754.

Morisset, C. E. (1993). Language and emotional milestones on the road to readiness (Report No. 18, Center on Families, Communities, Schools and Children's Learning). Arlington, VA: Zero to Three National Center for Clinical Infant Programs.

Mrazek, P. J., & Haggerty, R. J. (Eds.) (1994). *Reducing risks for mental disorders: Frontiers for preventive intervention research.* Washington, DC: National Academy Press.

Myers, H. F., Taylor, S., Alvy, K. T., Arrington, A., & Richardson, M. A. (1992). Parental and family predictors of behavior problems in inner-city black children. *American Journal of Community Psychology, 20,* 557–575.

Neighbors, B., Forehand, M. S., & McVicar, D. (1993). Resilient adolescents and interparental conflict. *American Journal of Orthopsychiatry, 63,* 462–471.

Nettles, S. M., & Pleck, J. H. (1994). Risk, resilience, and development: The multiple ecologies of black adolescents. In R. J. Haggerty, L. R. Sherrod, N. Garmezy, & M. Rutter (Eds.), *Stress, risk and resilience in children and adolescents: Processes, mechanisms and interventions* (pp. 147–181). New York: Cambridge University Press.

O'Donnell, J., Hawkins, J. D., & Abbott, R. D. (1995). Predicting serious delinquency and substance abuse among aggressive boys. *Journal of Consulting and Clinical Psychology, 63,* 529–537.

O'Dougherty, M., & Wright, F. S. (1990). Children born at medical risk: Factors affecting vulnerability and resilience. In J. Rolf, A. Masten, D. Cicchetti, K. H. Nuechterlein, & S. Weintraub (Eds.), *Risk and protective factors in the development of psychopathology* (pp. 120–140). New York: Cambridge University Press.

Office of Juvenile Justice and Delinquency Prevention. (1995, June). *Juvenile Justice Bulletin: OJJDP update on programs.* Washington, DC: U.S. Department of Justice, Office of Justice Programs.

O'Keefe, M. (1994). Adjustment of children from maritally violent homes. *Families in Society, 75,* 403–415.

Parker, S., Greer, S., & Zuckerman, B. (1988). Double jeopardy: The impact of poverty on early child development. *Pediatric Clinics of North America, 35,* 1127–1241.

Patterson, G. R. (1982). *Coercive family process.* Eugene, OR: Castalia.

Patterson, G. R., Reid, J. B., & Dishion, T. J. (1992). *Antisocial boys.* Eugene, OR: Castalia.

Pellegrini, D. S. (1990). Psychosocial risk and protective factors in childhood. *Developmental and Behavioral Pediatrics, 11*(4), 201–209.

Pellegrini, D. S., Kosisky, S., Nackman, D., Cytryn, L., McKnew, D. H., Gershon, E., Hamovit, J., & Cammuso, K. (1986). Personal and social resources in children of patients with bipolar affective disorder and children of normal controls. *American Journal of Psychiatry, 143,* 856–861.

Peoples, F., & Loeber, R. (1994). Do individual factors and neighborhood context explain ethnic differences in juvenile delinquency? *Journal of Quantitative Criminology, 10*(2), 141–157.

Radke-Yarrow, M., & Sherman, T. (1990). Hard growing: Children who survive. In J. Rolf, A. Masten, D. Cicchetti, K. H. Nuechterlein, & S. Weintraub (Eds.), *Risk and protective factors in the development of psychopathology* (pp. 97–119). New York: Cambridge University Press.

Rae-Grant, N., Thomas, B. H., Offord, D. R., & Boyle, M. H. (1989). Risk, protective factors, and the prevalence of behavioral and emotional disorders in children and adolescents. *Journal of the American Academy of Child and Adolescent Psychiatry, 28,* 262–268.

Rende, R., & Plomin, R. (1993). Families at risk for psychopathology: Who becomes affected and why? *Development and Psychopathology, 5,* 529–540.

Rutter, M. (1979). Protective factors in children's responses to stress and disadvantage. In J. S. Bruner & A. Garten (Eds.), *Primary prevention of psychopathology* (Vol. 3, pp. 49–74). Hanover, NH: University Press of New England.

Rutter, M. (1983). Statistical and personal interactions: Facets and perspectives. In D Magnusson & V. L. Allen (Eds.), *Human development: An interactional perspective* (pp. 295–320). New York: Academic Press.

Rutter, M. (1985). Family and school influences on behavioural development. *Journal of Child Psychology and Psychiatry, 26,* 349–368.

Rutter, M. (1987). Psychosocial resilience and protective mechanisms. *American Journal of Orthopsychiatry, 57,* 316–331.

Rutter, M. (1994). Stress research: Accomplishments and tasks ahead. In R. J. Haggerty, L. R. Sherrod, N. Garmezy, & M. Rutter (Eds.), *Stress, risk and resilience in children and adolescents: Processes, mechanisms and interventions* (pp. 354–386). New York: Cambridge University Press.

Sameroff, A. J., & Seifer, R. (1990). Early contributors to developmental risk. . In J. Rolf, A. Masten, D. Cicchetti, K. H. Nuechterlein, & S. Weintraub (Eds.), *Risk and protective factors in the development of psychopathology* (pp. 52–66). New York: Cambridge University Press.

Schteingart, J. S., Molnar, J., Klein, T. P., Lowe, C. B., & Hartman, A. H. (1995). Homelessness and child functioning in the context of risk and protective factors moderating child outcomes. *Journal of Clinical Child Psychology, 24,* 320–331.

Scott-Jones, D. (1991). Adolescent childbearing: Risks and resilience. *Education and Urban Society, 24*(1), 53–64.

Seifer, R., & Sameroff, A. J. (1987). Multiple determinants of risk and invulnerability. In E. J. Anthony & B. J. Cohler (Eds.), *The invulnerable child* (pp. 51–69). New York: Guilford Press.

Seifer, R., Sameroff, A. J., Baldwin, C. P., & Baldwin, A. (1992). Child and family factors that ameliorate risk between 4 and 13 years of age. *Journal of the American Academy of Child and Adolescent Psychiatry, 31,* 893–903.

Simeonsson, R. J. (1994). Toward an epidemiology of developmental, educational and social problems of childhood. In R. J. Simeonsson (Ed.), *Risk, resilience, and prevention: Promoting the well-being of all children* (pp. 13–32). Baltimore: Paul H. Brookes.

Sterling, S., Cowen, E. L., Weissberg, R. P., Lotyczewske, B. S., & Boike, M. (1985). Recent stressful life events and young children's school adjustment. *American Journal of Community Psychology, 13*(1), 87–98.

Stouthamer-Loeber, M., Loeber, R., Farrington, D. P., Zhang, Q., van Kammen, W., & Maguin, E. (1993). The double edge of protective and risk factors for delinquency: Interrelations and developmental patterns. *Development and Psychopathology, 5,* 683–701.

Taylor, R. D. (1994). Risk and resilience: Contextual influences on the development of African-American adolescents. In M. C. Wang & E. W. Gordon (Eds.),

Educational resilience in inner-city America: Challenges and prospects (pp. 119–130). Hillsdale, NJ: Lawrence Erlbaum.

Velez, C. N., Johnson, J., & Cohen, P. (1989). A longitudinal analysis of selected risk factors for childhood psychopathology. *Journal of the American Academy of Child and Adolescent Psychiatry, 28*, 861–864.

Vondra, J. I. (1990). Sociological and ecological factors. In R. T. Ammerman & M. Hersen (Eds.), *Children at risk: An evaluation of factors contributing to child abuse and neglect* (pp. 149–170). New York: Plenum Press.

Werner, E. E. (1984, November). Resilient children. *Young Children*, pp. 68–72.

Werner, E. E. (1992). The children of Kauai: Resiliency and recovery in adolescence and adulthood. *Journal of Adolescent Health, 13*(4), 262–268.

Werner, E. E. (1993). Risk, resilience, and recovery: Perspectives from the Kauai Longitudinal Study. *Development and Psychopathology, 5,* 503–515.

Werner, E. E., & Smith, R. S. (1977). *Kauai's children come of age.* Honolulu: University of Hawaii Press.

Werner, E. E., & Smith, R. S. (1982). *Vulnerable but invincible: A longitudinal study of resilient children and youth.* New York: Cambridge University Press.

Werner, E. E., & Smith, R. S. (1992). *Overcoming the odds: High risk children from birth to adulthood.* Ithaca, NY: Cornell University Press.

Widom, C. S. (1989). Does violence beget violence? A critical examination of the literature. *Psychological Bulletin, 106,* 3–28.

Wills, T. A., Baccara, D., & McNamara, G. (1992). The role of life events, family support, and competence in adolescent substance use: A test of vulnerability and protective factors. *American Journal of Community Psychology, 20,* 349–374.

Wolin, S., & Wolin, S. (1995). Resilience among youth growing up in substance-abusing families. *Pediatric Clinics of North America, 42,* 415–429.

Youngblade, L. M., & Belsky, J. (1990). Social and emotional consequences of child maltreatment. In R. T. Ammerman & M. Hersen (Eds.), *Children at risk: An evaluation of factors contributing to child abuse and neglect* (pp. 109–148). New York: Plenum Press.

3

METHODS IN THE ANALYSIS OF RISK AND PROTECTIVE FACTORS: LESSONS FROM EPIDEMIOLOGY

James K. Nash and Mark W. Fraser

An ecological approach to the study of social and health problems provides a framework for the assessment of risk and protective factors and for the design of more effective programs for children. This approach draws heavily from the social work concept of person-in-environment, which emphasizes the importance of identifying and assessing the role of individual and environmental factors that lead to or exacerbate social problems (Germain, 1991; Germain & Gitterman, 1980; Hollis & Woods, 1981). Also important is the identification and assessment of individual and environmental strengths and resources, from which flow effective social interventions that improve the degree of fit between a person and his or her environment.

Ecological perspectives are closely tied to the discipline of epidemiology, which is concerned with identifying and describing patterns of the occurrence of disease and health in human populations. From both ecological and epidemiological perspectives, researchers investigate the roles and interactions of physical, social, and biological factors in producing various health outcomes such as mortality and morbidity (Knox, 1979). This chapter explores epidemiological methods for the statistical analysis of case data on risk and protective factors.

AN EPIDEMIOLOGICAL PERSPECTIVE

Like research in the social sciences and social work, epidemiological research in public health seeks to generate new knowledge that can be put to practical use in prevention and treatment (Hennekens & Buring, 1987; Leaverton, 1991). It focuses on identifying causal agents of diseases, social problems, and health-related states. The purposes of modern epidemiology are to "(1) identify the etiology of deviations from health, (2) provide the data necessary to prevent or control disease through public health intervention, and (3) provide data necessary to maximize the timing and effectiveness of clinical interventions" (Valanis, 1992, p. 7).

The epidemiological literature yields three very useful ideas. To understand social and health problems more fully, we should focus on the distribution of wellness in addition to the distribution of problems and disorders in large groups and populations, attempt to identify potential causal agents, and produce knowledge that is practical, in that it can be used in the design of services. An epidemiological approach provides a framework for studying how frequently problems occur, for identifying factors that may lead to or exacerbate problems, and for developing strategies to address problems. More important, perhaps, it provides a means for the identification and assessment of factors that promote normative development and protect children and adolescents from risk.

LARGE GROUPS AND POPULATIONS

Epidemiology is concerned primarily with the occurrence of risk in large groups and populations, not with the course of a problem or disorder in an individual. This focus on populations led, historically, to the use of simple statistical techniques to determine whether the presence or absence of individual and environmental conditions was associated with the occurrence of health or disease. The key idea in epidemiology is that a large sample size is usually necessary to establish a reliable association between the existence of a factor (or agent) and the occurrence of an outcome. Determining that an association exists is the first step in establishing whether there is a causal relationship between two social or environmental conditions.

CAUSATION

The second element in an epidemiological approach is the identification of the causes of a condition or problem. Social problems, diseases, and disorders rarely have single causes (Knox, 1979; Leaverton, 1991). Rather, multiple environmental and individual factors are suspected to cause or increase the likelihood of problems or conditions. These factors may interact with one another and affect outcomes in ways that are difficult to observe or measure.

In this book we advocate that an ecological perspective be used to evaluate the roles of suspected causal agents. Basing their conclusions on findings across many studies, authors frequently contend that the presence of one or more factors is associated with an increased probability, risk, or odds of a future condition or problem. As we show later in this chapter, this concept of risk can be expressed mathematically.

PREVENTION, CONTROL, AND TREATMENT

From risk and odds data, scientists, scholars, and policymakers have attempted to develop interventions that will prevent the occurrence or spread of a problem or condition and that will result in more effective treatment. For some conditions—particularly some health problems—researchers can prove causality. They, along with policymakers, administrators, and practitioners, can develop and implement preventive and treatment strategies accordingly.

One need not, however, prove causality to develop and implement effective preventive and treatment strategies. It may not be possible to identify all the causes of many problems; moreover, causes may vary by child development, gender, and race or ethnicity. But once research has demonstrated that the presence of a particular factor consistently increases the risk or odds of the occurrence of the problem, strategies for prevention, control, and treatment target that factor and conditions associated with it. And when research has identified a protective factor, scholars, policymakers, and practitioners can design and implement strategies designed to enhance its effects.

These strategies are then tested. For example, when researchers determined that certain behaviors functioned as risk factors for the transmission of HIV, the precursor of AIDS, public health workers designed and evaluated the effectiveness of strategies targeting these high-risk behaviors (see chapter 10). In one study, researchers randomly divided gay men at high risk for HIV infection into two groups, an experimental group and a waiting-list control group. The members of the experimental group participated in 12 weekly instructional sessions designed to increase their knowledge of risk behaviors and to teach them strategies for avoiding high-risk circumstances. The authors found that the subjects who received training reported a significant decrease in the level of high-risk activities that may result in virus transmission (Kelly, St. Lawrence, Hood, & Brasfield, 1989).

ASSESSMENT OF RISK IN LARGE GROUPS AND IN INDIVIDUALS

The concepts of risk and protection are measurable, and can be expressed as a number, for groups and for individuals. By taking accurate measurements over time, researchers (including practitioners) can compare the occurrence of problem conditions in groups with and without risk and protective factors (Hennekens & Buring, 1987). For example, suppose a school social worker is responsible for several elementary schools and is concerned that student absences at two schools seem excessive when compared with other elementary schools in the district. In this situation, the social worker can invoke a large-number (that is, epidemiological) approach to measure risk and protection.

To test her idea about absentee rates, the social worker would have to determine the number of students enrolled in all schools and examine attendance records. By calculating respective attendance rates, she can confirm or reject her suspicion about excessive absences at two schools. If these schools do exhibit higher absentee rates, she can attempt to identify potential risk and protective factors that are associated with the different rates. To do this, she may draw on practice experience; knowledge about the schools and neighborhoods involved; interviews with teachers, students, and parents; and other sources of information. When the worker has identified and measured suspected factors, she can compare their occurrence at different schools to determine whether they function as risk or protective factors. We describe below several relatively simple methods for accomplishing this task. Each method yields a number expressing the estimated strength of risk and protective factors. Use of one or more of these methods can help practitioners more effectively target resources and energy. However, the resulting number expressing the estimated risk or protection cannot be generalized to other similar problems or to other communities unless additional studies produce similar results.

If a practitioner is concerned with developing an individual-focused intervention, measurement of risk and protective factors has a somewhat different meaning. For example, suppose the social worker is concerned about a particular student's excessive absences. The first step in intervention should be an individualized and comprehensive assessment that captures a wide range of data about the student and his or her environment. The presence or absence of identified risk and protective factors should be one important aspect of this assessment. To identify those risk and protective factors, the worker can complete one or more formal assessments. (In other chapters of this book are descriptions of numerous instruments designed to identify risk and protective factors for a range of social problems affecting children and adolescents.)

Of course, the scores on these instruments represent one of many components of an accurate and comprehensive assessment of an individual and his or her environment. An instrument may be excellent for identifying problems that are amenable to intervention and change and for highlighting strengths and resources residing within the student and the environment. But the instrument may also miss important factors unique to a particular individual or situation that contribute to the problem or that might promote a solution. Measuring the strength of risk and protective factors with standardized instruments cannot account for the total cluster of resources and problems that may be present. It is critical, then, that a comprehensive assessment employ a variety of methods, such as semistructured interviews, to develop a complete picture of the situation.

COMMON STATISTICS IN EPIDEMIOLOGY

Before describing methods for analyzing risk and protective factors for social problems, we define several basic terms readers will encounter throughout this book. A *ratio* is simply a fraction, with a numerator and a denominator. It expresses one quantity divided by a second quantity. There is no implication of a relationship between the numerator and denominator. For example, 1/3 means one divided by three. As a ratio, 1/3 does not imply one out of three.

A *proportion* is a special kind of ratio in which "those who are included in the numerator must also be included in the denominator" (Hennekens & Buring, 1987, p. 56). For example, if there are 10 adolescents in a math class, and five are known to be academically gifted, the proportion of academically gifted students in the class is 5/10, or five of ten. Proportions are often expressed as percentages: 50 percent of the students are academically gifted. A population-based example might involve the proportion of children in a state who have appeared in juvenile court. If there are 1 million children in the state, and 2,000 have appeared in juvenile court, the proportion of court-involved children is 2,000/1,000,000, or two per 1,000, or 0.2 percent.

A *rate* is a special kind of proportion. As in a proportion, those appearing in the numerator of a rate must appear also in the denominator; further, there is a relationship between the numerator and denominator that is expressed with respect to a specified unit of time. For example, a rate might express the number of days absent per 1,000 middle school children during a one-month period (Hennekens & Buring, 1987). In the juvenile court example (above), there is no way to know whether 0.2 percent of the state's children went to juvenile court last year or whether 0.2 percent of them have ever been to court. The proportion becomes a rate when it is expressed with respect to a specific unit of time (for example, the proportion of children who appeared in juvenile court in 1997).

In expressing a rate, it is important to define clearly what is being included in both the numerator and denominator (Hennekens & Buring, 1987). In a study of school violence, one might include the number of students per 1,000 enrolled who committed a violent act at school in the most recent month, the percentage of enrolled students who were assaulted at school over the past five school years, or the proportion of students committing an assault who were expelled during the most recent school year. All are rates and each is different. A study of the rate of assaults at school would have to specify what is being measured. Do assaults committed on the school bus count? If a student hits two peers during one incident, is this considered one act or two? Are assaults committed against staff treated in the same way as assaults committed against other students?

Prevalence is a rate often used in epidemiological studies and is defined as the number of existing cases of a condition at a given point in time divided by total population. The point in time can be "a specific point in calendar time" or a "fixed point in the course of events that varies in real time from person to person," such as the onset of puberty or the onset of menopause (Hennekens & Buring, 1987, p. 57). For example, one could measure the prevalence of gun ownership by adolescents by administering a survey to every adolescent in a city on the first of June, phrasing questions in terms of current ownership of a gun (that is, "Do you now own or have possession of a gun?"). The survey could be repeated each year on the first of June to measure year-to-year changes in the prevalence of gun ownership.

Incidence is also a rate, but it expresses new occurrences of a problem or condition within a time period. Incidence "quantifies the number of new events or cases of disease that develops in a population of individuals at risk during a specified time interval" (Hennekens & Buring, 1987, p. 57). Unlike prevalence, which gives the number of existing cases, incidence expresses the number of new cases. Incidence is calculated over an interval of time, in contrast to prevalence, which is calculated at a specific point in time. Incidence is commonly used in epidemiological studies.

In studying the problem of adolescent gun ownership, one could define incidence as the number of adolescents who acquired a gun, for the first time, during the period January 1 to May 31. The survey administered would reflect that definition with a suitably worded question (for example, "During the period from January 1 to May 31, did you buy or come into possession of a gun for the first time?"). Survey designers would need to decide exactly how to phrase questions to capture the specific desired information. For example, if an adolescent acquired a gun for the first time during the period, but immediately gave it away, would this count as a positive response?

Proportions, incidence rates, and prevalence rates are measurements commonly used in the assessment of the scope of child and adolescent social problems. For example, teachers concerned with the lack of after-school resources for children in a specific neighborhood can calculate a simple proportion to demonstrate the seriousness of the problem. By conducting an informal survey of other teachers, they can measure (approximately) the number of children from the neighborhood who have no caregivers in the home during the afternoon and who do not have access to an after-school program. This number, divided by the total number of children from the neighborhood who are enrolled in the school, gives the proportion of affected children. The teachers who collect such data might then report their results to community leaders in an effort to mobilize resources to address the problem.

Returning to the problem of school absenteeism, suppose that four schools keep records of absences and that you compile these data. The compiled data might look something like Table 3-1, which presents hypothetical data on the respective prevalences of absenteeism on a Monday.

This information confirms the suspicion that schools A and C have a higher rate of absenteeism, at least on one Monday. It would be useful to know whether these

Table 3-1. Student Absences on Monday, by School

SCHOOL	STUDENTS ABSENT	TOTAL STUDENTS	% ABSENT
A	30	300	10
B	6	300	2
C	45	300	15
D	12	300	4

numbers reflect the prevalence of absenteeism over time. To determine this, you could measure the prevalence each day of the month for several months. If the prevalence remains stable over time, one might reasonably conclude that schools A and C do have a problem with excessive absenteeism.

This latter procedure, measuring prevalence at different points, is not the same as calculating incidence, which measures the number of new cases over an interval of time. A nurse in a neonatal intensive care unit might be concerned with community services for babies born to mothers who are HIV positive. To demonstrate the scope of the problem he can calculate a monthly incidence rate by counting the number of these babies born (new cases) during the month (specified interval). This calculation would provide specific basic information about the problem. To obtain still more information about the scope of the problem and the need for services, he could calculate monthly incidence rates over an entire year, as shown in Table 3-2. These data suggest that the problem is growing, which could constitute evidence of the need for expanded services for this population.

Measures of Association: Relative Risk and Odds Ratio

Because child and adolescent behavior problems are almost always multiply determined, we will probably never fully understand all their causes. However, a risk-factor approach

Table 3-2. Incidence of Births to Women Who Are HIV Positive, over 12 Months

MONTH	NUMBER OF NEW CASES	MONTH	NUMBER OF NEW CASES
January	3	July	6
February	4	August	9
March	4	September	9
April	5	October	8
May	5	November	9
June	5	December	10

provides a broad framework for assessment. Knowledge of the existence and relative importance of risk and protective factors can inform efforts to design and implement more effective programs and interventions. In the linear (or additive) model, as opposed to an interactive one, the concept of risk factor is essentially identical to that of protective factor. As discussed in chapter 2, the distinction lies in the direction of the association between a factor and the occurrence of an outcome (desired or undesired). If a factor ("survivor of sexual abuse," for example) is associated with a higher likelihood of a negative outcome, it acts as a risk factor. If the factor ("has a positive relationship with an adult," perhaps) is associated with a higher likelihood of a positive outcome (or with the lower likelihood of a negative outcome), it is often considered a protective factor.

The assessment of risk or protective factors depends on one's ability to measure accurately the occurrence (usually incidence of prevalence) of a problem or condition in two groups in a population, accurately measure the presence or absence of a potential risk or protective factor in members of the groups, and compare these measures. From ecological and epidemiological perspectives, it is essential to identify those individual, family, school, neighborhood, community, and other factors that differentiate those who exhibit the problem or condition from those who do not (Leaverton, 1991).

For example, a social worker interested in analyzing potential risk and protective factors for adolescent pregnancy can begin by establishing the total number of adolescent girls in a selected area, perhaps using census data. She can measure (or estimate) pregnancy rates by contacting local health care providers or by conducting a survey in middle and high schools. Girls who become pregnant during the study period form one group and those who do not make up the second group. The social worker can identify potential risk and protective factors, such as "girl is doing well in school" (potential protective factor) or "girl's own mother was an adolescent mother" (potential risk factor). She must then measure the presence or absence of these factors in each girl in both groups. This yields the frequency with which the factor occurred for each group. By comparing the frequency in the first group with the frequency in the second group, the social worker can estimate the relative importance of the identified risk and protective factors.

This comparison can be made by combining the two frequencies into a single ratio that provides an estimation of the strength of the association between the presence of the risk or protective factor and the occurrence of the problem or condition (Hennekens & Buring, 1987). Two basic methodologies are involved in calculating this ratio: the cohort study and the case-control study (Leaverton, 1991). The cohort study produces a measure of relative risk for exposure to a risk factor. The case-control study produces an odds ratio, which can be used to estimate the relative risk.

Relative Risk

In its simplest form, a cohort study begins with two similar groups that differ in terms of their exposure to a potential risk or protective factor. One follows the two groups over time, observing whether the condition or problem of interest has developed. Next one compares the respective rates of incidence for the two groups to produce a measure of the relative risk of developing the problem for those with the risk factor, compared with those without the risk factor. The first step in calculating the relative risk is to estimate risk for each group, as shown in Table 3-3. This is defined as risk (R) = (number of

Table 3-3. Risk Factors from a Cohort Study

GROUP	PRESENCE OF PROBLEM	ABSENCE OF PROBLEM	TOTAL
Risk factor present	A	B	A + B
Risk factor absent	C	D	C + D
Total	A + C	B + D	N

individuals in the group who have the problem)/(total number in the group), or, for those with the risk factor, $R = A / (A + B)$. Similarly, for those without the risk factor, $R = C / (C + D)$. The relative risk (RR) then is calculated by $A / (A + B)$ divided by $C / (C + D)$. This ratio compares the likelihood of developing the problem in the group exposed to the risk vis-à-vis the group not exposed to the risk (Leaverton, 1991).

Suppose for a population of 1,000 10-year-old children, a case management team identifies a potential risk factor as "victim of parental physical abuse before age five." Team members also define the behavior problem of concern (condition), for example, "becoming aggressive in school by age 12." Those children with the risk factor make up one group and those without the risk factor form the second group. The members of the case management team can follow both groups over a two-year period. As shown in Table 3-4, team members can measure the respective number of children in each group who develop the condition of interest and compare the rates to estimate the relative risk for this factor.

The risk for those with the risk factor is estimated by $R = A / (A + B) = 200 / 300 = 2 / 3$. For those without the risk factor, it is estimated by $R = C / (C + D) = 100 / 700 = 1 / 7$. The relative risk for those with the risk factor, compared with those without the risk factor, is estimated by $A / (A + B)$ divided by $C / (C + D) = (2 / 3) / (1 / 7) = (2)(7) / (3)(1) = 14 / 3 = 4.67$. In other words, in this example and for this population of 1,000, children who were victims of abuse before age five were 4.67 times more likely than those who were not abused to become aggressive between ages 10 and 12.

If the relative risk in this example had turned out to be 1.0, then no risk would be associated with the identified factor. If the relative risk had been less than 1.0, then the factor would be associated with a lower likelihood of the occurrence of the condition—that is, it might be considered to serve a protective function.

Table 3-4. Relative Risk of Becoming Aggressive for Victims and Nonvictims of Early Child Abuse

GROUP	NUMBER AGGRESSIVE BY AGE 12	NUMBER NOT AGGRESSIVE BY AGE 12	TOTAL
Victim of early child abuse	200	100	300
Not a victim of early child abuse	100	600	700
Total	300	700	1,000

A relative risk greater than 1.0 does not imply that a causal relationship exists between the risk factor and the occurrence of the social problem or condition. It merely demonstrates that the presence of the risk factor is associated with a greater likelihood of the occurrence of the problem. Furthermore, the results of a single study can rarely be generalized to larger populations. That is, the results of the hypothetical study above do not necessarily imply that being a victim of abuse before age five is a risk factor for becoming aggressive for all 10-year-old children. Many more studies would be necessary to draw such a conclusion.

Although relative risk provides a useful summary statistic of the results of cohort studies, its importance must be assessed within the context of the absolute risk for the problem in the larger population (Leaverton, 1991). For example, consider a group of 1,000 adolescents who were retained in school at least once and a second group of adolescents who were not retained in school. Suppose that both groups of youths are followed for one year. Of the first group, three commit a felony during the year. Of the second group, one commits a felony during the year. Comparing these frequencies yields a relative risk of 3.0 for committing a felony when school failure is the risk factor, which might be considered fairly high. However, the difference in absolute risk (two per 1,000) is probably of little or no importance in addressing the problem of delinquency. By itself, a difference so small in absolute risk may not be sufficiently meaningful to warrant action.

ODDS RATIO

Cohort studies are often difficult and expensive to conduct. A related method, however, is somewhat easier to implement: in the case-control study, one begins by identifying a group of individuals in a defined population who already exhibit a problem or condition. These individuals are called the case group. One then selects a comparison group (or control group) from the same population, who do not exhibit the problem. Ideally, the presence or absence of a problem (outcome) will be the only difference between the case group and the control group. Otherwise the two groups should be as similar as possible.

In case-control studies, one measures the presence of a suspected risk factor in those who exhibit the problem or condition to calculate an exposure rate for the case group. Then the exposure rate is calculated for those who do not exhibit the problem (control group). Comparison of the respective exposure rates for the two groups (not, as in cohort studies, respective incidence rates) (Leaverton, 1991) yields a single parameter: the odds ratio. The odds in favor of an event are defined as "the frequency with which the event occurs divided by the frequency with which it does not occur" (Elston & Johnson, 1987, p. 45). In Table 3-5, the odds in favor of exposure for the group with the problem are *A/B* (that is, the frequency with which the event, or exposure, occurred, divided by the frequency with which it did not occur). The odds in favor of exposure in the group without the problem are *C/D*. The odds ratio (*OR*) is defined as (odds in favor of exposure in the problem group) / (odds in favor of exposure in the nonproblem group) = *(A/B) / (C/D)* = *AD/BC* (Valanis, 1992). To illustrate, consider a case-control study on adolescents who have dropped out of high school. If there are 100 such adolescents in a population (the case group), one can select a control group that is comparable to the case group

Table 3-5. Odds Ratio from a Case-Control Study

GROUP	RISK FACTOR PRESENT	RISK FACTOR ABSENT	TOTAL
Problem present	A	B	A + B
Problem absent	C	D	C + D
Total	A + C	B + D	N

except that the individuals in the control group have not dropped out of school. Suppose a school counselor, teacher, or social worker is interested in studying whether early school retention is associated with dropout rates. He can inspect the school records for individuals in both groups to determine who, in each group, was retained in school for at least one grade. Using the data shown in Table 3-6, he can calculate the odds ratio as follows: $OR = (A/B) / (C/D) = AD/BC = (50)(90) / (50)(10) = 4,500/500 = 9.0$. An odds ratio of 9.0 means that, in this group of 200, those students who dropped out were nine times more likely to have experienced early school retention than were students who did not drop out. Again, this finding does not show that a causal relationship exists between the risk factor and the outcome. Nevertheless, the odds ratio can be a useful tool in establishing whether an association exists between a potential risk factor and the occurrence of a problem or between a potential protective factor and the occurrence of a desired outcome (Hennekens & Buring, 1987).

Survival Analysis

Odds ratios and relative risks are useful in assessing the effects of risk and protective factors after a defined period of observation; however, they do not help us understand when, during a period of time, a risk or protective factor is likely to influence an outcome. Although the odds ratio demonstrated that students who dropped out were more likely to have experienced earlier school failure, a practitioner could draw no

Table 3-6. Odds of Early School Retention in Students Who Did and Did Not Drop Out of High School

GROUP	RETAINED AT LEAST ONE YEAR	NEVER RETAINED	TOTAL
Dropped out (case)	50	50	100
Did not drop out (control)	10	90	100
Total	60	140	200

conclusions about when, in the course of their high school careers, students were more likely to drop out. It would be helpful if the counselor or school social worker could determine whether there is a certain time when a youth is at particularly high risk of dropping out. Similarly, it would be helpful to know whether there is a period during which a protective factor has its greatest influence and whether the positive effects of the protective factor tend to wear off over time. It is critical, in fact, in designing interventions to know whether the potential effects of risk and protective factors change over time. Survival analysis is an increasingly common approach that combines time with odds ratios.

SURVIVAL TIME

Survival analysis was developed to increase understanding about the length of time patients diagnosed with a condition or receiving a specific treatment remained, or "survived," in good health. A central concept in survival analysis is the length of time from the onset of a condition or the beginning of a treatment to an outcome, such as death or remission. Survival data analysis is now used to study a variety of phenomena in social work (for example, days in foster care), sociology (duration of relationships), engineering (durability of electrical components), and criminology (recidivism). Survival time is defined as the length of time from the occurrence of one event to the occurrence of another event of interest (Lee, 1992). Hence it is sometimes called "event history analysis" (Allison, 1984).

Suppose, in the example of youth at risk of dropping out of high school, the counselor wishes to examine the data more closely to determine whether there is a certain period when the risk of dropping out is especially high for students with a particular risk factor. One approach is to measure the survival time for all the students who were at risk (those who had experienced early school failure). The first step is to divide the typical high school career (the period the youth is at risk) into intervals and examine each student's behavior (whether he or she dropped out) during each interval (Norusis, 1993).

The counselor can define an interval to be one semester, so each student is at risk for a total of eight semesters. The counselor must examine the record of each student and determine whether he or she dropped out during each semester. There also must be a rule by which to assign a value to each student's performance. For example, the counselor can decide to define survival time in terms of whether or not a student began a particular semester. A student who began the second semester, but dropped out during that semester, would have a survival time of two. To illustrate, consider data on 10 of the students who were defined as at risk (Table 3-7). Observing survival times, the counselor concludes that, for these students, the period of greatest risk comprised the first two semesters of their high school career.

Displaying data in this format provides a straightforward method for discerning high-risk periods when only a small number of students are involved. If the counselor is interested in looking at the experience of every youth at risk ($N = 60$, from Table 3-6), however, the format becomes cumbersome. For examining a large number of cases, it is more efficient to focus on the defined intervals of time and count how many individuals experienced the event in each interval.

Table 3-7. Survival Times for 10 Students Who Experienced Early School Failure

STUDENT	DROPPED OUT?	SEMESTER DROPPED OUT	SURVIVAL TIME (SEMESTERS)
1	Yes	2	2
2	Yes	1	1
3	No	NA	8
4	No	NA	8
5	Yes	2	2
6	Yes	2	2
7	No	NA	8
8	Yes	1	1
9	No	NA	8
10	Yes	1	1

NOTE: NA = not applicable.

LIFE TABLES

Survival data analysis often includes a statistical technique known as the follow-up life table (Norusis, 1993). To use the life-table method, one divides a period of observation into intervals, then, for each interval, counts the number of cases experiencing the event. Data for each interval can be presented in table form, as shown in Table 3-8.

To assess the effect of a risk or protective factor during each interval, the counselor or school social worker must estimate the probability of the occurrence of an

Table 3-8. Summary of School Withdrawal among Youths Who Experienced Early School Failure

SEMESTER	STUDENTS IN SCHOOL AT BEGINNING OF SEMESTER	AT-RISK STUDENTS WITHDRAWING DURING SEMESTER
1	60	15
2	45	20
3	25	10
4	15	4
5	11	1
6	10	0
7	10	0
8	10	0

event, given the presence of the factor for each interval. This probability estimate in turn provides an estimate of the magnitude of risk or protection. (Similarly, the relative risk and the odds ratio give estimates of risk or protection through the calculation of probabilities.) To estimate the probability of the event occurring for each interval, the counselor can determine the following ratio: (number of students experiencing event during interval) / (total number of students at risk during interval). The data in Table 3-9 show, for each interval, the estimated probability that a student dropped out during that interval. From this table the school counselor sees that, for these students, the period of highest risk was in the first four semesters, with relatively higher risk during the second and third semesters. After the fourth semester, the probability of a student withdrawing dropped sharply and was zero for the last three semesters of the high school career.

Data from life tables can also be presented graphically. Figure 3-1 shows the survival function for the data presented above. For each semester, it depicts the proportion of students in school at the beginning of that semester. This graph was generated by SPSS for Windows (Norusis, 1993), but it could easily be drawn by hand. Depicting the data graphically may help practitioners design interventions for specific populations at critical times. Practitioners can also use graphs when advocating for resources to address a problem such as dropping out of school. For example, the counselor might use the graph shown in Figure 3-1 in a presentation to school administrators or school board members aimed at securing funding for services that target at-risk ninth- and 10th-grade students.

In this example, the value of the survival function can change only at the beginning of a semester. The same data can be represented using the hazard function, which expresses the risk that an event will occur across an interval of time. Although the hazard function expresses risk over time, the function itself is not a probability because its value can exceed one. Calculation of the hazard function is relatively complex and will not be discussed in this text. Interested readers are referred to relevant textbooks on statistics (for example, Allison, 1984; Lee, 1992; or Norusis, 1993). SPSS for Windows calculates the value of the hazard function for an appropriate set of data and also generates the graph of the hazard function, as shown in Figure 3-2.

The graph of the hazard function shows how the risk of an event, such as dropping out of school, changes over a period of time. In this graph the risk of dropping

Table 3-9. Probability of an At-Risk Student Withdrawing, by Semester

SEMESTER	PROBABILITY OF STUDENT WITHDRAWING	SEMESTER	PROBABILITY OF STUDENT WITHDRAWING
1	15 / 60 = 0.25	5	1 / 11 = 0.09
2	20 / 45 = 0.45	6	0 / 10 = 0.00
3	10 / 25 = 0.40	7	0.00
4	4 / 15 = 0.27	8	0.00

Figure 3-1

Survival Plot of At-Risk Students Remaining in School

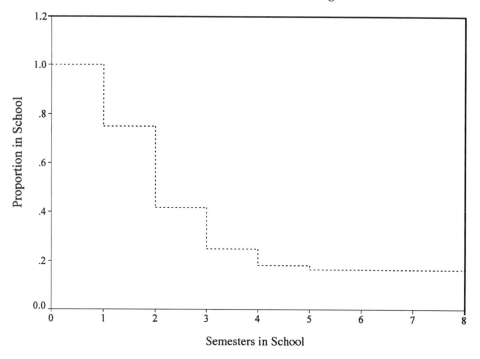

Figure 3-2

Hazard Function for Dropping Out for Students at Risk

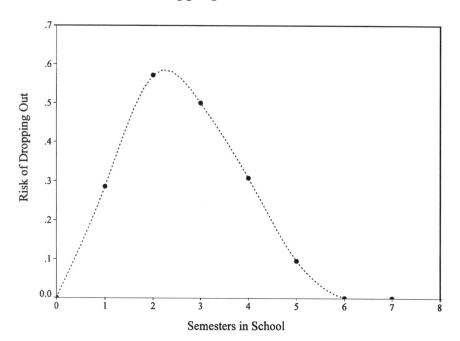

out increases sharply from *time = 0* (initial entry into high school) and reaches its peak at about *time = 2* (the second semester), at which point it begins to decrease (somewhat less sharply than it increased) until it approaches zero at *time = 6* (the sixth semester). The hazard function is a useful means of describing risk because it corresponds to "intuitive notions of risk" (Allison, 1984, p. 23). In this case it demonstrates that the peak period of risk is the second semester.

In summary, the hazard function and the survival function describe how probability and risk change over a period of time. The survival function is simpler to compute, and its graph can make risk trends explicit. The hazard function is more difficult to compute but its graph depicts the change in risk over time. Using both functions to identify combinations of risk and protective factors is one way of expressing the complexities of risk chains that shows great promise for the human services (Fraser, Jenson, Kiefer, & Popuang, 1994).

SUMMARY

This chapter has described a number of related methods for analyzing and quantifying risk and protection. By comparing the levels of a risk or protective factor in groups with and without a problem or condition, practitioners and researchers can calculate numerical values that estimate risk and protection. Quantifying risk and protective factors produces useful information that practitioners, policymakers, and researchers can use to develop interventions targeting specific groups or communities and to advocate for resources to address a specific problem. For practitioners working with a particular child or adolescent, this approach can also be used as one critical component of a comprehensive individualized assessment.

REFERENCES

Allison, P. D. (1984). *Event history analysis: Regression for longitudinal event data.* Beverly Hills, CA: Sage Publications.

Elston, R. C., & Johnson, W. D. (1987). *Essentials of biostatistics.* Philadelphia: F. A. Davis.

Fraser, M. W., Jenson, J. M., Kiefer, D., & Popuang, P. (1994). Statistical methods for the analysis of critical life events. *Social Work Research, 18,* 163–177.

Germain, C. B. (1991). *Human behavior in the social environment: An ecological view.* New York: Columbia University Press.

Germain, C., & Gitterman, A. (1980). *The life model of social work practice.* New York: Columbia University Press.

Hennekens, C. H., & Buring, J. E. (1987). *Epidemiology in medicine.* Boston: Little, Brown.

Hollis, F., & Woods, M. E. (1981). *Casework: A psychosocial approach* (3rd ed.). New York: Random House.

Kelly, J. A., St. Lawrence, J. S., Hood, H. V., & Brasfield, T. L. (1989). Behavioral intervention to reduce AIDS risk activities. *Journal of Consulting and Clinical Psychology, 57*, 60–67.

Knox, E. G. (1979). *Epidemiology in health care planning: A guide to the uses of a scientific method.* New York: Oxford University Press.

Leaverton, P. P. (1991). *A review of biostatistics: A program for self-instruction* (4th ed.). Boston: Little, Brown.

Lee, E. T. (1992). *Statistical methods for survival data analysis* (2nd ed.). New York: John Wiley & Sons.

Norusis, M. J. (1993). *SPSS for Windows: Advanced statistics release 6.0.* Chicago: SPSS.

Valanis, B. (1992). *Epidemiology in nursing and health care* (2nd ed.). Norwalk, CT: Appleton & Lange.

4

Risk and Protective Factors in Child Maltreatment

Barbara Thomlison

Maltreatment of children inflicts a huge toll on them, their families, and society. The detrimental developmental effects on children who have been maltreated include multiple impairments in behavioral, cognitive, affective, and social functioning (Ayoub, Willett, & Robinson, 1992; Kazdin, 1992; Kendall-Tackett & Eckenrode, 1996; Melton & Flood, 1994). The long-term consequences of child abuse and neglect are now considered to be one of the factors contributing to aggression and violence in adolescents and young adults (Widom, 1989a; 1989b) and to mental disorders (Bagley & Thomlison, 1991; Finkelhor, 1994; Finkelhor & Berliner, 1995). Victims of child abuse or neglect are 53 percent more likely than those who were not maltreated to be arrested as juveniles, and 38 percent more likely to have been arrested for a violent crime (Widom, 1989b). In addition, abused and neglected children more often have trouble with achievement in school and later in adulthood, and they more often encounter health problems and substance abuse (Kendall-Tackett & Eckenrode, 1996; Trupin, Tarico, Low, Jemelka, & McClellan, 1993).

Developmental psychopathology research identifies vulnerability for abuse and neglect as a function of specific child, family, and environmental risk factors within the context of various life settings (see, for example, Cicchetti & Carlson, 1989; Mrazek & Haggerty, 1994; Rutter, 1987; Seifer & Sameroff, 1987). The exact nature of the interactional processes among the risk factors is unclear. However, it is thought that in the absence of mediating factors, situational and predisposing contextual circumstances provide the opportunity for maltreatment to occur. This contextually dependent framework suggests that change is always possible for children and their parents (Howard, Beckwith, Rodning, & Kropenski, 1989).

Although much research has focused on the effects of child maltreatment, current research is increasingly focused also on the strengths and elements of the social environment that contribute to resilience in children and families where abuse has occurred or where the risk for abuse is high. Both biological and social competencies, it is clear, can act as mediating processes. Changing transactional patterns and circumstances for children and families is thought to reduce the effects of adversity and increase potential for successful coping (Anthony & Cohler, 1987; Coie et al., 1993; Hillson & Kuiper, 1994; Kopp & Kaler, 1989).

This chapter is written with two primary objectives. First, it seeks to identify the key risk and potential protective factors in child maltreatment, addressing factors that appear to produce maltreatment in the first place and factors that promote positive recovery after abuse or neglect. And second, it seeks to draw from this emerging knowledge implications for the design of capacity-building services that might protect children from maltreatment and help meet the needs of children and families as their circumstances change.

CONTEXT OF CHILD MALTREATMENT

Child maltreatment is differentially defined in the popular press and in the medical, child protection, legal, and research literature. But regardless of their derivation, definitions almost always refer to identifiable harm to a child inflicted by the caregiver, either by commission or omission (Finkelhor & Korbin, 1988; Giovannoni & Becerra, 1979; Korbin, 1994). In general, the literature refers to five types of maltreatment: physical abuse, sexual abuse, emotional or psychological abuse, neglect, and undifferentiated combinations of abuse and neglect. Throughout this chapter, the concept of harm to a child is used as the defining feature of child maltreatment, and the term maltreatment is used to refer to both abuse and neglect, although it is recognized that abuse and neglect often involve complex discrete processes.

DEFINING CHILD MALTREATMENT IN CONTEXT

The definition of child maltreatment shapes the response of the legal and protective service system to the identification of cases. This has a direct impact on the number of officially reported, substantiated cases and on estimates of the incidence and prevalence of child abuse and neglect. Broad, inclusive definitions of maltreatment are often thought to be advantageous for focusing political and public attention on the extent of child maltreatment. However, broad definitions create large errors in the search for predictors, because the factors that give rise to various types and degrees of maltreatment differ. Narrow definitions identify a smaller population, but one that is severely abused and neglected. These precise definitions are more likely than others to identify maltreatment within the at-risk population that makes up the referral base for protective services (Giovannoni & Becerra, 1979; Hutchison, 1994; Korbin, 1994; Lindsey, 1994).

The sociocultural context, which significantly affects childrearing practices, must be taken into account when defining maltreatment. The relationship between culture and child maltreatment is poorly understood. Korbin (1994) argued that "neither parental action nor physical injury is adequate in itself as a critical defining element of child maltreatment across cultures. . . . The process of defining child maltreatment and developing (often coercive) services related to child protection is complex because the same parental behavior may have different meaning and interpretations in different cultural contexts" (p.184). Across countries and cultures, definitions of maltreatment vary and the criteria for substantiation of maltreatment are often open to interpretation and public debate.

Whether it happens one time or many times in a family, child maltreatment is multidetermined—that is, maltreatment has multiple causes. No one situation, event, or circumstance can account for the complexity of individual and environmental conditions that produce harm to a child. In practice, each maltreatment event is likely to have a distinct explanation and conceptualization (Davies & Little, 1994; Finkelhor & Berliner, 1995). A definition of maltreatment must capture the changing circumstances of children and families over time, and it must emphasize the needs of children and their families that place them at risk. To have value, then, a definition must be specific and sensitive and possess predictive validity.

RATES OF CHILDHOOD MALTREATMENT

Prevalence and incidence rates of child maltreatment are markers of the social strength of a population. Abuse and neglect involves over 4 percent of all American children and their households. Moreover, rates of reported maltreatment showed a consistent yearly increase from 1976 to 1992 (McCurdy & Daro, 1993; U.S. Department of Health and Human Services, 1988, 1995). Over 1 million (35 percent) of the reported cases were substantiated by child protective services investigators as maltreatment (U.S. Department of Health and Human Services, 1988, 1995). The National Center on Child Abuse and Neglect categorized the prevalence of maltreatment in reported cases as follows: 49 percent consisted of neglect, 27 percent involved physical abuse, 14 percent were sexual abuse, and 7 percent reported emotional abuse. The incidence rate for child neglect is 14.6 per 1,000 children, 4.9 per 1,000 for physical abuse, and 2.1 per 1,000 for sexual abuse (U.S. Department of Health and Human Services, 1995). Overall, three children die each day from maltreatment. Child fatalities for 1992 included 1,262 deaths—the most extreme outcome of maltreatment—resulting from abuse incidents, a 54 percent increase (Lindsey, 1994). Children under five years of age were 79 percent of fatalities (McCurdy & Daro, 1993).

Age and Gender

Age, not gender, appears to be important in neglect cases; substantiated neglect reports decrease for older children. Most victims of maltreatment are seven years of age or younger (51 percent), and of this group 87 percent are under five years and 26 percent are three years old or younger. Adolescents (13 to 18 years old) represent about one in five victims. Of these, about half are females and 45 percent are males; in 5 percent of cases gender is unreported. Probably because they are better able to protect themselves using disclosure, placation, and avoidance, adolescents are only one-third as likely as preschool children to be struck by a parent (Finkelhor, 1995; U.S. Department of Health and Human Services, 1995; Wolfe, 1994).

Differences in gender and age are evident for physical and sexual abuse prevalence rates. When the onset of maltreatment begins early in the developmental process, younger males are more likely to be physically abused and younger females are more vulnerable to sexual abuse, except in the case of neglect, where young children of either gender are more vulnerable than older children. Boys with behavioral difficulties are more likely than girls to be at increased risk of maltreatment (Rutter, 1987). Girls in the school-aged population are twice as likely as boys to be sexually abused. The onset of sexual abuse is highest for preadolescents, that is, children ages eight to 12 (Finkelhor & Baron, 1986).

Poverty and Neglect

Because neglect is intricately tied to poverty and income, the poorest of the poor are at highest risk. The rate of known neglect is nine times greater in families with incomes under $15,000 than in families above that level (Gaudin, 1993).

Ethnicity, Race, and Culture

Ethnic and racial data on maltreatment indicate that about half (54 percent) of all incidents of child maltreatment in the United States involve white children, 25 percent of victims are African American, 9 percent are Hispanic, 2 percent are American Indian, and 2 percent come from other backgrounds; for 8 percent of incidents, race or ethnicity was not reported (U.S. Department of Health and Human Services, 1995). Studies controlled for poverty and other factors suggest that race, culture, and ethnicity are not directly related to rates of child maltreatment (Korbin, 1994), although children of color are more likely than others to encounter poverty, violence, crime, poor schools, racism, and other discriminatory experiences that may exacerbate other risk factors for abuse and neglect (Chaffin, Kelleher, & Hollenberg, 1996; Kendall-Tackett & Eckenrode, 1996; Pelton, 1994). Rates for sexual abuse are relatively consistent across cultures (Korbin, 1994). Curiously, white girls appear somewhat more vulnerable to sexual abuse in the preschool years, whereas African American girls appear somewhat more vulnerable to sexual abuse in the preteen years (Wyatt, 1985). The lifetime prevalence for sexual abuse has been reported equal for white and African American girls (Finkelhor & Baron, 1986; Wyatt, 1985).

Of course, the parenting techniques of some ethnic and racial groups may differ from those of the dominant culture, or they may even appear qualitatively different when they stem from the multiple disadvantages that often characterize groups of color in this culture (Garbarino & Kostelny, 1992). Different childrearing practices should not be construed as bad practices, as long as the safety of children is assured; such practices need to be placed in their cultural context.

RISK AND PROTECTIVE FACTORS

As suggested in chapter 2, child maltreatment is a social problem with a unique set of risk and protective factors, but it is also a risk factor for the development of a variety of problems later in life (see also Mrazek & Haggerty, 1994). Although they are not fully understood, risk and protective factors for maltreatment appear to act antagonistically or synergistically to produce a diversity of effects on children (Browne & Finkelhor, 1986; Coie et al., 1993; Emery, 1989; Garbarino, Dubrow, Kostelny, & Pardo, 1992). Protective factors need not be desirable or pleasant qualities, and environmental circumstances do not necessarily have to be positive or beneficial to act protectively (Kinard, 1995; Mrazek & Mrazek, 1987; Rutter, 1987). Each life setting exposes children to risk and protective factors as they interact with various events, processes, and relationships at differing times and intensities throughout childhood.

Risk and protective factors may be either enduring or transient. Enduring influences may be psychological, environmental, cultural, or biological factors that decrease or increase the odds for maltreatment (for a discussion of odds and odds ratios, see chapter 3). Enduring protective factors include a history of good parenting, positive marital support, and employment. Transient risk factors may be situations such as illness, injury, marital discord, or other life stressors—both perceived and actual—that may impair a vulnerable parent and lead to abuse or neglect of a child.

Child maltreatment is perhaps best conceptualized as a problem in the parent–child–environment system. To understand child maltreatment and its impact on children, one must analyze the ways in which environments respond to children. A poor developmental outcome is a child's response to multiple transactions. The child's response to maltreatment often depends on whether the parenting environment has adequate social and fiscal resources to change patterns of child care. From this perspective, intervention aims to reduce the magnitude of family risk factors while increasing protective factors.

PARENTAL RISK AND PROTECTIVE FACTORS

Childhood is usually a period of protection and safety wherein parents introduce children to healthy adaptation and prosocial behavior. Risk factors can change this. They may be personal qualities, attributes, or skills of a parent, or even the conditions of children's living environment. Researchers estimate that about 10 percent of American families have generic risk factors, such as exposure to inadequate resources, parental conflict, alcoholism, and employment stresses, which may elevate the odds for child maltreatment. But the presence of generic risk factors is not usually sufficient to produce maltreatment (Ayoub & Jacewitz, 1982; Browne & Saqui, 1988).

Individual Risk Factors

Psychological distress is the primary individual risk factor associated with child maltreatment. Included among these risk factors are parental affective disturbances, such as depression, withdrawal, anger, and aggression (Ayoub, Jacewitz, Gold, & Milner, 1983; Barth, 1991; Kotch et al., 1995); and low-self esteem, immaturity, rigid or unrealistic expectations, and excessive reliance on others, which places the parent's immediate needs in conflict with the child's needs (Faust, Runyan, & Kenny, 1995; Iverson & Segal, 1990). High levels of anxiety, lack of impulse control under stress, and low social supports are also implicated (Altemeier, O'Connor, Sherrock, & Tucker, 1986; Coohey, 1996; Garbarino et al., 1992; Kinard, 1995; Mrazek & Haggerty, 1994; Radke-Yarrow & Sherman, 1990; Rutter, 1987). Davies and Little (1994) concluded that parents who are low on warmth and nurturing and high on criticism are the most damaging.

These individual characteristics can amount to a parenting style that is characterized by distress, anger, and isolation (Kinard, 1995; Wolfe, 1985, 1994). Related risk factors that affect child maltreatment are found in the context of parental problems such as alcoholism and antisocial behavior (Smith & Saunders, 1995; Wolfe, 1991). As many as 80 percent of maltreating parents have past or current substance abuse problems (Cohn & Daro, 1987; Dore, Doris, & Wright, 1995; Jaudes, Ekwo, & Van Voorhis, 1995). The exact role these parental factors play in maltreatment is unclear, but it is thought that they influence interactions, perceptions, and other transactions in the environment. Regardless of culture, they increase risk for maltreatment when accompanied by mental disorder or a history of maltreatment (English & Pecora, 1994).

As suggested above, social and cognitive functioning is tied to maltreatment (Briere, Berliner, Bulkley, Jenny, & Reid, 1996). Rigid and unrealistic parental expectations about home, children, and self, and in particular a distorted perception of one's own history of care, have been associated with physical abuse and neglect (Crittenden, 1988a, 1988b). Other such factors include poor problem-solving ability in childrearing situations (Azar, Robinson, Hekimian, & Twentyman, 1984), inconsistent discipline and harsh or excessive physical punishment (Crittenden, 1988a), and poor attachment with the infant (Ayoub et al., 1983; Crittenden, 1988b).

Biological Risk Factors

Biological or genetic factors of the parent that result in physical problems during pregnancy or delivery or in chronic problems have often been linked to increased stress, which adds to the risk of physical abuse and neglect (Ayoub et al., 1992; Barth, 1991; Finkelhor, 1986; Iverson & Segal, 1990; Marks & McDonald, 1989). However, the nature and relative influence of the parent's biological difficulties need to be examined further within the context of broader environmental risks, such as the family structure and the quality of social supports.

Risk Factors for Types of Maltreatment

On balance, it is not yet clear how risk factors vary for child abuse, neglect, and sex abuse. Physical abuse appears to be associated with a childhood history of abuse or harsh physical punishment. Parents with a punitive family-of-origin history who encounter rapid and stressful life changes are at increased risk for engaging in abusive behavior (American Humane Association, 1994; Simons, Whitbeck, Conger, & Chyi-In, 1991). Apart from economic distress, a key risk factor in the etiology of neglect appears to be the lack of a support system. For sexual abuse, risk is significantly elevated by parental psychological distress, problems of communication, lack of emotional closeness, and inadequate social support (Briere et al., 1996; Coohey, 1996).

Parental Protective Factors

Parental factors that protect against maltreatment include functioning within normal boundaries on measures of behavior, social competence, and self-esteem and self-efficacy (Kinard, 1995; Rutter, 1987). Protective processes are determined primarily by the psychological well-being of the parent, which lets the attachment process between parent and child begin at birth (Belsky & Vondra, 1989). A supportive, helpful person at the birth of a child and a social network of relatives or friends are protective conditions (Alter-Reid, Gibbs, Lachenmeyr, Sigal, & Massoth, 1986; Quinton & Rutter, 1988). Similarly, emotionally satisfying relationships with others lead to satisfaction in the parenting role, which promotes resilience in the face of stress (Cicchetti, 1989; Quinton & Rutter, 1988; Wolfe, 1991). Generic protective factors in stressful environments include economic security and access to adequate health, education, and employment services (Mrazek & Mrazek, 1987).

CHILD RISK AND PROTECTIVE FACTORS

Risk and protective factors for children can be thought of as biological and psychosocial in nature. Biological risks include birth or health complications, low intellect, and developmental abnormalities (Kopp & Kaler, 1989). Infant health problems associated with physical abuse and neglect include prematurity (Kotch et al., 1995; Roberts, 1988), congenital physical or developmental disabilities (Iverson & Segal, 1990; Roberts, 1988), and characteristics such as gender or physical features that are counter to parental expectations (Ayoub et al., 1983; Roberts, 1988). These biological factors are identified as stressful for parents, and their presence is thought to elevate the potential of abusive or neglectful parenting behavior, or both. Increasingly, research suggests that biological factors may be more important during infancy and childhood than during middle childhood or adolescence (see, for example, Kopp & Kaler, 1989; Mrazek & Haggerty, 1994; Quinton & Rutter, 1988). The presence of biological risks may explain—at least in part—why children under the age of three are considered more vulnerable to physical abuse and neglect and, overall, why children under the age of five are at increased risk of death (McCurdy & Daro, 1993).

Psychosocial risk factors include a child's temperament, behavior, and mood; these are related to the difficulty of care and act as potential stressors. Infants who tend to be distressed and difficult to care for, because they do not have well-established eating or sleeping patterns, are three times more likely to be abused (Ayoub et al., 1983; Barth, 1991; Darmstadt, 1990; Marks & McDonald, 1989). In young children, temperament, aggression, and noncompliant behavior place them at increased risk of abuse, particularly when cultural or parental belief systems promote corporal punishment and violence (Garbarino et al., 1992; Marks & McDonald, 1989; Whiteman, Fanshel, & Grundy, 1987; Wolfe, 1994). Negative self-esteem, poor self-efficacy, and an external locus of control have been associated with increased vulnerability to sexual abuse (Faust, Runyon, & Kenny, 1995; Finkelhor, 1986). In the same vein, compared with children who are more outgoing, children who are emotionally distant, introverted, and socially isolated appear to be more vulnerable to sexual abuse (Finkelhor, 1986).

Research consistently emphasizes that parental characteristics afford comparatively greater protection than a child's individual characteristics (Briere et al., 1996; Chaffin, Kelleher, Hollenberg, 1996; Wolfe, 1994). Parental competency is therefore essential. However, Belsky and Vondra (1989) and Kinard (1995) noted that a distinct set of parental competencies has not been found to be either necessary or sufficient to distinguish maltreating from nonmaltreating parents. Other factors—some of which are clearly child-related—are involved.

Children's characteristics that appear to promote protective processes include competent behavior and competent social or cognitive functioning (Kinard, 1995). Characteristics such as being perceived as cuddly or affectionate in infancy, and of higher cognitive ability are also protective (Garbarino et al., 1992; Garmezy & Tellegen, 1984; Radke-Yarrow & Sherman, 1990; Rutter, 1981). Similarly, positive temperament and high self-esteem are both defined as a protective factors (Herrenkohl, Herrenkohl, & Egolf, 1994; Kinard, 1995; Mrazek & Haggerty, 1994; Rutter, 1987).

The older, more developmentally competent children are when they are exposed to the first maltreatment trauma, the more likely they will cope positively with stressors (Anthony & Cohler, 1987; Garbarino et al., 1992). Children who attempt to master stress rather than retreat from it also develop confidence and higher levels of self-esteem; they also appear to recover from maltreatment more quickly (Garbarino & Kostelny, 1994, p. 327; Hillson & Kuiper, 1994). Kinard (1995) argued that resilience changes over time and, although it may be present at one developmental level, it may disappear at the next.

Compared with children who have no bonds of attachment, children who have a deep sense of belonging and security are widely known to function more adaptively across settings (Belsky & Vondra, 1989; Crittenden, 1988a, 1988b; Kolko, 1996). Such attachments occur, first and foremost, because of a positive, caring caretaker from birth—a caretaker who is available in times of stress for support (Ainsworth, 1989; Garbarino & Kostelny, 1994; Garbarino et al., 1992; Kopp & Kaler, 1989; Mrazek & Mrazek, 1987; Rutter, 1987; Wekerle & Wolfe, 1993; Widom, 1989a). Yet the social, psychological, and environmental conditions that promote the construction of warm and supportive attachments are themselves protective factors, so it is not clear, to date, how family factors such as attachment interactions are distinguished from other variables that reduce risk (Kinard, 1995; Kolko, 1996). The importance of attachments is thus obvious but complicated.

ENVIRONMENTAL FACTORS RELATED TO MALTREATMENT

The structure and quality of social, emotional, and economic sources of support in the broad social environment or family setting contribute in major ways to the treatment, or maltreatment, of children (Coohey, 1996; Quinton & Rutter, 1988; Tracy, 1988; Tracy & McDonell, 1991).

Family Environment Risk Factors

The presence of violence, harsh punishment, marital discord, continuous threats of separation, poverty or lack of material resources, unemployment, and a conflictual social support network are associated with all types of maltreatment (Barnard, 1994; Belsky & Vondra, 1989; Emery, 1989; Garbarino et al., 1992; Kolko, 1996; Kotch et al., 1995; Wolfe, 1994). Family environments with limited positive interactions among family members are more likely to include children who model maladaptive parental behavior and perceive their social network system as unhelpful (Barnard, 1994; Coohey, 1996; Emery, 1989; Finkelhor & Berliner, 1995; Kowal et al., 1989; Widom, 1989a; Wolfe, 1994). Single-parent family structures, compared with two-parent family structures, often have higher levels of stress and difficulties and are more likely to lack the necessary financial resources to parent and meet child-care needs (Hay & Jones, 1994; Tracy, 1988; Tracy & McDonell, 1991; Wolfe, 1994). Being unemployed or unemployable, or experiencing poor living conditions such as housing and other material and household deficits, have been identified as sociodemographic risk factors for physical abuse and neglect (Ayoub et al., 1983; Kotch et al., 1995; Pelton, 1994). Poverty affects 14 million children in the United States and is the most frequently identified environmental factor that places children at increased risk of maltreatment (Kendall-Tackett & Eckenrode, 1996; Lindsey, 1994; U.S. Department of Health and Human Services, 1995).

The relationship between poverty and maltreatment is not well understood. Prolonged economic distress in the household is strongly related to all forms of childhood maltreatment and to the severity of maltreatment (Garbarino et al., 1992; Garbarino & Kostelny, 1994; Hay & Jones, 1994; Melton & Barry, 1994b; Pelton, 1994; U.S. Department of Health and Human Services, 1988, 1995). Although poverty is associated with neglect, it is very likely that the indirect stresses resulting from lack of money, food, and other necessities produce stress, shorten tempers, and contribute directly to poor parenting. To be sure, however, most children growing up in poverty are not abused, nor are most parents who are poor likely to be abusive. Pelton (1994) argued that "the probability of child abuse and neglect is largely dependent on the extent of one's ability to cope with poverty and its stressors" (p. 153).

Family Environment Protective Factors

Resilient children typically have parents who are models of resilience themselves and are available to children for providing comfort and reassurance (Kinard, 1995; Radke-Yarrow & Sherman, 1990). The availability of caring and emotionally supportive family, friends, siblings, teachers, and neighbors mediates stresses (Finkelhor & Berliner, 1995). Kotch and colleagues (1995) found that in the presence of stressful life events, the odds of child maltreatment decreased as social support increased. When parents are more involved with or participate in social networks, the stress of daily hassles and critical life events is moderated, reducing the likelihood of child maltreatment. Conditions such as family cohesiveness and family and marital harmony are factors that promote adaptation and coping (Briere et al., 1996). The presence of a positive adult role model in a child's life setting, as well as the amount of time spent with that role model, is an important influence (Maluccio, Abramczyk, & Thomlison, 1996; Quinton & Rutter, 1988; Wolfe, 1994). The presence of siblings has been shown to ease adjustment to conflicts and stresses by providing a positive source of reference and sense of support through sibling bonds (Anthony & Cohler, 1987; Bullock & Little, 1989; Hegar, 1988). Parenting is often defined as what parents do with a child, but how they do it appears to contribute to a child's ability to adapt and cope (Quinton & Rutter, 1988; Radke-Yarrow & Sherman, 1990; Rutter, 1987).

Community Risk Factors

Social environmental factors such as inaccessible and unaffordable health and child care, fragmented helping services, crime and violence, reduced or negative neighboring interactions, and sociocultural discrimination have been positively correlated with incidents of child maltreatment (Garbarino & Kostelny, 1992; Hay & Jones, 1994). Social disintegration and disorganization in neighborhoods—crime, gangs, vandalism, and substance abuse—add to family stress and worries. Socially impoverished communities have many more needs, and families must compete for limited resources.

More than the sheer physical resources of a community matters; local norms and values also appear related to child maltreatment. Communities that tolerate violence and physical aggression see increased maltreatment (Earls, McGuire, & Shay, 1994; Whiteman, Fanshel, & Grundy, 1987). The experience of traumatic events such as witnessing a murder can suppress developmental processes, which affects the child's ability to understand the world (Garbarino et al., 1992; Garbarino & Kostelny, 1994). Culturally promoted attitudes and behaviors have been identified as covert support for the dynamics of sexual abuse; these include a stereotype of male dominance in sexual relationships, social tolerance for sexual interest in children, and barriers to women's equality (Hay & Jones, 1994). Community norms can operate both to restrict opportunities for development and to promote violent dispute resolution. Each places children at risk.

Community Protective Processes

Conversely, community well-being is a protective factor. The level of employment and resources in a community establishes its economic and social strength. Influences such as stability and cohesiveness in neighborhoods are associated with coping and resilience in families and with lower rates of child maltreatment (Garbarino et al., 1992; Hay & Jones, 1994; Melton & Barry, 1994a, 1994b). Other sources of support can be found in positive peer models and supportive neighbors, teachers, and other positive adult role models. In neighborhoods with strong informal networks for social support, there is more positive parenting and less abuse and neglect (Pelton, 1994).

ASSESSING FOR MALTREATMENT RISK

Assessment of the risk for child maltreatment requires considering the various patterns of child maltreatment, risk and protective factors (including situational or contextual variables), and the multisystemic nature of family functioning. The aim of assessment is to identify what is needed for competence building in families, given the child, familial, and extrafamilial conditions. Assessments that are undertaken because maltreatment has been reported must first determine whether children can safely remain at home with their families. Second, they must determine how families will use services to address the conditions that produced maltreatment.

Safety, stability, physical and developmental well-being of the child, and parental functioning need to be measured. Issues of concern in any of these areas require identifying the resources and processes that are necessary and sufficient for enhancement of the parent, child, and environment. Assessment must then address whether or not there is a good enough fit between the needs of the child and the capacities of the parent to both protect the child and create a more positive family environment (Cicchetti, 1989; Wolfe, 1994).

ASSESSING FOR SAFETY AND BASIC FAMILY NEEDS

Determining the safety, security, and physical well-being of children within their own homes is the first step—a critical step—in determining whether children can remain at home. Assessment at this stage is investigative, and techniques involve gathering information to determine whether a child has been abused and to assess the potential of the parents for continued parenting. Activities include (1) interviewing the child, family members, and other caretakers to determine parenting and nurturing capacity, the stability of the home, and the resources of family members; (2) assessing parent–child interaction and parental performance to identify stress in the family and living environment and its contribution to current problems, including life cycle transitions, cultural issues, and adequacy of resources; (3) evaluating the type and quality of support available from relatives, friends, and neighbors in the immediate environment; (4) compiling physical evidence, medical assessments, and criminal records; and (5) making decisions about the need for court charges, respite care, ongoing services, and protective placements.

Many communities now provide local assessment sites where basic health and well-being can be assessed and evidential information can be obtained using medical and electronic technologies. Protocols usually describe the roles of investigative team members and the data to be obtained. Rural communities often share sites and have traveling assessment teams. Assessment centers usually offer a range of assessment and treatment services, including culturally sensitive investigations oriented to recovery from maltreatment.

Assessing for Developmental Needs

Developmental needs are best understood as those environmental conditions that are required for positive growth and child development. After a child's safety has been guaranteed, the emphasis shifts to assessing the potential for changing a child's living circumstances. Assessment of child development is intricately related to child care and parenting practices. British child welfare researchers identify assessment dimensions for outcomes in child life domains such as health, education, emotional and behavioral development, family and peer relationships, self-care and competence, identity, and social presentation (Parker, Ward, Jackson, Aldgate, & Wedge, 1991). Others, such as Clark and Clarke (1996), use the following developmental domains to define assessment: residence and culture and educational and vocational, family, social, emotional and psychological, safety, legal, spiritual, behavioral, and financial influences. Risk assessment should include, for example, information about the parent's child-rearing practices, activities of daily child care, cultural beliefs, knowledge of family and community supports, and home and family stresses.

Assessment must capture the potential for continued parenting by ascertaining resources in three areas. First to be explored is the parent's understanding of the unique caring and discipline responsibilities of parents. Next to be assessed is whether the parent understands a child's needs for continuing care, stimulation, and attachment. Third, sources of support and validation for parenting, both actual and perceived, must be identified; how parents feel about their strengths and vulnerabilities may be as important as what their strengths and abilities really are (Miller, 1994).

Dynamic Strengths Assessment Approach

Strengths assessment is necessarily multimodal. Validated tools and dynamic—that is, interactive—interviewing methods should be part of this staged process of assessment. The process can also include the structured case-assessment and monitoring method, clinical evaluation measures, observation, and information on environmental indicators discussed below. Often a team including the child and family and those close to family members is convened with professionals to assess strengths, resources, and supports within the context of various family life settings. To capture the breadth and depth of strengths, strengths assessments involve the use of multiple sources of information and multiple methods of data collection.

Risk Assessment for Future Maltreatment

Often heard in child welfare, the term "risk assessment" is usually applied to a class of methods for predicting whether a child is at risk of future reabuse (English &

Pecora, 1994). Risk assessment devices categorize families by an overall level of risk and specify keystone risk factors to be addressed in intervention. To date, four competing methods of risk assessment have emerged (Doueck et al., 1993; Pecora, 1991):

1. matrix models in which the severity of risk to the child is estimated (for example, Illinois CANTS 17B [Illinois Department of Social Services, 1985] and the Washington Assessment of Risk Matrix (WARM) [Miller, Williams, English, & Olmstead, 1987];

2. family risk assessment scales with which child, parent, and family functioning are investigated (for example, Child Well-Being Scales, Family Risk Scales [Magura & Moses, 1986; Magura, Moses, & Jones, 1987], and the Family Assessment Form [McCroskey & Nelson, 1989]);

3. empirical predictors modeling methods based on sets of risk factors (for example, Alameda County, CA [Johnson & L'Esperance, 1984]);

4. child at-risk field methods whereby an ecological approach covering the child, parent, family, maltreatment, and intervention domains are rated according to influences in specific situations (for example, Child at Risk Field [Holder & Corey, 1989]).

When used over time, risk measures have the potential to assess the level of change. But, at least for now, that potential is largely unrealized because risk factors are still difficult to measure and quantify. Moreover, they vary by the age and gender of the child. Still in development, risk assessment models such as WARM (Miller et al., 1987) will very likely improve in the future and, if they are based on understandings of risk and protective conditions, they will contribute to decisions on protective services (for critiques of current instruments for risk assessment, see Doueck et al., 1993; English & Pecora, 1994; Lawlor & Raube, 1995; Marks & McDonald, 1989; Pecora, 1991; Wald & Woolverton, 1990).

SELECTED CASE AND CLINICAL METHODS OF MEASUREMENT

Standardized clinical measures are also used increasingly in risk assessment. One multimodal assessment approach, the structured case review method developed by the state of Alabama, incorporates elements of single-subject design and clinical assessment (Groves & Foster, 1995). The structured case review method, which is a protocol for monitoring quality assurance rather than a single instrument, uses various clinical measurement tools (Corcoran & Vandiver, 1996; Groves & Foster, 1995). These include, among others, the Hudson Family Package, which measures family functioning (Hudson, 1982); the Multi-Problem Screening Inventory, which measures a wide range of child and family problems (Hudson, 1993); and the Ontario Child Neglect Index, which was designed for substantiation of child neglect (Trocme, 1996). More sensitivity to strengths and to cross-cultural influences is being built into instruments as the field of clinical measurement develops. The Behavioral and Emotional Strengths Scale (Epstein, Quinn, & Cumblad, 1992), for example, is a comparatively new instrument that assesses children's behavioral strengths on five dimensions: self-control, affective development, family involvement, school performance, and self-confidence. Coupled with long-standing clinical procedures such as family transitional mapping, ecomaps, and photogenograms, the recent emergence of clinical measurement packages that assess the wide range of risk and protective factors influencing maltreatment has created new and largely unexplored methods for case assessment and supervision (see Lawlor & Raube, 1995).

RECOVERY FROM CHILD MALTREATMENT

Because so many children are victimized each year, both prevention of and recovery from maltreatment have become high priorities. Although knowledge about recovery is limited, we do know that child welfare workers must determine when an intervention is necessary and insist that it be delivered in a timely manner and determine whether an intervention is sufficient to improve the conditions that led to the maltreatment. The emphasis of service must be switched from problems to needs to promote full family involvement (Corcoran & Vandiver, 1996).

STRENGTHENING FAMILIES

Parenting Enhancement

Specific parenting interventions for the child welfare worker include (1) training parents in behavioral and social skills, with an emphasis on immediate positive reinforcers; (2) helping set structured short-term goals with clearly defined activities; (3) using in-home teaching parent models and skills training approaches to improve interactions between parent and child; (4) addressing home management issues with homemakers; (5) working directly with the parent by, for example, role playing, reviewing videotapes, and commenting correctively about parent–child interaction; and (6) working one-to-one with the parent on social skills (using modeling, coaching, and rehearsal techniques, for example) before moving to a group approach for training (Gaudin, 1993; Melton & Barry, 1994a; Wolfe, 1994).

Supporting Child Caring

Strength-based family interventions are highly individualized needs-based services focused on improving family functioning. The creation of networks for parental and family support and positive communication styles are associated with recovery from physical abuse (Bronfenbrenner, 1986; Clark & Clarke, 1996; Garbarino & Kostelny, 1992, 1994). Promotion of positive parent roles and family life develops structure, routine, and consistency in discipline and assists in protective functions. Social support from outside the family is important for prosocial adaptation. For example, in-home teaching of family models helps parents understand how to care for and interact with a child as they build skills in nurturing and parenting. Cognitive behavioral approaches decrease aggressive and hostile behaviors and increase positive behavior and attachment between parents and children (Wolfe, 1994). Activities that strengthen bonds between parents and children while enhancing child care and supervision appear to reduce risks for maltreatment (Chadwick, 1996; Wolfe, 1994).

Recovery from Sexual Abuse

Recovery from child abuse and neglect is often painful and difficult. But recovery from sexual abuse, which is equally painful and difficult, is complicated by the fact that some children appear to be asymptomatic or experience "sleeper" effects. They do not show symptoms until much later and this has implications for service (Finkelhor & Berliner, 1995). Referral for treatment is often made when sexual abuse is disclosed, rather than when social, cognitive, or other developmental problems emerge. Because children may limit the extent of their disclosure and because disclosure may occur after years of self-blame, recovery from sexual abuse often proceeds slowly. High rates of family conflict or family violence confound recovery, as do the age of the child at the last episode of abuse—abuse at different ages produces different problems—and the degree of severity of the abuse (Kazdin, 1992; Wyatt & Newcomb, 1990). The factors that appear to promote a child's recovery from sexual abuse include support from a nonoffending, caring parent or adult; a high level of parental upset; early help-seeking responses to the family crisis; a family history of skillful conflict management; and high family cohesion.

Recovery from Neglect

Although neglect is the most common form of child maltreatment, interventions with neglectful families have not been thoroughly studied. Programs are far from effective and have high rates of recidivism—in some studies as many of 66 percent of program participants are subsequently investigated for neglect (Garbarino et al., 1992; Gaudin, 1993, Kendall-Tackett & Eckenrode, 1996; Kinard, 1995; Pelton, 1994). Daro and McCurdy (1994) concluded that, regardless of the type of intervention, the level of severity of family problems was the best predictor of treatment outcome. More effective interventions use in-home instruction. They begin by teaching attachment behaviors and focus on consistent feeding and child care, infant–toddler stimulation, money management, and nutrition (Wekerle & Wolfe, 1993). Research suggests that home-based interventions that monitor parents and provide support and skills training need to be introduced during pregnancy for high-risk families (those with, for example, a history of neglect). These should be followed with services in the postpartum period and reintroduced when children enter the school system (Gaudin, 1993; Kendall-Tackett & Eckenrode, 1996). Not much information is available yet about the effectiveness of these programs, but the use of risk and protective factors in their design is promising (see, for example, Olds & Henderson, 1990).

CHILD-CENTERED INTERVENTIONS

Abused and neglected children often need educational and social services when they first enter school and during their middle-school years. Kendall-Tackett and Eckenrode (1996) predicted low levels of achievement for children without these services. Very young children in neglectful families often benefit from therapeutic day care services in preschool, early (at preschool entry) interventions such as parent–child educational play, and, if safety is a concern, out-of-home placement (Daro & McCurdy, 1994; Kendall-Tackett & Eckenrode, 1996; Kinard, 1995). Schools can serve as a model for family support systems. Particularly helpful programs for the middle-school child aim at fostering an open and educational climate; they are often nontraditional in the presentation of curricula. Other promising programs attempt to change bullying behavior, prevent drug abuse, and inform children about depression and suicide (Mrazek & Haggerty, 1994). Programs to enhance social competence must focus on self-control, communication and problem solving, and resistance to negative social influences.

STRENGTHENING THE SOCIAL SUPPORT ENVIRONMENT

Direct and indirect social support interventions focused on the family system have increasing empirical support (Daro & McCurdy, 1994). Social support efforts should focus on promoting connections for family members across the major domains of community—housing, education and vocation, health, safety, religious or spiritual organizations, social services, and cultural organizations and agencies. Direct work with the parent—for example, providing information and strengthening skills—appears more effective than group approaches (Garbarino et al., 1992; Gaudin, 1993; Melton & Barry, 1994a, 1994b).

IMPLICATIONS FOR PREVENTION, EARLY INTERVENTION, AND TREATMENT

If the range of risk and protective factors that influence child maltreatment is to be properly addressed, the current service system needs to be better coordinated, more comprehensive, and less categorical. Services for all children should focus on building self-esteem and self-efficacy, reducing parental and family stress, breaking negative risk chains, and increasing opportunities for learning through positive child-care and educational experiences. Protective processes that build bonds of attachment to parents and others should be nurtured across life settings and at key stages in child development. Early intervention that promotes positive developmental outcomes is likely to minimize the negative chain reactions that disadvantage many children (Kinard, 1995; Rutter, 1987).

Public policy that underpins community-based services needs to ensure that both family preservation and support services are integrated into community institutions such as schools, churches, and recreational organizations serving families. Community-based service models are not unique, but the way in which communities organize and involve participants to develop plans for safe communities and families is critical to reducing maltreatment and its impact (see, for example, Hawkins & Catalano, 1992). As suggested in chapter 13, communities need to assess their level of risk factors and the resources directed at reducing those risk factors. They must then establish programs to address the risk factors endangering the greatest number of children. Risk-focused programming should do the following:

- prevent the accumulation of risk factors
- establish and maintain prosocial situations and opportunities
- focus on resilience and adaptation

- facilitate active involvement of parents, children, and others in planning
- ensure that services to at-risk populations are both necessary and sufficient
- provide timely, careful, and expert evaluation, assessment (including assessment of strengths), and follow-up services throughout the formative childhood years
- build safe, stable environments to permit families to establish structure, routines, rituals, and organization.

Summary

Risk and protective factors that affect rates of child maltreatment can be identified in every life setting—in the family and with peers and in schools, neighborhoods, and communities. Data about protective factors are just emerging, and conclusions about what factors and circumstances produce resilience are limited. Resilience appears to be affected by both environmental and biological conditions, but resilience is dynamic—it changes under differing conditions and over time. We do know that

- there is a strong link between poverty or disadvantaged circumstances and child maltreatment
- access to good health, education, and social services moderates environmental stressors associated with child maltreatment
- attachment to a supportive adult promotes recovery from child maltreatment
- feeling loved and cared for gives many children who have been victimized the strength, optimism, and sense of spirituality to see them through difficulties
- a secure, stable, and safe environment in family, neighborhood, and community fosters recovery, coping, and resilience
- social support helps connect children with others outside the family and provides models of prosocial behavior.

It is important to acknowledge that we have much to learn about how these risk and protective factors actually operate in different families and environments, and we need to know more about how to respond to those needs and situations. Nevertheless, what we do know sets the foundation for fostering a positive environment for children and their families.

References

Ainsworth, M. S. (1989, April). Attachments beyond infancy. *American Psychologist,* pp. 709–716.

Altemeier, W., O'Connor, S., Sherrock, K., & Tucker, E. (1986). Outcome of abuse during childhood among pregnant low income women. *Child Abuse & Neglect, 10,* 319–330.

Alter-Reid, K., Gibbs, M. S., Lachenmeyr, J. R., Sigal, J., & Massoth, N. A. (1986). Sexual abuse of children: A review of the empirical findings. *Clinical Psychology Review, 6,* 249–266.

American Humane Association (1994, March). *Child protection leader*. Englewood, CO: Author.

Anthony, E. J., & Cohler, B. (1987). *The invulnerable child*. New York: Guilford Press.

Ayoub, C., & Jacewitz, J. (1982). Families at risk of poor parenting: A descriptive study of sixty at-risk families in a model prevention program. *Child Abuse & Neglect, 6*, 413–422.

Ayoub, C., Jacewitz, M., Gold, R., & Milner, J. (1983). Assessment of a program's effectiveness in selecting individuals "at risk" for problems in parenting. *Journal of Clinical Psychology, 39*, 334–339.

Ayoub, C., Willett, J., & Robinson, D. (1992). Families at risk of child maltreatment: Entry-level characteristics and growth in family functioning during treatment. *Child Abuse & Neglect, 16*, 495–511.

Azar, S., Robinson, D., Hekimian, E., & Twentyman, C. (1984). Unrealistic expectations and problem-solving ability in maltreating and comparison mothers. *Journal of Consulting and Clinical Psychology, 52*, 687–691.

Bagley, C., & Thomlison, R. J. (1991). *Child sexual abuse: Critical perspectives on prevention, intervention, and treatment*. Toronto: Wall & Emerson.

Barnard, C. (1994). Resiliency: A shift in our perception? *American Journal of Family Therapy, 22*, 135–144.

Barth R. P. (1991). An experimental evaluation of in-home child abuse prevention services. *Child Abuse & Neglect, 15*, 363–375.

Belsky, J., & Vondra, J. (1989). Lessons from child abuse: The determinants of parenting. In D. Cicchetti & V. Carlson (Eds.), *Child maltreatment: Theory and research on the causes and consequences of child abuse and neglect* (pp. 153–202). New York: Cambridge University Press.

Briere, J., Berliner, L., Bulkley, J., Jenny, C., & Reid, T. (1996). *The APSAC handbook on child maltreatment*. Thousand Oaks, CA: Sage Publications.

Bronfenbrenner, U. (1986). Ecology of the family as a context for human development research perspectives. *Developmental Psychology, 22*, 723–742.

Browne, K., & Finkelhor, D. (1986). The impact of child sexual abuse: A review of the research. *Psychological Bulletin, 99*, 66–77.

Browne, K., & Saqui, S. (1988). Approaches to screening for child abuse and neglect. In K. Browne, C. Davies, & P. Stratton (Eds.), *Early prediction and prevention of child abuse* (pp. 57–85). New York: John Wiley & Sons.

Bullock, R., & Little, M. (1989). Managing the family contacts of children absent in care, professional and legislative issues: The experience of England and Wales. In J. Hudson & B. Galaway (Eds.), *The state as parent: International research perspectives on interventions with young persons* (NATO ASI Series, pp. 83–93). Boston: Kluwer Academic.

Chadwick, D. (1996). Community organization of services needed to deal with child abuse. In J. Briere, L. Berliner, J. Bulkley, C. Jenny, & T. Reid, T. (Eds.), *The APSAC handbook on child maltreatment* (pp. 398–409). Thousand Oaks, CA: Sage Publications.

Chaffin, M., Kelleher, K., & Hollenberg, J. (1996). Onset of physical abuse and neglect: Psychiatric, substance abuse, and social risk factors from prospective community data. *Child Abuse & Neglect, 20,* 191–203.

Cicchetti, D. (1989). How research on child maltreatment has informed the study of child development: Perspectives from developmental psychopathology. In D. Cicchetti & V. Carlson (Eds.), *Child maltreatment: Theory and research on the causes and consequences of child abuse and neglect* (pp. 377–431). New York: Cambridge University Press.

Cicchetti, D., & Carlson, V. (Eds.) (1989). *Child maltreatment: Theory and research on the causes and consequences of child abuse and neglect.* New York: Cambridge University Press.

Clark, H. B., & Clarke, R. T. (1996). Research on the wraparound process and individualized services for children with multi-system needs. *Journal of Child and Family Studies, 5,* 1–5.

Cohn, A. H., & Daro, D. (1987). Is treatment too late: What ten years of evaluative research tell us. *Child Abuse & Neglect, 11,* 433–442.

Coie, J., Watt, N., West, S., Hawkins, J. D., Asarnow, J., Markman, H., Ramey, S., Shure, M., & Long, B. (1993). The science of prevention: A conceptual framework and some directions for a national research program. *American Psychologist, 48,* 1013–1022.

Coohey, C. (1996). Child maltreatment: Testing the social isolation hypothesis. *Child Abuse & Neglect, 20,* 241–254.

Corcoran, K., & Vandiver, V. (1996). *Maneuvering the maze of managed care.* New York: Free Press.

Crittenden, P. M. (1988a). Families and dyadic patterns of functioning in maltreating families. In K. Browne, C. Davies, & P. Stratton (Eds.), *Early prediction and prevention of child abuse* (pp. 161–189). New York: John Wiley & Sons.

Crittenden, P. M. (1988b). Relationships at risk. In J. Belsky & T. Nezworski (Eds.), *Clinical implications of attachment* (pp. 136–174). Hillsdale, NJ: Lawrence Erlbaum.

Darmstadt, G. (1990). Community-based child abuse prevention. *Social Work, 35,* 487–489.

Daro, D., & McCurdy, K. (1994). Preventing child abuse and neglect: Programmatic interventions. *Child Welfare, 73*(Special issue), 405–431.

Davies, C., & Little, M. (1994). Child abuse and child protection: Recent research findings and their implications—A study in research management. In *Seminar: Research on social programmes for children, youth, and families* (pp. 23–33). Leicester, England: Norwegian Ministry of Children and Family Affairs.

Dore, M. M., Doris, J. M., & Wright, P. (1995). Identifying substance abuse in maltreating families: A child welfare challenge. *Child Abuse & Neglect, 19,* 531–543.

Doueck, H. J., English, D., DePanfilis, D., & Moote, G. T. (1993). Decision-making in child protective services: A comparison of selected risk-assessment systems. *Child Welfare, 72,* 441–452.

Earls, F., McGuire, J., & Shay, S. (1994). Evaluating a community intervention to reduce the risk of child abuse: Methodological strategies in conducting neighborhood surveys. *Child Abuse & Neglect, 18,* 473–487.

Emery, R. (1989). Family violence. *American Psychologist, 44,* 321–328.

English, D., & Pecora, P. (1994). Risk assessment as a practice method in child protective services. *Child Welfare, 73*(Special issue), 451–475.

Epstein, M., Quinn, K., & Cumblad, C. (1992). *Program initiatives to improve special education services for students with behavior disorders/emotional disorders: Evaluation plans.* DeKalb, IL: Educational Research and Services Center.

Faust, J., Runyon, M., & Kenny, M. (1995). Family variables associated with the onset and impact of intrafamilial childhood sexual abuse. *Clinical Psychology Review, 15,* 443–456.

Finkelhor, D. (1986). Prevention: A review of programs and research. In D. Finkelhor & Associates (Eds.), *A sourcebook on child sexual abuse* (pp. 224–254). Beverly Hills, CA: Sage Publications.

Finkelhor, D. (1994). The international epidemiology of child sexual abuse. *Child Abuse & Neglect, 18,* 409–417.

Finkelhor, D. (1995). The victimization of children: A developmental perspective. *American Journal of Orthopsychiatry, 65,* 177–193.

Finkelhor, D., & Baron, L. (1986). High-risk children. In D. Finkelhor (Ed.), *A sourcebook on child sexual abuse.* Beverly Hills, CA: Sage Publications.

Finkelhor, D., & Berliner, L. (1995). Research on the treatment of sexually abused children: A review and recommendations. *Journal of the American Academy of Child and Adolescent Psychiatry, 34,* 1–16.

Finkelhor, D., & Korbin, J. (1988). Child abuse as an international issue. *Child Abuse & Neglect, 11,* 397-407.

Garbarino, J., Dubrow, N., Kostelny, K., & Pardo, C. (1992). *Children in danger: Coping with the consequences of community violence.* San Francisco: Jossey-Bass.

Garbarino, J., & Kostelny, K. (1992). Child maltreatment as a community problem. *Child Abuse & Neglect, 16,* 455–464.

Garbarino, J., & Kostelny, K. (1994). Neighborhood-based programs. In G. B. Melton & F. D. Barry (Eds.), *Protecting children from abuse and neglect: Foundations for a new national strategy.* New York: Guilford Press.

Garmezy, N., & Tellegen, A. (1984). Studies of stress-resistant children: Methods, variables, and preliminary findings. In F. J. Morrison, G. Lord, & D. P. Keating (Eds.), *Applied developmental psychology* (pp. 231–287). Orlando, FL: Academic Press.

Gaudin, J. (1993). Effective intervention with neglectful families. *Criminal Justice and Behavior, 20,* 66–89.

Giovannoni, J., & Becerra, R. (1979). *Defining child abuse.* New York: Free Press.

Groves, I., & Foster, R. (1995). *Creating a new system of care: Building a stronger child and family partnership* (Assessment process, R.C. Monitoring Protocol, Version 3.0). Birmingham: Alabama Department of Human Resources, Division of Family and Children's Services.

Hawkins, J. D., & Catalano, R. F., Jr. (1992). *Communities that care.* San Francisco: Jossey-Bass.

Hay, T., & Jones, L. (1994). Societal interventions to prevent child abuse and neglect. *Child Welfare, 73*(Special issue), 379–405.

Hegar, R. L. (1988). Legal and social work approaches to sibling separation in foster care. *Child Welfare, 57,* 113–121.

Herrenkohl, E., Herrenkohl, R., & Egolf, B. (1994). Resilient early school-age children from maltreating homes: Outcomes in late adolescence. *American Journal of Orthopsychiatry, 64,* 301–309.

Hillson, J., & Kuiper, N. (1994). A stress and coping model of child maltreatment. *Clinical Psychology Review, 14,* 261–285.

Holder, W., & Corey, M. (1989). *The Child at Risk Field system: A family preservation approach to decision making in child protective services.* Charlotte, NC: ACTION for Child Protection.

Howard, J., Beckwith, L., Rodning, C., & Kropenski, V. (1989). The development of young children of substance-abusing parents: Insights from seven years of intervention and research. *Zero to Three, 9*(5), 8–12.

Hudson, W. (1982). *The clinical measurement package: A field manual.* Chicago: Dorsey.

Hudson, W. (1993). *Multi-problem screening inventory.* Tempe, AZ: Walmyr Publishing.

Hutchison, E. (1994). Child maltreatment: Can it be defined? In R. Barth, J. Berrick, & N. Gilbert (Eds.), *Child welfare research review* (pp. 5–15). New York: Garland.

Illinois Department of Social Services. (1985). *Child abuse and neglect investigation decisions handbook.* Springfield, IL: Author.

Iverson, T. J., & Segal, M. (1990). *Child abuse and neglect: An information and reference guide.* New York: Garland.

Jaudes, P. K., Ekwo, E., & Van Voorhis, J. (1995). Association of drug abuse and child abuse. *Child Abuse & Neglect, 19,* 1065–1075.

Kazdin, A. E. (1992). Child and adolescent dysfunction and paths toward maladjustment: Targets for intervention. *Clinical Psychology Review, 12,* 795–817.

Kendall-Tackett, K., & Eckenrode, J. (1996). The effects of neglect on academic achievement and disciplinary problems: A developmental perspective. *Child Abuse & Neglect, 20,* 161–171.

Kinard, M. (1995, July). *Assessing resilience in abused children.* Paper presented at the Fourth International Family Violence Research Conference, Durham, NH.

Kolko, D. J. (1996). Child physical abuse. In J. Briere, L. Berliner, J. Bulkley, C. Jenny, & T. Reid (Eds.). *The APSAC handbook on child maltreatment* (pp. 21–50). Thousand Oaks, CA: Sage Publications.

Kopp, C., & Kaler, S. (1989). Risk in infancy: Origins and implications. *American Psychologist, 44,* 224–230.

Korbin, J. (1994). Sociocultural factors in child maltreatment. In G. B. Melton & F. D. Barry (Eds.), *Protecting children from abuse and neglect: Foundations for a new national strategy* (pp. 182– 223). New York: Guilford Press.

Kotch, J., Browne, D., Ringwalt, C., Stewart, P., Ruina, E., Holt, K., Lowman, B., & Jung, J. (1995). Risk of abuse or neglect in a cohort of low-income children. *Child Abuse & Neglect, 19,* 1115–1130.

Kowal, L., Kottimeier, C., Ayoub, C., Komives, J., Robinson, D., & Allen, J. (1989). Characteristics of families at risk of problems in parenting: Findings from a home-based secondary prevention program. *Child Welfare, 68,* 529–538.

Lawlor, E., & Raube, K. (1995). Social interventions and outcomes in medical effectiveness research. *Social Service Review, 69,* 383–404.

Lindsey, D. (1994). *The welfare of children.* New York: Oxford University Press.

Magura, S., & Moses, B. S. (1986). *Outcome measures for child welfare services. Theory and applications.* Washington, DC: Child Welfare League of America.

Magura, S., Moses, B. S., & Jones, M. A. (1987). *Assessing risk and measuring change of families: The family risk scales.* Washington, DC: Child Welfare League of America.

Maluccio, A. M., Abramczyk, L., & Thomlison, B. (1996). Family reunification of children in out-of-home care: Research perspectives. *Children and Youth Services Review, 18,* 4–5.

Marks, J., & McDonald, T. (1989). *Risk assessment in child protective services: 4. Predicting recurrence of child maltreatment.* Portland: University of Southern Maine.

McCroskey, J., & Nelson, J. (1989). Practice-based research in a family support program. The Family Connection Project example. *Child Welfare, 68,* 573–587.

McCurdy, M., & Daro, D. (1993). *Current trends in child abuse reporting and fatalities: The results of the 1992 annual fifty-state survey.* Chicago: National Committee for the Prevention of Child Abuse.

Melton, G. B., & Barry, F. D. (1994a). Neighbors helping neighbors: The vision of the U.S. Advisory Board on Child Abuse and Neglect. In G. B. Melton & F. D. Barry (Eds.), *Protecting children from abuse and neglect: Foundations for a new national strategy* (pp. 1–14). New York: Guilford Press.

Melton, G. B., & Barry, F. D. (Eds.). (1994b). *Protecting children from abuse and neglect. Foundations for a new national strategy.* New York: Guilford Press.

Miller, J. S., Williams, K. M., English, D. J., & Olmstead, J. (1987). *Risk assessment in child protection: A review of the literature.* Olympia, WA: Department of Social and Health Services, Division of Children and Family Services.

Miller, N. B. (1994). *Nobody's perfect.* Baltimore: Paul H. Brookes.

Mrazek, P. J., & Haggerty, R. J. (Eds.). (1994). *Reducing risks for mental disorder: Frontiers for preventive intervention research.* Washington, DC: National Academy Press.

Mrazek, P. J., & Mrazek, D. A. (1987). Resilience in child maltreatment victims: A conceptual exploration. *Child Abuse & Neglect, 11,* 357–366.

Olds, D., & Henderson, C. (1990). The prevention of maltreatment. In D. Cicchetti & V. Carlson (Eds.), *Child maltreatment* (pp. 722–763). New York: Cambridge University Press.

Parker, R., Ward, H., Jackson, S., Aldgate, J., & Wedge, P. (1991). *Looking after children: Assessing outcomes in child care.* London: Her Majesty's Stationery Office.

Pecora, P. (1991). Investigating allegations of child maltreatment: The strengths and limitations of current risk assessment systems. *Child and Youth Services, 15*(2), 73–92.

Pelton, L. (1994). The role of material factors in child abuse and neglect. In G. B. Melton & F. D. Barry (Eds.), *Protecting children from abuse and neglect: Foundations for a new national strategy* (pp. 131–181). New York: Guilford Press.

Quinton, D., & Rutter, M. (1988). *Parenting breakdown: The making and breaking of intergenerational links.* Aldershot, England: Gower.

Radke-Yarrow, M., & Sherman, T. (1990). Hard growing: Children who survive. In J. Rolf, A. S. Masten, D. Cicchetti, K. H. Nuechterlein, & S. Weintraub (Eds.), *Risk and protective factors in the development of psychopathology* (pp. 97–119). Cambridge: Cambridge University Press.

Roberts, J. (1988). Why are some families more vulnerable to child abuse? In K. Browne, C. Davies, & P. Stratton (Eds.), *Early prediction and prevention of child abuse* (pp. 43–56). New York: John Wiley & Sons.

Rutter, M. (1981). Stress, coping, and development: Some issues, and some perspectives. *Journal of Child Psychology and Psychiatry, 22,* 323–356.

Rutter, M. (1987). Psychosocial resilience and protective mechanisms. *American Journal of Orthopsychiatry, 57,* 316–330.

Seifer, R., & Sameroff, A. J. (1987). Multiple determinants of risk and invulnerability. In E. J. Anthony & B. J. Cohler (Eds.), *The invulnerable child* (pp. 51–69). New York: Guilford Press.

Simons, R. L., Whitbeck, L. B., Conger, R. D., & Chyi-In, W. (1991). Intergenerational transmission of harsh parenting. *Developmental Psychology, 27,* 159–171.

Smith, D. W., & Saunders, B. E. (1995). Personality characteristics of father/perpetrator and non-offending mothers in incest families: Individual and dyadic analyses. *Child Abuse & Neglect, 19,* 607–617.

Tracy, E. (1988). Social support resources of at-risk families: Implementation of social support assessments in an intensive family preservation program. *Dissertation Abstracts International, 49,* 2813-A. (University Microfilms No. DA88-26430).

Tracy, E., & McDonell, J. (1991). Home-based work with families: The environmental context of family intervention. *Journal of Independent Social Work, 5*(3/4), 93–108.

Trocme, N. (1996). Development and preliminary evaluation of the Ontario Child Neglect Index. *Child Maltreatment 1,* 145–155.

Trupin, E. W., Tarico, V. S., Low, B. P., Jemelka, R., & McClellan, J. (1993). Children on child protective service caseloads: Prevalence and nature of serious emotional disturbance, *Child Abuse & Neglect, 17,* 345–355.

U.S. Department of Health and Human Services, National Center on Child Abuse and Neglect. (1988). *Study findings: Study of national incidence and prevalence of child abuse and neglect.* Washington, DC: U.S. Government Printing Office.

U.S. Department of Health and Human Services, National Center on Child Abuse and Neglect. (1995). *Child maltreatment 1993: Reports from the states to the*

National Center on Child Abuse and Neglect. Washington, DC: U.S. Government Printing Office.

Wald, M., & Woolverton, N. (1990). Risk assessment. *Child Welfare, 69,* 483–511.

Wekerle, C., & Wolfe, D. (1993). Prevention of child physical abuse and neglect: Promising new directions. *Clinical Psychology Review, 13,* 501–540.

Whiteman, M., Fanshel, D., & Grundy, J. F. (1987). Cognitive–behavioral interventions aimed at anger of parents at risk of child abuse. *Social Work, 32,* 469–474.

Widom, C. S. (1989a). Does violence beget violence? A critical examination of the literature. *Psychological Bulletin, 6,* 3–28.

Widom, C. S. (1989b). Child abuse, neglect, and adult behavior: Research design and findings on criminality, violence, and child abuse. *American Journal of Orthopsychiatry, 59,* 355–367.

Wolfe, D. (1985). Child abusive parents: An empirical review and analysis. *Psychological Bulletin, 97,* 462–482.

Wolfe, D. (1991). *Preventing physical and emotional abuse of children.* New York: Guilford Press.

Wolfe, D. (1994). The role of intervention and treatment services in the prevention of child abuse and neglect. In G. B. Melton & F. D. Barry (Eds.), *Protecting children from abuse and neglect: Foundations for a new national strategy* (pp. 224–304). New York: Guilford Press.

Wyatt, G. E. (1985). The sexual abuse of Afro-American and White-American women in childhood. *Child Abuse & Neglect, 9,* 507–519.

Wyatt, G. E., & Newcomb, M. (1990). Internal and external mediators of women's sexual abuse in childhood. *Journal of Consulting and Clinical Psychology, 58,* 758–767.

5

ATTENTION DEFICIENCY AND HYPERACTIVITY

S. Rachel Dedmon

For nearly a century professionals who serve children have struggled with the conceptualization and cause of a condition that hinders the ability of many children to adapt to and function in their environments. Characteristically, these children tend to leave tasks incomplete, appear disorganized and messy, squirm and fidget in their seats, talk excessively, engage in potentially dangerous behavior without apparent concern for consequences, interrupt adults and peers, and have trouble keeping quiet—all with little or no insight into how these activities cause them frequently to be misunderstood, excluded, and behind on deadlines. In 1902 Dr. George Still described such a group of children, mostly boys, as restless and apt to get in trouble. In what was probably the first documentation of hyperactivity, Still reported to the Royal College of Physicians in London that he believed these children lacked moral control (Kohn, 1989). Over the years the list of symptoms characterizing the disorder has been revised, and the focus of theories about its causes has shifted from Still's "moral functioning" to the current emphasis on biological functioning. The name of the condition has been refined also. It is known today as "attention-deficit hyperactivity disorder" (ADHD).

Early in the century there was growing concern that some of the unruly behaviors Dr. Still described could be the result of central nervous system dysfunction caused by conditions such as encephalitis, epilepsy, and lead poisoning (Gordon & Asher, 1994). By midcentury opinion had shifted. The thought then was that these children could be suffering from minimal brain damage—later framed as brain dysfunction—even though the exact damage and dysfunction were difficult to measure and thus hard to prove. In the 1960s the disorder became known as "hyperkinetic reaction of childhood" (Rapport, 1995), perhaps because the excess motor activity so visible in these children was easier to quantify than brain dysfunction. The diagnosis, so stated, was recorded in the second edition of the American Psychiatric Association's *Diagnostic and Statistical Manual of Mental Disorders* (DSM-II) (American Psychiatric Association [APA], 1968).

Research on child mental health, which increased after the publication of DSM-II, found that children with hyperkinesis had trouble attending to stimuli in the environment, and by the time DSM-III was published, the condition had been renamed attention deficit disorder (APA, 1980). It was thought to present with or without hyperactivity and probably to always reflect some impulsivity (Rapport, 1995). Then came a decade of debate over whether there was a common clinical presentation or whether heterogeneous conditions were grouped under one diagnostic umbrella (Kohn, 1989). Specifically, researchers questioned whether hyperactivity was always present to some degree or whether attention difficulties could present alone, in which case the clinical condition would be totally different.

Case studies reflected mixtures of the chief manifestations that were eventually recognized—attention deficiency, hyperactivity, and impulsivity—which resulted in the current name of the condition: attention-deficit hyperactivity disorder. ADHD can present with a predominance of inattention, a predominance of hyperactivity and impulsivity, or as a combination of all three difficulties (APA, 1994). The many labels and opinions that have been used over the years to name and describe this condition weave an interesting backdrop to the perception that ADHD is a many-featured, complex problem that responds to more than a single solution (Attention Deficit Disorder—Part I, 1995; Kaplan, Sadock, & Grebb, 1994).

Nature of the Problem

According to the DSM-IV, ADHD is a condition marked by a "persistent pattern of inattention and/or hyperactivity-impulsivity that is more frequent and severe than is typically observed in individuals at a comparable level of development" (APA, 1994, p. 78). This overarching definition makes it clear that the disorder has more than a singular nature. Somewhat more frequent in boys than in girls, ADHD varies according to which manifestation is prominent, the developmental stage of the child, and the circumstances of the child.

Hyperactivity

Hyperactivity is the most frequent manifestation of ADHD, and it is the one most likely to first alert parents and professionals to a potential problem (Kaplan et al., 1994). Children with hyperactivity seem driven in their interactions with the environment—they talk excessively, move their hands and feet almost constantly, and have difficulty keeping quiet even in low-key play (APA, 1994). Not only do such children frequently find it hard to remain seated and still during school, but the wiggling and repositioning persist at mealtimes, while riding in a car, and even when sleeping (Rapport, 1995). As a group, children who experience the disorder with hyperactivity have more pervasive and severe behavioral problems, and less behavioral inhibition, than children with the disorder but without hyperactivity. Ratings by parents and teachers of children with the disorder rank the former group (+H) as more aggressive and antisocial than children in the latter group (-H). Testing shows the +H children to have no particular problems with perceptual motor speed; they can therefore respond well when stimulated. They do, however, appear to be impaired in vigilance and behavioral inhibition, which could produce problems with inattention and failure to understand when and how to stop ongoing problematic behavior (Barkley, DuPaul, & McMurray, 1991). They also have higher rates of noncompliance with rules and requests and experience more peer rejection; they are also more likely to be placed in classrooms with students with severe emotional disturbances and to be suspended from school (DuPaul & Stoner, 1994).

Hyperactivity varies according to a child's age and stage of development, and, with caution, it can be assessed in very young children. As infants, children at risk of ADHD are more active in their cribs and sleep less than the average baby their age (Kaplan et al., 1994), and they can be difficult to hold and soothe (Barkley et al., 1991). As toddlers, they run soon after learning to walk and are constantly on the go and into everything—darting out open doors, running in the house, and climbing and jumping on the furniture more than their peers. As school-aged children they fidget with objects, tap their feet, shake their legs, and show little change in behaviors when going from a permissive environment to one requiring more social compliance (APA, 1994). Their fidgeting often consists of whole body movements that sweep wider and cover a greater expanse than those of comparison children (Teicher, Ito, Glod, & Barber, 1996).

Sometimes hyperactivity appears in one setting, such as home or school, but not in others, such as religious or recreational facilities. When children at risk of ADHD are involved in a structured activity—a one-on-one game of skill, for example—they tend to adapt with far less overactivity than in unstructured situations such as free play. The hyperactivity is more than just a brief and transient incident of overactivity in response to life stressors (Kaplan et al., 1994). It usually lasts for years and is evidenced in multiple settings.

INATTENTION

The major problem with attention tends to be with sustained attention, which is the capacity to keep focused on an age-appropriate activity whether at work or at play (Barkley et al., 1991). There seem to be fewer problems with selective attention— that is, the ability to focus on a specific stimulus while ignoring competing stimuli— and with attention capacity, which is the ability to attend to information in short-term memory (Hinshaw, 1994). Because of sustained attention deficits, the child cannot focus on an assignment long enough to take in all the details or instructions, makes careless mistakes doing the work, does not persist with tasks until they are completed, shifts from one uncompleted activity to another, has poor work habits, and frequently loses or damages materials needed to complete a task (APA, 1994).

Compared with children with hyperactivity, children with attention difficulties alone have greater problems recalling events and responding speedily to perceptual motor demands (DuPaul & Stoner, 1994). Although these children may initially maintain the work pace of comparison children, they begin to flag as the demands for attention go on. Personally selected tasks that can be completed at the child's own rate are done best; paced tasks selected by someone else and those of little interest to the child are the most difficult (Hinshaw, 1994). The child is likely to try to avoid homework and school desk work because of the inherent difficulties involved, but the avoidance is not seen as opposition to the work, although secondary opposition may occur (APA, 1994). The attention problem persists across settings, academic and social.

Opinions differ about whether ADHD is really an attention problem. Some see it as lack of direction (Attention Deficit Disorder—Part I, 1995). Barkley (1994) expressed the belief that it is a problem of "a delay in the development of response inhibition" (p. vii). In part, neuropsychological delay accounts for difficulties in sustaining mental images, referencing the past, imagining outcomes to events, making plans, and avoiding non-goal-directed behavior. Thus, ADHD, according to Barkley (1994), is a disorder "of not doing what you know rather than of not knowing what to do" (p. viii). It is most severely experienced in environments requiring personal discipline, organization, and performance. In school, it appears as a discrepancy between a child's tested IQ and adaptive functioning (DuPaul & Stoner, 1994).

Levine (1987) argued that the internal control systems that regulate learning and adaptation are weak in people with attention difficulties. These weakened systems cause problems for focus (perseveration on unimportant matters or insufficient focus on relevant ones, for example); sensory perceptions (visual, auditory, or tactile distractibility, or all three); associative processes (daydreaming); appetite (insatiability and difficulty in delaying gratification); social interactions (failure to "filter out" peers); motor control (inefficient or non-goal-directed activity); behavioral issues (unpremeditated opposition or disruption); communicative operations (lack of verbal inhibition); and affective behavior (wide and unpredictable mood swings). Across children at risk of ADHD, control system problems vary in intensity and are influenced by individual and environmental circumstances.

IMPULSIVITY

The third primary characteristic of ADHD, impulsivity, means more than just being impatient and having difficulty delaying responses. It can have a cognitive component, which frequently clusters with inattention. At-risk children attempt to move ahead in assignments before they have completed basic tasks, and they often become distracted by activities other than the main subject. They tend to skip around with ideas and become frustrated, needing help to organize tasks cognitively so that there can be a logical progression toward reaching a goal. Consequently, they need close, preferably one-on-one, instruction and supervision to complete academic work.

Impulsivity can also have a behavioral component that frequently meshes with hyperactivity. Children may blurt out a response before a question is completed, jump out of line while awaiting an event, and talk so much that no one else can enter the conversation (Hinshaw, 1994). At-risk children make comments out of turn, talk at inappropriate times, touch things when instructed not to do so, and intrude on others' privacy. They break and spill things frequently and get in potentially dangerous situations without considering outcomes (they might, for example, try flips on a skateboard when they have no skating experience, no helmet, and no protective pads). Such behaviors seem associated less with thrill seeking than with acting without thinking of the consequences (Parker, 1992).

DIAGNOSTIC SUBTYPES

Based on symptom patterns that last at least six months, three subtypes of ADHD may be identified: predominantly inattentive, predominantly hyperactive–impulsive, or a combination of the two. The first two patterns require six or more symptoms of the designated type of manifestation for diagnosis; the latter requires six or more manifestations of both inattention and hyperactivity–impulsivity. The symptoms usually present before the age of seven and cause the child to feel maladapted (a feeling of distress or disability) or put the child at increased risk for conditions that interfere with school, play, and relationships. For a diagnosis of ADHD, impairment must be present in two or more settings, such as school and home (APA, 1994).

Secondary problems are frequent in such areas as academics, peer relations, and self-esteem (Barlow & Durand, 1995). As schoolwork demands grow with advancing grade levels, the child's difficulty with staying on task and assuming personal responsibility for learning can prove problematic. Studies have shown that adolescents with unremediated hyperactivity are often two academic years behind peers without the disorder (Munoz-Millan & Casteel, 1989). Making and keeping friends is difficult, especially if the child barges into activities without invitation and loses his or her temper when frustrated. Not surprisingly, given the frequent negative feedback from parents, teachers, and peers—which is complicated by the frustration of trying unsuccessfully to do things right—children with ADHD often suffer from low self-esteem.

The comorbidity of ADHD with conduct disorder, including oppositional defiant disorder, is hotly debated. Some professionals think that ADHD is not a freestanding diagnosis but merely part of a more inclusive diagnosis such as conduct disorder (Munoz-Millan & Casteel, 1989). Externalizing behaviors, such as defiance, disruption, inattention, overactivity, and antisocial activities, characterize all three conditions. However, Hinshaw (1987) showed that despite the overlap in characteristics, there is evidence that the three constitute independent or different diagnoses. The co-occurrence, or comorbidity, of conduct disorder among children with ADHD has been reported at rates from 20 percent (Barkley, 1990) to 60 percent (Biederman, Munir, & Knee, 1987). The co-occurrence of ADHD in children with conduct disorder, however, is significantly higher—90 percent (Abikoff, Klein, Klass, & Ganeles, 1987).

Prevalence

It is estimated that 3 percent to 5 percent of preadolescent school-aged children in the United States have ADHD (APA, 1994; Barlow & Durand, 1995). At the elementary school level, however, the prevalence was recently estimated to be as high as 15 percent to 20 percent (Gordon & Asher, 1994). ADHD is one of the main reasons children are seen in mental health services, constituting up to 40 percent of child referrals (Barlow & Durand, 1995; DuPaul & Stoner, 1994), with boys outnumbering girls 6 to 1 in clinical settings and 3 to 1 in community settings (Barlow & Durand, 1995).

Outcome research, which looks today at adults who had been assessed in childhood as having ADHD, must be interpreted with care. A diagnosis of ADHD made 15 or 20 years ago was based on a different set of criteria; thus, the sample on which outcomes were collected is not representative of children with ADHD today. Current assessment tools reflect refinement over the years, and more children are being identified with milder symptoms and possibly better prognoses. In fact, studies show that the expanded criteria for ADHD in DSM-IV (APA, 1994) produced as much as 56 percent more diagnoses of the disorder than did those in DSM-III, Revised (APA, 1987) (Wolraich, Hannah, Pinnock, Baumgaertel, & Brown, 1996).

The research to date suggests that over half of all children with ADHD will continue to experience manifestations of the disorder in adulthood (Barkley, 1995), although the manner and intensity of the manifestations may change with maturity. Mannuzza et al. (1991), replicating an earlier study (Mannuzza, Klein, Konig, & Giampino, 1989), studied 111 subjects with a childhood assessment of hyperactivity and 115 control subjects who had no psychiatric diagnosis; the mean age of both groups was 18 years. Ninety-four of the probands received a mental health diagnosis of attention deficit disorder (43 percent), antisocial personality disorder/conduct disorder (32 percent), and substance use disorder (14 percent). All diagnoses were significantly more prevalent in the probands than in the controls. Only 1 percent had an affective disorder, and 1 percent had another type of personality disorder—data not significantly different from the controls. It is important to note that for substance use disorders, an antisocial syndrome preceded a substance problem in 97 percent of the cases. This finding negates concerns that medication for hyperactivity might lead to later substance abuse (Mannuzza et al., 1991). Clearly, ADHD is a condition that probably persists into adulthood, although many people learn how to cope with the energy and distraction of the disorder and adapt successfully to their environments.

In spite of the evidence, questions persist about the appropriateness of ADHD diagnoses. Some studies re-evaluating children diagnosed with ADHD have reported that most did not have the disorder or that it was not their primary problem (Cotugno, 1993; Sabatino & Vance, 1994). Sabatino and Vance studied 75 children who had been referred to a hospital clinic with a diagnosis of ADHD, according to criteria from DSM-III, Revised (APA, 1987), and a history of unsatisfactory response to medical and educational interventions. Senior staff teams from departments of pediatrics, neurology, and psychology re-evaluated the children and determined, with a high level of interrater reliability (r = .89), that only 31 of the children (41 percent) actually had ADHD. Of the 44 children re-evaluated as not having ADHD, 68 percent had impulsivity that evaluators believed related to conduct disorder, oppositional defiant disorder, and a variety of anxiety disorders. There were two other subgroups: 30 percent were found to have information-processing problems associated with learning disabilities, and 23 percent had central auditory processing or receptive language problems. This study and others like it raise concern that the ADHD diagnosis is being used as a medical assessment of children who simply move too much and are easily distracted (Creemers, 1990; Rosemond, 1995; Sabatino & Vance, 1994). This view remains controversial, because it is not yet supported by a significant body of research.

DESCRIPTION OF RISK FACTORS

The greatest potential for understanding the risk factors for ADHD as well as the complexity and variability of the disorder lies in an ecological perspective. This perspective promotes viewing the child at risk and the entire environment in which the child lives as a unitary system and examining the impact of one on the other (Germain & Gitterman, 1995). There is no linear causation to this condition, which continues to defy simple description. It is much more the result of multiple risk interactions that account for the presence and variation of the disorder among children. An ecological perspective also allows the disorder to be understood dynamically, as a matter of fitting in the environment over time (Germain & Gitterman, 1995). Children with ADHD change in their expression of the disorder as they age. There are also differences among children sharing similar social environments at the same developmental stage. ADHD represents a child's unique biosocial interaction with the environment at a particular point in time.

Increased research on attention deficiency and hyperactivity in the past two decades has identified a number of risk factors, although the findings for many of these are more suggestive than confirmed. Proposed but without substantial empirical support are theories of the effects of sugar, food additives, toxins, and exposure to cool-white fluorescent lighting and to radioactive rays emitted from television (Rapport, 1995). Some of these poorly documented risk factors, many believe, may exacerbate the conditions of some children with ADHD, but their general effect is limited.

FAMILY HISTORY

One of the clearest risk traits for ADHD is to be born into a family in which some members have the disorder. Various family-genetic studies have demonstrated the increased risk, whether the family members' ADHD symptoms are concurrent or past (Anastopoulos & Barkley, 1988; Biederman et al., 1992; Faraone, Biederman, Keenan, & Tsuang, 1991; Goodman & Stevenson, 1989). Biederman et al. (1992) examined 140 male children with ADHD and their 454 first-degree, both-gender relatives and 120 normal male controls and their 368 first-degree, both-gender relatives. ADHD was found in the relatives of probands five times more frequently than in the relatives of control subjects. These rates held when controlled for the potentially confounding variables of age of proband, age of relative, socioeconomic status, percentage of intact families, and number of siblings. Twin studies provide even more persuasive data on the strength of genetic influence. Gillis, Gilger, Pennington, and Defries (1992) reported that when one monozygotic twin had been diagnosed with ADHD, in 79 percent of cases the other twin also had ADHD. The same was true for 32 percent of dizygotic twins, a rate approximately 10 times higher than that of the general public. On balance, scientific data suggest that family-genetic influences are strong and independent of psychosocial conditions. But even though genetic predisposition may be a risk factor, it is believed highly unlikely that a single inheritable gene can account for all cases of ADHD and equally unlikely that genetic factors can be disentangled from congenital and familial influences.

THYROID HORMONE

A specific biological condition has been found to predispose some children to ADHD. Hauser et al. (1993) reported on the correlation between generalized resistance to thyroid hormone and the presence of ADHD. Comparing 49 subjects with generalized resistance to thyroid hormone with their 55 relatives who did not have it, they discovered that, despite very similar genetic and environmental backgrounds, adults with the resistance were 15 times more likely to have ADHD than their adult relatives and that children with the resistance were 10 times more likely to have the disorder than their child relatives. Because the thyroid gland is essential for energy consumption through the basal metabolic rate and for normal mental development, this finding is important even though it affects only a small percentage of people with the disorder (Attention Deficit Disorder—Part I, 1995).

BRAIN FUNCTIONS

Brain dysfunction was suspected but difficult to prove in the 1950s, but today's brain imaging and mapping technologies have produced evidence suggesting a connection between ADHD and brain activity or structure (or both). Lou, Henriksen, and Bruhn (1984) and Lou, Henriksen, Bruhn, Borner, and Nielsen (1989) used single-photon emission computed tomography to measure blood flow in the brain (the more active or more functional the brain section, the greater the blood flow to the section). In the studies of children with ADHD, they found low activity in the frontal lobes and basal ganglia—areas important to inhibiting behavior and sustaining attention and to controlling emotions, motivation, and memory. They also discovered overactivity in the primary sensory and sensorimotor regions, areas obviously important to movement and activity levels. Work by Zametkin et al. (1990) using positron emission tomography supports the finding of frontal lobe abnormality; this research noted reduced glucose metabolism in several regions of the brain, including the frontal lobes.

The frontal lobe affects thinking, reasoning, remembering, and social abilities (Barlow & Durand, 1995). It has been theorized that the frontal lobes do not adequately perform their inhibitory functions in children with ADHD (Kaplan et al., 1994). Difficulties in brain functioning might be caused by abnormal development or by brain injury (Barkley, 1995), which could be the result of subtle stressors during the fetal and perinatal periods (Kaplan et al., 1994). Alternatively, Kaplan, Sadock, and Grebb suggested that the abnormal development could result from insults to the central nervous system caused by infection, inflammation, or injury during early infancy. All of these problems with brain function could be related to psychosocial as well as physiological risks.

A related area of brain research posits a neurochemical predisposition to ADHD involving neurotransmitters, which are chemical agents released by the brain's message-bearing cells—neurons—to transport messages from one neuron to another. Three specific neurotransmitters—dopamine, norepinephrine, and serotonin—are particularly important. They are associated with such behaviors as attention, motivation, and inhibition of the motor system. Stimulant medication, which has a positive effect on ADHD, increases the amount of these particular neurotransmitters (Riccio, Hynd, Cohen, & Gonzalez, 1993). The fact that frontal–limbic connections of the brain have relatively high amounts of dopamine and norepinephrine strengthens the findings of those studies of brain activities described above that show problems in the frontal lobes.

The information from studies of the brain is consistent: There is a biological component in the etiology of ADHD. What the data cannot specify, however, is exactly how that connection works. It is possible that different manifestations of ADHD (that is, some with hyperactivity, some without hyperactivity) have different neuroanatomical or neurochemical bases for the disorder.

Psychosocial Factors

Family stability and environmental stress have long interested scientists searching for an etiology of ADHD (Rende & Plomin, 1993). Data suggest that stresses in the family system and in the broader social environment may elevate risk for early onset and may contribute to maintenance of the condition. However, it does not appear that family and environmental stress are causal (Kaplan et al., 1994). The diathesis–stress and reciprocal gene–environmental models of examining influences on behavior offer explanations for the correlation. According to the diathesis–stress conceptualization, children with a genetic or biological predisposition for hyperactivity could experience an acceleration of overactivity or maintain an overactive state when faced with environmental stress. The reciprocal gene–environmental model suggests that the genetic predisposition for ADHD may actually increase the likelihood that the child with ADHD will interact with the environment in ways that increase the chances of encountering stressors (Barlow & Durand, 1995). Exacerbating contextual effects associated with such interactions include low maternal education, low parental socioeconomic status, single parenthood, and abandonment by the father (Barkley, 1995).

The study by Biederman et al. (1992) found that other characteristics of the family might result in stressful events for the child with ADHD. Relatives were at risk not only for having ADHD themselves, but also for major depression, antisocial disorders, substance dependence, and anxiety disorders—all conditions that have the potential to increase stress levels in the family environment. Jacobvitz and Stroufe (1987), in a study of impoverished inner-city families, connected overstimulating mother–infant interactions with the child being diagnosed with ADHD several years later. Such a connection is likely to be more complex than a linear explanation suggests, however. The mothers were primarily teenage; they could have been genetically predisposed to impulsivity, which could have put them at risk of pregnancy as well as overstimulation of their infants (Hinshaw, 1994). In addition, parenthood at such an age and in such economic conditions might have created critical life stressors for the mother, which would certainly affect the infant's environment. Whatever the circumstances, it is easily conceivable that children with ADHD not only may react to unrest in the environment, but also may be the source of stressful relationships and environments in their homes. The interaction can be circular and it can snowball, exemplifying reciprocated causation in multifactorial models of risk.

DESCRIPTION OF PROTECTIVE FACTORS

Like risk factors, protective factors have only recently been identified and are best understood when viewed from an ecological perspective. The ability of a child with ADHD to effect a good fit with the environment—to be adaptive—probably reflects resilience of the "overcoming the odds" type, as proposed by Masten, Best, and Garmezy (1990). Most factors serve as what Luthar (1991) identified as additive interactions, which enhance the child's likelihood of having positive experiences in life (see chapter 2).

ACADEMIC ACHIEVEMENT

One of the strongest predictors of any child growing up to be a well-functioning adult is academic achievement (Rutter & Quinton, 1984). This is an area of difficulty for most children with ADHD, particularly if they also have conduct disorder (Rapport, 1995). Although no study has proved a relationship between ADHD and deficits in academic skills (that is, learning disabilities), empirical evidence indicates that approximately one of every three children with ADHD will have a specific learning disability (DuPaul & Stoner, 1994). Approximately 40 percent of children with the disorder are placed in special education programs; approximately one-third are retained in at least one grade before reaching high school; and an estimated 10 percent to 30 percent quit school and do not graduate (DuPaul & Stoner, 1994; Rapport, 1995). Their standardized achievement test scores are often below normal in the basics (reading, spelling, and mathematics) (Rapport, 1995). All of this occurs in a group in which the range of intellectual capabilities is identical to that of the general population. Some scientists deduce that promoting scholastic success through direct instruction in academic areas is critical to the success of children with ADHD (DuPaul & Stoner, 1994; Hinshaw,

1992). On the basis of studies of children with reading disabilities (for example, Gittelman & Feingold, 1983), it appears logical that instruction in deficient academic skills, such as oral and written language, can have a wide-ranging positive effect.

LEGAL SUPPORT

Three federal laws provide the protection needed to ensure the availability of education for children with ADHD: (1) Section 504 of the Rehabilitation Act of 1973, (2) the Individuals with Disabilities Education Act of 1992 (IDEA, successor to P.L. 94-142 and P.L. 99-457), and (3) the Americans with Disabilities Act (ADA), enacted in 1990. Section 504, a civil rights law prohibiting discrimination against people with disabilities, ensures that schools address the needs of children with disabilities as adequately as they address those of nondisabled children. Disability is defined as any physical or mental impairment that limits major life activities, including learning. With a "Policy Clarification Memorandum" of September 16, 1991, the U. S. Department of Education clarified that children with ADHD may qualify for special education and related services solely on the basis of their having ADHD when it significantly impairs their educational performance. The children are eligible under IDEA's category of "other health impaired." If an evaluation is needed to determine eligibility, it must be provided at no cost to the parents, regardless of available health insurance coverage. Title II of ADA prohibits educational institutions from denying educational services and activities to people with disabilities (Asch & Mudrick, 1995; Children & Adults with Attention Deficit Disorders, 1993). These legal mandates are intended to create environments that help children with special needs—such as those with ADHD—reach their potential.

DIFFERENCES IN RISK AND PROTECTIVE FACTORS BY AGE, GENDER, AND RACE OR ETHNICITY

Although boys with ADHD greatly outnumber girls with the disorder in both community and clinical settings, it is not completely clear that gender accounts for the difference in the base rate. There is a paucity of epidemiological studies on girls with ADHD. In fact, some important family studies, such as the one by Biederman et al. (1992), excluded females. Others have such small samples of girls that the data cannot be examined for the effects of gender (see, for example, Barkley, DuPaul, & McMurray, 1990, 1991). James and Taylor (1990) noted that girls with ADHD had higher rates of cognitive impairment, language dysfunction, and compromised neurological status than boys with the disorder, who displayed more variation in symptoms. Boys may be assessed more quickly than girls because of the expansiveness or breadth of their symptoms; likewise, they reportedly are more likely than girls to experience comorbidity for behavioral disorders (Berry, Shaywitz, & Shaywitz, 1985; James & Taylor, 1990). If that is true, behavioral disruptions alone could be the reason boys are seen more often for services and diagnosed more frequently with the disorder. In addition, teachers reportedly assess inattention and hyperactivity much more frequently when a child displays oppositional or disruptive behaviors, regardless of the presence of inattention or hyperactivity (Hinshaw, 1994). It is therefore possible that teachers underidentify girls with the disorder because of the lesser evidence of behavioral problems. Moreover, tests that do not differentiate gender might fail to detect girls with the disorder as quickly as they do boys because the thresholds for diagnosis are too high.

Some studies have reported similarities in the ways boys and girls experience ADHD. One found that girls and boys experience the manifestations of the disorder in fundamentally the same ways, allowing for the greater comorbidity of behavioral problems in boys (McGee, Williams, & Silva, 1987). Also, their families have been reported to have similar psychopathologies in male and female members (Befera & Barkley, 1985; Faraone et al., 1991). Even though the majority of work to date supports the idea that the disorder is similarly expressed in boys and girls, the question of difference clearly needs more investigation (Hinshaw, 1994).

The effect of socioeconomic status (SES) on ADHD is unclear. Biederman et al. (1992) in the family-genetic studies excluded the lowest SES level "to minimize the potential confounds of psychosocial chaos" (p. 729). SES proved not to be a significant difference for the children accepted as subjects, who varied between SES levels I and IV. Barkley et al. (1990) studied the differences among children having ADHD with hyperactivity, those having ADHD without hyperactivity, children with learning disabilities, and normal control children. Findings showed no significant difference among the four groups on the Hollingshead Two-Factor Index of Social Position. However, to the degree that lower SES levels imply poverty and hence stress, one can theorize that a child in adverse socioeconomic conditions who has ADHD might experience an exacerbation and continuance of symptoms.

ADHD is reported across cultures. Studies from Australia, Germany, Great Britain, New Zealand, and the United States have used comparable rating scales, although the cultural standards for determining the normality of behavior are quite different. For example, mental health professionals in distinct cultures differ in their judgments about whether behavior is hyperactive or disruptive. Reviewing four videotapes of eight-year-old boys, two from Honolulu and two from Tokyo, Chinese and Indonesian professionals gave higher scores for hyperactive or disruptive behaviors than did Japanese and American mental health professionals (Mann et al., 1992). These differences about the intensity of behavior required to constitute a diagnosis make it difficult to compare international findings.

Witnessing or being the object of violence in the home appears to be related to, and probably exacerbates, symptoms of ADHD. In a study of 22 boys and 23 girls, ages five to 12 years, from maritally violent families in which the mother had been physically victimized in the past 12 months, high levels of parent–child aggression were statistically associated with attention problems, conduct problems, and motor excess in boys ($p < .05$) but not in girls (Jouriles, Barling, & O'Leary, 1987). Moreover, the relationship of parent–child aggression to those behavior problems of both boys and girls remained significant when age of the child and interspousal aggression were controlled ($p < .01$). In a larger study of 185 children ages seven to 13 years, O'Keefe (1994) determined that the amount and frequency of marital violence witnessed by children and the experience of mother–child aggression were associated with severe behavior problems. There were no gender differences in the scores and no difference between external behaviors (aggression, for example) and internal behaviors (depression, for example). In this study, which included Hispanic (37 percent), black (21 percent), and white (42 percent) children, race was significantly related to externalizing behavior; white children scored significantly higher than black children on externalizing behavior.

Another form of violence, sexual abuse, raises a question about whether behaviors that look like ADHD symptoms truly are evidence of ADHD. In a study comparing 26 sexually abused children seen in a sex-abuse diagnostic and treatment service with 23 nonsexually abused children referred for psychiatric services, 46 percent of the sexually abused group and 30.4 percent of the nonabused group had ADHD. It was the most common disorder found in both groups—its occurrence was greater than posttraumatic stress disorder, which had been hypothesized to be the most common for the abused children. Unlike most studies focusing on ADHD, this one found that most of the subjects with ADHD in both groups were girls (58 percent of the abused group and 70 percent of the nonsexually abused group) (McLeer, Callaghan, Henry, & Wallen, 1994).This study raises the question of whether some children, particularly girls, could be showing ADHD-like manifestations that emanate from the trauma of abuse.

ASSESSING RISK AND PROTECTIVE FACTORS

No single measurement tool can identify ADHD. Rather, multiple assessment tools and clinical wisdom are used to obtain a broad database and to evaluate findings to determine whether the composite picture comprises signs and symptoms of the disorder. Two factors complicate that process: the variability of the data from completed research and the normalcy of the symptoms. As the conceptualization of the disorder has changed over time, so have the areas being measured. Data gathered at earlier stages in the conceptualization (for example, when hyperactivity was viewed as always present or when attention deficiency was the primary manifestation) reflect now-unaccepted interpretations of ADHD; thus, they cannot be compared with current findings, nor can assessments be based on them. The second complication arises because the symptoms that now define ADHD—attention deficiency, hyperactivity, and impulsivity—are seen to some degree in most children, especially during elementary school years. Diagnostic assessments are therefore made, not on the presence of a particular behavior, but on the determination that the behavior is "more frequent and severe than is typically observed in individuals at a comparable level of development" (APA, 1994, p. 78). That determination is fraught with the potential for observer subjectivity, if not bias. It also emphasizes the need for informed and skilled observers who can view changing behaviors in children at different stages of development and still recognize the shifting patterns of symptoms of the disorder, a process known as "heterotypic continuity" (Hinshaw, 1994).

RATING SCALES

Rating scales are often used to obtain information from significant individuals in a child's life. Parents and teachers, for example, always have views that are vital to understanding the child, and they can report behaviors over time. Use of scales alone is not acceptable for diagnostic purposes, but an assessment would be incomplete without them; they also can be helpful later in monitoring intervention response. The Conners Parent and Teacher Rating Scales (CPRS and CTRS, respectively) developed by Dr. C. Keith Conners (Conners, 1985; Goyette, Conners, & Ulrich, 1978) and the Child Behavior Checklist (CBCL) developed by Drs. Thomas Achenbach and Craig Edelbrock (Achenbach, 1991) are frequently used to assess children believed to have problems with hyperactivity.

The CPRS comes in two versions, one with 48 questions and the other with 93. Scales in both versions address issues in addition to hyperactivity, such as conduct problems and learning problems. The shorter version (CPRS-R) has normative data for children ages three to 17 years, divided by gender. The CTRS also has two versions, 28 and 39 items, with the shorter version (CTRS-R) having normative data for ages three to 17 years, both sexes. Like the companion parent scale, it provides a useful measure of externalizing behaviors such as hyperactivity and conduct problems (Conners, 1985). Both parent and teacher rating scales appear to have a "practice effect"—scores decline from initial levels at subsequent administration. Consequently, data collection for evaluation usually begins with the third or later administration (Barkley, 1988). As noted earlier, teachers may infer hyperactivity when they observe disruptive behavior (Hinshaw, 1994). Even though each measure has been proved to be reliable and valid, parent–teacher agreement is reported at .49, but this is considered satisfactory because raters appraise the child in different environments, which could produce divergent behaviors (Barkley, 1988; Hinshaw, 1994).

Some prefer the CBCL because it has a larger item pool (138) and covers both internalizing and externalizing behaviors. The parent and teacher versions are structured similarly so that cross-informant agreement can be examined, along with agreement among three age groups between four and 16 years, for both male and female children (Achenbach, 1991). The test is available in various languages and used in numerous cultures (Canino & Spurlock, 1994).

INTERVIEWS

Interviews, structured and unstructured, are a second assessment strategy. They are usually conducted with the child, parents, and teachers. Although children tend to underreport key manifestations of the disorder (Loeber, Green, Lahey, & Stouthamer-Loeber, 1991), their information on internal feelings is important and cannot be learned from other informants. A popular, and the most researched, interview guide is the Diagnostic Interview Schedule for Children (DISC), which is keyed to the *Diagnostic and Statistical Manual of Mental Disorders* (DISC-3 is keyed to DSM-IV) (Hinshaw, 1994). This fully structured guide, which is applicable for children ages eight to 17 years, gathers information on symptoms present in the past six months (Kaplan et al., 1994). It was developed by the National Institute of Mental Health. Because the test prespecifies the coding of items, lay interviewers with little training can administer it effectively (Edelbrock & Costello, 1988).

OBSERVATION

A third assessment area, and one in which new measurements are continually being introduced, is that of observation systems to document frequency and duration of behaviors salient to ADHD and other aspects of adjustment. A trained observer using an audio recorder, a paper-and-pen checklist, or an electronic keypunch, for example, can unobtrusively observe a child and note each episode of a particular behavior. The observation can be continuous for an entire activity or made at defined intervals (for example, 10- to 30-minute observations spread throughout the week) or points (a brief observation made every 30 minutes, for example). In their review of observational measures for ADHD, Platzman et al. (1992) learned that data collected from classroom observations were better than those from clinic observations at discriminating between children with ADHD and controls. Moreover, they observed that three observations consistently discriminated differences: off-task behavior, excessive gross motor activity, and negative vocalizations. Because girls, who had not been included in many studies, tend to express ADHD with fewer aggressive behaviors, Platzman et al. recommended that interpretations of off-task behavior might need to be sexually differentiated.

The revised ADHD behavior coding system (Barkley, 1990) is an observation tool that keys on the variables that reliably identify ADHD. Specifically, it observes off-task behavior (that is, breaking eye contact for at least three consecutive seconds), fidgeting (at least four nonpurposeful motions of legs, arms, hands, buttocks, or trunk), task-relevant vocalization (noise or vocalization relevant to the task), task-irrelevant vocalization (noise or vocalization not relevant to the task), and out-of-seat activity (child rises from the flat surface of the seat).

Hyperactivity can now be documented with objective, reliable recordings of movements. An infrared motion-analysis system, such as the one used by Teicher, Ito, Glod, and Barber (1996), tracks the child during continuous classroom performance. By fixing on reflective markers on the child's cap and clothing (shoulder, back, and elbow), a high-resolution video camera, infrared strobe, and video processor track movements up to 50 times per second and feed data into a computer for analysis. Patterns and total movements can be analyzed. These measures could aid in the development of an objective measure for hyperactivity and in specifying particular movements for treatment (Teicher et al., 1996).

Other tools that round out the assessment process are cognitive measures, such as the Wechsler Intelligence Scale for Children (Wechsler, 1991) and the Woodcock–Johnson Psychoeducational Battery–Revised (Woodcock & Johnson, 1990). These are well-known measures for testing intellectual functioning and academic achievement.

Implications for Prevention, Early Intervention, and Treatment

Given the increasing evidence that ADHD is a biologically predisposed condition, it is not surprising that the major intervention is biochemical, involving in particular the use of psychostimulants (that is, medicine that can arouse the central nervous system). This intervention has only short-term effects—it is not a cure. But it has proven to position the child in ways that allow a better and more productive connection with the immediate environment. In essence, it can empower the child to adapt, or, in other words, it can enhance resilience.

Medication

More than 2 percent of the school-aged children in the United States take stimulant medications and stay on them from two to seven years, depending on the age of the child at the initiation of medication (DuPaul & Stoner, 1994). The most commonly prescribed stimulants, in order of use, are methylphenidate (Ritalin), d-amphetamine (Dexedrine), and pemoline (Cylert). The precise way that the medicine influences the brain is not known. The suspected interaction is that the stimulant increases either the supply or activity levels of dopamine and norepinephrine in the frontal lobes. With this increase, the brain functions more effectively. Approximately 70 percent to 90 percent of children with ADHD experience improved behavior when treated with stimulants—specifically, by exhibiting less hyperactivity and impulsivity (DuPaul & Costello, 1995) and less aggressive behavior (Abikoff et al., 1988). Most children also experience more sustained attention and persistence with work efforts, which means that they are better organized to learn and to show what they have learned (DuPaul & Costello, 1995). However, medications have not yet been shown to significantly improve performance on standardized achievement tests (Hinshaw, 1994).

Ritalin does not need build-up time in the bloodstream. It tends to affect cognitive and behavior performance within 30 or 45 minutes and peaks in one to three hours; it then begins to dissipate and is washed from the system in 24 hours. It can be given in sustained-release form with a life of six to eight hours. The optimal dose does not depend on body weight; treatment usually begins at a low dose, which is increased until the optimal level is reached (that is, the level at which symptoms decrease and task performance improves but side effects are absent or minimal) (Barkley et al., 1991). Common side effects are difficulty getting to sleep and reduced appetite (especially with the noon meal) (Barlow & Durand, 1995). The small weight loss that can occur tends to level out by the second year of medication. Contrary to earlier concerns, stimulants do not appear to stunt growth. Consequently, drug holidays—times when the medication is not administered, such as weekends or summer vacations—are not currently considered important, even for children with severe symptoms. Stimulants are also sometimes associated with headaches, stomach aches, nausea, tics, and insomnia; there can be a rebound effect of mild irritability and slight hyperactivity as the effects of the medication wear off (Kaplan et al, 1994).

Antidepressants have proved helpful for some children who do not respond to stimulants. In addition, a hypotensive agent, Catapres (clonidine), may be used when the child appears to have a predisposition to a tic condition such as Tourette's syndrome (Kaplan et al., 1994).

BEHAVIOR MANAGEMENT

The short-term gains achieved with medications, especially stimulants, are impressive, but they do not reach clinically significant levels as the sole intervention. Behavior management is widely used as an additional strategy to secure short-term gains and to promote academic and social success. This strategy appears to have preventive as well as maintenance-focused effects. A good management program operates at least at school and at home. It involves close communication among the child, parents, teachers, physician, and other professionals working with the child and family.

The school is a logical site for management efforts, which should begin with antecedent efforts aimed at making the environment conducive to prosocial behaviors. Suggestions by Gordon and Asher (1994) addressed such things as seating (choosing row rather than cluster seating and placing the child with ADHD at front in the center), classroom rules (involving children in stating and posting expectations that are simple, positive, situationally specific, and have consequences), and location (choosing a classroom that is as far as possible from external noises or outside activities that might distract the child).

The teacher's management of the classroom has received much attention. The teacher's motivation and willingness to work closely with the child and the community of care have the greatest effect on academic achievement. Evidence shows that when a task is motivating and within the child's achievement range and can be completed in a reasonable amount of time, attention and focus are easier for the child to maintain. This approach seems to work best when teachers search for exercises that interest the child with ADHD, emphasize the strengths of all students, replace workbooks with personalized work plans, and use tests sparingly and make appropriate adjustments to testing conditions (Weaver, 1992). Such environmental modifications promote success and well-being in the child with ADHD while retaining the rigor of the educational process.

Reducing disruptiveness does not necessarily result in academic achievement, but academic achievement is positively associated with a reduction in the frequency of disruptiveness (Rapport, 1995). Positive behavior should be recognized, yet there is some concern that constantly giving positive feedback not only takes a great deal of the teacher's time but also draws the child off task. Several mechanisms are being introduced to help the child personally monitor behavior. One such device is the attentional training system (ATS), a small electric counter that sits on the child's desk, tallies a point per minute, and displays accumulated points in a window that the child can see easily. The teacher glances at the child periodically and, using criteria known to the child, notes whether the child is on task. If so, the teacher does nothing; if not, the teacher reduces the point count by remote control. The student can use accumulated points to select from a pre-established personal list of learning activities (for example, using the computer or viewing a video) (Rapport, 1995). The child is thus empowered to achieve goals, and the child's success leads to enhanced self-esteem. The entire process protects against ongoing risks.

To achieve maximum effectiveness, behavior management must continue at home, and to succeed there it must be designed with the individual family's schedule and lifestyle in mind. Usually recommended is some method of charting behavior according to points earned and lost, similar to the system used in the classroom. Points are given for positive behavior and deducted for negative behavior—again, the procedure ought to be familiar to and negotiated with the child. At the end of designated time periods, or when a specified total has been reached, the child may use the accumulated points for a personally selected activity. One such program introduces a "very special time," which is 10 to 15 minutes of a parent's undivided attention for an at-home, nondestructive activity of the child's choosing (Greenberg & Horn, 1991).

Important factors for success of the management program at home and at school are that the child is involved in the planning and that the system works on an earn–loss basis, whereby the whole day need not be lost because of one episode of problem behavior. Just as with stimulant medication, the effects of a behavior management program are short-term. Efforts must be continued until the child matures enough to make personal choices that reflect positive behavior.

SKILLS TRAINING

Improvement in social skills can be targeted in both school and home programs for behavior management, of course, but peer groups especially organized for social skills training have been found effective also. Curricula for such training often focus on positive entry into groups, conversational skills, conflict resolution, and anger-coping abilities. Studies show an increase in children's social skills within the group, but specific efforts must be made to translate those gains to life outside the group. One way to begin that translation is to use real-life scenarios in group discussions, but it takes work from teachers and parents to prompt and reinforce the newly acquired skills enough to make it happen (Guevremont, 1990).

PARENTS AS PARTNERS

Working with the parents of a child with ADHD is vital to any intervention. Parents (and, indeed, the child) should be seen as partners in the whole service-delivery system, beginning with assessment. Efforts to bring together parents with representatives of all the child-helping services (from school and mental health facilities as well as any other involved agency, such as juvenile court or health services) in one place embodies ecological interdependence. In such a setting parents, the best source of information about the child's behavior, can offer their unique perspective on their child's difficulties, and they can also learn about ADHD. They can help explain this condition to the wider family and to others who have contact with the child, some of whom may view the child's behavior as simply mean or the result of inadequate discipline. All parents can gain from further knowledge about the condition; even parents who have ADHD themselves may not understand it from a biosocial perspective.

In addition to information on ADHD, parents frequently need and benefit from training in strategies for behavior management. They need to know, among other things, about the reciprocal nature of parent–child interactions, principles of positive and differential reinforcement, the workings of home token systems, and management of misbehavior in public settings (DuPaul & Stoner, 1994). Support groups for parents of children with ADHD often provide practical help, as parents talk about how best to make day-to-day management techniques work, gain access to local resources, and prepare for conferences on IEPs (individualized educational plans) authorized through IDEA (K. Kustra, parent, personal communication, October 31, 1995). Life is frequently difficult for families in which someone (or some two or three or more) has ADHD. Providing education, training, counseling, and support to the parents and other family members can facilitate direct intervention with the child with ADHD.

CONCLUSION

Although there has been almost a century of effort to understand and learn how to intervene successfully in ADHD, much remains to be done. There is no known cause, no known cure, and no definitive explanation for why stimulant medication works. ADHD clearly is a "condition in the making." Hyperactivity, attention deficiency, and impulsivity are its hallmark symptoms, but the variations among symptoms, coupled with a series of secondary problems, create a disorder that has many expressions. As such, it requires a multimodal intervention that assesses the child in the environment and adopts procedures—medication, behavioral management, family support, and special educational efforts—to address the risks and strengthen protective factors. Work continues.

REFERENCES

Abikoff, H., Ganeles, D., Reiter, G., Blum, C., Foley, C., & Klein, R. G. (1988). Cognitive training in academically deficient ADHD boys receiving stimulant medication. *Journal of Abnormal Child Psychology 16*, 411–432.

Abikoff, H., Klein, R., Klass, E., & Ganeles, D. (1987, October). *Methylphenidate in the treatment of conduct disordered children*. Paper presented at the annual meeting of the American Academy of Child and Adolescent Psychiatry, Washington, DC.

Achenbach, T. M. (1991). *Manual for the Child Behavior Checklist/4–18 and 1991 profile*. Burlington: University of Vermont, Department of Psychiatry.

American Psychiatric Association. (1968). *Diagnostic and statistical manual of mental disorders* (2nd ed.). Washington, DC: Author.

American Psychiatric Association. (1980). *Diagnostic and statistical manual of mental disorders* (3rd ed.). *I*. Washington, DC: Author.

American Psychiatric Association. (1987). *Diagnostic and statistical manual of mental disorders* (3rd ed.-rev.). Washington, DC: Author.

American Psychiatric Association. (1994). *Diagnostic and statistical manual of mental disorders* (4th ed.). Washington, DC: Author.

Americans with Disabilities Act of 1990, P.L. 101-336, 104 Stat. 327.

Anastopoulos, A. D., & Barkley, R. A. (1988). Biological factors in attention-deficit hyperactivity disorder. *Behavior Therapist, 11*, 47–53.

Asch, A., & Mudrick, N. R. (1995). Disability. In R. L. Edwards (Ed.-in-Chief), *Encyclopedia of social work* (19th ed., Vol. 1, pp. 752–761). Washington, DC: NASW Press.

Attention Deficit Disorder—Part I. (1995). *Harvard Mental Health Letter, 11* (10), 1–4.

Barkley, R. A. (1988). Child behavior rating scales and checklists. In M. Rutter, A. H. Tuma, & I. S. Lann (Eds.), *Assessment and diagnosis in child psychopathology* (pp. 113–155). New York: Guilford Press.

Barkley, R. A. (Ed.). (1990). *Attention deficit hyperactivity disorder: A handbook for diagnosis and treatment*. New York: Guilford Press.

Barkley, R. A. (1994). Foreword. In G. J. DuPaul & G. Stoner (Eds.), *ADHD in the schools: Assessment and intervention strategies* (pp. vii–xi). New York: Guilford Press.

Barkley, R. A. (1995). *Taking charge of ADHD: The complete authoritative guide for parents*. New York: Guilford Press.

Barkley, R. A., DuPaul, G. J., & McMurray, M. B. (1990). Comprehensive evaluation of attention deficit disorder with and without hyperactivity as defined by research criteria. *Journal of Consulting and Clinical Psychology, 58*, 775–789.

Barkley, R. A., DuPaul, G. J., & McMurray, M. B. (1991). Attention deficit disorder with and without hyperactivity: Clinical response to three dose levels of methylphenidate. *Pediatrics, 87*, 519–531.

Barlow, D. H., & Durand, V. M. (1995). *Abnormal psychology: An integrative approach*. Pacific Grove, CA: Brooks/Cole.

Befera, M. S., & Barkley, R. A. (1985). Hyperactive and normal boys and girls: Mother-child interaction. *Journal of Child Psychology & Psychiatry, 26,* 439–452.

Berry, C. A., Shaywitz, S. E., & Shaywitz, B. A. (1985). Girls with attention deficit disorder: A silent minority? A report on behavioral and cognitive characteristics. *Pediatrics, 76,* 801–809.

Biederman, J., Munir, K., & Knee, D. (1987). Conduct and oppositional disorder in clinically referred children with attention deficit disorder: A controlled family study. *Journal of the American Academy of Child & Adolescent Psychiatry, 26,* 724–727.

Biederman, J., Faraone, S. V., Keenan, K., Benjamin, J., Knifcher, B., Moore, C., Sprich-Buckminster, S., Ugaglia, K., Jellinek, M. S., Steingard, R., Spencer, T., Norman, D., Kolony, R., Kraus, I., Perrin, J., Keller, M. B., & Tsuang, M. T. (1992). Further evidence for family-genetic risk factors in attention deficit hyperactivity disorder: Patterns of comorbidity in probands and relatives in psychiatrically and pediatrically referred samples. *Archives of General Psychiatry, 49,* 728–738.

Canino, I. A., & Spurlock, J. (1994). *Culturally diverse children and adolescents.* New York: Guilford Press.

Children & Adults with Attention Deficit Disorders. (1993). *CH.A.D.D. Facts 4: Educational rights for children with ADD.* Plantation, FL: Author.

Conners, C. K. (1985). *The Conners rating scales: Instruments for the assessment of childhood psychopathology.* Unpublished manuscript.

Cotugno, A. J. (1993). The diagnosis of attention deficit hyperactivity disorder (ADHD) in community mental health centers: Where and when. *Psychology in the Schools, 30,* 338–344.

Creemers, D. (1990, February 7). Disorder turns life into a distraction: Hyperactivity dulls children's attention spans. *The News & Observer* [Raleigh, NC], p. 12A.

DuPaul, G. J., & Costello, A. (1995). The stimulants. In R. A Barkley (Ed.), *Taking charge of ADHD: The complete authoritative guide for parents* (pp. 249–262). New York: Guilford Press.

DuPaul, G. J., & Stoner, G. (1994). *ADHD in the schools: Assessment and intervention strategies.* New York: Guilford Press.

Edelbrock, C., & Costello, A. J. (1988). Structured psychiatric interviews for children. In M. Rutter, A. H. Tuma, & I. S. Lann (Eds.), *Assessment and diagnosis in child psychopathology* (pp. 87–112). New York: Guilford Press.

Faraone, S., Biederman, J., Keenan, K., & Tsuang, M. T. (1991). A family-genetic study of girls with DSM-III attention deficit disorder. *American Journal of Psychiatry, 148,* 112–117.

Germain, C. B., & Gitterman, A. (1995). Ecological perspective. In R. L. Edwards (Ed.-in-Chief), *Encyclopedia of social work* (19th ed., Vol. 1, pp. 816–824). Washington, DC: NASW Press.

Gillis, J. J., Gilger, J. W., Pennington, B. F., & Defries, J. C. (1992). Attention deficit disorder in reading-disabled twins: Evidence for a genetic etiology. *Journal of Abnormal Child Psychology, 20,* 303–315.

Gittelman, R., & Feingold, I. (1983). Children with reading disorders: Effects of reading instruction. *Journal of Child Psychology & Psychiatry, 24,* 167–191.

Goodman, R., & Stevenson, J. (1989). A twin study of hyperactivity. II: The etiological role of genes, family relationships, and perinatal adversity. *Journal of Child Psychology & Psychiatry, 30,* 691–709.

Gordon, S. B., & Asher, M. J. (1994). *Meeting the ADD challenge: A practical guide for teachers.* Champaign, IL: Research Press.

Goyette, C. H., Conners, C. K., & Ulrich, R. F. (1978). Normative data on revised Conners parent and teacher rating scales. *Journal of Abnormal Child Psychology, 6,* 221–236.

Greenberg, G. S., & Horn, W. F. (1991). *Attention deficit hyperactivity disorder: Questions and answers for parents.* Champaign, IL: Research Press.

Guevremont, D. C. (1990). Social skills and peer relationship training. In R. A. Barkley (Ed.), *Attention-deficit hyperactivity disorder: A handbook for diagnosis and treatment* (pp. 540–572). New York: Guilford Press.

Hauser, P., Zametkin, A. J., Martinez, P., Benedetto, V., Matochik, J. A., Mixson, A. J., & Weintraub, B. D. (1993). Attention deficit-hyperactivity disorder in people with generalized resistance to thyroid hormone. *New England Journal of Medicine, 328,* 997–1001.

Hinshaw, S. P. (1987). On the distinction between attentional deficits/hyperactivity and conduct problems/aggression in child psychopathology. *Psychological Bulletin, 101,* 443–463.

Hinshaw, S. P. (1992). Academic underachievement, attention deficits, and aggression: Comorbidity and implications for intervention. *Journal of Consulting and Clinical Psychology, 60,* 893–903.

Hinshaw, S. P. (1994). *Attention deficits and hyperactivity in children.* Beverly Hills, CA: Sage Publications.

Individuals with Disabilities Education Act, P.L. 101-476, 104 Stat. 1142 (1990).

Jacobvitz, D., & Stroufe, L. A. (1987). The early caregiver–mother relationship and attention deficit disorder with hyperactivity in kindergarten: A prospective study. *Child Development, 58,* 1488–1495.

James, A., & Taylor, E. (1990). Sex differences in the hyperkinetic syndrome of childhood. *Journal of Child Psychology & Psychiatry, 31,* 437–446.

Jouriles, E. N., Barling, J., & O'Leary, D. O. (1987). Predicting child behavior problems in maritally violent families. *Journal of Abnormal Child Psychology, 15*(2), 165–173.

Kaplan, H. I., Sadock, B. J., & Grebb, J. A. (1994). *Synopsis of psychiatry: Behavioral sciences and clinical psychology* (7th ed.). Baltimore: Williams & Wilkins.

Kohn, A. (1989, March). Suffer the restless children. *Atlantic Monthly,* pp. 90–100.

Levine, M. G. (1987). Attention deficits: The diverse effects of weak control systems in childhood. *Pediatric Annals, 16*(2), 117–131.

Loeber, R., Green, S. M., Lahey, B. B., & Stouthamer-Loeber, M. (1991). Differences and similarities between children, mothers, and teachers as informants on disruptive behavior disorders. *Journal of Abnormal Child Psychology, 19,* 75–95.

Lou, H. C., Henriksen, L., & Bruhn, P. (1984). Focal cerebral hypoperfusion in children with dysphasia and/or attention deficit disorder. *Archives of Neurology, 41,* 825–829.

Lou, H. C., Henriksen, L., Bruhn, P., Borner, H., & Nielsen, J. B. (1989). Striatal dysfunction in attention deficit and hyperkinetic disorder. *Archives of Neurology, 46*, 48–52.

Luthar, S. S. (1991). Vulnerability and resilience: A study of high-risk adolescents. *Child Development, 62*, 600–616.

Mann, E. M., Ikeda, Y., Mueller, C. W., Takahashi, A., Tao, K. T., Humris, E., Li, B. L., & Chin, D. (1992). Cross-cultural differences in rating hyperactive-disruptive behaviors in children. *American Journal of Psychiatry, 149*, 1539–1542.

Mannuzza, S., Klein, R. G., Bonagura, N., Malloy, P., Giampino, T. L., & Addalli, K. A. (1991). Hyperactive boys almost grown up. V: Replications of psychiatric status. *Archives of General Psychiatry, 48*, 77–83.

Mannuzza, S., Klein, R. G., Konig, P. H., & Giampino, T. L. (1989). Hyperactive boys almost grown up. IV: Criminality and its relationship to psychiatric status. *Archives of General Psychiatry, 46*, 1073–1079.

Masten, A., Best, K. M., & Garmezy, N. (1990). Resilience and development: Contributions from the study of children who overcame adversity. *Development and Psychopathology, 2*, 425–444.

McGee, R., Williams, S., & Silva, P. A. (1987). A comparison of girls and boys with teacher-identified problems of attention. *Journal of the American Academy of Child and Adolescent Psychiatry, 26*, 711–717.

McLeer, S. V., Callaghan, M., Henry, D., & Wallen, J. (1994). Psychiatric disorders in sexually abused children. *Journal of the American Academy of Child and Adolescent Psychiatry, 33*, 313–319.

Munoz-Millan, R. J., & Casteel, C. R. (1989). Attention-deficit hyperactivity disorder: Recent literature. *Hospital and Community Psychiatry, 40*, 699–712.

O'Keefe, M. (1994). Linking marital violence, mother–child/father–child aggression, and child behavior problems. *Journal of Family Violence, 9*(1), 63–78.

Parker, H. C. (1992). *A.D.D. fact sheet*. Plantation, FL: CH.A.D.D.

Platzman, K. A., Stoy, M. R., Brown, T. T., Coles, D. D., Smith, I. E., & Felek, A. (1992). Review of observational methods in attention deficit hyperactivity disorder (ADHD): Implications for diagnosis. *School Psychology Quarterly, 7*, 155–177.

Rapport, M. D. (1995). Attention-deficit hyperactivity disorder. In M. Hersen & R. T. Ammerman (Eds.), *Advanced abnormal child psychology* (pp. 353–374). Hillsdale, NJ: Lawrence Erlbaum.

Rehabilitation Act of 1973, P.L. 93-112, 87 Stat. 355.

Rende, R., & Plomin, R. (1993). Families at risk for psychopathology: Who becomes affected and why? *Development and Psychopathology, 5*, 529–540.

Riccio, C. A., Hynd, G. W., Cohen, M. J., & Gonzalez, J. J. (1993). Neurological basis of attention deficit hyperactivity disorder. *Exceptional Children, 60*(2), 118–124.

Rosemond, J. (1995, November 16). Psychologist calls attention deficit disorder a myth. *Herald-Sun* [Durham, NC], p. E6.

Rutter, M., & Quinton, D. C. (1984). Long-term follow-up of women institutionalized in childhood: Factors promoting good functioning in adult life. *British Journal of Developmental Psychology, 18*, 225–234.

Sabatino, D. A., & Vance, H. B. (1994). Is the diagnosis of attention deficit/hyperactivity disorders meaningful? *Psychology in the Schools, 31*, 188–196.

Teicher, M. H., Ito, Y., Glod, C. A., & Barber, N. I. (1996). Objective measurement of hyperactivity and attentional problems in ADHD. *Journal of the American Academy of Child and Adolescent Psychiatry, 35*, 334–343.

Weaver, C. (1992). The promise of whole language education for students with ADHD. *The CH.A.D.D.ER Box, 5*(4), 1, 7–8.

Wechsler, D. (1991). *Wechsler Intelligence Scale for Children* (3rd ed.). San Diego: Harcourt Brace Jovanovich.

Wolraich, M. L., Hannah, J. N., Pinnock, T. Y., Baumgaertel, A., & Brown J. (1996). Comparison of diagnostic criteria for attention-deficit hyperactivity disorder in a county-wide sample. *Journal of the American Academy of Child and Adolescent Psychiatry, 35*, 334–342.

Woodcock, R. W., & Johnson, M. B. (1990). *Woodcock–Johnson Psychoeducational Battery–Revised.* Allen, TX: DLM Teaching Resources.

Zametkin, A. J., Nordahl, T. E. , Gross, M., King, A. C., Sempe, W. E., Rumsey, J., Hamburger, S., & Cohen, R. M. (1990). Cerebral glucose metabolism in adults with hyperactivity of childhood onset. *New England Journal of Medicine, 323*, 1361–1366.

6

School Failure: An Ecological–Interactional–Developmental Perspective

Jack M. Richman and Gary L. Bowen

Many students today experience difficulty adjusting to school and acquiring the social and academic skills necessary for pursuing advanced education and training. As a result their opportunity for functioning successfully as adults in work and family roles is being jeopardized. With limited means and opportunities to achieve self-sufficiency through employment, many of these young adults are unable either to participate meaningfully in society or to find personal satisfaction and purpose. Poverty and welfare dependency become a way of life for many, especially females (Bowen, Desimone, & McKay, 1995; Harris, 1991). For others, the future is even more bleak: school failure has been associated with higher mortality rates, higher incidence of suicide, and more frequent admissions to state mental hospitals (Brenner, 1976; Rumberger, 1987).

The impact of school failure has consequences for society as well for the individual, including a waste of human capital, loss of national income, loss of tax revenues, earlier involvement in sexual intercourse, higher risks of sexually transmitted disease, increased use of and demand for social services, more crime, reduced political participation, and higher health care costs (Carnahan, 1994; Levin & Bachman, 1972; O'Malley, 1977; Santelli & Beilenson, 1992). In addition to these concerns, business leaders have noted that many students either graduate or leave school before graduation without the basic competencies to perform even rudimentary tasks in industry, much less to hold positions requiring more technical ability or knowledge (Slavin, Karweit, & Madden, 1988). Such a loss of human capital places a heavy weight on the U.S. economy and greatly restricts this nation's competitiveness in the world economy. Helping to keep students in school and to promote academic success are critical steps toward promoting greater and more competent adult role performance. These aims have important implications for the individual, the family system, the economy, and the general well-being of society.

It is interesting to note that the heightened interest in school dropout and school success by researchers, politicians, educators, business and community leaders, and consumers comes at a time of declining nationwide dropout rates. In 1900, 4 percent of the population completed high school; by 1950 that figure had risen to 50 percent,

The authors would like to thank the BellSouth Foundation of Atlanta, Georgia, and the John S. and James L. Knight Foundation of Miami, Florida, for their support of the development of the School Success Profile.

and the graduation rate now stands at approximately 75 percent in the United States (Carnahan, 1994; Wehlage & Rutter, 1986).

Given these positive trends for the past 100 years, why are school success and educational resilience such important issues in America today? Several possible explanations exist. Chief among them is the fact that school failure appears to have more severe consequences for individuals and society today than it did for prior generations (Ekstrom, Goertz, Pollack, & Rock, 1986; Hepburn & White, 1990; Levin & Bachman, 1972; O'Malley, 1977; Rumberger, 1987; Wehlage & Rutter, 1986). Furthermore, school failure seems to affect poor people and individuals of color disproportionately more than economically stable and heterogenous populations. The implications of not acquiring minimal high school competencies in the context of prevailing social and economic realities place young people in much greater jeopardy of failing to achieve the entry-level abilities necessary to function as competent adults in a complex society.

This chapter considers an individual's resilience as a central protective factor that promotes his or her successful adaptation to the challenges and demands faced in school and in the larger social environment. After discussing the concept of school failure and the profile of students most likely to experience difficulty in academic settings, this chapter advances an ecological–interactional–developmental perspective to explain variations in levels of resilience across individuals.

At the center of an ecological–interactional–developmental perspective is the person–environment fit, a dominant viewpoint in a variety of helping professions. Concepts from this perspective are used to discuss social structural experiences that may promote the development of resilience in children and how these experiences can become the foci of prevention, early intervention, and remedial efforts to reduce school failure. Last, we discuss the development and implementation of the School Success Profile, an assessment instrument informed by the ecological–interactional–developmental perspective.

NATURE OF THE PROBLEM

CONCEPT OF SCHOOL FAILURE

Comparisons of definitions of school failure by both practitioners and academicians reveal a great deal of conceptual confusion. Indicators and predictors of school failure often overlap; other times they are used interchangeably. For example, one study may emphasize poor grades as a predictive variable of school failure (Rumberger, 1983), whereas another uses grades as an indicator of school achievement (Steinberg, Elman, & Mounts, 1989; Wehlage & Rutter, 1986). Some authors avoid distinguishing between indicators and predictors altogether by talking more generally about correlations and associations.

Although the school dropout problem should not be overlooked or minimized, it is only one manifestation of school failure. Large numbers of students stay in school but do not or cannot participate in ways that enable them to acquire the requisite skills to function even at basic educational levels. Some researchers have postulated that the number of "academically marginal students" (Alpert & Dunham,

1986) or "interior dropouts" (Martz, 1992) is equal to the number of students who actually drop out of school (Martz, 1992). Alpert and Dunham (1986) define academically marginal students as those youths in school who display low attendance, low grade-point averages, and low scores on achievement tests. Therefore, the problem is not only preventing school dropout but also maximizing school success. As Wehlage and Rutter (1986) stated, "The problem is not simply to keep educationally at-risk youth from dropping out but, more importantly, to provide them with educationally worthwhile experiences" (p. 375). Redefining the focus from dropping out to maximizing school success greatly increases the area of concern, because a focus on school success includes the entire school-aged population, that is, school dropouts, academically marginal students (interior dropouts), and students who function at acceptable educational levels or higher.

Our perspective of school failure encompasses both school dropout (physical absence) and poor attendance, low achievement, and grade retention (psychological absence). It is possible to construct a simple typology of school failure by treating physical presence and psychological involvement in school as dichotomous variables (see Boss, 1988, from which this typology is adapted). Physical dropout from school is a dichotomous variable that assesses whether a student is physically enrolled (present) or withdrawn (absent). Poor attendance, low achievement, and grade retention are defined as indicators of psychological investment in school.

This typology reveals four categories of students. The first group includes those students who have both physically and psychologically withdrawn from school. For these students, dropping out of school merely formalized their psychological withdrawal as manifested in poor attendance, low achievement, and grade retention. For example, data from the National Longitudinal Study (NELS) of 1988 suggest that a high percentage of students who leave school drop out, in part, because they are failing school and could not keep up with their schoolwork (U.S. Department of Education, 1990, 1992). These students probably will not return to a traditional school setting.

The second group involves students who physically drop out of school but remain psychologically invested in their education; these students, while attending school, evidenced at least satisfactory academic progress. These students may have dropped out of school because of situational circumstances or structural constraints, such as pregnancy. For example, many girls who participated in NELS and who dropped out of school reported a family-related reason for dropping out of school: became pregnant, became a parent, got married, or had to support the family or care for a family member (U.S. Department of Education, 1990, 1992). In the context of tangible support and encouragement, students in this group probably will either return to school to complete their education or pursue alternative educational opportunities.

Martz's (1992) label of "interior dropouts" perhaps best captures the next group of students, those who are physically enrolled in school but who are psychologically withdrawn. It is this group of students who often require the most help from school officials and who, without intervention, are very likely to join the first group of students.

This logical typology is completed by the fourth group of students, who represent what may be used to describe school success—students who are both physically and psychologically involved in school. This cell in the typology shifts the perspective from a pathological model of school failure to a model of school success that is oriented to the study of health, well-being, and successful coping (Antonovsky, 1991). An important goal of school-based interventions is to help students move from the first three groups into the fourth group or to move them into alternative educational or career opportunities that will increase their economic prospects.

Profile of School Failure

Although no student is immune to school problems, students more vulnerable to academic problems and poor psychosocial adjustment in school are those from racial and ethnic minority groups and lower socioeconomic levels (Rumberger, 1987). These composite group effects (or contextual variables) are highly confounded with one another, and they are related to other predictors of school failure, such as family structure (Mulkey, Crain, & Harrington, 1992). Contextual variables serve as proxies for the more specific situational and behavioral variables associated with the structural variable in question. Each informs the social reality of individuals through its influence on the system of opportunities and constraints that individuals experience in society, as well as through its association with the normative system of values and beliefs that informs behavioral choices (Bowen & Pittman, 1995).

In the following analysis of data from the Bureau of the Census, dropout rates are an important criterion for school failure across racial or ethnic groups and socioeconomic status (Livingston & Miranda, 1995). Gender is not a major correlate of school failure and therefore is not included in the body of this discussion. (There has been a steady upward trend in the past 20 years for both male and female students in grades 10–12 to stay in school, although female students remain in school at a slightly high rate than male students.)

Racial or Ethnic Group

When the percentages of people 25 to 29 years old who completed high school are compared by racial or ethnic group identity in 1973, 1983, and 1993, it is evident that there has been a steady increase in the high school graduation rates of white, black, and Hispanic students (Figure 6-1). Although the proportion of white students who graduate from high school (91.2 percent) remains higher than that for either black students (82.7 percent) or Hispanic students (60.9 percent), black students have shown the largest percentage gain from 1973 to 1993 (a 29 percent increase). The comparative increases for white students and Hispanic students were 8.6 percent and 16.4 percent, respectively. In considering the relationship between recent immigration status, language, and school success or failure, Frase (1992) noted that many Hispanic students face special challenges in school that help explain their lower graduation rates. She stated that 45 percent of the Hispanic population between the ages of 16 and 24 in 1989 were born outside the United States. In addition, she noted that 73.9 percent of Hispanics in the same age range in 1992 reported that Spanish was the language spoken in their home.

Socioeconomic Status

Figure 6-2 illustrates the association between socioeconomic status (SES) and high school completion. Socioeconomic status is divided into three categories: low (bottom 20 percent of all family incomes), middle (middle 60 percent), and high (upper 20 percent). Across the three successive cohorts of students (1973, 1983, and 1993) who were in grades 10 to 12 and between ages 15 and 24, a smaller proportion of low

Figure 6-1

The Percentage of 25- to 29-Year-Olds Who Have Completed High School, by Race or Ethnicity

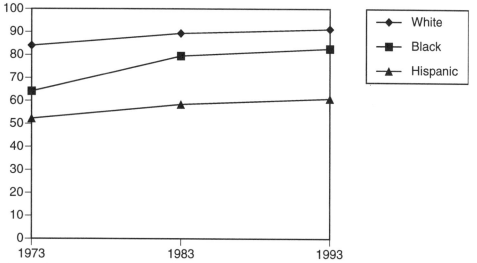

SOURCE: Livingston, A. M., & Miranda, S. (Eds.). (1995). *The condition of education, 1995.* Washington, DC: U.S. Department of Education, National Center for Education Statistics.

Figure 6-2

Percentage of High School Students in Grades 10 to 12, Ages 15 to 24, Enrolled the Previous October Who Were Enrolled Again the Following October, by Family Income

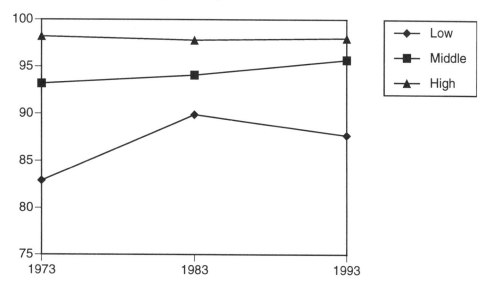

SOURCE: Livingston, A. M., & Miranda, S. (Eds.). (1995). *The condition of education, 1995.* Washington, DC: U.S. Department of Education. National Center for Education Statistics.
NOTE: Low income is the bottom 20 percent of all family incomes; high income is the top 20 percent of all family incomes; and middle income is the 60 percent in between.

SES students maintained continuous enrollment from one October to the next October. Further, Figure 6-2 suggests that while the continuous enrollment differential between middle and high family income is closing, the gap between students from middle- and high-income families and students from low-income families is widening. These results suggest that children living in families with low SES are five times more likely to drop out of school than those in higher SES families (cited in Carnahan, 1994). It is likely that a stable and sufficient family income provides children with a set of experiences, as well as an opportunity and resource base, that reinforces the importance of education and an orientation toward the future (Livingston & Miranda, 1995).

Wehlage and Rutter (1986) considered the relationship between racial or ethnic group identity and school failure to be spurious, explained by the association between racial or ethnic group identity and SES. After adjusting for SES, they maintained, the relationship between racial or ethnic group identity and school dropout disappears. Support for this conclusion was found in data from the U.S. Department of Commerce, which compares dropout rates among youth ages 16 to 24 by family income and race or ethnicity. As Figure 6-3 shows, racial or ethnic group differences diminish as family income increased. Dropout rates for white, black, and Hispanic youths from high-income families were 2.5 percent, 3.9 percent, and 6.0 percent, respectively; only 3.5 percent separates the lowest from the highest group. For low-income families, the percentages are 19.1 percent, 24.5. percent, and 41.3 percent and the lowest and highest groups are differentiated by 22.9 percent (Livingston & Miranda, 1995).

Figure 6-3

Dropout Rates among Youths Ages 16 to 24, by Income and Race or Ethnicity

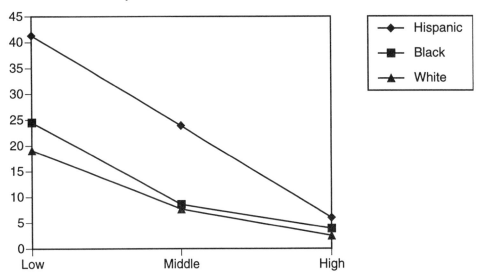

SOURCE: Livingston, A. M., & Miranda, S., (Eds.). (1995). *The condition of education, 1995.* Washington, DC: U.S. Department of Education, National Center for Education Statistics.

NOTE: Low income is the bottom 20 percent of all family incomes; high income is the top 20 percent of all family incomes; and middle income is the 60 percent in between.

BEATING THE ODDS

Of course, not all students who possess one or more of the risk factors related to school failure actually experience school failure. Whatever their particular adversities, the majority of students graduate from high school, including lower-income Hispanic and black youths. More attention has been paid in recent years to those students who seem to "beat the odds" (Wang, Haertel, & Walberg, 1994, p. 46). In the search for protective factors that buffer the potential effects of risks and promote the positive adaptation of individuals, the concept of resilience has been introduced into the literature as a psychological construct (Garmezy, 1993; Wang et al., 1994; Werner & Smith, 1982). Although several behavioral and social scientists have offered nominal definitions of resilience in agreement with Garmezy (1993)—"The central element in the study of resilience lies in the power of recovery and in the ability to return once again to those patterns of adaptation and competence that characterized the individual prior to the pre-stress period" (p. 129)—some authors attempt to define resilience by identifying the selective individual or situational characteristics that promote such recovery. For example, Beardsless (1989) considered self-understanding to be the essential feature of resilience: "Resilient individuals have a total organizing conceptualization of who they are and how they came to be" (p. 275). In some cases, authors have attempted to provide more situation-specific definitions of resilience, paralleling Bandura's (1982) treatment of self-efficacy as a more situation-specific concept. For example, Wang, Haertel, and Walberg (1994) defined educational resilience as "the heightened likelihood of success in school and other life accomplishments, despite environmental adversities brought about by early traits, conditions, and experiences" (p. 46). Yet, as discussed in earlier chapters, definitional ambiguity is the rule rather than the exception in definitions of resilience. Researchers often fail to distinguish between resilience as an outcome and resilience as a process, as well as between its indicators and its predictors. In critiquing the literature on resilience, Lavee (1995) asked whether resilience implies "being," "doing," or "having."

TOWARD A NOMINAL DEFINITION OF RESILIENCE

If resilience is a major discriminator between students who succeed at school and students who do not, it seems critical for purposes of intervention to better understand variations in this variable. Thus, this chapter focuses on resilience as a dependent outcome. *Resilience* is defined as a general frame of reference or belief system through which individuals appraise events and situations in the environment. It allows them to define situations from their environment as a challenge and an opportunity and to act with understanding, confidence, and persistence in overcoming or rebounding from the consequences of associated adversities through environmental mastery and individual adaptation. It is conceptualized as a variable that may range from low to high; following the distinction between "primitive" and "higher-order" beliefs (Lazarus & Folkman, 1984), it is derived more from accumulated experiences than from conformity to external authority, and it is subject to influence from new experiences, reinterpretation of earlier events, and knowledge of the experiences of others.

This definition of resilience parallels definitions of similar constructs in the literature, including Antonovsky's "sense of coherence," Bandura's "self-efficacy," Kobasa's "hardiness," and Rotter's "locus of control" (see Antonovsky, 1991, for a discussion of the similarities and distinctions among these concepts). Each of these related constructs reflects a "salutogenic" perspective, which focuses attention on explaining health and well-being rather than sickness and pathology. Like resilience, each is best understood in the context of specific stressors faced by the individual at particular points in life (compare Rutter, 1987). Sense of coherence, self-efficacy, hardiness, and locus of control may be conceptualized as manifest indicators of resilience. Benard (1991) used a similar conceptualization when she wrote that the profile of the resilient child included "social competence," "problem-solving skills," "autonomy," and "sense of purpose and future" (pp. 3–6). This idea may be especially attractive because operational measures have been developed for each of these related constructs.

Why are some children more resilient than other children when confronted with stressors and risk factors in their environments? Newspapers are filled with stories about children who somehow seem to rise above their problematic situations. On the other hand, there are also stories about other children who fail to thrive or who fall victim in even the most advantageous situations. How do we understand such differences in the outcomes that children experience? The following discussion of the ecological–interactional–developmental perspective attempts to address this issue of individual differences.

AN ECOLOGICAL–INTERACTIONAL–DEVELOPMENTAL PERSPECTIVE

The study of individual differences has been informed by two rich traditions in the behavioral and social sciences: the "human factors" approach and the "situational" approach. The human factors approach focuses attention on those more-or-less stable and enduring features of individuals, including needs, values, expectations, beliefs, motives, traits, feelings, abilities, and attitudes (Chatman, 1989). From this perspective, individual outcomes are best understood as reflecting variations in the internal characteristics of individuals.

From the situational perspective, individual differences are explained by considering individuals in the context of the social structures that frame and inform their individual orientations and behavioral choices (Bowen & Pittman, 1995). Such biographical, social, political, economic, and historical forces are typically viewed as more dynamic than individual-level features and are therefore more open to change and intervention.

Although studies of resilience reflect the perspectives of both human factors and situations, the additive and interactive nature of individual and situational variables also needs to be addressed to develop explanatory and predictive models of resilience. In social work and other fields, the interplay between the features of individuals and the features of their situations is often captured from the perspective of a person–environment fit. Yet to fully comprehend this complex interplay it is necessary to conceptualize the nature of the situation beyond the immediate environments of the individual (neighborhood, school, friends, and family) to include broader structural and normative influences. Such a viewpoint is perhaps best seen in the ecological approach (Bronfenbrenner, 1979; Garbarino, 1992). Also, the nature of the fit between person and environment must be conceptualized as dynamic to reflect the ways that the individual and the situation, as well as their interaction, change and evolve over time. Each of the components of the ecological–interactional–developmental perspective is discussed below.

AN ECOLOGICAL PERSPECTIVE

In capturing the process of mutual adaptation and accommodation that takes place between individuals and their environment, a person–environment fit perspective by definition reflects an ecological approach. As defined by Bronfenbrenner (1979), "The ecology of human development involves the scientific study of the progressive, mutual accommodation between an active, growing human being and the changing properties of the immediate settings in which the developing person lives, as this process is affected by relations between these settings, and by the larger contexts in which the settings are embedded" (p. 21). Bronfenbrenner conceptualized the environment as a set of four regions, each of which is embedded within the next and defined from the perspective of their proximity to the individual: microsystem, mesosystem, exosystem, and macrosystem.

The *microsystem* is the environment in which the person directly participates and interacts (activities, roles, and relationships), such as neighborhood, school, family, and friends (Bronfenbrenner, 1979). Because children's experiences in the microsystem most directly shape their views of the world and are incorporated into their beliefs about self (Garbarino, 1992), events in the microsystem play a decisive role in contributing to the development of resilience in children.

The *mesosystem* represents the connections between the microsystems in which children participate. Bronfenbrenner (1979) noted that the mesosystem "comprises the interrelations among two or more settings in which the developing person actively participates" (p. 25). An important mesosystem for adolescents is the relationship between their parents and friends. Strong and positive connections between various microsystems provide a supportive context for the child's development; weak connections or the existence of value conflicts between various microsystems may place the child at a disadvantage for developing those attitudes and behaviors that are associated with developmental success.

The child does not participate directly in the next setting, the exosystem; however, events in the exosystem reverberate to influence situations and circumstances in the microsystem. Bronfenbrenner (1979) defined the *exosystem* as "one or more settings that do not involve the developing person as an active participant, but in which events occur that affect, or are affected by, what happens in the setting containing the developing person" (p. 25). For example, a sibling's experience at school or a parent's experience at work will affect the developing youth even though the child does not directly participate in the specific environment.

The *macrosystem* is the environment most distal from the developing child and reflects the broad ideological and institutional patterns in society. It is important to underscore that the "environment" goes well beyond the immediate environments that individuals inhabit: it also includes the economic, political, and sociocultural environments (Jessor, 1993). Forces in the environment that limit opportunities for children or weaken the operation of environments at the lower levels (national policies that tolerate families living in poverty, for example) place a child at developmental risk and provide a poor context for the development of resilience.

AN INTERACTIONAL PERSPECTIVE

An interactional perspective focuses on the "goodness-of-fit" between the characteristics of individuals and the characteristics of their environment. Goodness-of-fit is a variable that ranges from favorable to unfavorable, and its evaluation is made in the context of the individual's development and within the broader sociocultural–historical milieu (Germain & Gitterman, 1995). The ecological–interactional–developmental perspective assumes that resilience is a consequence of favorable "goodness of fit" over time, which "promotes continued development and satisfying social functioning and sustains or enhances the environment" (Germain & Gitterman, 1995, p. 817).

At least two levels of fit can be specified: needs–supplies and demands–competencies (Caplan, 1983, 1987; French, Caplan, & Harrison, 1982; Harrison, 1978; Moos, 1987). First, individuals have certain needs related to their physical and psychological survival. For example, Maslow's (1954) hierarchy includes needs that are physiological, social, and affiliative, as well as needs for safety and security, esteem and recognition, and self-actualization. Maslow suggested that individuals are motivated to meet these needs and that needs at a higher level are not motivating until needs at the lower level are satisfied. The first type of fit considers these needs in the context of the opportunities, resources, and supplies available in the environment to meet them: the needs–supplies fit. It is likely, for example, that children find it hard to develop resilience in environments that are so unpredictable and chaotic that basic needs for safety and security cannot be met.

The second type of fit considers the level of congruency between demands and requirements from the environment and a child's competencies, capacities, and skills for meeting these demands: the demands–competencies fit. Like their adult counterparts, children occupy social positions (student, for example) with intrinsic expectations for performance that tend to become more ambitious as children move across the developmental life span. At the same time, children have certain competencies at particular developmental points that are based on the interplay of heredity, learning, and maturation. A goodness-of-fit is achieved when children are faced with demands from their environment that are appropriate to their abilities. It is important to note that environments may be overdemanding as well as underdemanding in the context of a child's abilities. Children who face environmental demands that they lack the competencies to meet are likely to feel self-doubt, frustration, hopelessness, and despair. On the other hand, children who face situations that fail to challenge them and mobilize their skills and capabilities may become bored and seek out experiences with negative implications for their own development, well-being, and social functioning. The resulting behaviors also have negative implications for their host communities. In either of these incongruous situations, the development of resilience may be impaired.

These two types of person–environment fit are not always independent of each other. For example, citing Caplan (1983), Kulik, Oldham, and Hackman (1987) concluded that "reducing the demands of the environment in order to provide a better match with the person's abilities may result in a lessened capacity of that environment to satisfy the person's needs for growth and development" (p. 279). It is also important to distinguish between the objective reality and the reality as perceived by the child (Caplan, 1987; Harrison, 1978). Children's views of themselves as well as their perceptions of their environments may be more or less congruent with assessments by independent observers. Nevertheless, it is their subjective reality that children respond to and that forms the basis for their development of resilience. Last, the nature of person–environment fit must be seen as dynamic. Individuals are constantly working to increase the level of fit between themselves and their environments through coping strategies that are directed toward the environment, self, or both (Germain & Gitterman, 1995; Harrison, 1978).

A DEVELOPMENTAL PERSPECTIVE

From a developmental perspective, children are not just passive agents within their environments. They act, as well as react, in response to their surroundings. The nature of this interaction and its consequences for the individual and society must be understood from a perspective that captures the dynamic interplay between individuals and their environments over time, which Werner and Smith (1982) described as "the shifting balance between risk, stress, and protective factors in the child and his caregiving environment" (p. 133). This continuous interaction between individual and environmental forces over the course of a child's physical, cognitive, emotional, and social development provides the context and experiences for the development of resilience.

From a developmental perspective, it is important to focus on the timing as well as the nature of events in a child's life (Rutter, 1989). For example, the ability of children to understand and cope with parental divorce depends in part on their developmental maturity (Richman, Chapman, & Bowen, 1995). Events that happen at nonnormative times, such as pregnancy in the teenage years, may spill over to disrupt progress along parallel trajectories, such as education.

The ecological–interactional–developmental perspective provides a broad conceptual lens from which to view resilience as a dynamic construct. It also offers some clues about the types of experiences that may promote the development of resilience in childhood, which is directly associated with school success and is a buffer between individual and situational risk factors and school success.

IMPLICATIONS FOR PREVENTION, EARLY INTERVENTION, AND TREATMENT

The areas or environments of strength regularly identified in the research as characteristic of resilient children include the individual, the family, the peer group, the school, and the community (Benard, 1991; Wang et al., 1994). Practitioners who want to intervene with students who are at risk of school failure might find it helpful, from an ecological–interactional–developmental viewpoint, to assess, with the client, the individual student (addressing values, beliefs, skills, and competencies, for example), his or her interactions with the various layers of the ecosystems, and his or her developmental stage. The goal is to begin to develop interventions that support and strengthen the student and the microsystems in which the student is embedded. We believe that the most efficient course for the practitioner is to attempt to intervene in the social environment to effect change in the individual student, as outlined by the ecological–interactional–developmental perspective. That is, the practitioner should work with the family, peer group, school, and community to produce positive change and to help promote the development of resilience within the student. As discussed by Antonovsky (1991), the environment needs to provide the student with three types of protective conditions—stability, load balance, and participation.

STABILITY

A consistent finding in the literature is that stable, close, and caring relationships between parent and child, as well as supportive relationships outside the family, play a protective role in the development of resilience (Werner & Smith, 1982; Wyman et al., 1992). Coleman (1988) referred to the strengths and supports that individuals have available from these relationships as "social capital," a resource that may be accumulated and, if needed, mobilized to meet internal needs and respond to external demands. Although the parent–child relationship is an important source of social capital for children, social capital may come also from sources both within and outside the household environment, as well as from linkages between the microsystems in which children are embedded (Coleman, 1988). The stabilizing and supportive role of teachers (Bingham, Heywood, & White, 1991; Werner, 1990), the peer group (Felsman, 1989), the school (Offord, 1991), the extended family and neighbors (Tracy, Whittaker, Boylan, Neitman, & Overstreet, 1995), and the community (Brook, Normura, & Cohen, 1989) for building resilience is documented in the literature.

LOAD BALANCE

Load balance for children and youths concerns how well the demands of the environment fit with the capabilities of the individual student (Antonovsky, 1991). The ecosystem in which the student is embedded can provide care and support or it can be a source of risk and stress. Each youth may or may not possess the individual competencies or resources to respond to the stressors presented. For example, parent employment may require that a child be left at home without adult supervision for several hours after school. The concept of load balance would examine whether or not the child is capable of managing that time alone at home. Rutter (1987) suggested that one way to achieve a good load balance is to shield children against risk factors in their environment. Other researchers (Chess, 1989; Wallerstein, 1983) noted that when one environment is highly stressful (the family, perhaps), children need to cope with that negative situation by seeking greater support from other microsystems (peer group, teachers and school, or the community, for example).

PARTICIPATION

Research suggests that resilience is encouraged and developed when children and youth have opportunities to meaningfully participate in and contribute to the environments that embody their microsystems. When families, schools, peer groups, and community all communicate the expectation that children and youths can and will handle their responsibilities successfully and participate in valued ways, the youths respond by developing a sense of autonomy, independence, heightened social competence, and—in a word—resilience (Benard, 1991; Wang et al., 1994; Wehlage, 1989). Werner and Smith (1982) describe this sense of involvement and participation as developing and enabling the social relationships that provide meaning for life and a reason for caring.

The three types of interactive protective conditions that arise from interaction of the student with her or his environment—stability, load balance, and participation—can provide keys and direction to planning interventions that help students at risk for school failure move toward greater resilience. These three protective conditions, together with the focus on the family, school, peer group, and community, can help practitioners and educational specialists begin to design intervention strategies that will strengthen a student's social competencies, problem-solving skills, autonomy, and sense of purpose.

A Practice Planning Form

The practice planning form depicted in Figure 6-4 can be used to target the ecological systems (family, school, peer group, and community) listed at the left of the form with interventions that promote the interactive protective conditions of stability, load balance, and participation. The practitioner can plan strategies that address the relevant intersects, which will ultimately influence the individual resilience factors listed at the right of the planning form. For example, in the family–stability intersect, the practitioner might plan interventions that attempt to enhance stability and caring within the family; in the school–participation intersect, the worker might intervene to try to increase a student's meaningful participation in school activities. The important point is that the practitioner must assess the student's environment for areas of strength or potential and then work with the student to develop practice strategies that target the identified intersect. This process should produce greater individual resilience. Examples of such targeted interventions are shown in Figure 6-4; each of the intersects displays a potential intervention strategy.

It should be remembered that nothing takes the place of professional expertise and judgment. The examples given in the practice planning form are probably most relevant for middle and high school students who are still engaged in school and are developmentally on target. They are provided as examples only—the practitioner must assess the client and his or her ecosystem and stage of development in planning and implementing appropriate and mutually acceptable interventions that will promote stability, load balance, and participation.

Assessing Risk and Resilience: The School Success Profile

Professionals who attempt to intervene with their clients to foster resilience may need to evaluate their progress. Increased accountability can be a critical aspect of program planning and development and often helps to ensure that programs use resources in the most efficient and effective manner. Many initiatives in schools function without outcome measures, but a measurement instrument can prove useful in some instances for monitoring the progress of program participants.

In 1992 BellSouth Foundation awarded a grant to the School of Social Work at the University of North Carolina at Chapel Hill to work with representatives from Communities-In-Schools (CIS) at the national, state, and local levels to develop and field test assessment instruments that local CIS representatives can use to monitor their success in achieving objectives. CIS is the largest dropout prevention program in the

Figure 6-4
Practice Planning Form

	Stability	Load Balance	Participation
Family	Home visit—Intervene with family to develop more positive relationship between student and his or her parent(s)/guardian. Parent education—Invite parents to a meeting where the importance of family stability is discussed and explored.	Home visit—Work with the student and family to develop a reasonable set of expectations regarding free time versus supervised time. Explore the student's role as a main provider of family child care and try to negotiate a lower load balance of responsibility.	Parent and student education intervention—Invite parents to a meeting where the importance of their child participating in family life is discussed and explored. Brainstorm with students and families on how this goal might be accomplished.
School	Teacher and staff intervention—Provide the teachers and administrative staff with a training and renewal program that emphasizes the direct correlation between a student's positive relationship and attachment to teachers and staff and his or her successful school performance.	Teacher intervention—Work with teachers to understand the family overload that student may be facing. Develop ways that the teachers can be more supportive of student, for example, provide an afterschool tutoring program that allows the student to complete homework in a less stressful environment.	Teacher and staff intervention—Work with teachers and administrators to encourage student participation in school activities and recognize the importance of seeing students as consumers. Support students in their choices and stand as a role model in valuing student participation.
Peer Group	Social support group—A student social support group could develop out of a tutoring or an intramural program. The goal is to have peers become supportive of each other as they deal with issues such as pregnancy/parenting, family stress or disengagement, or academic concerns.	Peer group stress audit—Work with students in groups to evaluate their peer involvement. What is gained by their involvement with their peer group (for example, belonging or support) and what stress might be increased because of their peer group affiliations (for example, exposure to violence, conflict with parents)?	Psychoeducational peer discussions—Develop time-limited discussion groups where students are invited to share their experiences and expertise concerning how they deal with problems they face (for example, drugs, violence, sexuality, and grades).
Community	Volunteer program—Involve the student in a community volunteer program similar to Big Brother or Big Sister. Try to get a one- or two-year commitment on the part of the volunteer and the student.	Neighborhood safety and involvement assessment—Work with neighborhood leaders (for example, police, public housing officials, school administrators, youths, and residents) to develop a list of common safety and neighborhood involvement issues. Use this list as the basis for creating a community task force to generate solutions.	Community group involvement—Work with community organizations to reach out to youth and encourage them to become involved in community projects (such as Habitat for Humanity), volunteer in homeless shelters, tutor younger children, or participate on planning boards.

⇨

Individual Resiliency Outcomes

Social Competence
- flexible
- empathy and caring
- communication skills
- visualize and generate alternatives
- develop positive relationships

Problem-Solving Skills
- alternative solutions
- planning skills

Autonomy
- sense of power
- self-esteem
- self-efficacy
- impulse control and self-discipline
- adaptive distancing

Sense of Purpose
- healthy expectations
- some control over one's environment
- goal directedness

SOURCE: Richman, J. M., & Bowen, G. L. (1997). *The Communities-in-School Evaluation Project: The development of the School Success Profile.* Chapel Hill: University of North Carolina.

nation. The School Success Profile (SSP) is a survey questionnaire developed by Bowen and Richman, coprincipal investigators for the project, to help program staff describe those students selected for program participation; inform the process by which each student is provided a comprehensive program of academic services, social services, and employment and life-skills training; monitor changes in program participants over time; develop effective and responsive programs; and increase accountability to the major stakeholders.

Consistent with an ecological perspective, the SSP emphasizes students' perceptions of their four primary microsystems: neighborhood, school, friends, and family. It is designed to be used with middle school and high school students (11 to 18 years of age), and it results in two profiles: the Social Environment Profile and the Individual Adaptation Profile (see Figure 6-5). Each subdimension on the SSP has a positive label (neighborhood satisfaction, for example) and scores are coded to range from negative (low) to positive (high).

Special care was taken to keep the wording of instructions and survey items and response formats simple and to avoid highly sensitive subjects and questions that may violate community sensitivities. The SSP has been successfully field tested in middle schools and high schools in North Carolina and Florida. Validity and reliability of the measures on the SSP have been empirically established and supported.

The SSP is designed to yield group or program and individual profiles by school. The group score is scaled from 0 to 100 on each profile subdimension, which represents the percentage of the maximum score possible (average score across students divided by the maximum score possible). Each middle school is compared to a summary score representing the combined score from other middle schools, and each high school is compared to the combined score from other high schools. For example, if the average student score for George Washington Middle School on "neighborhood safety" is 75 percent and the combined average for other middle schools is 85 percent, students in George Washington Middle School reportedly feel less safe in their neighborhood than "average" middle school students. Practitioners can accordingly assess the areas of greatest concern and the relative level of risk factors for each individual student and the program or group as a whole.

The information on the group profile alerts practitioners to areas that may warrant group interventions and allows them to plan change strategies in these areas. Site coordinators are encouraged to meet with students who completed the SSP to discuss group findings and their validity, however, before using results from the SSP to plan interventions.

The SSP compiles a two-page individual profile in addition to a group profile, a feature that distinguishes it from other student profiles. The first page is the social environment profile; the second page is the individual adaptation profile. Information at the bottom of each page includes the student's ID number, gender, race or ethnicity, age, grade level, and proportion of valid responses.

Individual profiles are not scored in the same way as group profiles. Students receive a standard score on each profile subdimension (a T-score) that reflects their individual score in the context of scores from other students at the same grade level. Scores on each profile subdimension range from 20 to 80, with the average score being 50. Any score above 50 means that a student did better than average when compared

Figure 6-5

School Success Profile: Social Environment and Individual Adaptation Profiles

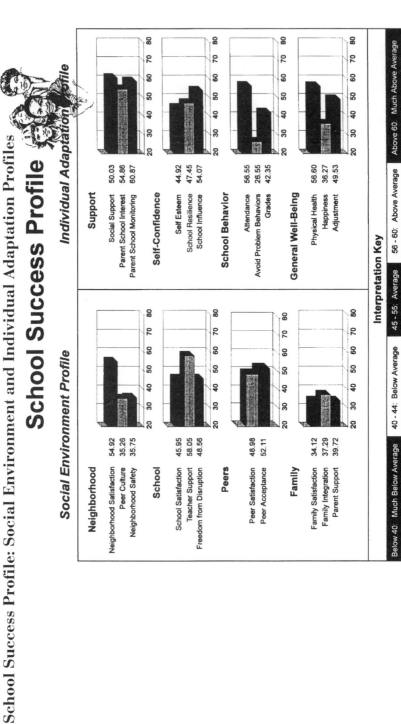

SOURCE: Richman, J. M. & Bowen, G. L. (1997). *The Communities-in-School Evaluation Project: The development of the School Success Profile.* Chapel Hill: University of North Carolina.

with other students; any score below 50 means that a student did worse than average. Of course, "better" and "worse" are relative terms. Because all components on the SSP are coded from low to high, the higher the score, the better; the lower the score, the worse. A key to interpreting scores is shown on the profile.

The SSP is designed to be administered more than once. Most often, students are given the SSP at the beginning and end of the academic year. These repeated administrations make it possible to calculate change scores for both group and individual profiles. These change scores help practitioners determine the extent to which their interventions are producing the desired effects.

Site coordinators are encouraged to meet with each student who completes the SSP and review the profile results. These results, of course, represent only one way to look at the life of the student, and practitioners should take care to establish whether the findings have any validity from the student's perspective. The SSP is designed to augment practitioners' ongoing observations of and dialogue with students. It is not a substitute for this process—it is designed to enhance and support that process. The intervention planning and monitoring form that accompanies the SSP helps the practitioner develop intervention plans with each student who completes the SSP. The form is designed to inform and monitor intervention activities that are directly connected to the data in the social environment and individual adaptation profiles (see Figure 6-6).

Two requirements help ensure the quality of the SSP experience. First, practitioners who wish to use the SSP must attend a two-day training session to learn about its administration, interpretation, and use in informing practice interventions and monitoring the effectiveness of those interventions over time. Second, students must get parental consent before the SSP is administered.

CONCLUSION

This chapter has attempted to accomplish the following five goals: to define the relationship between resilience and school success, to provide a profile of school failure, to present the ecological–interactional–developmental perspective as a theoretical viewpoint that helps explain individual variation in the level of resilience as a factor in school success, to suggest a practice framework that may help develop strategies and interventions leading to greater resilience in students, and to describe and discuss the SSP, an assessment instrument that has been useful in evaluating and monitoring programs and interventions that attempt to promote school success and increased levels of student resilience.

Promoting school success for all children and youth requires developing, supporting, and maintaining safe, caring, and challenging environments in which students can participate fully and gain a sense of acceptance and belonging as they prepare to assume adult roles. Many human services professionals, educators, and business and government leaders have joined together to find effective methods of helping our youth maximize their potential. Continued efforts are needed to promote a social context in which students can build resilience, succeed in school, and move successfully into adult roles and responsibilities.

Figure 6-6

School Success Profile: Intervention Planning and Monitoring Form

Student's first name and initial of last name _____

School _____

SSP ID # _____

A. Targeted Individual Adaptation Area(s) for change (☑ all appropriate areas):

Support	Self-Confidence	School Behavior	General Well-Being
☐ Social Support	☐ Self Esteem	☐ School Attendance	☐ Physical Health
☐ P-S Interest	☐ School Resilience	☐ Misbehavior Avoidance	☐ Happiness
☐ P-S Monitoring	☐ School Influence	☐ Grades	☐ Adjustment

B. Targeted Social Environment Area(s) for change (☑ all appropriate areas):

Neighborhood	School	Friends	Family
☐ Satisfaction	☐ Satisfaction	☐ Satisfaction	☐ Satisfaction
☐ Peer Culture	☐ Teacher Support	☐ Peer Group Acceptance	☐ Integration
☐ Safety	☐ Safety		☐ Parent Support

C. After reviewing the Individual Adaptation and Social Environment profiles with the student, please list the three or four areas you and the student have checked ☑ (in sections A and B above), and chosen to target for intervention and change during the next several months.

Area 1. _____

Area 2. _____

Area 3. _____

Area 4. _____

SOURCE: Richman, J. M., & Bowen, G. L. (1997). *The Communities-in-School Evaluation Project: The development of the School Success Profile.* Chapel Hill: University of North Carolina.

REFERENCES

Alpert, G., & Dunham, R. (1986). Keeping academically marginal youths in school. *Youth & Society, 17,* 346–361.

Antonovsky, A. (1991). The structural sources of salutogenic strengths. In C. L. Cooper & R. Payne (Eds.), *Personality and stress: Individual differences in the stress process* (pp. 67–104). Chichester, England: John Wiley & Sons.

Bandura, A. (1982). Self-efficacy: Mechanism in human agency. *American Psychologist, 37,* 122–147.

Beardsless, W. R. (1989). The role of self-understanding in resilient individuals: The development of a perspective. *American Journal of Orthopsychiatry, 59,* 266–278.

Benard, B. (1991). *Fostering resilience in kids: Protective factors in the family, school, and community.* Portland, OR: Western Center for Drug-Free Schools and Communities.

Bingham, R. D., Heywood, J. S., & White, S. B. (1991). Evaluating schools and teachers based on student performance: Testing an alternative methodology. *Evaluation Review, 15,* 191–218.

Boss, P. (1988). *Family stress management.* Newbury Park, CA: Sage Publications.

Bowen, G. L., Desimone, L. M., & McKay, J. K. (1995). Poverty and the single mother family: A macroeconomic perspective. *Marriage and Family Review, 20* (1–2), 115–142.

Bowen, G. L., & Pittman, J. F. (1995). Introduction. In G. L. Bowen & J. F. Pittman (Eds.), *The work and family interface: Toward a contextual effects perspective* (pp. 1–13). Minneapolis: National Council on Family Relations.

Brenner, M. H. (1976). *Estimating the costs of national economic policy* (Study prepared for the Joint Economic Committee, U.S. Congress, 94th Congress, 2nd Session). Washington, DC: U.S. Government Printing Office.

Bronfenbrenner, U. (1979*). The ecology of human development: Experiments by nature and design.* Cambridge, MA: Harvard University Press.

Brook, J., Normura, C., & Cohen, P. (1989). A network of influences on adolescent drug involvement: Neighborhood, school, peer, and family. *Genetic, Social, and General Psychology Monographs, 115,* 303–321.

Caplan, R. D. (1983). Person–environment fit: Past, present, and future. In C. L. Cooper (Ed.), *Stress research* (pp. 35–78). New York: John Wiley & Sons.

Caplan, R. D. (1987). Person–environment fit theory and organizations: Commensurate dimensions, time perspectives, and mechanisms. *Journal of Vocational Behavior, 31,* 248–267.

Carnahan, S. (1994). Preventing school failure and dropout. In R. J. Simeonsson (Ed.), *Risk resilience & prevention: Promoting the well-being of all children* (pp. 103–123). Baltimore: Paul H. Brookes.

Chatman, J. A. (1989). Improving interactional organizational research: A model of person–organization fit. *Academy of Management Review, 14,* 333–349.

Chess, S. (1989). Defying the voice of doom. In T. Dugan & R. Coles (Eds.), *The child in our times* (pp. 179–199). New York: Brunner/Mazel.

Coleman, J. S. (1988). Social capital in the creation of human capital. *American Journal of Sociology, 94*(Suppl.), S95–S120.

Ekstrom, R. B., Goertz, M. E., Pollack, J. M., & Rock, D. A. (1986). Who drops out of high school and why? Findings from a national study. *Teachers College Record, 87*, 356–373.

Felsman, J. K. (1989). Risk and resilience in childhood: The lives of street children. In T. Dugan & R. Coles (Eds.), *The child in our times* (pp. 56–80). New York: Brunner/Mazel.

Frase, M. (1992). *Are high Hispanic dropout rates a result of recent immigration?* Washington, DC: U.S. Department of Education, National Center for Education Statistics.

French, J. R. P., Jr., Caplan, R. D., & Harrison, R. V. (1982). *The mechanisms of job stress and strain.* Chichester, England: John Wiley & Sons.

Garbarino, J. (1992). *Child and families in the social environment.* New York: Aldine de Gruyter.

Garmezy, N. (1993). Children in poverty: Resilience despite risk. *Psychiatry, 56*, 127–136.

Germain, C. B., & Gitterman, A. (1995). Person-in-environment. In R. L. Edwards (Ed.-in-Chief), *Encyclopedia of social work* (19th ed., Vol. 2, pp. 1818–1827). Washington, DC: NASW Press.

Harris, K. M. (1991). Teenage mothers and welfare dependency: Working off welfare. *Journal of Family Issues, 12*, 492–518.

Harrison, R. V. (1978). Person–environment fit and job stress. In C. L. Cooper & R. Payne (Eds.), *Stress at work* (pp. 175–205). Chichester, England: John Wiley & Sons.

Hepburn, L. R., & White, R. A. (1990). *School dropouts: A two-generation problem.* Athens: University of Georgia, Carl Vinson Institute of Government.

Jessor, R. (1993). Successful adolescent development among youth in high-risk settings. *American Psychologist, 48*, 117–126.

Kulik, C. T., Oldham, G. R., & Hackman, J. R. (1987). Work design as an approach to person–environment fit. *Journal of Vocational Behavior, 31*, 278–296.

Lavee, Y. (1995, November). *Discussant's comments on Dale R. Hawley and Laura De Haan's "Toward a definition of family resilience: Integrating life-span and family perspectives."* Paper presented at the National Council on Family Relations Theory Construction and Research Methodology Workshop, Portland, OR.

Lazarus, R. S., & Folkman, S. (1984). *Stress, appraisal, and coping.* New York: Springer.

Levin, H. M., & Bachman, J. G. (1972). *The costs to the nation of inadequate education* (A report prepared for the Select Committee on Equal Educational Opportunity, U.S. Senate). Washington, DC: U.S. Government Printing Office.

Livingston, A. H., & Miranda, S. (Eds.). *The condition of education, 1995.* Washington, DC: U.S. Department of Education, National Center for Education Statistics.

Martz, L. (1992). *Making schools better.* New York: Times Books.

Maslow, A. (1954). *Motivation and personality.* New York: Harper & Row.

Moos, R. H. (1987). Person–environment congruence in work, school, and health care settings. *Journal of Vocational Behavior, 31,* 231–247.

Mulkey, L. M., Crain, R. L., & Harrington, A. J. (1992). One-parent households and achievement: Economic and behavioral explanations of a small effect. *Sociology of Education, 65,* 48–65.

Offord, D.R. (1991, February). *Conference summary of the Research and Training Center for Children's Mental Health of the Florida Mental Health Institute,* Tampa, FL.

O'Malley, P. M. (1977). *Five years and beyond high school: Causes and consequences of educational attainment: Final Report.* Ann Arbor, MI: Michigan University, Ann Arbor Survey Research Center.

Richman, J. M., Chapman, M. V., & Bowen, G. L. (1995). Recognizing the impact of marital discord and parental depression on children: A family centered approach. In W. L. Coleman & E. H. Taylor (Eds.*),* *Family focused pediatrics: Issues, challenges, and clinical methods* (pp. 167–180). Philadelphia: W. B. Saunders.

Rumberger, R. W. (1983). Dropping out of high school: The influences of race, sex, and family background. *American Educational Research Journal, 20*(2), 199–220.

Rumberger, R. W. (1987). High school dropouts: A review of issues and evidence. *Review of Educational Research, 57*(2), 101–121.

Rutter, M. (1987). Psychosocial resilience and protective mechanisms. *American Journal of Orthopsychiatry, 57,* 316–331.

Rutter, M. (1989). Pathways from childhood to adult life. *Journal of Child Psychology and Psychiatry, 30*(1), 23–51.

Santelli, J. S., & Beilenson, P. (1992). Risk factors for adolescent sexual behavior, fertility, and sexually transmitted diseases. *Journal of School Health, 62,* 271–279.

Slavin, R. E., Karweit, N. L., & Madden, N. A. (1988). *Effective programs for students at risk.* Boston: Allyn & Bacon.

Steinberg, L., Elman, J., & Mounts, N. (1989). Authoritative parenting, psychological maturity, and academic success among adolescents. *Child Development, 60,* 1424–1436.

Tracy, E. M., Whittaker, J. K., Boylan, F., Neitman, P., & Overstreet, E. (1995). Network interventions with high-risk youth and families throughout the continuum of care. In I. M. Schwartz & P. AuClaire (Eds.), *Home-based services for troubled children* (pp. 55–72). Lincoln: University of Nebraska Press.

U.S. Department of Education, National Center for Education Statistics. (1990). *National Education Longitudinal Study of 1988: First follow-up survey.* Unpublished data. Washington, DC.

U.S. Department of Education, National Center for Education Statistics. (1992). *Second follow-up survey.* Unpublished data. Washington, DC.

Wallerstein, J. (1983). Children of divorce: The psychological tasks of the child. *American Journal of Orthopsychiatry, 53,* 230–243.

Wang, M. C., Haertel, G. D., & Walberg, H. J. (1994). Educational resilience in inner cities. In M. C. Wang & E. W. Gordon (Eds.), *Educational resilience in inner-*

city America: Challenges and prospects (pp. 45–72). Hillsdale, NJ: Lawrence Erlbaum.

Wehlage, G. G. (1989). *Reducing the risk: Schools as communities of support.* Philadelphia: Falmer Press.

Wehlage, G. G., & Rutter, R. A. (1986). Dropping out: How much do schools contribute to the problem? *Teachers College Record, 87,* 374–391.

Werner, E. E. (1990). Protective factors and individual resilience. In S. M. Meisels & J. Shonkoff (Eds.), *Handbook of early childhood intervention* (pp. 97–116). New York: Cambridge University Press.

Werner, E. E., & Smith, R. S. (1982). *Vulnerable but invincible: A longitudinal study of resilient children and youth.* New York: McGraw-Hill.

7

Risk and Protective Factors for Alcohol and Other Drug Use in Childhood and Adolescence

Jeffrey M. Jenson

More and more American youths are growing up in life circumstances that place them at risk of alcohol and other drug problems. Identifying factors that decrease their risk and protect them against alcohol and drug abuse is a critical step in preventing adolescent drug abuse.

Scope of the Problem

Most data about the prevalence of alcohol and drug use among American youths comes from the Monitoring the Future Study (Johnston, O'Malley, & Bachman, 1994), sponsored by the National Institute on Drug Abuse and the University of Michigan. The study is an annual assessment of alcohol and drug use in a random sample of 16,000 of the nation's public school students. In-school surveys of nationally representative samples of high school seniors have been conducted since 1975; eighth- and 10th-grade students have been surveyed since 1991.[1]

12th-Grade Students

Lifetime illicit drug use peaked among high school seniors in 1981.[2] Sixty-six percent of 12th graders in 1981 used an illicit drug at least once in their life; 43 percent used an illicit drug other than marijuana. Lifetime use of illicit drugs reached its lowest point in 1992, when only 41 percent of seniors used any illicit drug, and 25 percent used an illicit drug other than marijuana. In 1993 seniors reversed a decade-long pattern of declining illicit drug use: 43 percent used an illicit drug, and 27 percent used an

---

[1] The Monitoring the Future Study may underestimate the magnitude of substance use among high school seniors in the United States because it does not include school dropouts (an estimated 15 percent to 20 percent of students in this age group), a group at high risk of alcohol and drug use. Estimates of drug and alcohol use among adolescents of color may be particularly affected, because more American Indian and Hispanic students drop out of school than do African American or white students (Wallace & Bachman, 1991).

[2] Illicit drug use includes any use of marijuana, hallucinogens, cocaine, heroin or other opiates, and stimulants, barbiturates, or tranquilizers not prescribed by a doctor.

illicit drug other than marijuana. Figure 7-1 shows the lifetime prevalence of illicit drug use for 12th graders between 1975 and 1993.

Lifetime alcohol and tobacco use by seniors reached its highest level in the late 1970s and early 1980s. Approximately 93 percent of seniors reported alcohol use in the eight consecutive years between 1977 and 1984. Lifetime prevalence of alcohol use decreased between 1985 and 1993; 87 percent of students in the class of 1993 used alcohol. Lifetime cigarette smoking peaked in 1977: 76 percent of seniors smoked cigarettes that year, compared with 62 percent of seniors in 1992 and 1993.

In 1993, 51 percent of seniors reported drinking alcohol in the past month; 16 percent reportedly used marijuana, and 3 percent used hallucinogens over the same period. Fewer than 1 percent of high school seniors reported daily use of any illicit drug other than marijuana, however; 2 percent reportedly used marijuana daily in 1993.

EIGHTH-GRADE STUDENTS

Knowledge of drug use prevalence among eighth-grade students is important to practitioners, because alcohol and drug use by young adolescents may be a precursor of drug use trends among future high school students. Awareness of the prevalence of

Figure 7-1.

Lifetime Prevalence of Illicit Drug Use by 12th Graders, 1975–1993

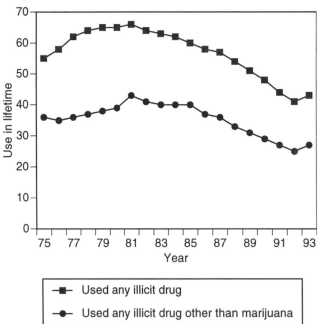

SOURCE: Data are from the Monitoring the Future Study conducted annually by the University of Michigan and the National Institute on Drug Abuse (Johnson, O'Malley, & Bachman, 1994). Use of "any illicit drugs" includes any use of marijuana, hallucinogens, cocaine, heroin or other opiates, stimulants, barbituates, or tranquilizers not prescribed by a doctor.

Figure 7-2.

Lifetime Prevalence of Use of Various Drugs by Eighth Graders, 1991–1993

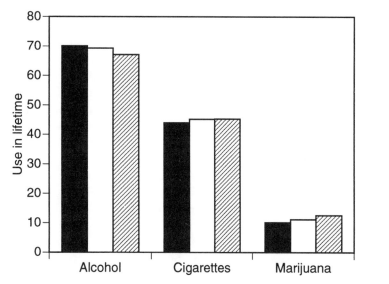

SOURCE: Data are from the Monitoring the Future Study conducted annually by the University of Michigan and National Institute on Drug Abuse (Johnston, O'Malley, & Bachman, 1994).

drug use among eighth graders may also inform the content and direction of prevention and treatment programs.

In 1993, 67 percent of adolescents had used alcohol by the time they reached eighth grade; 26 percent said they had been drunk at least once. Forty-five percent used cigarettes, 19 percent tried inhalants, and 13 percent smoked marijuana. Lifetime prevalence of marijuana and inhalant use increased significantly between 1992 and 1993; cigarette use remained at or near 1992 levels, and alcohol use decreased (Figure 7-2).

Five percent of eighth graders reported having used marijuana in the past month. Five percent had used inhalants, 26 percent drank alcohol, and 17 percent smoked cigarettes. Eight percent of eighth-grade students reported daily use of cigarettes. These data suggest that use of gateway drugs such as alcohol, cigarettes, inhalants, and marijuana is common among youths 13 and 14 years old. Longitudinal studies of drug use prevalence among children and youths indicate that many youths who experiment with gateway drugs proceed to other drugs such as hallucinogens, cocaine, amphetamines, and heroin (Kandel, Simcha-Fagan, & Davies, 1986; Loeber, 1990). These findings suggest that many eighth-graders are already at risk of continued drug use.

DIFFERENCES BY GENDER AND ETHNICITY

Early studies of alcohol and other drug use among adolescents indicated that substance use was more prevalent among boys than among girls (Johnston et al., 1985), but recent results from Monitoring the Future surveys show a decrease in gender differences. Female high school seniors are more likely than their male counterparts to smoke cigarettes and use amphetamines, and they use alcohol and marijuana at nearly the same rates as male seniors. Boys continue to be more involved in heavy drinking and drunk driving than girls (Johnston et al.,1994).

Survey results indicate that alcohol and drug use are more prevalent among white 12th graders than among African American or Hispanic high school seniors (Johnston et al., 1994). The 1993 prevalence of marijuana use ranged from 14 percent for African American to 26 percent for white adolescents. Twenty-four percent of Hispanic seniors had used marijuana during the past year in 1993. White teenagers also had the highest annual prevalence of alcohol use, 80 percent versus 77 percent for Hispanics and 64 percent for African Americans. White seniors were also more likely to have drunk five or more drinks in a row in the past two weeks; 31 percent reported having done so. Twenty-seven percent of Hispanics and 13 percent of African Americans reported binge drinking.

Long-term trends in cigarette smoking reveal interesting differences by ethnicity. Daily smoking rates in the late 1970s were similar for white, Hispanic, and African American seniors: 29 percent of white students, 25 percent of African American students, and 22 percent of Hispanic students smoked daily in 1977. All three groups showed declines between 1977 and 1981. Since 1981 the smoking rates for African American and Hispanic youths have shown a consistent decline, but smoking rates have changed little for white youths. The 1993 rates show that 21 percent of white students, 12 percent of Hispanic students, and 4 percent of African American students smoked cigarettes daily.

Differences in rates of alcohol and drug use among ethnic groups should be interpreted with caution. African American and Hispanic inner-city youths, particularly males, are often underrepresented in national surveys. Other sources reveal that African American men account for one-third of admissions to emergency rooms for drug-related episodes (Institute of Medicine, 1990), and that substance use rates are highest among Hispanic men (Anthony, 1991). Evidence also indicates that American Indian youths, a group not included in annual Monitoring the Future surveys, consume alcohol and use drugs at higher levels than all other racial or ethnic groups (Institute of Medicine, 1990).

SUMMARY OF PREVALENCE STUDIES

Results from these studies reflect important patterns and trends in adolescent alcohol and drug use. First, national surveys of youths enrolled in school showed a decrease in the prevalence of most drug use between 1981 and 1992 (Johnston et al., 1994). Such results suggest that prevention efforts and social norms favoring drug abstinence during the 1980s may have helped curb adolescent alcohol and drug use. Second, recent increases in illicit drug use signal a reversal of a decade-long pattern of decreasing substance use among the nation's youths. Deteriorating social and economic conditions for children and reduced policy attention to drug abuse prevention may be responsible for increased drug use (National Research Council, 1993). Recent findings should remind policymakers that drug abuse is a recurring problem that must be addressed over the long run. Despite the improvements in rates in the 1980s, secondary school students in 1993 showed a level of drug involvement exceeding that of any other industrialized nation (Johnston et al., 1994). Third, disparities in alcohol and drug use between males and females have decreased. Finally, substance use appears to be more prevalent among white and American Indian youths than among Hispanic and African American youths.

RISK AND PROTECTIVE FACTORS FOR ADOLESCENT ALCOHOL AND DRUG ABUSE

Reviews of risk and protective factors for alcohol and drug abuse suggest that multiple factors contribute to the problem behavior (Hawkins, Catalano, & Miller, 1992b; Jessor, 1992). This section summarizes the evidence regarding risk factors for the use of drugs and alcohol during adolescence. Factors protecting against drug use also are identified.

RISK FACTORS FOR ALCOHOL AND DRUG ABUSE

Chapter 2 laid out an ecological perspective for describing risk and protective factors for childhood social problems. Some factors are environmental or background conditions (for example, poverty or lack of prosocial opportunities) that increase the likelihood of childhood problems; other factors are family, school, neighborhood, or individual characteristics (for example, family conflict or biomedical conditions) that increase the risk for problem behavior. A multisystems framework, which offers a way both to understand etiological factors of drug abuse and to inform assessment strategies for identifying drug problems, is used below to classify risk factors at environmental, interpersonal, social, and individual levels. Risk factors for alcohol and drug abuse are summarized in Table 7-1.

Environmental Risk Factors for Drug Abuse

Community laws and norms favorable to drug use—a low legal drinking age and low taxes on alcoholic beverages, for example—increase the risk of drug use during adolescence (Joksch, 1988). Studies examining the relationship between legal age for drinking and adolescent drinking and driving have shown that lowering the drinking age increases underage drinking and adolescent traffic fatalities (Joksch, 1988; Saffer & Grossman, 1987). Laws and norms that express intolerance for use of alcohol and illicit drugs by adolescents are associated with a lower prevalence of drug use (Johnston, 1991).

In 1990 nearly 10 million children under age six lived in poor and near-poor families (National Center for Children in Poverty, 1992). Extreme and persistent poverty is associated with many unfavorable adolescent outcomes, including conduct problems, delinquency, and unwanted pregnancy (Farrington, Gallagher, Morley, St.

Table 7-1. Risk Factors for Adolescent Alcohol and Drug Abuse

Environmental Factors

Laws and Norms
  * Taxation of alcohol and drugs
  * Regulation of alcohol and drugs
  * Criminal laws for alcohol and drug use
  * Cultural norms about alcohol and drug use
  * Hyperactivity

Availability of Alcohol and Drugs

Poverty and Economic Deprivation

Low Economic Opportunity

Neighborhood Factors
  * Neighborhood disorganization
  * Low neighborhood attachment
  * Residential mobility
  * High population density
  * High adult crime rates

Interpersonal and Social Factors

Family Factors
  * Family conflict
  * Poor parent–child bonding
  * Poor family management practices
  * Family communication
  * Family alcohol and drug use

School Factors
  * School failure
  * Low commitment to school

Peer Factors
  * Rejection by conforming peer group
  * Association with drug-using peers

Individual Factors

Psychosocial and Biological Factors
  * Family history of alcoholism
  * Sensation-seeking orientation
  * Poor impulse control
  * Attention deficits

Leger, & West, 1988). Interestingly, research on social class and drug use has produced conflicting results about the association between poverty and drug use prevalence. Several studies have reported a negative relationship between extreme poverty and alcohol and drug use (Murray, Richards, Luepker, & Johnson, 1987; Robins & Ratcliff, 1979), suggesting that children raised in poor households and neighborhoods are at increased risk of adolescent drug abuse. Also, poverty may have an indirect effect on adolescent drug use, because family income is associated with many other risk factors for drug use (for example, poor parenting practices and academic difficulties). Nevertheless, other studies have indicated that adolescents from nonpoor families use drugs more often than youths from poor families (Adams, Blanken, Ferguson, & Kopstein, 1990).

Low neighborhood attachment, school transitions, and residential mobility are associated with drug and alcohol abuse (Felner, Primavera, & Cauce, 1981; Murray, 1983). Neighborhoods with high population density and high rates of adult crime also have high rates of adolescent crime and drug use (Simcha-Fagan & Schwartz, 1986). Neighborhood disorganization may also indirectly affect risk for drug abuse by eroding the ability of parents to supervise and control their children.

Interpersonal and Social Risk Factors for Drug Abuse

Interpersonal and social risk factors for adolescent drug abuse occur in family, school, and peer settings. Children whose parents or siblings engage in serious alcohol or illicit drug use are themselves at greater risk for these behaviors (Brook, Whiteman, Gordon, & Brook, 1988); so are children raised in families with lax supervision, excessively severe or inconsistent disciplinary practices, and little communication and involvement between parents and children (Baumrind, 1983). Similarly, studies have shown that parental conflict is related to subsequent alcohol or drug use by adolescent family members (Kumpher & DeMarsh, 1986).

School failure, a low degree of commitment to education, and lack of attachment to school have been identified as school-related factors that increase the risk of drug abuse during adolescence (Fleming, Kellam, & Brown, 1982; Holmberg, 1985). Studies also indicate that adolescent drug users are more likely than nondrug users to skip classes, be absent from school, and perform poorly (Gottfredson, 1981; Kim, 1979).

Association with friends who use drugs is among the strongest predictors of adolescent alcohol or drug abuse (Elliott, Huizinga, & Ageton, 1985; Barnes & Welte, 1986). Peer rejection in elementary grades is associated with school problems and delinquency (Coie, 1990; Kupersmidt, Coie, & Dodge, 1990), which are also risk factors for drug abuse (Hawkins, Jenson, Catalano, & Lishner, 1988). Some investigators hypothesize that rejected children form friendships with other rejected children and that such groups become delinquent during adolescence (Tremblay, 1988), but this hypothesis has not been adequately tested for adolescent drug use outcome measures.

Individual Risk Factors for Drug Abuse

Psychosocial and biological factors are related to drug and alcohol abuse during adolescence. For example, evidence from adoption, twin, and half-sibling studies supports the notion that alcoholism is an inherited disorder (Cadoret, Cain, & Grove, 1980). There is evidence that a sensation-seeking orientation predicts the start of and continued use of alcohol and other drugs (Cloninger, Sigvardsson, & Bohman, 1988). Research also indicates that attention deficit disorders, hyperactivity, and poor impulse control before the age of 12 predict the age of onset of drinking and drug use (Shedler & Block, 1990). Although individual factors may increase risk for alcohol and drug use, they probably interact with environmental, interpersonal, and social risk factors in the etiology of substance abuse.

SUMMARY OF RISK FACTORS

Current knowledge of risk factors for drug abuse is correlational in nature, not causal. The presence of risk factors only increases the likelihood that an adolescent will develop problem alcohol or drug use. The interaction and the overlap of risk factors during adolescence are not well understood (Hawkins et al., 1992b), and many investigators argue that such factors may be consequences of drug abuse rather than characteristics that increase the risk for drug use (Macdonald, 1989). Despite these limitations, several conclusions about risk factors for alcohol and drug abuse can be drawn.

First, risk factors have been shown to be stable during the past 20 years. The factors summarized above have consistently predicted alcohol and drug use, even though social norms about the acceptability of substance use changed several times during this period. Second, research indicates that the more the risk factors in a child's life, the greater the risk that child will have for alcohol or drug problems (Bry, McKeon, & Pandina, 1982; Vega, Zimmerman, Warheit, Apospori, & Gil, 1993). These findings suggest that prevention programs should target risk factors at multiple levels, including differential vulnerability, poor childrearing practices, school achievement, social influences, social learning, and broad social norms.

Third, early initiation of drug and alcohol use is a key factor in the development of drug abuse problems. The early onset of any drug use increases the subsequent frequency of drug use and the probability of involvement in deviant activities such as selling drugs. Children who begin to use drugs before the age of 15 are twice as likely to develop problems with drugs than are children who delay experimentation until age 19 (Robins & Pryzbeck, 1985).

PROTECTIVE FACTORS AGAINST ALCOHOL AND DRUG ABUSE

Many adolescents develop healthy relationships and succeed in school and in the community despite being exposed to risk factors. Identifying individual and environmental characteristics that reduce risk for drug abuse among children has been a focus of research for the past decade (Garmezy, 1985; Rutter, 1985, 1990; Smith, Lizotte, Thornberry, & Krohn, 1995; Werner, 1994). Such characteristics, often called protective factors, mediate or moderate the effects of exposure to drug abuse or to risk factors for abuse (Cowen & Work, 1988; Garmezy, 1985; Hawkins, Catalano, & Associates, 1992a). When identified in children and adolescents, protective factors can be manipulated or enhanced to reduce risks for drug abuse. Longitudinal research with adolescents exposed to multiple risks has identified environmental, interpersonal, social, and individual protective factors (Garmezy, 1985; Coie, Watt, West, Hawkins, et al., 1993) (Table 7-2).

Environmental, Interpersonal, and Social Protective Factors against Drug Abuse

Environmental, interpersonal, and social protective factors are attributes that buffer community, neighborhood, family, school, and peer risk factors. The most comprehensive study of protective factors among children was conducted by Werner and colleagues (Werner, 1994; Werner & Smith, 1989). Werner and Smith began following a cohort of high-risk children in Kauai, Hawaii, in 1955. Analysis of the children's outcomes as adolescents and adults has contributed to knowledge about factors that prevent youths from engaging in drug abuse.

Werner (1994) found that being raised in a family with four or fewer children, experiencing low parental conflict, and being a firstborn child buffer the effects of poverty and other risk factors for drug abuse. Children who abstained from drug use

Table 7-2. Protective Factors against Adolescent Alcohol and Drug Abuse

Environmental, Interpersonal, and Social Factors
* Being a firstborn child
* Being raised in a small family
* Experiencing low parental conflict
* Caring relationships with siblings
* Caring relationships with extended family
* Social support from nonfamily members
* Attachment to parents
* Commitment to school
* Involvement in conventional activities
* Belief in prosocial norms and values

Individual Factors
* Social and problem-solving skills
* Attitude
* Temperament
* High intelligence
* Low childhood stress

during adolescence and early adulthood were found to have had positive parent–child relationships in early childhood and caring relationships with siblings and grandparents. Children abstaining from alcohol and other drugs also received social support and frequent counsel from teachers, ministers, and neighbors (Werner, 1994).

A positive family milieu and community supports are protective factors for drug abuse among children exposed to multiple risk factors. Garmezy (1985) found low childhood stress among high-risk children living in supportive family environments and in adolescents who had strong external support systems. Because stress increases risk of drug use in later adolescence and early adulthood (Rutter, 1985), such findings have implications for preventing childhood and early adolescent drug abuse.

Strong social bonds to parents, teachers, and prosocial peers are significant factors in children's resistance to drug use (Berrueta-Clement, Schweinhart, Barnett, Epstein, & Weikhard, 1984; Hawkins et al., 1992a). Four elements of the social bond have been found to be inversely related to adolescent drug abuse: (1) strong attachments to parents (Brook, Brook, Gordon, Whiteman, & Cohen, 1990); (2) commitment to school (Hawkins, Doueck, & Lishner, 1988); (3) involvement in prosocial activities, such as those carried out by church or community organizations (Gottfredson, 1981); and (4) belief in the generalized norms and values of society (Krohn & Massey, 1980).

Understanding the processes by which strong social bonds develop is necessary for devising strategies that increase healthy bonding in high-risk youths. Social learning (Bandura, 1989) and social development (Hawkins et al., 1992a) theorists indicate that three conditions are critical to the formation of strong social bonds: (1) opportunities for involvement in prosocial activities, (2) possession of the behavioral and cognitive skills necessary for achieving success in such activities, and (3) rewards or recognition for positive behaviors. To promote healthy bonds, practitioners should use intervention strategies that provide opportunities, enhance skills, and offer rewards to high-risk youths.

Individual Protective Factors against Drug Abuse

Individual protective factors are psychosocial and biomedical characteristics that inhibit drug use. Competence in social and problem-solving situations is associated with abstinence and reductions in teenage drug use and delinquency (Jenson & Howard, 1990). In a sample of high-risk urban children, Rutter (1985) found that problem-solving skills and strong self-efficacy were associated with successful adolescent outcomes. Youths who possessed adequate problem-solving skills, and the ability to use skills, were less likely to engage in drug use and delinquency. Jenson, Wells, Plotnick, Hawkins, and Catalano (1993) found that, among adjudicated delinquents, strong self-efficacy decreased the likelihood of drug use six months following drug treatment. These findings suggest that social and problem-solving skills moderate the effects of multiple risk factors for drug abuse and other adverse adolescent outcomes.

Attitude and temperament can be protective factors for drug abuse; positive social orientation and positive temperament reduced the likelihood of adolescent drug abuse in several studies of high-risk youths. Low intelligence (Werner, 1994) is also sometimes associated with drug use.

SUMMARY OF PROTECTIVE FACTORS

Research identifying factors protecting children and adolescents from alcohol and drug abuse is relatively new. Studies are being conducted to better understand the reciprocal nature of risk and protective factors (Jessor, 1993; Stouthamer-Loeber, Loeber, Farrington, Zhang, van Kammen, & Maguin, 1993; Tolan, Guerra, & Kendall, 1995). These investigations typically do not view risk and protective factors as distinct constructs. Rather, protective factors are viewed as characteristics that affect individual responses to a given amount of exposure to risk. This interpretation provides an opportunity to test the mediating effect of protective factors on risk and to examine nonlinear and interactive relationships among risk and protective factors. Additional research is needed to increase our understanding of risk and protective factors and our knowledge about the multiple pathways to teenage substance abuse.

DIFFERENCES IN RISK AND PROTECTIVE FACTORS BY AGE AND RACE OR ETHNICITY

Few etiological studies of adolescent drug abuse devote attention to characteristics such as age, race, or ethnicity (Feldman & Elliott, 1990). Most of what is known about risk and protective factors for adolescent drug abuse has been drawn from studies of white junior and senior high school students residing in middle-class neighborhoods. Prevention and treatment programs often assume that risk and protective factors related to alcohol and drug use are the same for different adolescent populations. However, age and ethnic minority status are central issues in the developmental process of children and adolescents and clearly warrant more research attention.

AGE

Different risk and protective factors are salient at different stages in a child's development (Coie et al., 1993; Hawkins et al., 1992b). For example, aggressiveness in children as young as five predicts later drug use (Kellam & Brown, 1982), and association with deviant peers in early adolescence is strongly related to drug use in later adolescence and early adulthood (Dishion, 1990). Poor parenting and family management practices are related to drug use during childhood and adolescence (Kendziora & O'Leary, 1993), and community supports and extended family members are protective factors against drug abuse for older adolescents (Werner, 1994).

Knowledge of developmental differences in the saliency of risk and protective factors must be considered in prevention and treatment efforts. Factors that are predictive of drug use in early childhood differ considerably from factors that are the most important in later stages of adolescence, so practitioners must be familiar with the saliency of risk and protective factors across all developmental stages. Proximal or situational risk factors are generally the best predictors of problem behaviors such as drug abuse (Coie et al., 1993).

RACE OR ETHNICITY

Adolescents in the United States receive differential exposure to risk based on racial and ethnic characteristics. Youths of color are overrepresented in persistent poverty (Sawhill, 1992) and are more likely than white youths to be incarcerated (Pope & Feyerherm, 1993). Youths of color are also more likely than white adolescents to be victims of violent crime (Snyder & Sickmund, 1995) and to be raised in single-parent households (National Research Council, 1993). Differential exposure to predisposing factors because of race or ethnicity may increase the risk for alcohol and drug abuse among youths of color. Research has only begun to examine racial and ethnic differences in risk and protective factors for adolescent drug abuse (Jessor, 1993).

The Social Development Research Group examined racial differences in individual and family risk factors related to drug use among white, African American, and Asian American adolescents (Catalano, Hawkins, Krenz, Gillmore, & Morrison, 1993; Catalano et al., 1992; Gillmore et al., 1990; Wells et al., 1992). Data were drawn from a longitudinal study of drug use and delinquency among public school children in Seattle between 1981 and 1986. Subjects were in the fifth grade at the time of analysis. Tobacco and alcohol use was highest among the white students: 23 percent of white students, 19 percent of African American students, and 9 percent of Asian American students had used tobacco by the fifth grade. Figures for alcohol use were 49 percent, 40 percent, and 17 percent for white, African American, and Asian American students, respectively (Gillmore et al., 1990).

Differences in family factors related to drug use were found for the three groups; white and African American children reported significantly better family communication than did Asian American students, and African American children reported a significantly higher proportion of deviant siblings than did the other two groups (Catalano et al.,

1992). Asian American children had the lowest, and African American children the highest, involvement in family work and activities (Catalano et al., 1992). White youths reported less use of proactive family management practices by their parents than did youths in the other two groups (Catalano et al., 1993). These findings suggest that families of different racial groups do not always influence their children in the same way.

Wells et al. (1992) examined the relationship between antisocial behaviors and attitudes and early initiation of drug use for white, African American, and Asian American students. Self-reported antisocial behaviors and attitudes were the strongest predictors of drug use for fifth-grade Asian American children. Teacher ratings of antisocial behavior were significantly related to drug use for white but not African American or Asian American students. African American youths were perceived by their teachers to be more aggressive than other students, but this perception was not related to self-reported initiation of tobacco, alcohol, or marijuana use.

Gillmore et al. (1990) examined exposure to risk factors for white, African American, and Asian American fifth graders. White children reported the greatest access to marijuana, greatest parental tolerance of drug use, and greatest intention to use drugs in the future. No racial differences were found in the number of children's friends who used alcohol or other drugs.

Differences between risk and protective factors for Hispanic and non-Hispanic adolescents have been examined. Jenson (1993) found that strong family bonds among Hispanic families acted as a buffer against drug use among adjudicated delinquents. Parent involvement and family communication were significantly higher among delinquents of Hispanic origin than among non-Hispanic delinquent youths.

At least one study examined the relationship between number of risk factors and drug use by racial or ethnic groups. Vega and colleagues (1993) examined risk factors for drug use among sixth- and seventh-grade Cuban and other Hispanic, African American, and white youths. African American youths were the least likely to have no risk factors and the most likely to have three to six risk factors; African American youths also had the highest mean number of risk factors across groups. Low self-esteem and delinquency were related to drug use among the group "other Hispanics." Depression symptoms predicted alcohol use among white youths, and parental drug use was a strong predictor of drug use among African American youths. Low family pride and willingness to engage in antisocial behavior were related to alcohol use in all groups.

These findings suggest that prevention and treatment programs may need to be tailored to different racial or ethnic groups. For example, parent bonding and family communication appear to be salient protective factors against drug abuse for Hispanic children and youths (Gilbert, 1989; Jenson, 1993). Hispanic youths at risk of drug abuse may benefit from family-based programs that enhance family strengths. Poor parent modeling of alcohol use in some African American families may place youths at high risk of drug abuse (Institute of Medicine, 1990). Prevention efforts aimed at African American youths might include intervention strategies that address appropriate modeling practices for alcohol use. These and other racial or ethnic differences in risk factors should be systematically included in intervention strategies for high-risk youths.

Research is only beginning to address racial or ethnic differences in risk and protective factors. Additional studies are needed to provide the empirical base necessary for the design of culturally sensitive prevention and treatment programs.

Assessing Risk and Protective Factors

Assessing the prevalence of risk and protective factors in children and communities is an essential part of targeting and designing prevention and treatment programs. Risk indices, comprehensive inventories, and standardized measures have been used to assess risk for drug abuse.

Risk Indices

Self-report indices that seek information about multiple risk or protective factors is one method of assessing an adolescent's propensity to use drugs. Farrell and colleagues (Farrell, 1993; Farrell, Anchors, Danish, & Howard, 1992a; Farrell, Danish, & Howard, 1992b) developed a risk factor index for youths ages 12 to 17 based on a subset of nine risk factors for drug abuse: (1) home alone after school, (2) friends approve of drug use, (3) friends use drugs, (4) youth knows adults who use drugs, (5) feel pressure to use drugs, (6) history of trouble with the police, (7) delinquent behavior, (8) intentions to use drugs, and (9) inadequate coping and social skills. Self-report interviews in which adolescents respond to questions assessing each of these risk factors are used to determine a subject's risk for drug abuse. Farrell has demonstrated the predictive validity of the index in studies of rural and urban adolescents (Farrell et al., 1992a, 1992b).

Several investigators have used a multiple-gating process to identify youths at high risk of drug abuse or antisocial behavior (Lochman & the Conduct Problems Prevention Research Group, 1995; Loeber, Dishion, & Patterson, 1984). The first step (gate) in multiple gating is usually a basic screening of a specified population (for example, children in the fifth grade). Subsequent screening steps (gates) are conducted with a smaller pool of youths that the previous step identified as likely to be at risk.

Multiple-gating procedures using child self-reports—plus teacher and parent ratings of child behavior—have been accurate in predicting subsequent antisocial behavior. Loeber, Dishion, and Patterson (1984) successfully identified 86 percent of recidivists using teacher and parent reports of child behavior. Lochman and associates (1995) used teacher and parent ratings of child behavior to predict negative behaviors among children in early elementary school. Multiple-gating methods have seldom been used to identify high-risk adolescent drug abusers or to predict drug use among adolescents, however. Such studies are needed.

Assessments of risk and protective factors for drug abuse may be enhanced by using more than one method for data collection. Patterson and associates at the Oregon Social Learning Center have combined teacher, parent, peer, and child self-reports to predict antisocial behavior in longitudinal studies of high-risk youths (Capaldi & Patterson, 1989; Patterson, Reid, & Dishion, 1992). A unique feature of their longitudinal investigations is the inclusion of in-home and school observations of early childhood behavior. Their results have important implications for assessing risk for antisocial behaviors such as drug abuse (Patterson et al., 1992).

Using ratings of risk and protective factors to predict subsequent involvement in drug abuse is complex. Many predictions are false positive: Not all children who are at risk of drug abuse actually engage in drug use during adolescence (Dodge, 1993). Teachers and community members may treat youths who are labeled "high risk" differently from other youths, which could have negative effects on young people's behavior. Conversely, some predictions are false negative: Some children do not exhibit patterns of drug use until late in their development, precluding early intervention efforts. Additional research is needed so that indicators of risk and resilience can be assessed more accurately.

INVENTORIES AND STANDARDIZED INSTRUMENTS

Inventories and standardized measures are other ways to evaluate risk and protective factors and predict the likelihood of drug abuse. The Personal Experience Inventory (PEI) is a self-report measure of psychosocial risk factors associated with adolescent drug involvement (Winters, Stinchfield, & Henly, 1993a). The inventory includes five scales: (1) personal involvement with drug use, (2) effects from drug use, (3) social benefits of drug use, (4) personal consequences of drug use, and (5) polydrug use. Each of the five scales has a range of eight to 29 items; all have demonstrated reliability and validity. Studies of the PEI indicate that the scales are significantly related to DSM-III-R criteria for substance use disorders and treatment recommendations (Henly & Winters, 1988; Winters et al., 1993b). The PEI has also classified high-risk adolescents into outpatient or inpatient treatment referral subgroups (Winters et al., 1993b).

Winters (1992) developed the Personal Experience Screening Questionnaire (PESQ) to meet the need for a quick adolescent screening tool. The PESQ is used to determine the need for a comprehensive assessment of risk and protective factors associated with drug use. Psychometric properties have been established for an 18-item and a 38-item PESQ (Winters, 1992; Winters, Weller, & Meland, 1993b). The PESQ is a paper-and-pencil screening tool written at the fourth-grade reading level. The test is scored for problem severity, drug use history, and psychological problems. Response options are based on a 4-point scale ranging from 1 = never to 4 = often. The total score for problem severity gets either a green flag or a red flag. The red flag score suggests the need for further assessment. A discriminant function analysis was used to identify the score—the red flag—that most often correctly classified adolescents into relevant criterion groups (need for a comprehensive assessment versus no need for a comprehensive assessment).

The Problem Oriented Screening Instrument for Teenagers (POSIT) is designed to identify risk and protective factors for drug abuse that may require additional assessment (Rahdert, 1991). The POSIT is intended to operate as a first screen for drug use problems. Ten functional areas incorporating many of the risk and protective factors discussed in this chapter are assessed in the POSIT: substance use and abuse, physical health, mental health, family relationships, peers, educational status, vocational status, social skills, leisure and recreation, and aggressive behavior. Scores exceeding the established cutoff point for each area may indicate that a problem with drug use exists. The POSIT scoring system is based on expert clinical judgment. Studies establishing psychometric properties of the instrument are in progress (Hall, Grinstead, Fortney, Rembert, & Richardson, 1995).

Inventories That Assess Individual Risk or Protective Factors

Many assessment instruments are designed to assess single risk or protective factors (for example, family functioning or peer relations). These instruments do not provide an overall "risk or protective score" across multiple factors; rather, they offer comprehensive assessments of specific factors that protect children or place them at risk of alcohol or drug abuse.

The Family Assessment Measure (FAM) includes three interrelated measures that provide a comprehensive profile of family functioning (Skinner, Steinhauer, & Santa-Barbara, 1983). Each of the three instruments addresses dimensions of task accomplishment, role performance, communication, affective expression, involvement, control, and values. The FAM has established psychometric properties, and parents and youths can complete it with little or no supervision (Skinner, 1987).

The Piers-Harris Children's Self-Concept Scale is a commonly used measure that provides an assessment of a youth's peer relations (Piers, 1984). The scale was established in the early 1960s and has acceptable reliability and validity. The Revised Problem Behavior Checklist (RPBC) offers practitioners an assessment of the deviance orientation of an adolescent's peer group (Hagbord, 1990). The RPBC also contains subscales assessing conduct disorder, attention problems or immaturity, anxiety withdrawal, psychotic behavior, and motor excess. The instrument is completed by parents, teachers, social workers, or other adults. Psychometric properties for the RPBC are well established (Hagbord, 1990).

The Social Skills Rating System (SSRS) is a checklist that provides student, parent, and teacher ratings of cooperation, assertion, responsibility, empathy, and self-control skills (Elliot, Gresham, Freeman, & McCloskey, 1988). Elementary and secondary school versions of the SSRS have been standardized on 4,000 youths between ages three and 18.

The Adolescent Problem Situation Inventory (APSI), an audiotaped skills inventory, evaluates social, behavioral, and cognitive abilities (Wells, Jenson, Hurwitz, Catalano, & Hawkins, 1988). Subjects listen and respond to role-playing situations that place youths at risk for drug use or delinquency; for example an item from the APSI is the following scenario:

> You are getting ready for a concert that you have been looking forward
> to for a long time. You are thinking about what it would be like to get
> high at the concert. What would you say to yourself?

Responses to this and 30 other items are independently scored by two or more raters to assess a youth's skill level. The instrument has been used to accurately identify skill deficits in delinquent and drug-abusing youths (Hawkins, Jenson, Catalano, & Wells, 1991).

Measures of Aggressive Behavior and Delinquency

The Child Behavior Checklist (CBC) measures a variety of child disturbances and behaviors (Achenbach & Edelbrock, 1990). The Youth Self-Report contained in the CBC assesses aggressive and delinquent behaviors among adolescents, outcomes that are strongly correlated with drug use.

Investigators have also developed self-report inventories to examine childhood aggression. Coie, Lochman, Terry, and Hyman (1992) successfully predicted adolescent behavior problems using self-report and teacher ratings of aggression and peer rejection for elementary school children. Cicchetti and Richters (1993), Dodge (1993), and

Lochman and associates (1995) have developed self-report inventories that measure childhood aggressive behavior. Studies of early childhood aggression have focused on the relationship between early aggression and later delinquency; research into the role of aggression in adolescent drug abuse problems is needed.

Implications for Prevention, Early Intervention, and Treatment

Knowledge gained from studies on risk and protective factors for adolescent drug abuse should be put to work in prevention and treatment programs. This chapter establishes that there is empirical evidence of the stability of risk and protective factors for drug abuse. The next step requires social work and other human services practitioners to apply this evidence to practice.

The multisystems ecological framework for understanding childhood social problems presented in chapter 2 is an effective tool for using what is known about risk and protective factors. Identifying those environmental, interpersonal and social, and individual factors associated with drug abuse allows practitioners to examine their own interventions and ask, Do my intervention efforts with high-risk adolescents address multiple risk and protective factors for drug abuse? If not, how can I incorporate risk-focused strategies in practice? How can I enhance existing protective factors among the children and families I serve? How can I incorporate concepts of risk and resilience in practice? To implement programs or strategies based on risk and protective factors, practitioners should do the following:

- Focus on known risk factors for adolescent drug abuse. Practitioners must first identify the risk and protective factors that are most prevalent in their communities (Hawkins, 1995). Once factors are identified, prevention and treatment efforts can be tailored to target the specific factors that are most salient for local youths.
- Initiate intervention efforts before drug use problems stabilize or become serious. Risk and protective factors provide practitioners with the tools to predict and assess drug use. Factors in early childhood and elementary schools should be targeted by practitioners to prevent serious drug abuse during adolescence.
- Adjust interventions to developmental stages of childhood and adolescence. This review identifies risk and protective factors that are salient at different stages of child development. For example, evidence suggests that factors such as early signs of aggressive behavior should be addressed when a child is four to six years old. At the adolescent stage of development, a different predictor of drug use becomes especially important: association with antisocial peers. Skills to resist peer pressure should therefore be emphasized during adolescent development.
- Be sensitive to racial and ethnic differences. Traditionally, intervention efforts targeting alcohol and drug abuse have paid little attention to race or ethnicity. Research is beginning to uncover racial and ethnic differences in exposure to risk and protective factors, however, and practitioners must consider these

differences when intervening to prevent or treat adolescent drug abuse (Jenson, Howard, & Yaffe, 1995).

CONCLUSION

Risk and resilience in childhood and adolescence are key concepts in assessment techniques and interventions for high-risk youths. Strategies that practitioners in schools, clinics, the community, and other settings use in prevention and treatment programs for youths at risk of drug abuse need to be based on those factors that mitigate risk and promote resilience. Multicomponent strategies can delay the initiation of alcohol and drug use among high-risk children and reduce substance use among adolescents who already engage in drug use. No one strategy can be applied successfully in every instance—approaches should be tried in various combinations and evaluated for their efficacy in preventing the initiation and continuance of alcohol and drug use.

REFERENCES

Achenbach, T. M., & Edelbrock, C. (1990). The classification of child psychopathology: A review and analysis of empirical efforts. *Psychological Bulletin, 85,* 1275–1301.

Adams, E. H., Blanken, A. J., Ferguson, L. D., & Kopstein, A. (1990). *Overview of selected drug trends.* Rockville, MD: National Institute on Drug Abuse.

Anthony, J. C. (1991). The epidemiology of drug addiction. In N. S. Miller (Ed.), *Comprehensive handbook of drug and alcohol addiction* (pp.55–86). New York: Marcel-Dekker.

Bandura, A. (1989). Human agency in social cognitive theory. *American Psychologist, 44,* 1175–1184.

Barnes, G. M., & Welte, J. W. (1986). Patterns and predictors of alcohol use among 7–12th grade students in New York state. *Journal of Studies on Alcohol, 47,* 53–62.

Baumrind, D. (1983, October). *Why adolescents take chances—and why they don't.* Paper presented at a meeting at the National Institute for Child Health and Human Development, Bethesda, MD.

Berrueta-Clement, J. R., Schweinhart, L. J., Barnett, W. S., Epstein, A. S., & Weikhard, D. P. (1984). *Changed lives: The effects of the Perry Preschool Program on youths through age 19.* Ypsilanti, MI: High/Scope Press.

Brook, J. S., Brook, D. W., Gordon, A. S., Whiteman, M., & Cohen, P. (1990). The psychosocial etiology of adolescent drug use: A family interactional approach. *Genetic, Social and General Psychology Monographs* (No. 116, Whole No. 2).

Brook, J. S., Whiteman, M., Gordon, A. S., & Brook, D. W. (1988). The role of older brothers in younger brothers' drug use viewed in the context of parent and peer influences. *Journal of Genetic Psychology, 151,* 59–75.

Bry, B. H., McKeon, P., & Pandina, R. J. (1982). Extent of drug use as a function of number of risk factors. *Journal of Abnormal Psychology, 91*, 273–279.

Cadoret, R. J., Cain, C. A., & Grove, W. M. (1980). Development of alcoholism in adoptees raised apart from alcoholic biologic relatives. *Archives of General Psychiatry, 37*, 561–563.

Capaldi, D. M., & Patterson, G. R. (1989). *Psychometric properties of fourteen latent constructs from the Oregon Youth Study.* New York: Springer-Verlag.

Catalano, R. F., Hawkins, J. D., Krenz, C., Gillmore, M. R., & Morrison, D. M. (1993). Using research to guide culturally appropriate drug abuse prevention. *Journal of Consulting and Clinical Psychology, 61*, 804–811.

Catalano, R. F., Morrison, D. M., Wells, E. A., Gillmore, M. R., Iritani, B., & Hawkins, J. D. (1992). Ethnic differences in family factors related to early drug initiation. *Journal of Studies on Alcohol, 53*, 208–217.

Cicchetti, D., & Richters, J. E. (1993). Developmental considerations in the investigation of conduct disorder. *Development and Psychopathology, 5*, 331–344.

Cloninger, C. R., Sigvardsson, S., & Bohman, M. (1988). Childhood personality predicts alcohol abuse in young adults. *Alcoholism, 12*, 494–503.

Coie, J. D. (1990). Towards a theory of peer rejection. In S. R. Asher & J. D. Coie (Eds.), *Peer rejection in childhood* (pp. 365–398). New York: Cambridge University Press.

Coie, J. D., Lochman, J. E., Terry, R., & Hyman, C. (1992). Predicting early adolescent disorder from childhood aggression and peer relations. *Journal of Consulting and Clinical Psychology, 60*, 783–792.

Coie, J. D., Watt, N. F., West, S. G., Hawkins, J. D., Asarnow, J. R., Markman, H. J., Ramey, S. L., Shure, M. B., & Long, B. (1993). The science of prevention: A conceptual framework and some directions for a national research program. *American Psychologist, 48*, 1013–1022.

Cowen, E. L., & Work, W. (1988). Resilient children, psychological wellness, and primary prevention. *American Journal of Community Psychology, 16*, 591–607.

Dishion, T. J. (1990). The peer context of troublesome behavior in children and adolescents. In P. Leone (Ed.), *Understanding troubled and troublesome youth* (pp. 128–153). Newbury Park, CA: Sage Publications.

Dodge, K. A. (1993). The future of research on the treatment of conduct disorder. *Development and Psychopathology, 5*, 311–319.

Elliott, D. S., Huizinga, D., & Ageton, S. A. (1985). *Explaining delinquency and drug use.* Beverly Hills, CA: Sage Publications.

Elliott, S. N., Gresham, F. M., Freeman, T., & McCloskey, G. (1988). Teachers' and observers' ratings of children's social skills. *Journal of Psychoeducational Assessment, 6*, 225–235.

Farrell, A. D. (1993). Risk factors for drug use in urban adolescents: A three-wave longitudinal study. *Journal of Drug Issues, 23*, 443–462.

Farrell, A. D., Anchors, D. M., Danish, S. J., & Howard, C. W. (1992a). Risk factors for drug use in rural adolescents. *Journal of Drug Education, 22*, 313–328.

Farrell, A. D., Danish, S. J., & Howard, C. W. (1992b). Risk factors for drug use in urban adolescents: Identification and cross-validation. *American Journal of Community Psychology, 20*, 263–275.

Farrington, D. P., Gallagher, B., Morley, L., St. Leger, R., & West, D. (1988). Are there any successful men from criminogenic backgrounds? *Psychiatry, 51*, 116–130.

Feldman, S. S., & Elliott, G. R. (1990). *At the threshold: The developing adolescent.* Cambridge, MA: Harvard University Press.

Felner, R. D., Primavera, J., & Cauce, A. M. (1981). The impact of school transitions: A focus for preventive efforts. *American Journal of Community Psychology, 9*, 449–459.

Fleming, J. P., Kellam, S. G., & Brown, C. H. (1982). Early predictors of age at first use of alcohol, marijuana, and cigarettes. *Drug and Alcohol Dependence, 9*, 285–303.

Garmezy, N. (1985). Stress-resistant children: The search for protective factors. In J. E. Stevenson (Ed.), *Recent research in developmental psychology* (pp. 213–233). Tarrytown, NY: Pergamon Press.

Gilbert, M. J. (1989). Alcohol use among Latino adolescents: What we know and what we need to know. In *Perspectives on adolescent drug use.* Binghamton, NY: Haworth Press.

Gillmore, M. R., Catalano, R. F., Morrison, D. M., Wells, E. A., Iritani, B., & Hawkins, J. D. (1990). Racial differences in acceptability and availability of drugs and early initiation of substance use. *American Journal of Drug and Alcohol Abuse, 16*, 185–206.

Gottfredson, G. D. (1981). Schooling and delinquency. In S. E. Martin, L. B. Sechrest, & R. Redner (Eds.), *New directions in the rehabilitation of criminal offenders* (pp. 424–469). Washington, DC: National Academy Press.

Hagbord, W. J. (1990). The Revised Problem Behavior Checklist and severely emotionally disturbed adolescents: Relationship to intelligence, academic achievement, and sociometric ratings. *Journal of Abnormal Child Psychology, 18*, 47–53.

Hall, J. A., Grinstead, D. M., Fortney, M. A., Rembert, J. K., & Richardson, B. B. (1995). *Using the POSIT to identify substance use risk factors among rural adolescents.* Unpublished manuscript, School of Social Work, University of Iowa, Iowa City.

Hawkins, J. D. (1995, August). Controlling crime before it happens: Risk-focused prevention. *National Institute of Justice Journal* (U.S. Department of Justice, Office of Justice Programs). Washington, DC: U.S. Government Printing Office.

Hawkins, J. D., Catalano, R. F., & Associates. (1992a). *Communities that care: Action for drug abuse prevention.* San Francisco: Jossey-Bass.

Hawkins, J. D., Catalano, R. F., & Miller, J. Y. (1992b). Risk and protective factors for alcohol and other drug problems in adolescence and early adulthood: Implications for substance abuse prevention. *Psychological Bulletin, 112*, 64–105.

Hawkins, J. D., Doueck, H. J., & Lishner, D. M. (1988). Changing teaching practices in mainstream classrooms to improve bonding and behavior of low achievers. *American Educational Research Journal, 25*, 31–50.

Hawkins, J. D., Jenson, J. M., Catalano, R. F., & Lishner, D. L. (1988). Delinquency and drug abuse: Implications for social services. *Social Service Review, 62*, 258–284.

Hawkins, J. D., Jenson, J. M., Catalano, R. F., & Wells, E. A. (1991). Effects of skills training intervention with juvenile delinquents. *Research on Social Work Practice, 1*, 107–121.

Henly, G. A., & Winters, K. C. (1988). Development of problem severity scales for the assessment of adolescent alcohol and drug abuse. *International Journal of the Addictions, 23*, 65–85.

Holmberg, M. B. (1985). Longitudinal studies of drug abuse in a fifteen-year-old population: I. Drug career. *Acta Psychiatrica Scandanavia, 71*, 67–79.

Institute of Medicine (1990). *Broadening the base of treatment for alcohol problems.* Washington, DC: National Academy Press.

Jenson, J. M. (1993, November). *Factors related to gang membership among juvenile probationers.* Paper presented at the annual meeting of the American Society of Criminology, Phoenix, AZ.

Jenson, J. M., & Howard, M. O. (1990). Skills deficits, skills training, and delinquency. *Children and Youth Services Review, 12*, 213–238.

Jenson, J. M., Howard, M. O., & Yaffe, J. (1995). Treatment of adolescent substance abusers: Issues for practice and research. *Social Work in Health Care, 21*(2), 1–18.

Jenson, J. M., Wells, E. A., Plotnick, R. D., Hawkins, J. D., & Catalano, R. F. (1993). The effects of skills and intentions to use drugs on posttreatment drug use of adolescents. *American Journal of Drug and Alcohol Abuse, 19*, 1–17.

Jessor, R. (1992). Risk behavior in adolescence: A psychosocial framework for understanding and action. In D. E. Rogers & E. Ginzberg (Eds.), *Adolescents at risk: Medical and social perspectives* (pp. 19–34). Boulder, CO: Westview Press.

Jessor, R. (1993). Successful adolescent development among youth in high-risk settings. *American Psychologist, 48*, 117–126.

Johnston, L. D. (1991). Toward a theory of drug epidemics. In L. Donohew, H. E. Sypher, & W. J. Bukoski (Eds.), *Pervasive communication and drug abuse prevention* (pp. 93–131). Hillsdale, NJ: Lawrence Erlbaum.

Johnston, L. D., O'Malley, P. M., & Bachman, J. G., (1985). *Drug use, drinking, and smoking: National survey results from high school, college, and young adult populations.* Washington, DC: U.S. Government Printing Office.

Johnston, L. D., O'Malley, P. M., & Bachman, J. G. (1994). *Drug use, drinking, and smoking: National survey results from high school, college, and young adult populations.* Washington, DC: U.S. Government Printing Office.

Joksch, H. C. (1988). *The impact of severe penalties on drinking and driving.* Washington, DC: AAA Foundation for Traffic Safety.

Kandel, D., Simcha-Fagan, O., & Davies, M. (1986). Risk factors for delinquency and illicit drug use from adolescence to young adulthood. *Journal of Drug Issues, 60*(1), 67–90.

Kellam, S .G., & Brown, H. (1982, December). *Social adaptational and psychological antecedents of adolescent psychopathology ten years later.* Paper presented at a research workshop on prevention aspects of suicide and affective disorders among adolescents and young males, Harvard School of Public Health and Harvard School of Medicine, Boston.

Kendziora, K. T., & O'Leary, S. G. (1993). Dysfunctional parenting as a focus for prevention and treatment of child behavior problems. In T. H. Ollendick & R. J. Prinz (Eds.), *Advances in clinical child psychology* (Vol. 15, pp. 121–149). New York: Plenum Press.

Kim, S. (1979). *An evaluation of ombudsman primary prevention program on student drug abuse.* Charlotte, NC: Charlotte Drug Education Center.

Krohn, M. D., & Massey, J. L. (1980). Social control and delinquent behavior: An examination of the elements of the social bond. *Developmental Psychology, 18,* 359–368.

Kumpher, K. L., & DeMarsh, J. (1986). Family-oriented interventions for the prevention of chemical dependency in children and adolescents. In S. Ezekoye, K. L. Kumpher, & W. Bukoski (Eds.), *Childhood and chemical abuse: Prevention and intervention* (pp. 117–152). New York: Haworth Press.

Kupersmidt, J. B., Coie, J. D., & Dodge, K. A. (1990). The role of poor peer relationships in the development of disorder. In S. R. Asher & J. D. Coie (Eds.), *Peer rejection in childhood* (pp. 274–305). New York: Cambridge University Press.

Lochman, J. E., & the Conduct Problems Prevention Research Group. (1995). Screening of child behavior problems for prevention programs at school entry. *Journal of Consulting and Clinical Psychology, 63,* 549–559.

Loeber, R. (1990). Development and risk factors of juvenile antisocial behavior and delinquency. *Clinical Psychology Review, 10,* 1–41.

Loeber, R., Dishion, T. J., & Patterson, G. R. (1984). Multiple gating: A multistage assessment procedure for identifying youths at risk for delinquency. *Journal of Research on Crime and Delinquency, 21,* 7–32.

Macdonald, D. I. (1989). *Drugs, drinking, and adolescents* (2nd ed.). Chicago: Year Book Medical Publishers.

Murray, C. A. (1983). The physical environment and community control of crime. In J. Q. Wilson (Ed.), *Crime and public policy* (pp. 107–122). San Francisco: Institute for Contemporary Studies.

Murray, D. M., Richards, P. S., Luepker, R. V., & Johnson, C. A. (1987). The prevention of cigarette smoking in children: Two and three-year follow-up comparisons of four prevention strategies. *Journal of Behavioral Medicine, 10,* 595–611.

National Center for Children in Poverty. (1992). *Five million children: 1992 update.* New York: Columbia University, School of Public Health.

National Research Council. (1993). *Losing generations. Adolescents in high-risk settings.* Washington, DC: National Academy Press.

Patterson, G. R., Reid, J. B., & Dishion, T. J. (1992). *Antisocial boys.* Eugene, OR: Castalia.

Piers, E. V. (1984). *Piers-Harris Children's Self-Concept Scale: Revised manual.* Los Angeles: Western Psychological Services.

Pope, C., & Feyerherm, W. (1993). *Minorities in the juvenile justice system* (Office of Juvenile Justice and Delinquency Prevention). Washington, DC: U.S. Government Printing Office.

Rahdert, E. R. (1991). *The adolescent assessment/referral system manual.* Washington, DC: Alcohol, Drug Abuse, and Mental Health Administration.

Robins, L. N., & Pryzbeck, T. R. (1985). Age of onset of drug use as a factor in drug and other disorders. In C. L. Jones & R. J. Battjes (Eds.), *Etiology of drug abuse: Implications for prevention* (pp. 178–192). Washington, DC: U.S. Government Printing Office.

Robins, L. N., & Ratcliff, K. S. (1979). Continuation of antisocial behavior into adulthood. *International Journal of Mental Health, 7,* 96–116.

Rutter, M. (1985). Resilience in the face of adversity: Protective factors and resistance to psychiatric disorder. *British Journal of Psychiatry, 147,* 598–611.

Rutter, M. (1990). Psychosocial resilience and protective mechanisms. In J. Rolf, A. Masten, D. Cichetti, K. H. Nuechteerlein, & S. Weintraub (Eds.), *Risk and protective factors in the development of psychopathology* (pp. 181–214). Cambridge, England: Cambridge University Press.

Saffer, H., & Grossman, M. (1987). Beer taxes, the legal drinking age, and youth motor vehicle fatalities. *Journal of Legal Studies, 16,* 351–374.

Sawhill, I. (1992). Young children and families. In H. J. Aaron & C. L. Schultze (Eds.), *Setting domestic priorities: What can governments do?* (pp. 147–184). Washington, DC: Brookings Institution.

Shedler, J., & Block, J. (1990). Adolescent drug use and psychological health: A longitudinal inquiry. *American Psychologist, 45,* 612–630.

Simcha-Fagan, O., & Schwartz, J. E. (1986). Neighborhood and delinquency: An assessment of contextual effects. *Criminology, 24,* 667–703.

Skinner, H. (1987). Self-report instrument for family assessment. In T. Jacob (Ed.), *Family interaction and psychopathology: Theories, methods, and findings* (pp. 143–187). New York: Plenum Press.

Skinner, H., Steinhauer, P., & Santa-Barbara, J. (1983). The family assessment measure. *Canadian Journal of Community Mental Health, 2,* 91–105.

Smith, C. A., Lizotte, A. J., Thornberry, T. P., & Krohn, M. (1995). Resilient youth: Identifying factors that prevent high-risk youth from engaging in delinquency and drug use. In J. Hagen (Ed.), *Delinquency in the life course* (pp. 67–94). Greenwich, CT: JAI Press.

Snyder, H. N., & Sickmund, M. (1995). *Juvenile offenders and victims: A national report.* Washington, DC: Office of Juvenile Justice and Delinquency Prevention.

Stouthamer-Loeber, M., Loeber, R., Farrington, D. P., Zhang, Q., van Kammen, W., & Maguin, E. (1993). The double edge of protective and risk factors for delinquency: Interrelations and developmental patterns. *Development and Psychopathology, 5,* 683–701.

Tolan, P. H., Guerra, N. G., & Kendall, P. C. (1995). A developmental–ecological perspective on antisocial behavior in children and adolescents: Toward a unified risk and intervention framework. *Journal of Consulting and Clinical Psychology, 63,* 579–584.

Tremblay, R. (1988). *Peers and the onset of delinquency.* Paper prepared for the Onset Working Group Program on Human Development and Criminal Behavior, Castine, ME.

Vega, W. A., Zimmerman, R. S., Warheit, G. J., Apospori, E., & Gil, A. G. (1993). Risk factors for early adolescent drug use in four ethnic and racial groups. *American Journal of Public Health, 83,* 185–189.

Wallace, J. M., & Bachman, J. G. (1991). Explaining racial/ethnic differences in adolescent drug use: The impact of background and lifestyle. *Social Problems, 38,* 333–357.

Wells, E. A., Jenson, J. M., Hurwitz, H. A., Catalano, R. F., & Hawkins, J. D. (1988). *The Adolescent Problem Situation Inventory.* Seattle: University of Washington, Center for Social Welfare Research.

Wells, E. A., Morrison, D. M., Gillmore, M. R., Catalano, R. F., Iritani, B., & Hawkins, J. D. (1992). Race differences in antisocial behaviors and attitudes and early initiation of substance use. *Journal of Drug Education, 22,* 115–130.

Werner, E. E. (1994). Overcoming the odds. *Developmental and Behavioral Pediatrics, 15*(2), 131–136.

Werner, E. E., & Smith, R. S. (1989). *Vulnerable but invincible: A longitudinal study of resilient children and youth.* New York: Adams, Bannister & Cox.

Winters, K. A. (1992). Development of an adolescent alcohol and other drug abuse screening scale: Personal Experience Screening Questionnaire. *Addictive Behaviors, 17,* 479–490.

Winters, K. A., Stinchfield, R. D., & Henly, G. A. (1993a). Further validation of new scales measuring adolescent alcohol and other drug abuse. *Journal of Studies on Alcohol, 54,* 534–541.

Winters, K. A., Weller, C. L., & Meland, J. A. (1993b). Extent of drug abuse among juvenile offenders. *Journal of Drug Issues, 23,* 515–524.

8

RISK AND PROTECTIVE FACTORS IN THE DEVELOPMENT OF DELINQUENCY AND CONDUCT DISORDER

James Herbert Williams, Charles D. Ayers, and Michael W. Arthur

Juvenile delinquency and conduct disorder, particularly violent behavior, continue to plague America. They are major social problems that the American public wants solved, but as those involved in the prevention, intervention, and treatment of such behavior know, solutions do not come easily. Consensus has been building, however, on the focus of efforts at prevention and intervention. From the Institute of Medicine (1994) to the Office of Juvenile Justice and Delinquency Prevention, U.S. Department of Justice (1965–1994), a risk–protective factor perspective is taking hold.

As suggested in chapter 2, a risk–protective strategy implies that certain individual and social characteristics, variables, and hazards (risk factors) present in an individual's life make it more likely that the person will engage in delinquent activity or develop mental health disorders (conduct disorder, for example). Other characteristics and variables (protective factors) are known to reduce an individual's risk level or buffer an individual from the effects of risk. Risk and protective factors for juvenile delinquency and conduct disorder are known to exist in all domains of a youth's life, including family, school, community, and peer group, as well as within individuals themselves. Consequently, the risk–protective factor perspective is consistent with ecological theory and provides a conceptual framework for prevention, intervention, and treatment based on the person-in-environment model.

This chapter reviews the research literature on risk and protective factors of juvenile delinquency and conduct disorder, and it discusses their implications for prevention, intervention, and treatment efforts. To provide a foundation, the chapter defines juvenile delinquency and conduct disorder and puts those terms in a sociological context by reviewing recent behavioral trends, purported developmental pathways of delinquent behavior, and critical life periods. Risk factors are then presented by social domain—community, family, school, peer group—and by genetic and biological factors. Protective factors are reviewed as well. The chapter concludes with a review of some of the strategies used to assess risk and protective factors and a discussion of the implications of the risk–protective strategy for prevention, intervention, and treatment of delinquency and conduct disorder.

NATURE OF THE PROBLEM

Juvenile delinquency is defined as illegal acts committed by persons under 18 years of age, including some acts which, if committed by someone 18 or older, would not be illegal (status offenses). The Federal Bureau of Investigation (1993) classified delinquent acts into three categories based on the severity of the offense. The most serious of the three categories is violent index crimes. *Violent index crimes* include forcible rape, robbery, aggravated assault, murder, and nonnegligent manslaughter. *Property index crimes*, the second most serious level of offense, include burglary, larceny (theft), motor vehicle theft, and arson. All other delinquent acts are categorized as nonindex offenses. *Nonindex offenses* include forgery, vandalism, gambling, driving under the influence, drunkenness, disorderly conduct, vagrancy, and status offenses such as running away and violating curfew.

Conduct disorder is a clinical mental health diagnosis; it subsumes delinquent behavior, but not all delinquency constitutes conduct disorder. The essential feature of *conduct disorder*, as defined by the *Diagnostic and Statistical Manual of Mental Disorders—Fourth Edition* (DSM-IV) (American Psychiatric Association [APA], 1994), is a "repetitive and persistent pattern of behavior in which the basic rights of others or the major age-appropriate societal norms or rules are violated" (p. 85). Such behaviors are classified into four groups: (1) aggressive behavior that causes or threatens physical harm to other people or animals, (2) nonaggressive behavior that causes property loss or damage, (3) deceitfulness or theft, and (4) serious violations of rules. A clinical diagnosis of conduct disorder is made when children or adolescents under the age of 18 have exhibited three or more characteristic behaviors during the past 12 months, with at least one behavior having been present in the past six months. Consequently, even though all delinquent acts are classified in the behavioral grouping of conduct disorder, not all individuals engaging in delinquent activities meet clinical criteria for conduct disorder. The specific guidelines for a clinical diagnosis of conduct disorder, as defined in DSM-IV (APA, 1994), are detailed in Table 8-1.

GENERAL TRENDS

In 1992, 1.9 million juveniles were arrested in the United States. More than 110,000 of these arrests were for violent index crimes (murder and nonnegligent manslaughter, forcible rape, robbery, and aggravated assault). Another 600,000 were for property index crimes (burglary, larceny–theft, motor vehicle theft, and arson). Arrests of juveniles accounted for 16.3 percent of all arrests in 1992, including 17.5 percent of violent index crime arrests and 33.1 percent of property index crime arrests (Bureau of Justice Statistics, 1994).

Over the 10-year period from 1983 to 1992, the juvenile arrest rate for violent crimes increased 50.5 percent, from 139.1 to 209.4 per 100,000. In those 10 years the murder and nonnegligent manslaughter arrest rate jumped 132.4 percent, from 7.4 to 17.2 per 100,000 (Bureau of Justice Statistics, 1994; Federal Bureau of Investigation, 1994). Despite these figures, the proportion of adolescents involved in serious violent offenses has increased only slightly—from 8 percent to 10 percent—over the past decade (Elliott, 1994a).

What has increased over this period is the lethality of violent acts, a result of increased handgun use in violent adolescent interactions (Elliott, 1994a; Jones & Krisberg, 1994). During the 1980s the rate of homicide by firearms among young

Table 8-1. DSM-IV Diagnostic Criteria for Conduct Disorder

- initiate frequent physical fights
- use a weapon that can cause physical harm (for example, a bat, brick, broken bottle, knife, or gun)
- physically cruel to people or animals
- steal while confronting a victim (for example, mugging, purse snatching, extortion, or armed robbery)
- force someone into sexual activity
- physical violence (for example, rape, assault, and, in rare cases, homicide)
- fire setting
- deliberate destruction of other people's property
- deceitfulness or theft (for example, breaking and entering, car vandalism, or burglary)
- frequent lying (for example, "conning" other people)
- stealing items of nontrivial value without confronting the victim (for example, shoplifting, forgery)
- running away from home, staying out late despite parental prohibitions

Criteria for Severity of Conduct Disorder

Mild: Few if any conduct problems in excess of those required to make the diagnosis are present, and conduct problems cause relatively minor harm to others (for example, lying, truancy, staying out after dark without permission).

Moderate: The number of conduct problems and the effect on others are intermediate between "mild" and "severe" (for example, stealing without confronting a victim, or vandalism).

Severe: Many conduct problems in excess of those required to make the diagnosis are present, or conduct problems cause considerable harm to others (for example, forced sex, physical cruelty, use of a weapon, stealing while confronting a victim, breaking and entering).

SOURCE: Reprinted with permission from the *Diagnostic and statistical manual of mental disorders—Fourth edition* (American Psychiatric Association, 1994, pp. 90–91). Copyright 1994 American Psychiatric Association.

people ages 15 to 19 increased 61 percent. The non–firearm homicide rate decreased by 29 percent (National Coalition of State Juvenile Justice Advisory Groups, 1993).

Although sobering enough, these official statistics fail to portray the full extent of childhood and adolescent delinquency and conduct disorder. According to self-report data, a majority of America's youths will commit at least one delinquent act by the time they reach adulthood (Elliott, Huizinga, & Ageton, 1985; Farrington et al., 1990; Feldman, Caplinger, & Wodarski, 1983; Johnston, O'Malley, & Bachman, 1994). The rate of conduct disorder in the general child and adolescent population runs about 6 percent to 16 percent for boys and 2 percent to 9 percent for girls (APA, 1994). It is responsible for about one-third to one-half of all child and adolescent clinical referrals (Herbert, 1987; Robins, 1981). This prevalence of criminal involvement not only makes juvenile delinquency statistically normative, but also makes juveniles one of the most criminal segments of our population.

Of course, most of the youths who account for the high prevalence of delinquency and conduct disorder have committed offenses that are relatively minor and infrequent. Furthermore, the vast majority will terminate their criminal careers during the normal course of adolescent development. In this sense, delinquency represents a transient response to adolescence, a response that most youths will outgrow (Elliott, Huizinga, & Menard, 1989). On the other hand, a very small proportion of adolescents engage in frequent and serious offending over a long time. This subpopulation, estimated to constitute between 5 percent and 12 percent of the adolescent population (Dunford & Elliott, 1984; Farrington, 1983; Tracy, Wolfgang, & Figlio, 1985; West & Farrington, 1977), accounts for a substantial amount of the total incidence of juvenile offending (Elliott et al., 1985; Wolfgang, 1983) and the bulk of all serious and violent offenses (Office of Juvenile Justice and Delinquency Prevention, 1993).

In the National Youth Survey (NYS) study, serious juvenile offenders made up fewer than 5 percent of the study sample in 1980, but they accounted for 83 percent of all index offenses committed and half of all offenses reported (Elliott, 1994a). Wolfgang, Figlio, and Sellin (1972) found that although "chronic offenders" (five or more police contacts) constituted only 6 percent of their study's 1945 birth cohort and 18 percent of the delinquents, they were responsible for 52 percent of all offenses and about two-thirds of all violent offenses. Other studies have found similar results (Farrington, 1983; Farrington & West, 1990, 1993; Hamparian, Schuster, Dinitz, & Conrad, 1978; Huizinga, Loeber, & Thornberry, 1993; Shannon, 1988, 1991; Snyder, 1988; Tracy, Wolfgang, & Figlio, 1990).

DEMOGRAPHICS OF DELINQUENCY AND CONDUCT DISORDER

Regardless of the source of the data, either official arrest statistics or self-reports, it is clear that the prevalence of delinquent involvement and conduct disorder is much greater among males than females (Elliott et al., 1989). This is especially true for more serious offenses. In 1992 males represented 76.9 percent of all juveniles arrested and 87.5 percent of all arrestees for violent index crimes (Bureau of Justice Statistics, 1994). However, criminal propensity is not restricted to boys. Over the past several decades, dramatic increases in antisocial behavior have been noted for girls (Robins, 1991; Rutter & Giller, 1983). In fact, between 1983 and 1992, the arrest rate of girls rose faster than the rate for boys (25 percent and 15 percent, respectively). The arrest rate of juvenile females for violent crimes jumped 82 percent over that 10-year period (U.S. Department of Justice, 1965–1994).

Unlike data on gender, official and self-report information on ethnic or racial differences conflict. According to official arrest data, African American youths are much more likely to be arrested than their white, European American counterparts. In 1992 the arrest rate for African American adolescents (2,565 per 100,000) was 2.33 times higher than that of white adolescents (1,095 per 100,000). For violent index crimes, African American youths were arrested at almost five and a half times the rate of white youths—677 and 126 per 100,000, respectively (U.S. Department of Justice,

1965–1994). Huizinga, Loeber, and Thornberry (1993), using official arrest data, also reported higher arrest rates among African Americans, yet they reported no racial or ethnic differences in analyses of self-reports of criminal involvement.

In fact, with the exception of higher prevalence rates for serious offenses such as felony assault, robbery, and total index offenses for African Americans, most self-report studies have not found significant racial differences in illegal behavior (Elliott et al., 1989). These results suggest that, in officially reported arrest data, racial differences may actually be indicators of other social processes and conditions, such as socioeconomic status and system response bias. Research by Pope and Feyerherm (1990a, 1990b, 1993), which suggested that youths of color are more likely than other youths to become involved with the juvenile justice system—which is not racially neutral—supports this conclusion.

Conduct disorder is the most common disorder seen in child mental health clinics (Institute of Medicine, 1994). The six-month and one-year prevalence rates obtained from clinic populations range from 1.5 percent to 11.9 percent. Boys are diagnosed more frequently with conduct disorder than girls. Many times conduct disorder occurs in conjunction with other disorders, such as attention-deficit hyperactivity disorder, and it can persist into late adolescence and adulthood (Offord et al., 1992).

Developmental Pathways, Critical Periods of Delinquency, and Conduct Disorder

Whether overt (aggressive), covert (concealing), or both, the delinquent activities of most youths follow a common pattern of initiation, escalation, de-escalation, and desistance, with less serious behaviors generally preceding more moderate, consequential behaviors (Elliott et al., 1989; Loeber, Stouthamer-Loeber, van Kammen, & Farrington, 1991). It is uncertain, however, whether this pattern of involvement is explained by a single behavioral pathway encompassing both types of behavior (overt and covert) or whether the pattern of involvement differs for each behavioral type.

Reviewing the literature, Loeber (1988) concluded that evidence supports a dual pathway model with an aggressive–versatile pathway (aggressive and concealing behavior) and a nonaggressive, antisocial pathway (nonaggressive, covert behavior only). More recently, empirical support for three pathways in the development of delinquency and conduct disorder has been reported (Loeber & Stouthamer-Loeber, 1993). These include the authority conflict pathway (stubborn behavior, defiance, and authority avoidance), the covert pathway (minor covert behaviors such as lying and shoplifting, property damage, and moderate to serious delinquency), and the overt pathway (aggression, physical fighting, and violence). However, membership in one pathway did not exclude membership in another. In fact, dual and triple pathway membership was not uncommon.

Historically, the peak age for the onset of delinquency has been decreasing. The peak age of onset for the cohort panel in studies by Wolfgang, Figlio, and Sellin (1972) and Wolfgang, Thornberry, and Figlio (1987) was 16 years. Elliott and Huizinga (1984) found the peak age for their panel to be 13 to 15 years. More recent studies have found that most youths engaging in delinquent behavior began their delinquency around ages 12 and 13 (Thornberry, 1996; Wilson & Herrnstein, 1985). However, for many the onset of delinquent activity occurs even before the teenage years. Sixty percent of 11-year-olds in the NYS reported participating in general delinquency, and 20 percent reported participating in index offenses (Elliott et al., 1989).

Self-report studies suggest that initiation of serious violent offending generally occurs between ages 14 and 17, with the highest risk of initiation at 15 to 16 years old. The risk of initiating serious violent offending decreases to nearly zero after age 20 (Elliott, 1994b). Both prevalence and offending rates for general delinquent involvement tend to peak around mid- to late adolescence, or ages 15 to 17 (Hirschi, 1969; Thornberry, 1996; Wilson & Herrnstein, 1985). Elliott (1994b) reported that the prevalence of self-reported violent behavior peaks at age 17 for males and around ages 15 and 16 for females.

Half of the youths in the NYS who had been involved in delinquent activity before age 18 discontinued those activities for one or more years while still under age 18; they had not resumed general offending by ages 18, 19, or 20, depending on the study cohort (Elliott et al., 1989). More than 50 percent of the sample was not involved in general delinquency by age 18, and more than 90 percent either terminated or did not initiate index offending by age 17. Elliott (1994b) found peak termination to occur between ages 18 and 19. A steeper decline in involvement was noted for females. Elliott (1994b) reported that in the NYS, involvement differentials between boys and girls increased from 2 to 1 at age 12 to 3 to 1 at age 18 and 4 to 1 at age 21. After age 17, participation rates dropped dramatically for both boys and girls. Eighty percent of those who had engaged in serious violent offending had not done so again by age 21 (Elliott, 1994b).

RISK FACTORS FOR DELINQUENCY AND CONDUCT DISORDER

Risk factors predict the increased probability of a subsequent undesirable outcome (Barnes & Farrell, 1992; Elliott et al., 1989; Farrington & West, 1993; Gillmore, Hawkins, Catalano, Day, & Abbott, 1991; Hawkins, Catalano, & Miller, 1992a; Hawkins, Jenson, Catalano, & Lishner, 1988; Institute of Medicine, 1994; Stouthamer-Loeber, Loeber, & Farrington, 1993). Extensive research has identified risk factors for delinquency and conduct disorder (Dryfoos, 1990; Forehand, Wierson, Frame, Kempton, & Armistead, 1991; Hawkins et al., 1992b; Robins, 1966; Yoshikawa, 1994). These factors can be divided into two categories: contextual or community risk factors and interpersonal or individual risk factors. Contextual factors are associated with the structure and values within the social environment of the individual and his or her peer group. Risk factors that exist in the social context include cultural or community norms or laws that foster delinquency, availability of drugs or weapons, poverty, and neighborhood disorganization (Alexander, Massey, Gibbs, & Altekruse, 1985; Garbarino, DuBrow, Kostelny, & Pardo, 1992; Hawkins et al., 1992b; Loftin, McDowell, & Wiersema, 1993; Loftin, McDowell, Wiersema, & Cottey, 1991; Sampson, 1986; Yoshikawa, 1994). Individual risk factors are associated with the adolescent's personal environment—his or her family, peers, school, and genetic factors (Cadoret, Cain, & Crowe, 1983; Cairns, Cairns, Neckerman, Ferguson, & Gariepy, 1989; Farrington, 1991; McCord, 1988). Among the risk factors for an adolescent are family management problems, family conflict, early onset of problem behavior, academic failure, low commitment to school, association with antisocial peers, alienation, rebelliousness, favorable attitudes toward delinquent behavior, physiological abnormalities, temperamental behavior, cognitive and neuropsychological deficits, and hyperactivity (Earls, 1981; Hawkins et al., 1992a; Institute of Medicine, 1994, Kandel, Simcha-Fagan, & Davies, 1986; Rutter, 1978; Rutter & Giller, 1983; White, Moffitt, & Silva, 1989; Yoshikawa, 1994).

Risk factors for delinquency and conduct disorder have been identified in many longitudinal studies (for example, Hawkins et al., 1992; Kandel et al., 1986; Tolan & Guerra, 1994; Yoshikawa, 1994). Contemporary research has given far too little attention to comparative study of the factors influencing delinquency and conduct disorder across racial groups, in part because adequate multiethnic samples are lacking. Antisocial behaviors among white youths are considered to have a strong correlation with emotional or psychological dysfunction, whereas social risk factors are more prevalent among African Americans (Dembo, Williams, & Schmeidler, 1994).

COMMUNITY RISK FACTORS

Community norms and levels of crime in a neighborhood help determine whether youths will thrive or develop antisocial behaviors (Garbarino et al., 1992; Williams, Stiffman, & O'Neal, 1996). Community norms—the attitudes and policies a community holds concerning crime and violence—are communicated through formal means (for example, laws or written policies) and informal practices (social practices or community expectations, for example) (Alexander et al., 1985; National Research Council, 1993). Chronic community violence can have a long-term impact on children's development and level of functioning (Garbarino et al., 1992). Poverty, too, is an important risk factor for many problem behaviors (Simcha-Fagan & Schwartz, 1986). Adolescents who live in economically deprived neighborhoods characterized by extreme poverty, poor living conditions, and high unemployment are more likely to engage in delinquent behavior than adolescents living in less deprived neighborhoods (Yoshikawa, 1994). The quality of housing in these communities is often poor and the levels of violence and crime high. Access to health care, social services, and good schools is often limited for people who live in poverty (Yoshikawa, 1994). Statistics for arrest, mortality, and morbidity have long suggested that ethnic minority youths have higher rates of delinquent behavior, but racial differences tend to vanish when findings are controlled for poverty (National Research Council, 1993). Because researchers have found it difficult to separate the influences of race and community from those of poverty, it has been a challenge for them to make a strong argument for the relationship between poverty and delinquency (National Research Council, 1993).

Neighborhood characteristics such as high population density and mobility, physical deterioration, low attachment to the community, and high crime rates are related to juvenile participation in delinquent behavior (Bursik & Webb, 1982; Farrington et al., 1990). Neighborhoods with high residential mobility usually have higher rates of juvenile crime (Wilson & Herrnstein, 1985), and when neighborhoods undergo rapid residential shifts, victimization and crime rates increase (Sampson, 1986). Research has shown that children who reside in disorganized communities with high population density, physical deterioration, and low levels of attachment to the neighborhood are at higher risk of delinquent behavior than those who do not live in such communities (Laub & Sampson, 1988; Sampson & Laub, 1994).

FAMILY RISK FACTORS

The influence of family is another correlate of antisocial behavior. Family management problems, family conflict, family history of high-risk behaviors, and parents' inappropriate modeling behavior (including attitudes and involvement in problem behaviors) are associated with delinquent behavior and conduct disorder. Poor family management practices include unspecified expectations for behavior, inadequate supervision and monitoring, and excessively severe or inconsistent punishment. Children exposed to poor family management practices are at higher risk of developing conduct disorder and engaging in delinquent behavior (Farrington, 1991; Patterson & Dishion, 1985; Thornberry, 1994). Lack of parental monitoring and supervision has been found to increase the likelihood that a child will develop aggressive and violent patterns of behavior during adolescence and early adulthood (Farrington, 1991). A comprehensive review of parenting behavior by Loeber and Stouthamer-Loeber (1986) found that two of the strongest correlates of conduct disorder in children were poor parental supervision and lack of parental involvement in their child's activities. Other studies of delinquent children have supported these findings (Cernkovich & Giordano, 1987; Voorhis, Cullen, Mathers, & Garner, 1988). Harsh, abusive forms of discipline and inconsistent discipline also have been linked to severe conduct problems (Patterson, 1982; Patterson & Stouthamer-Loeber, 1984; Robins, 1991; Voorhis et al., 1988).

Parental conflict and coercive family interaction create a situation that reinforces aggressiveness and coercive behavior (Farrington, 1991; Loeber & Dishion, 1984; Patterson & Dishion, 1985). Furthermore, Loeber and Dishion found that domestic violence increases the likelihood of an adolescent's involvement in violent behavior. In their study, boys who lived in homes characterized by parental conflict or marital discord had a high predilection for fighting.

Adolescents who experience family instability because of divorce also have higher rates of delinquent behavior (Rutter & Giller, 1983; Williams et al., 1996). Divorce can create disruption and conflict, of course, but the major life transition necessitated by a divorce is perhaps more consequential. Divorce can reduce risk that is attributable to family conflict, but risk caused by the major transition in the child's life might be heightened. If resolving family conflict by some means other than divorce is an option, then that route should be considered. If such a solution is not feasible, however, removing the conflict through divorce is preferable to letting the conflict remain. Keep in mind that although family management problems are a risk factor for conduct disorder and delinquency, family structure is not. Although it may be harder for a single parent to manage the family unit, the children of single parents are at no greater risk than those of two-parent families strictly because of family composition. Risk factors for delinquency may increase over time—many times, the outcome of divorce is poverty, and poverty exerts a direct contextual influence on children and their families. But all else being equal, the children of divorce may in fact be at less risk than those who remain with two parents in conflict.

Other risk factors in the family domain include problematic parental attitudes toward antisocial behavior, parental involvement in problem behavior, parental discord, and parental psychopathology. Parental norms and attitudes toward crime and antisocial behavior influence the behavior of children (Hawkins & Weis, 1985). Children of criminal and alcoholic parents are at increased risk of conduct disorder (Rutter, 1985). According to Robins (1991), the risk factor of parental criminal or substance-using behavior is a more striking indicator when the mother rather than the father is affected. Finally, children (especially boys) who display aggressive and antisocial behavior have been found to be more likely to come from families where the parents are suffering from depression (Biederman, Munir, & Knee, 1987; Frick et al., 1992; Robins, 1991).

SCHOOL-RELATED RISK FACTORS

Early and persistent antisocial behavior, academic failure in elementary school, and low degree of commitment to school are risk factors within the school domain that are predictors of adolescent delinquent behavior. Studies have found that individuals who exhibit aggressive behavior, negative moods, and temper tantrums in early childhood are more likely to have problems with aggressive behavior in adolescence and early adulthood (Cairns & Cairns, 1991; Farrington, 1991; Institute of Medicine, 1994; Loeber, 1988; Robins, 1978). Farrington found that 57 percent of boys identified as aggressive at ages 12 to 14 had been convicted of a violent crime by age 32.

No matter what its cause (for example, learning disability, boredom, or a poor teacher–student match, for example), school failure is a common risk factor identified in children diagnosed with conduct disorder (Robins, 1991). Poor academic performance is related to the prevalence and onset of delinquency, and the converse is true as well (Maguin & Loeber, 1996). Maguin and Loeber found that 35 percent of low-performing children became delinquent, but only 21 percent of high-performing children did so. They also found that the relationship between academic performance and delinquent behavior was stronger for white students than for African American students and stronger for males than for females. Farrington (1991) found that boys who were low achievers in school or had low levels of intelligence had an increased chance of developing aggressive behavior. Beginning at grade four, academic achievement is a stable predictor of later behavior problems (Hawkins, Catalano, & Brewer, 1995b; Yoshikawa, 1994).

The level of an individual's commitment to education is considered one of the best predictors of delinquent behavior for adolescents (Gottfredson, 1986). Children who have discipline problems and who display a lack of commitment to school (as defined by a lack of motivation to achieve) were more likely than other children to develop problem behavior (Farrington, 1991). Cairns and colleagues (1989) found that both boys and girls who were rated as aggressive and who had academic problems were much more likely than others to drop out of school early.

INDIVIDUAL AND PEER GROUP RISK FACTORS

Research indicates that adolescents who think favorably of delinquent behaviors and associate with delinquent peers are more likely than most other adolescents to engage in delinquent behaviors themselves (Cairns et al., 1989; Elliott et al., 1989; Farrington, 1991; Hawkins et al., 1992; Williams et al., 1996). The socialization perspective of delinquent behavior posits that peer affiliation provides the environment for learning and reinforcing attitudes and beliefs and behavior. Delinquent peers and delinquent beliefs, it is widely agreed, are strongly correlated with delinquent behavior. This correlation creates a consistent environment for the onset and continuation of delinquent behavior (Elliott et al., 1985; Matsueda, 1982; Thornberry, Lizotte, Krohn, Farnworth, & Jang, 1994). Attitudes and beliefs favorable toward deviance are considered to be risk factors for violent offending behavior (Elliott, 1994a).

Research has shown that peer influence, including friendship and group affiliation, has a significant effect on delinquent behaviors (Cairns et al., 1989; Elliott & Menard, 1992; Matsueda & Heimer, 1987; Thornberry et al., 1994; Williams, 1994). Peers serve an important role in the socialization and social development of adolescents. Furthermore, research demonstrates that adolescents tend to associate with peers of similar background (in terms of age, gender, and socioeconomic status, for example), and with peers whose values concerning delinquent behavior are similar to their own (Cairns et al., 1989; Elliott et al., 1985). Studies by Agnew (1991) and Elliott et al.(1985), using the National Youth Study, found a strong association between delinquent peers and delinquent behavior. However, the strength of this association may vary by race or ethnicity. Matsueda and Heimer (1987) found that, as a predictor, delinquent peers had a greater effect for white youths than for African American youths. More research is needed on racial and gender differences, but it is clear that high levels of delinquent behavior are strongly correlated with high levels of association with delinquent friends (Menard & Elliott, 1994); thus, peer-related social interactions appear to strongly affect delinquent behavior.

GENETIC OR BIOLOGICAL RISK FACTORS

Research literature suggests that biological and congenital predispositions for delinquent behavior exist. In her study of families, Robin (1966) found that one of the best predictors of antisocial behavior in boys was the criminal arrest of their fathers. Other methods of studying genetic influences have also shown promising results. In comparing identical, or monozygotic (MZ), twins with dizygotic (DZ) twins, Mednick and Volavka (1980) found that MZ twins had a much higher concordance rate for delinquent behavior than did DZ twins. In an effort to isolate the effects of hereditary and environmental influences, Mednick, Gabrielli, and Hutchings (1984) studied a cohort of 14,427 nonfamilial children adopted in Denmark between 1924 and 1947. They found that the correlations of conviction rates for biological fathers and their adopted-away sons were much higher than those for the adoptive fathers and their adopted sons.

Other genetic and biological factors related to delinquency include perinatal trauma, neurotoxins, and alcohol or drug use by the mother (Hawkins et al., 1992; Institute of Medicine, 1994). Litt (1971) discovered that perinatal trauma predicted impulsive criminal offenses. Antecedent factors associated with hyperactivity and impulsivity include exposure of children to neurotoxins such as lead, early malnutrition, low birthweight, and mother's substance use during pregnancy (Breslau, Klein, & Allen, 1988; Needleman, 1982), and children with hyperactivity and impulsive behaviors are at greater risk of developing antisocial behaviors (Loeber, 1990). (For a further review of biological and genetic risk factors for antisocial behaviors, see Farrington, 1994).

The role of genetics and biology in the development of conduct disorder continues to be sorted out by researchers. Some studies support a role for genetic factors, but the data are often inconsistent, inconclusive, and methodologically flawed. Conduct disorder is a relatively new diagnosis—it appeared in the DSM for the first time in 1968—and practitioners are not always fully consistent in their assessment of the diagnosis. Despite these limitations, some research studies have found both genetic and environmental predictors of individuals' involvement in antisocial behavior (Cadoret et al., 1983, Earls & Jung, 1987; Offord et al., 1987). In two studies, one on adopted children (Cadoret et al., 1983) and one on biological fathers and male adoptees (Mednick, Gabrielli, & Hutchings, 1983), researchers concluded that there is a genetic predisposition to conduct disorder.

Conduct disorder occurs at a much higher rate in boys than in girls (Robins, 1991), and these differences in rates have remained stable over time. In the Ontario Child Health Study, Offord et al. (1987) found that among children ages six to 11, boys had a rate of conduct disorder that was six times that of girls. These gender differences were not as pronounced in older adolescents (Offord & Waters, 1983). It is not clear whether the differences for gender are caused by behavioral influences or by differences in socialization that result in different expectations for boys and girls (Institute of Medicine, 1994).

Results of the investigation of racial differences in the prevalence of conduct disorder have been mixed. Rutter (1978) found racial differences among 10-year-old children in London. In the United States, studies have shown no differences in the proportions of African American and white youths who reported three or more symptoms of conduct disorder before age 15 (Robins, 1991). Although African Americans are overrepresented in the criminal justice system as juvenile delinquents, data collected on self-reported delinquent acts has shown no differences in involvement across racial groups (Elliott et al., 1985; Elliott, Huizinga, & Morse, 1986).

Other risk factors that are common in children who are diagnosed with conduct disorder include attention deficit hyperactivity disorder (ADHD), difficult temperament, poor coordination and motor skills, developmental delays, and low IQ (Offord et al., 1992; Robins, 1991). The literature shows a significant relationship between ADHD and conduct disorder: In the Ontario Child Health Study, 40 percent of the children with an initial diagnosis of ADHD had symptoms of conduct disorder four years later (Offord et al., 1992). Although Rutter and Quinton (1984) found that children with difficult temperaments were more likely to develop later behavioral problems, overall research on childhood temperament as a risk factor for conduct disorder has been inconclusive. Other possible antecedents to conduct disorder identified in the research literature include difficulty with language, low level of intelligence, neurological impairment, and low birthweight (Breslau et al., 1988; Loeber, 1990; Robins, 1991; White et al., 1989).

PROTECTIVE FACTORS FOR EFFECTIVE RISK REDUCTION

Criminologists and others have researched the implications of protective factors associated with the prevention and treatment of delinquent behavior and conduct disorder (Farrington & Hawkins, 1991; Farrington & West, 1993; Minde, 1992; Rutter, 1985; Stouthamer-Loeber, Leober, & Farrington, 1993; Werner & Smith, 1992). Protective factors can be conceptualized in different ways (Cowen & Work, 1988; Rutter, 1985; Werner, 1989). One might think of them as the opposite of risk factors.

For example, poor parental supervision would be considered a risk factor, whereas proactive family management would be a protective factor. Some might consider them to be freestanding, with no corresponding risk factor. Last, protective factors may be viewed as variables that interact or buffer the effect of risk factors. Some have theorized that protective factors are processes that inhibit the onset of antisocial behavior (Rutter, 1990; Werner, 1989). As discussed in chapter 2, protective factors are related to the concept of resilience and associated with successful adaptation to stressful life situations (Rutter, 1985, 1990).

The protective factors that reduce the chance that a child at risk will become involved in delinquent behavior include female gender, strong attachment to parents, commitment to family, resilient or positive temperament or disposition, ability to adjust and recover, supportive family environment, strong external support system that reinforces children's coping efforts, healthy beliefs, prosocial orientation (easy disposition and enjoyment of social interaction, for example), and social problem-solving skills (Farrington, 1994; Hawkins et al., 1992; Hawkins et al., 1995b). The literature highlights some protective factors that reduce the chances that an at-risk child will develop conduct disorder: moderate intelligence, easy disposition, social skills, strong bond with parent, prosocial peer group, academic success, and self-discipline (Minde, 1992; Robins, 1991; Rutter, 1979; Werner & Smith, 1992).

ASSESSING RISK AND PROTECTIVE FACTORS FOR CONDUCT DISORDER AND DELINQUENCY

ASSESSMENT STRATEGIES

The choice of strategy for assessing risk and protective factors for conduct disorder and delinquency depends on the purpose of the assessment and the age of the target population. For example, conduct disorder can have an early onset marked by aggressive and disruptive behavior in the preschool years, or it can develop during late childhood or adolescence as a pattern of delinquent behavior or substance abuse (Institute of Medicine, 1994). Purposes of the assessment might be, among other things, to assess the clinical intake of children or the risk and protective factors in a population (for epidemiological studies or for decision making in the judicial system, for example) or to test etiological theory (Achenbach & Edelbrock, 1983; Loeber & Stouthamer-Loeber, 1986, 1987; Office of Juvenile Justice and Delinquency Prevention, 1995). Assessment procedures can follow either a clinical or an empirical approach; both approaches predict the likelihood of conduct problems based on current levels of risk and protective factors. This chapter explores three different empirically based assessment instruments used for different purposes.

THE CHILD BEHAVIOR CHECKLIST

One widely used instrument for assessing children's conduct problems and competencies is the Child Behavior Checklist (CBCL) developed by Achenbach and Edelbrock (1983). The original form, designed to be completed by a parent in about 15 minutes, consists of 118 items describing problematic child behaviors and four items asking about behavioral competencies (Achenbach & Edelbrock, 1983). Empirical analyses of CBCL responses concerning children assessed at intake for clinical services were used to construct scales for rating problem behavior at different ages for both genders. Three competence scales (activities, school, social) reflecting the content of the items were also developed. All scales were normed on nonclinical samples and subjected to extensive validation analyses. Two more versions of the CBCL have been developed recently, one reporting teacher responses and the other responses from youths (see, for example, Achenbach, 1991; Achenbach & Edelbrock, 1986).

The CBCL is noteworthy because of the extensive empirical work that has gone into its development and because of its widespread use for assessing conduct problems in young (even four-year-old) children. It is useful for clinicians assessing children referred for treatment, for research into behavior problems, and for epidemiological assessments of the prevalence of problem behaviors in children. It has been used to assess the risk factor of early and persistent behavior problems and the protective factor of social competence in studies predicting delinquency (Atkins & Stoff, 1993; Edelbrock, 1986; Hawkins et al., 1992; Lizotte, Chard-Wierschem, Loeber, & Stern, 1992). It is easy for parents, teachers, and youths to complete, and the evidence that it reveals is reliable and valid for different age, gender, racial, and socioeconomic groups (Achenbach, 1991; Achenbach & Edelbrock, 1983).

Because the CBCL focuses entirely on the youth's behavior, however, its use as an ecological assessment of risk and protective factors has thus far been limited. The CBCL reflects the historical focus on the individual in the prevention and treatment of conduct disorder and delinquency. Within an ecological approach to problem behaviors, the CBCL is best considered as only a small part of a comprehensive assessment of risk and protection. Nevertheless, the CBCL is useful for the construction of a standardized profile of a youth's behavior that can be compared to normative data. This can be a valuable, albeit incomplete, part of an assessment of risk and protective factors.

JUVENILE PROBATION AND AFTERCARE ASSESSMENT OF RISK

Unlike the CBCL, which offers an extensive assessment of behavior, risk assessment instruments used in the juvenile justice system typically supply only cursory information. The purpose of justice system assessments depends on the stage of processing and the primary concerns of that stage (Office of Juvenile Justice and Delinquency Prevention, 1995). For example, the Juvenile Probation and Aftercare Assessment of Risk (Baird, 1984) seeks to classify offenders into one of three levels of risk for reoffending, so that the appropriate level of supervision can be determined for probationers or parolees. The instrument includes eight items shown by empirical research to predict recidivism (age at first adjudication, prior criminal behavior, prior institution placements, drug use, alcohol use, inadequate parental control, school disciplinary problems, problematic peer relationships). A similar instrument developed for the state of Michigan successfully discriminated between high-, medium-, and low-risk offenders in Wayne County, Michigan. The recidivism rate among the high-risk group was 76 percent, 39 percent for the medium-risk group, and 19 percent for the low-risk group (Office of Juvenile Justice and Delinquency Prevention, 1995).

Other empirical instruments are also beginning to be widely used in the juvenile justice system. In placement and custody decisions, for example, policies must consider the appropriate sanctions for the juvenile's offense, as well as the chances that the juvenile will commit other offenses. Assessment tools designed to inform placement and custody decisions typically give more weight to the seriousness of the current offense than would be justified by the weak relationship between offense seriousness and risk of reoffending. Instruments for needs assessment, which typically present a complete array of risk and protective factors related to potential areas of intervention (family relationships, parental problems and skills, level of academic achievement, school problems, peer relationships, life and vocational skills, for example), are also being used in the juvenile justice system to guide case planning and workload decisions (Office of Juvenile Justice and Delinquency Prevention, 1995). In contrast, risk screening for detention decisions focuses on the relative likelihood that an offender will represent a threat to the community or run away during the period between arrest and adjudication. Risk screening in decisions concerning placement includes assessment of the seriousness of the offense, risk of reoffending, and risk for behavior problems during placement.

In each instance, however, the primary focus of these measures is on assessment of the individual offender's behavior and a few characteristics of his or her immediate social environment. Although these measures offer a broader view of the risk and protective factor ecology than do behavioral assessment tools such as the CBCL, they still provide a fairly limited picture of the ecology of risk and protection. They are useful for classifying individuals within certain defined levels of risk and need, which is valuable for both treatment and policy decision making. However, they are less useful for planning ecologically based delinquency prevention strategies for populations whose members have not yet exhibited conduct problems. Given the apparent effectiveness of prevention strategies that are environmentally and population-focused—they reduce risk for delinquency, violence, and substance abuse (see, for example, Brewer, Hawkins, Catalano, & Neckerman, 1995; Hawkins, Arthur, & Catalano, 1995a)—methods for assessing a broader array of risk and protective factors should be used by communities, juvenile justice personnel, and others concerned with the prevention of delinquency and interventions for conduct disorders.

STUDENT SURVEY OF RISK AND PROTECTIVE FACTORS AND ADOLESCENT ANTISOCIAL BEHAVIOR

The Center for Substance Abuse Prevention (CSAP) recently funded efforts to develop and validate an epidemiological assessment tool designed to cover a comprehensive array of risk and protective factors for delinquency and substance abuse (Pollard, Hawkins, Catalano, & Arthur, 1995). The self-report instrument contains 129 items measuring 22 risk factors and 11 protective factors in the community, school, family, and peer and individual domains. It is designed for 10- to 18-year-old youths and can be completed by most students in school during one class period (45 to 50 minutes). The instrument was developed, pretested, pilot tested, and administered to statewide samples of students in grades six through 12 in six states under a contract with CSAP (Pollard et al., 1995). The survey scales have been validated for the samples within and across states, and work is proceeding to test the reliability and validity of the scales and constructs within various demographic subgroups within the total sample. (A copy of the six-state student survey is available from the Social Development Research Group, School of Social Work, University of Washington, Seattle.)

This instrument differs markedly in both content and purpose from the others discussed in this chapter. The focus of this instrument is on epidemiological assessment of risk and protective factors in a group or population; it does not seek to assess individuals' characteristics to predict behavior. Much of the content of survey items reflects respondents' ratings of community, school, family, and peer-group environments. Such assessments are useful in identifying specific populations at high risk for the development of conduct problems, including delinquency and substance abuse, and for identifying specific risk and protective factors that are either elevated or depressed in the assessed populations. This information can be used to direct more prevention services to high-risk populations and to select prevention strategies that focus on the risk or protective factors identified as priorities. Thus, this instrument is particularly useful in designing interventions that address population-level needs rather than individual-level needs.

ISSUES IN ASSESSMENT OF RISK AND PROTECTIVE FACTORS

Several important issues should be considered before assessing risk and protective factors for behavior problems. First, it should be understood that risk and protective factors are probabilistic, not perfect, predictors of conduct disorder and delinquency. The accurate prediction of a specific individual's conduct problems is typically problematic, characterized by high false-positive rates along with false negatives (Loeber & Stouthamer-Loeber, 1987). That is, many youths whose current risk and protective status would indicate high risk of behavior problems do not develop conduct problems, whereas some low-risk youths do develop serious behavior problems. The implications of this fact are serious indeed: Prevention and treatment programs that target individuals based on assessments of risk and protective factors might exclude low-risk youths who need intervention, and high-risk youths who otherwise would have avoided conduct problems might not do so because of the iatrogenic effects of labeling and net widening.

MULTIPLE GATING

One method advocated for reducing errors in prediction is multiple gating (Loeber, 1988; Loeber, Dishion, & Patterson, 1984; Loeber & Hay, 1994; Loeber et al., 1991). This stepwise assessment procedure uses an inexpensive, broad assessment (a school or teacher survey, for example) as the first gate. Individuals identified at the first gate as potentially at risk of conduct problems are then reassessed some time later through a more intensive assessment procedure (for example, a parent survey). The youths passing through the second gate still classified as high risk can be assessed again through an even more intensive process (interview with the parent or child or both) to determine the need for intervention to reduce risk for conduct problems. Loeber, Dishion, and Patterson (1984) demonstrated that such procedures could considerably improve the accuracy of prediction while minimizing the costs of risk assessment.

POPULATION-LEVEL PROGRAMS

Another approach to the issue of imperfect prediction is to focus the assessments for risk and protective factors at the population level rather than the individual level. Universal programs can still address specific factors that the assessment identified within the population as particularly elevated (risk) or depressed (protection) (Hawkins et al.,1992b). This is consistent with an ecological approach to prevention and promotion of well-being, wherein the focus of programs is on reducing risk and enhancing protection in the physical and social environment, not on changing the individual. This approach also minimizes the potential for labeling and for the problems associated with net widening, because the goal of the intervention is to protect and promote health in the entire population.

METHODOLOGICAL LIMITATIONS

A third issue concerns the validity of instruments for assessing risk and protective factors across demographic groups. Gottfredson and her colleagues (1995), in their assessment of promising instruments for measuring risk and protective factors for adolescent drug abuse, noted that few of the instruments have been validated with different racial and ethnic groups. Questions about how differences in age and socioeconomic status affect the validity and appropriateness of assessment tools also need to be answered. Current research, such as that by Gottfredson and Koper (1993), the six-state consortium (Pollard et al., 1995), and others should soon shed light on these issues.

IMPLICATIONS FOR PREVENTION, EARLY INTERVENTION, AND TREATMENT

Recent advances in knowledge about risk factors for delinquency and conduct disorder have important implications for intervention and prevention. Risk factors are found all across the social ecology of childhood, in the domains of the individual, family, school, peers, and community. Moreover, the greater the number of risks in an individual's life, the greater the probability of involvement in delinquent behavior (Institute of Medicine, 1994). Thus, to be most effective, prevention and treatment interventions must focus on a comprehensive approach that includes individual, family, school, peer-cluster, and community risk factors. Program development should emphasize the reduction of risk factors and, at the same time, the enhancement of identified protective factors.

Current strategies use three approaches for implementing intervention and prevention programs focusing on risk and protection for at-risk individuals and groups. The first approach is universal preventive interventions. Universal interventions are targeted at a whole population group that has not been identified on the basis of individual risk (Institute of Medicine, 1994). Universal interventions are desirable when their per-person cost is low and the risk of negative effects from the intervention is minimal. These interventions are good for everyone in the population. Risk factors such as poverty, exposure to toxins, problematic laws and norms, poor family management practices, and inadequate parenting skills can be lessened through a broad approach. Programs focused on providing training in parenting and social skills can universally enhance protective factors without targeting a specific population (Institute of Medicine, 1994). Other programs and policies targeted toward decreasing poverty, improving policing strategies, developing more effective educational systems, limiting exposure to neurotoxins, and reducing the availability of handguns and drugs are considered to be universal precautions (Loftin et al., 1991; Loftin et al., 1993).

The second approach, selective preventive interventions, uses programs primarily focused on at-risk populations. Selective interventions are targeted to individuals or groups whose risk of becoming delinquent or having conduct disorder is higher than average. These programs also use intervention with the ultimate goal of minimizing risks and enhancing or increasing protective factors. The third approach, indicated preventive interventions, are targeted to high-risk individuals thought to have a predisposition for delinquency or conduct disorder. Indicated interventions are targeted to individuals whose symptoms appear early but who have not initiated delinquent acts or do not meet the diagnostic criteria for conduct disorder. Indicated interventions have historically been referred to as early interventions. The underpinnings of universal, selected, and indicated prevention interventions are identified risk factors. Several researchers have reviewed well-designed evaluations of preventive interventions targeting delinquent behavior (Hawkins & Catalano, 1992; Hawkins et al., 1992b; Howell et al., 1995; Institute of Medicine, 1994).

Reducing delinquency and conduct disorder requires a multifaceted, coordinated approach; early intervention is a critical step. Although strategies for delinquency prevention or intervention focus on all social domains, strategies for conduct disorder intervention focus primarily on the individual and family. However, because conduct disorder and delinquency exhibit common risk factors (aggressive behavior, school failure, poor family management, and family conflict), and because behaviors are similar and overlapping in the two disorders, intervention strategies within the individual and family domains overlap.

INDIVIDUAL AND FAMILY INTERVENTIONS

Programs for prenatal and perinatal health and parent education provide health and parenting education, job and education counseling, and emotional and social support during and after pregnancy (Olds, Henderson, Tatelbaum, & Chamberlin, 1986). The main goal of prenatal and parenting education programs is to minimize biological or genetic risk factors and to increase protective factors such as parenting and job skills. Evaluations of prenatal programs have been favorable. Results from program participation include decreased perinatal difficulties and fewer referrals for child abuse or neglect, as well as higher birthweight and increased parent employment (Greenwood, Model, Rydell, & Chiesa, 1996; Olds, Henderson, Chamberlin, & Tatelbaum, 1986).

Intensive family preservation services are short-term crisis interventions for families whose children are at risk of out-of-home placement. These programs address the risk factors of poor family management practices and family conflict as they simultaneously enhance family bonding and social supports (Bergquist, Szwejda, &

Pope, 1993; Henggeler & Borduin, 1990; Henggeler, Melton, & Smith, 1992). Interventions such as intensive family preservation services have been shown to be effective for reducing family conflict and children's antisocial behavior and for improving family management practices (Dumas, 1989; Henggeler & Borduin, 1990; Henggeler et al., 1992; Rossi, 1992; Shadish, 1992). Other interventions include marital and family services and training to improve parent–child interaction by minimizing the risk factors of family conflict, poor family management practices, and family instability (Dumas, 1989; Strayhorn & Weidman, 1991).

PEER CLUSTER INTERVENTIONS

Interventions specifically targeted at peer-group relationships should build social skills, acceptable techniques for conflict resolution, and skills for avoiding problem behavior (Prothrow-Stith & Weissman, 1991). Sound conflict-resolution and violence-prevention curriculums attempt to minimize early aggressive behavior and association with delinquent peers and to enhance the protective factors of skills in childhood social problem-solving skills and anger management. Many such curriculums have been extensively evaluated. Results from these evaluation studies indicate some effectiveness, but more studies are needed to address possible interaction effects and cultural relevancy.

Empowering Children to Survive and Succeed (ECSS) (Brennan, 1992) and Second Step (Committee for Children, 1992) are two curriculums that target elementary schoolchildren. Both programs emphasize interpersonal problem solving, appropriate social behavior, and self-control and self-confidence. The evaluation of ECSS showed mixed results, whereas the evaluation of the Second Step program showed improvement for students who received the structured lessons (Brennan, 1992; Committee for Children, 1988, 1992).

Think First and Fighting Fair are programs developed for students in middle school. They focus on mediation, negotiation, control of anger and aggression, problem solving, and school attendance incentives (Larson, 1992; Marvel et al., 1993). Both programs were effective in decreasing problem behaviors within the school settings where they were administered (Marvel et al., 1993; Larson, 1992). Positive Adolescents Choices Training (PACT) is a violence-prevention program specifically designed for African American youths in middle school (Hammond & Yung, 1991, 1993). PACT seeks to develop social skills for resisting peer pressure and for problem solving and negotiation, using African American role models and culturally relevant vignettes. Evaluation studies showed decreases in physical and verbal aggression and lower rates of juvenile court-recorded offenses for program participants (Hammond & Yung, 1993).

Dealing with Conflict and Violence Prevention are two curriculums specifically targeted at high school students. Activities in these curriculums build participant trust, group cohesion, and ability to identify and articulate consequences and alternatives to violence (Bretherton, Collins, & Ferretti, 1993; Prothrow-Stith, 1987; Webster, 1993). Student participants in both curriculums had significantly decreased self-reported violent behavior and fighting in comparison to a control group (Bretherton et al., 1993; Webster, 1993). Both curriculums showed promising results, but concerns about methodology require more extensive evaluation studies.

Peer mediation programs and peer counseling are two other programs used to address problem-solving abilities and peer culture (Gottfredson, 1987). Such programs are often carried out in conjunction with programs for conflict resolution and violence prevention. Peer mediation programs address risk factors of early and persistent antisocial behavior and association with antisocial peers (Lam, 1989); peer counseling addresses risk factors of favorable attitudes toward delinquency, alienation, rebelliousness, and association with delinquent peers (Gottfredson, 1987). Protective factors, including problem solving to resolve conflicts, healthy beliefs, and clear expectations for behavior, are the enhancement goals of peer mediation and peer counseling programs; peer counseling also seeks to enhance opportunities and skills to communicate. Lam's (1989) review of 14 peer mediation programs suggests that they had positive effects on knowledge, attitudes, and behaviors. The research on peer counseling has produced mixed results (Gottfredson, 1987).

INTERVENTIONS IN EDUCATIONAL SETTINGS

Intervention strategies in the school domain—classroom organization, classroom management, and instructional strategies, for instance—promote the protective factors of bonding to school, opportunities for achievement, and involvement with prosocial peers. These strategies seek to reduce the risk factors of academic failure, low commitment to school, and early antisocial behavior (Hawkins et al., 1992b; Slavin, 1994). The "good behavior game," which uses motivational tools to decrease aggressive behavior and reward learning and prosocial behavior, has been introduced to children in elementary school (Kellam, Rebok, Ialongo, & Mayer, 1994). The good behavior game is an example of an educational program that seeks to advance cognitive and social development in younger children. Kellam, Rebok, Ialongo, and Mayer (1994) found that children enrolled in classes using this program showed significantly less aggressive behavior than the control group. The Seattle Social Development Project (SSDP), a longitudinal study developed to prevent delinquency, used a multicomponent prevention program in selected elementary school classrooms (Hawkins & Lam, 1987). The strategies of the program included cooperative learning, proactive classroom management, and interactive teaching. Results indicate that SSDP produced significant effects in various areas, including a reduction in aggressive behavior; moreover, longitudinal analysis revealed that children in the program classrooms were less likely to have initiated delinquent behavior (Hawkins et al., 1992b).

There are many other research studies on prevention strategies within the educational setting—too many, in fact, to allow extensive coverage in this chapter. In brief, other strategies shown to be effective include behavioral monitoring, attendance reinforcement, special education placements, and graduation incentives (Brooks, 1975; Bry, 1982; Hahn, Leavitt, & Aaron, 1994; Safer, 1990; Taggart, 1995).

COMMUNITY STRATEGIES

Strategies developed for use in the community domain attempt to address the risk factors of community disorganization, low neighborhood attachment, and norms that are tolerant of crime. These strategies include regulations restricting the carrying, sale, and transfer of firearms; mandatory sentencing; community mobilization; and new, innovative policing strategies. Regulations and restrictions regarding firearms and mandatory sentencing are universal in nature. Policing strategies and community mobilization are often implemented in high-risk communities, where the goals are to enhance opportunities for involvement and bonding with police and to promote the prosocial skills needed to monitor and influence the neighborhood. Community policing and neighborhood block watch programs are currently being implemented in high-risk communities to decrease delinquent behavior. Evaluations of community policing programs show mixed results for effectiveness (Rosenbaum, Yeh, & Wilkinson, 1994; Thurman, Giacomazzi, & Bogen, 1993). Neighborhood block watch programs have been shown to be effective in decreasing victimization rates of burglary and vandalism (Lindsay & McGillis, 1986).

Conclusion

Many of these interventions in various domains show significant or mixed effectiveness at addressing risk factors, and evaluation studies, although inadequate, have noted positive program effects. It is apparent that more rigorous design and methods will be needed to determine the preventive effectiveness of these interventions. Previous research indicates the various domains in which interventions will be useful, but more work is necessary to learn what will facilitate more effective approaches and where gaps might be in our knowledge base. For instance, few studies have investigated the relationship of race and gender to delinquent behavior and the effectiveness of prevention interventions across racial or cultural groups and gender. Critical issues of racial disparities in delinquency require more research using a risk-factor approach. Studies are also needed to investigate causal factors that may explain racial and gender differences in the prevalence of and participation in delinquent behavior. Notwithstanding the need for further research, the effectiveness of programs reviewed here and elsewhere warrants their continued use by practitioners who work to mitigate risk factors and enhance protective factors for children.

References

Achenbach, T. M. (1991). *Manual for the Teacher's Report Form and 1991 Profile.* Burlington: University of Vermont, Department of Psychiatry.

Achenbach, T. M., & Edelbrock, C. (1983). *Manual for the Child Behavior Checklist and revised Child Behavior Profile.* Burlington, VT: University Associates in Psychiatry.

Achenbach, T. M., & Edelbrock, C. (1986). *Manual for the Teacher's Report Form and teacher's version of the Child Behavior Profile.* Burlington, VT: University Associates in Psychiatry.

Agnew, R. (1985). Social control theory and delinquency: A longitudinal test. *Criminology, 23,* 47–61.

Agnew, R. (1991). A longitudinal test of social control theory and delinquency. *Journal of Research in Crime and Delinquency, 28*(2), 126–156.

Alexander, G. R., Massey, R. M., Gibbs, T., & Altekruse, J. M. (1985). Firearm-related fatalities: An epidemiological assessment of violent death. *American Journal of Public Health, 75,* 165–168.

American Psychiatric Association. (1994). *Diagnostic and statistical manual of mental disorders* (4th ed.). Washington, DC: Author.

Atkins, M. S., & Stoff, D. M. (1993). Instrumental and hostile aggression in childhood disruptive behavior disorders. *Journal of Abnormal Child Psychology, 21,* 165–178.

Baird, S. C. (1984). *Classification of juveniles in corrections: A model systems approach.* Madison, WI: National Council on Crime and Delinquency.

Barnes, G. M., & Farrell, M. P. (1992). Parental support and control as predictors of adolescent drinking, delinquency and related problem behaviors. *Journal of Marriage and the Family, 54,* 763–776.

Bergquist, C., Szwejda, D., & Pope, G. (1993). *Evaluation of Michigan's Families First Program: Summary report.* Lansing: Michigan Department of Social Services.

Biederman, J., Munir, K., & Knee, D. (1987). Conduct and oppositional disorder in clinically referred children with attention deficit disorder: A controlled family study. *Journal of the American Academy of Child and Adolescent Psychiatry, 26,* 724–727.

Brennan, T. (1992). *Project evaluation: ECSS program of the Lesson One Foundation beginners' curriculum (pre-kindergarten to third grade).* Boston: Lesson One Foundation.

Breslau, N., Klein, N., & Allen, L. (1988). Very low birth weight: Behavioral sequelae at nine years of age. *Journal of the American Academy of Child and Adolescent Psychiatry, 67,* 605–612.

Bretherton, D. L., Collins, L., & Ferretti, C. (1993). Dealing with conflict: Assessment of a course for secondary school students. *Australian Psychologist, 28,* 105–111.

Brewer, D. D., Hawkins, J. D., Catalano, R. F., & Neckerman, H. J. (1995). Preventing serious, violent, and chronic juvenile offending: A review of evaluations of selected strategies in childhood, adolescence, and the community. In J. C. Howell, B. Krisberg, J. D. Hawkins, & J. J. Wilson (Eds.), *Sourcebook on serious, violent, & chronic juvenile offenders* (pp. 61–142). Thousand Oaks, CA: Sage Publications.

Brooks, B. D. (1975). Contingency management as a means of reducing school truancy. *Education, 95,* 206–211.

Bry, B. H. (1982). Reducing the incidence of adolescent problems through preventive intervention: One- and five-year follow-up. *American Journal of Community Psychology, 10,* 265–276.

Bureau of Justice Statistics. (1994). *Bureau of Justice Statistics sourcebook of criminal justice statistics.* Washington, DC: Author.

Bursik, R. J., Jr., & Webb, J. (1982). Community change and patterns of delinquency. *American Journal of Sociology, 88,* 24–42.

Cadoret, R. J., Cain, C. A., & Crowe, R. R. (1983). Evidence for gene–environment interaction in the development of adolescent antisocial behavior. *Behavior Genetics, 13,* 301–310.

Cairns, R. B., & Cairns, B. D. (1991). Social cognition and social networks: A developmental perspective. In D. Pepler & K. H. Rubin (Eds.), *The development and treatment of childhood aggression* (pp. 249–278). Hillsdale, NJ: Lawrence Erlbaum.

Cairns, R. B., Cairns, B. D., Neckerman, H. J., Ferguson, L. L., & Gariepy, J. L. (1989). Growth and aggression: Childhood to early adolescence. *Developmental Psychology, 25,* 320–330.

Cernkovich, S. A., & Giordano, P. C. (1987). Family relationships and delinquency. *Criminology, 25,* 295–319.

Committee for Children. (1988). *Second Step, grades 1–3, pilot project 1987–88: Summary report.* Seattle: Author.

Committee for Children. (1992). *Evaluation of Second Step, preschool–kindergarten: A violence prevention curriculum kit.* Seattle: Author.

Cowen, E., & Work, W. (1988). Resilient children, psychological wellness, and primary prevention. *American Journal of Community Psychology, 16,* 591–607.

Dembo, R., Williams, L., & Schmeidler, J. (1994). Psychosocial, alcohol/other drug use, and delinquency differences between urban black and white male high-risk youth. *International Journal of Addictions, 29,* 461–483.

Dryfoos, J. G. (1990). *Adolescents at risk: Prevalence and prevention.* New York: Oxford University Press.

Dumas, J. E. (1989). Treating antisocial behavior in children: Child and family approaches. *Clinical Psychology Review, 9,* 197–222.

Dunford, F. W., & Elliott, D. S. (1984). Identifying career offenders using self-reported data. *Journal of Research in Crime and Delinquency, 21,* 57–86.

Earls, F. (1981). Temperament characteristics and behavior problems in three-year-old children. *Journal of Nervous and Mental Disease, 169,* 367–373.

Earls, F., & Jung, K. (1987). Temperament and home environment characteristics as causal factors in the early development of childhood psychopathology. *Journal of the American Academy of Child and Adolescent Psychiatry, 26,* 491–498.

Edelbrock, C. (1986). Behavioral rating of children diagnosed for attention deficit disorder. *Psychiatric Annals, 16,* 36–40.

Elliott, D. S. (1994a). *Youth violence: An overview.* Boulder: University of Colorado, Center for the Study and Prevention of Violence.

Elliott, D. S. (1994b). Serious violent offenders: Onset, developmental course and termination—the American Society of Criminology 1993 presidential address. *Criminology, 32,* 1–21.

Elliott, D. S., Huizinga, D., & Ageton, S. (1985). *Explaining delinquency and drug use.* Beverly Hills, CA: Sage Publications.

Elliott, D. S., Huizinga, D., & Menard, S. (1989). *Multiple problem youth: Delinquency, substance, and mental health problems.* New York: Springer-Verlag.

Elliott, D. S., Huizinga, D., & Morse, B. (1986). Self-reported violent offending—A descriptive analysis of juvenile violent offenders and their offending careers. *Journal of Interpersonal Violence, 1,* 472–514.

Farrington, D. P. (1983). Offending from 10 to 25 years of age. In K. T. Van Dusen & S. A. Mednick (Eds.), *Prospective studies of crime and delinquency* (pp. 17–37). Boston: Kluwer-Nijhoff.

Farrington, D. P. (1991). Childhood aggression and adult violence. In D. Pepler & K. H. Rubin (Eds.), *The development and treatment of childhood aggression* (pp. 2–29). Hillsdale, NJ: Lawrence Erlbaum.

Farrington, D. P. (1994). Early developmental prevention of juvenile delinquency. *Criminal Behaviour and Mental Health, 4,* 209–227.

Farrington, D. P., & Hawkins, J. D. (1991). Predicting participation, early onset, and later persistence in officially recorded offending. *Criminal Behaviour and Mental Health, 1,* 1–33.

Farrington, D. P., Loeber, R., Elliott, D. S., Hawkins, J. D., Kandel, D. B., Klein, M. W., McCord, J., Rowe, D. C., & Tremblay, R. E. (1990). Advancing knowledge about the onset of delinquency and crime. In B. B. Lahey & A. E. Kazdin (Eds.), *Advances in clinical child psychology* (Vol. 13, pp. 283–342). New York: Plenum Press.

Farrington, D. P., & West, D. J. (1990). The Cambridge Study in delinquent development. In H. J. Kerner & G. Kaiser (Eds.), *Criminality: Personality, behavior and life history* (pp. 115–138). Berlin: Springer-Verlag.

Farrington, D. P., & West, D. J. (1993). Criminal, penal, and life histories of chronic offenders: Risk and protective factors in early identification. *Criminal Behaviour and Mental Health, 3,* 492–523.

Federal Bureau of Investigation. (1993). *Crime in the United States, 1992.* Washington, DC: U.S. Government Printing Office.

Federal Bureau of Investigation. (1994). *Age-specific arrest rates and race-specific arrests for selected offenses, 1965–1992.* Washington, DC: U.S. Government Printing Office.

Feldman, R. A., Caplinger, T. E., & Wodarski, J. S. (1983). *The St. Louis conundrum: The effective treatment of antisocial youths.* Englewood Cliffs, NJ: Prentice-Hall.

Forehand, R., Wierson, M., Frame, C., Kempton, T., & Armistead, L. (1991). Juvenile delinquency entry and persistence: Do attention problems contribute to conduct problems? *Journal of Behavior Therapy & Experimental Psychiatry, 22*(4), 261–264.

Frick, P. J., Lahey, B. B., Loeber, R., Stouthamer-Loeber, M., Christ, M. G., & Hanson, K. (1992). Familial risk factors to oppositional defiant disorder and conduct disorder: Parental psychopathology and maternal parenting. *Journal of Consulting and Clinical Psychology, 60,* 49–55.

Garbarino, J., DuBrow, N., Kostelny, K., & Pardo, C. (1992). *Children in danger: Coping with the consequences of community violence.* San Francisco: Jossey-Bass.

Gillmore, M. R., Hawkins, J. D., Catalano, R. F., Day, L. E., & Abbott, R. D. (1991). Structure of problem behaviors in preadolescence. *Journal of Consulting and Clinical Psychology, 59,* 499–506.

Gottfredson, D. C. (1986). An empirical test of school-based environmental and individual intervention to reduce the risk of delinquent behavior. *Criminology, 24,* 705–731.

Gottfredson, D. C. (1987). An evaluation of an organization development approach to reducing school disorder. *Evaluation Review, 11,* 739–763.

Gottfredson, D. C., Harmon, M. A., Gottfredson, G. D., Jones, E. M., & Celestin, J. A. (1995). *ATOD prevention program outcomes and instrument selection system*

(CSAP draft). Rockville, MD: National Center for the Advancement of Prevention.

Gottfredson, D. C., & Koper, C. S. (1993). *Race and sex differences in the measurement of risk for delinquency and substance abuse.* Paper presented at the annual meeting of the American Society of Criminology, Phoenix, AZ.

Greenwood, P. W., Model, K. E., Rydell, C. P., & Chiesa, J. (1996). *Diverting children from a life of crime: Measuring costs and benefits.* Santa Monica, CA: Rand Corporation.

Hahn, A., Leavitt, T., & Aaron, P. (1994). *Evaluation of the Quantum Opportunities Program (QOP): Did the program work? A report on the postsecondary outcomes and cost-effectiveness of the QOP program (1989–1993).* Waltham, MA: Brandeis University.

Hammond, W. R. & Yung, B. R. (1993). *Evaluation and activity report: Positive Adolescents Choice Training (PACT) program.* Dayton, OH: Wright State University, School of Professional Psychology.

Hammond, W. R. & Yung, B. R. (1991). Preventing violence in at-risk African American youth. *Journal of Health Care for the Poor and Underserved, 2*, 359–373.

Hamparian, D., Schuster, R., Dinitz, S., & Conrad, J. (1978). *The violent few: A study of dangerous juvenile offenders.* Lexington, MA: Lexington Books.

Hawkins, J. D., Arthur, M. W., & Catalano, R. F. (1995a). Prevention of substance abuse. In M. Tonry & D. Farrington (Eds.), *Crime and justice: An annual review of research* (Vol. 18*)*. Chicago: University of Chicago Press.

Hawkins, J. D., & Catalano, R. F. (1992). *Communities that care: Action for drug abuse prevention.* San Francisco: Jossey-Bass.

Hawkins, J. D., Catalano, R. F., & Brewer, D. D. (1995b). Preventing serious, violent, and chronic juvenile offending: Effective strategies from conception to age 6. In J. C. Howell, B. Krisberg, J. D. Hawkins, & J. J. Wilson (Eds.), *Sourcebook on serious, violent, and chronic juvenile offenders* (pp. 47–61). Thousand Oaks, CA: Sage Publications.

Hawkins, J. D., Catalano, R. F., & Miller, J. Y. (1992a). Risk and protective factors for alcohol and other drug problems in adolescence and early adulthood: Implication for substance abuse prevention. *Psychological Bulletin, 112*, 64–105.

Hawkins, J. D., Catalano, R. F., Morrison, D. M., O'Donnell, J., Abbott, R. D., & Day, L. E. (1992b). The Seattle Social Development Project: Effects of the first four years on protective factors and problem behaviors. In J. McCord & R. Tremblay (Eds.), *The prevention of antisocial behavior in children* (pp. 139–161). New York: Guilford Press.

Hawkins, J. D., Jenson, J. M., Catalano, R. F., & Lishner, D. M. (1988). Delinquency and drug use: Implications for social services. *Social Service Review, 62*, 258–284.

Hawkins, J. D., & Lam, T. (1987). Teacher practices, social development, and delinquency. In J. D. Burchard & S. N. Burchard (Eds.), *Prevention of delinquent behavior.* Newbury Park, CA: Sage Publications.

Hawkins, J. D., & Weis, J. G. (1985). The social development model: An integrated approach to delinquency prevention. *Journal of Primary Prevention, 6*(2), 73–97.

Henggeler, S. W., & Borduin, C. M. (1990). *Family therapy and beyond: A multisystemic approach to treating the behavior problems of children and adolescents.* Pacific Grove, CA: Brooks/Cole.

Henggeler, S. W., Melton, G. B., & Smith, L. A. (1992). Family preservation using multisystemic therapy: An effective alternative to incarcerating serious juvenile offenders. *Journal of Consulting and Clinical Psychology, 60,* 953–961.

Herbert, M. (1987). *Conduct disorders of childhood and adolescence: A social learning perspective* (2nd ed.). Chichester, England: John Wiley & Sons.

Hirschi, T. (1969). *Causes of delinquency.* Berkeley: University of California Press.

Howell, J. C., Krisberg, B., Hawkins, J. D., & Wilson, J. J. (Eds.). (1995). *Sourcebook on serious, violent and chronic juvenile offenders.* Thousand Oaks, CA: Sage Publications.

Huizinga, D., Loeber, R., & Thornberry, T. (1993). *Urban delinquency and substance abuse.* Washington, DC: Office of Juvenile Justice and Delinquency Prevention.

Institute of Medicine. (1994). *Reducing risks for mental disorders: Frontiers for preventive intervention research.* Washington, DC: National Academy Press.

Johnston, L. D., O'Malley, P. M., & Bachman, J. G. (1994). *National survey results on drug use from the Monitoring the Future Study, 1975–1993.* Rockville, MD: National Institute on Drug Abuse.

Jones, M. A., & Krisberg, B. (1994). *The facts about youth and violence in America.* San Francisco: National Council on Crime and Delinquency.

Kandel, D., Simcha-Fagan, O., & Davies, M. (1986). Risk factors for delinquency and illicit drug use from adolescence to young adulthood. *Journal of Drug Issues, 16,* 67–90.

Kellam, S. G., Rebok, G. W., Ialongo, N., & Mayer, L. S. (1994). The course and malleability of aggressive behavior from early first grade into middle school: Results of a developmental epidemiologically based preventive trial. *Journal of Child Psychology and Psychiatry, 35,* 259–281.

Lam, J. A. (1989). *The impact of conflict resolution programs on schools: A review and synthesis of the evidence.* Amherst, MA: National Association for Mediation in Education.

Larson, J. D. (1992). Anger and aggression management techniques through the Think First Curriculum. *Journal of Offender Rehabilitation, 18,* 101–117.

Laub, J. H., & Sampson, R. J. (1988). Unraveling families and delinquency: A reanalysis of the Gluecks' data. *Criminology, 26,* 355–380.

Lindsay, B., & McGillis, D. (1986). Citywide community crime prevention: An assessment of the Seattle program. In D. P. Rosenbaum (Ed.), *Community crime prevention: Does it work?* (pp. 46–67). Beverly Hills, CA: Sage Publications.

Litt, S. M. (1971). *Perinatal complications and criminality.* Unpublished doctoral dissertation, University of Michigan, Ann Arbor.

Lizotte, A. J., Chard-Wierschem, D. J., Loeber, R., & Stern, S. B. (1992). A shortened Child Behavior Checklist for delinquency studies. *Journal of Quantitative Criminology, 8,* 233–245.

Loeber, R. (1990). Development and risk factors of juvenile antisocial behavior and delinquency. *Clinical Psychology Review, 10,* 1–41.

Loeber, R. (1988). Natural histories of conduct problems, delinquency, and associated substance use: Evidence for developmental progressions. In B. B. Lahey & A. E. Kazdin (Eds.), *Advances in clinical child psychology* (Vol. 11, pp. 73–124). New York: Plenum Press.

Loeber, R. (1990). Development and risk factors of juvenile antisocial behavior and delinquency. *Clinical Psychology Review, 10,* 1–41.

Loeber, R., & Dishion, T. J. (1984). Boys who fight at home and school: Family conditions influencing cross-setting consistency. *Journal of Consulting and Clinical Psychology, 52,* 759–768.

Loeber, R., Dishion, T. J., & Patterson, G. R. (1984). Multiple gating: A multistage assessment procedure for identifying youths at risk for delinquency. *Journal of Research on Crime and Delinquency, 24,* 7–32.

Loeber, R., & Hay, D. F. (1994). Developmental approaches to aggression and conduct problems. In M. Rutter & D. F. Hay (Eds.), *Development through life: A handbook for clinicians* (pp. 488–516). Oxford: Blackwell Scientific.

Loeber, R., & Stouthamer-Loeber, M. (1986). Family factors as correlates and predictors of juvenile conduct disorder and delinquency. In M. Tonry & N. Morris (Eds.), *Crime and justice* (Vol. 7, pp. 29–149). Chicago: University of Chicago Press.

Loeber, R., & Stouthamer-Loeber, M. (1987). The prediction of delinquency. In H. C. Quay (Ed.), *Handbook of juvenile delinquency* (pp. 325–382). New York: John Wiley & Sons.

Loeber, R., & Stouthamer-Loeber, M. S. (1993). Developmental progressions. In D. Huizinga, R. Loeber, & T. Thornberry (Eds.), *Urban delinquency and substance abuse: Technical report* (chap. 7). Washington, DC: Office of Juvenile Justice and Delinquency Prevention.

Loeber, R., Stouthamer-Loeber, M. S., van Kammen, W., & Farrington, D. P. (1991). Initiation, escalation, and desistance in juvenile offending and their correlates. *Journal of Criminal Law and Criminology, 82,* 36–82.

Loftin, C., McDowell, D., & Wiersema, B. (1993). Evaluating effects of changes in gun laws. *American Journal of Preventive Medicine, 9*(Suppl.: Firearms injuries: A public health approach), 39–43.

Loftin, C., McDowell, D., Wiersema, B., & Cottey, T. J. (1991). Effects of restrictive licensing of handguns on homicide and suicide in the District of Columbia. *New England Journal of Medicine, 23,* 1615–1620.

Maguin, E., & Loeber, R. (1996). Academic performance and delinquency. In M. Tonry (Ed.), *Crime and justice: Vol. 20. A review of research* (pp. 145–264). Chicago: University of Chicago Press.

Marvel, J., Moreda, I., & Cook, I. (1993). *Developing conflict resolution skills in students: A study of the Fighting Fair model.* Miami: Peace Education Foundation.

Matsueda, R. L. (1982). Testing control theory and differential association: A causal modeling approach. *American Sociological Review, 47,* 489–504.

Matsueda, R. L., & Heimer, K. (1987). Race, family structure, and delinquency: A test of differential association and social control theories. *American Sociological Review, 52*, 826–840.

McCord, J. (1988). Parental behavior in the cycle of aggression. *Psychiatry, 51*, 14–23.

Mednick, S. A., Gabrielli, W. F., & Hutchings, B. (1984). Genetic influences in criminal convictions: Evidence from an adoption cohort. *Science, 224*, 891–894.

Mednick, S., Moffitt, T., Gabrielli, W. F., Jr., & Hutchings, B. (1983). Genetic influence in criminal behavior: Evidence from an adoption cohort. In K. T. Van Dusen & S. A. Mednick (Eds.), *Prospective studies of crime and delinquency* (pp. 39–56). Boston: Kluwer-Nijhoff.

Mednick, S. A., & Volavka, J. (1980). Biology and crime. In N. Morris & M. Tonry (Eds.), *Crime and justice: An annual review of research* (Vol. 2, pp. 85–158). Chicago: University of Chicago Press.

Menard, S., & Elliott, D. S. (1994). Delinquent bonding, moral beliefs, and illegal behavior: A three-wave panel model. *Justice Quarterly, 11*, 173–188.

Minde, K. (1992). Aggression in preschoolers: Its relation to socialization. *Journal of the American Academy of Child and Adolescent Psychiatry, 31*, 853–862.

National Coalition of State Juvenile Justice Advisory Groups. (1993). *Myths and realities: Meeting the challenges of serious violent and chronic juvenile offenders: 1992 annual report*. Washington, DC: Author.

National Research Council. (1993). *Losing generations: Adolescents in high-risk settings*. Washington, DC: National Academy Press.

Needleman, H. L. (1982). The neuropsychiatric implications of low level exposure to lead. *Psychological Medicine, 12*, 461–463.

Office of Juvenile Justice and Delinquency Prevention. (1993). *Comprehensive strategy for serious, violent, and chronic juvenile offenders (OJJDP Program Summary)*. Washington, DC: U. S. Department of Justice.

Office of Juvenile Justice and Delinquency Prevention. (1995). *Guide for implementing the comprehensive strategy for serious, violent, and chronic juvenile offenders*. Washington, DC: U.S. Department of Justice.

Offord, D. R., Boyle, M. H., Racine, Y. A., Fleming, J. E., Cadman, D. T., Blum, H. M., Byrne, C., Links, P. S., Lipman, E. L., & Macmillan, H. L. (1992). Outcome, prognosis and risk in a longitudinal follow-up study. *Journal of the American Academy of Child and Adolescent Psychiatry, 31*, 916–923.

Offord, D. R., Boyle, M. H., Szatmari, P., Rae Grant, N. I., Links, P. S., Cadman, D. T., Byles, J. A., Crawford, J. W., Blum, H. M., Byrne, C., Thomas, H., & Woodward, C. A. (1987). Ontario Child Health Study: Six month prevalence of disorder and rates of service utilization. *Archives of General Psychiatry, 44*, 832–836.

Offord, D. R., & Waters, B. G. (1983). Socialization and its failure. In M. D. Levine, W. B. Carey, A. C. Crocker, & R. T. Gross (Eds.), *Developmental–behavioral pediatrics* (pp. 650–682). Philadelphia: W. B. Saunders.

Olds, D. L., Henderson, C. R., Jr., Chamberlin, R., & Tatelbaum, R. (1986). Preventing child abuse and neglect: A randomized trial of nurse home visitation. *Pediatrics, 78*, 65–78.

Olds, D. L., Henderson, C. R., Jr., Tatelbaum, R., & Chamberlin, R. (1986). Improving the delivery of pre-natal care and outcomes of pregnancy: A randomized trial of nurse home visitation. *Pediatrics, 77*, 16–27

Patterson, G. R. (1982). *Coercive family process.* Eugene, OR: Castalia.

Patterson, G. R., & Dishion, T. J. (1985). Contributions of families and peers to delinquency. *Criminology, 23*, 63–77.

Patterson, G. R. & Stouthamer-Loeber, M. (1984). The correlation of family management practices and delinquency. *Child Development, 55*, 1299–1307.

Pollard, J. A., Hawkins, J. D., Catalano, R. F., & Arthur, M. W. (1995). *Development of a school-based survey measuring risk and protective factors predictive of substance abuse in adolescent populations.* Unpublished manuscript, Social Development Research Group, University of Washington, Seattle.

Pope, C. E., & Feyerherm, W. (1990a). Minority status and juvenile justice processing: An assessment of the research literature (Part 1). *Criminal Justice Abstracts, 22,* 327–336.

Pope, C. E., & Feyerherm, W. (1990b). Minority status and juvenile justice processing: An assessment of the research literature (Part 2). *Criminal Justice Abstracts, 22,* 527–542.

Pope, C. E., & Feyerherm, W. (1993). *Minorities and the juvenile justice system.* Washington, DC: Office of Juvenile Justice and Delinquency Prevention.

Prothrow-Stith, D. (1987). *Violence prevention curriculum for adolescents.* Newton, MA: Education Development Center.

Prothrow-Stith, D., & Weissman, M. (1991). *Deadly consequences: How violence is destroying our teenage population and a plan to begin solving the problem.* New York: HarperCollins.

Robins, L. N. (1966). *Deviant children grown up: A sociological and psychiatric study of sociopathic personality.* Baltimore: Williams & Wilkins.

Robins, L. N. (1978). Sturdy childhood predictors of adult anti-social behavior: Replications from longitudinal studies. *Psychological Medicine, 8*, 611–622.

Robins, L. N. (1981). Epidemiological approaches to natural history research: Antisocial disorder in children. *Journal of the American Academy of Child Psychiatry, 20,* 566–580.

Robins, L. N. (1991). Conduct disorder. *Journal of Child Psychology and Psychiatry and Allied Disciplines, 32,* 193–212.

Rosenbaum, D. P., Yeh, S., & Wilkinson, D. L. (1994). Impact of community policing on police personnel: A quasi-experimental test. *Crime & Delinquency, 40,* 331–353.

Rossi, P. H. (1992). Assessing family preservation programs. *Children and Youth Services Review, 14,* 77–97.

Rutter, M. (1978). Family, area, and school influences in the genesis of conduct disorders. In L. A. Hersov and M. Berger, (Eds.), *Aggression and antisocial behaviour in childhood and adolescence.* (pp. 95–114). London: Pergamon Press.

Rutter, M. (1979). Protective factors in children's responses to stress and disadvantage. In M. W. Kent & J. E. Rolf, (Eds.), *Primary prevention of psychopathology, Vol. 3: Social competence in children.* Hanover, NH: University Press of New England.

Rutter, M. (1985). Resilience in the face of adversity: Protective factors and resistance to psychiatric disorder. *British Journal of Psychiatry, 147,* 598–611.

Rutter, M. (1990). Psychosocial resilience and protective mechanisms. In J. Rolf (Ed.), *Risk and protective factors in the development of psychopathology.* Cambridge, England: Cambridge University Press.

Rutter, M., & Giller, H. (1983). *Juvenile delinquency: Trends and perspectives.* New York: Penguin Books.

Rutter, M., & Quinton, D. (1984). Parental psychiatric disorders: Effects on children. *Psychological Medicine, 14,* 853–880.

Safer, D. J. (1990). A school intervention for aggressive adolescents. In L. J. Hertzberg, G. F. Ostrum, & J. R. Field (Eds.), *Violent behavior: Vol. 1. Assessment and intervention.* Great Neck, NY: PMA Publishing.

Sampson, R. J. (1986). Crimes in cities: The effects of formal and informal social control. In A. J. Reiss & M. Tonry (Eds.), *Crime and justice: An annual review of research: Vol. 8: Communities and crime* (pp. 271–311). Chicago: University of Chicago Press.

Sampson, R. J., & Laub, J. H. (1994). Urban poverty and the family context of delinquency: A new look at structure and process in a classic study. *Child Development, 65,* 523–540.

Shadish, W. R., Jr. (1992). Do family and marital psychotherapies change what people do? A meta-analysis of behavioral outcomes. In T. D. Cook, H. Cooper, D. S. Cordray, H. Hartmann, L. V. Hedges, R. J. Light, T. A. Louis, & F. Mosteller (Eds.), *Meta-analysis for explanation: A casebook* (pp. 129–208). New York: Russell Sage Foundation.

Shannon, L. W. (1978). A longitudinal study of delinquency and crime. In S. Wellford (Ed.), *Quantitative studies in crime.* Beverly Hills, CA: Sage Publications.

Shannon, L. W. (1988). *Criminal career continuity: Its social context.* New York: Human Sciences Press.

Shannon, L. W. (1991). *Changing patterns in delinquency and crime: A longitudinal study in Racine.* Boulder, CO: Westview Press.

Simcha-Fagan, O., & Schwartz, J. E. (1986). Neighborhood and delinquency: An assessment of contextual effects. *Criminology, 24,* 667–703.

Slavin, R. E. (1994). School and classroom organization in beginning reading: Class size, aides, and instructional grouping. In R. E. Slavin, N. L. Karweit, & B. A. Wasik (Eds.), *Preventing early school failure: Research, policy, and practice* (pp. 122–142). Boston: Allyn & Bacon.

Snyder, H. (1988). *Court careers of juvenile offenders.* Washington, DC: Office of Juvenile Justice and Delinquency Prevention.

Stouthamer-Loeber, M., Loeber, R., & Farrington, D. P. (1993). The double edge of protective and risk factors for delinquency: Interrelations and developmental patterns. *Development & Psychopathology, 5,* 683–690.

Strayhorn, J. M., & Weidman, C. S. (1991). Follow-up one year after Parent-Child Interaction Training: Effects on behavior of preschool children. *Journal of American Academy of Child and Adolescent Psychiatry, 30,* 138–143.

Taggart, R. (1995). *Quantam Opportunity Program*. Philadelphia: Opportunities Industrialization Centers of America.

Thornberry, T. P. (1994). *Violent families and youth violence* (Fact Sheet 21). Washington, DC: Office of Juvenile Justice and Delinquency Prevention.

Thornberry, T. P. (1996). Empirical support for interactional theory: A review of the literature. In J. D. Hawkins (Ed.), *Delinquency and crime: Current theories* (pp. 198–236). New York: Cambridge University Press.

Thornberry, T. P., Lizotte, A. J., Krohn, M. D., Farnworth, M., & Jang, S. J. (1994). Delinquent peers, beliefs, and delinquent behavior: A longitudinal test of interactional theory. *Criminology, 32*, 47–83.

Thurman, Q. C., Giacomazzi, A., & Bogen, P. (1993). Research note: Cops, kids, and community policing: An assessment of a community policing demonstration project. *Crime & Delinquency, 39*, 554–564.

Tolan, P., & Guerra, N. (1994). *What works in reducing adolescent violence: An empirical review of the field* (Report submitted to the Center for the Study and Prevention of Violence). Chicago: University of Illinois at Chicago.

Tracy, P. E., Wolfgang, M. E., & Figlio, R. M. (1985). *Delinquency in two birth cohorts*. Washington, DC: National Institute of Juvenile Justice and Delinquency Prevention.

Tracy, P. E., Wolfgang, M. E., & Figlio, R. M. (1990). *Delinquency in two birth cohorts*. Washington, DC: National Institute of Juvenile Justice and Delinquency Prevention.

U.S. Department of Justice, Federal Bureau of Investigation. (1965–1994). *Uniform crime reports of the United States*. Washington, DC: U.S. Government Printing Office.

Voorhis, P. V., Cullen, F. T., Mathers, R. A., & Garner, C. C. (1988). The impact of family structure and quality on delinquency: A comparative assessment of structural and functional factors. *Criminology, 26*, 235–248.

Webster, D. W. (1993). The unconvincing case for school-based conflict resolution programs for adolescents. *Health Affairs, 12*, 126–141.

Werner, E. E. (1989). High risk children in young adulthood: A longitudinal study from birth to 32 years. *American Journal of Orthopsychiatry, 59*, 72–81.

Werner, E. E., & Smith, R. S. (1992). *Overcoming the odds: High risk children from birth to adulthood*. Ithaca, NY: Cornell University Press.

West, D. J., & Farrington, D. P. (1977). *The delinquent way of life*. London: Heinemann.

White, J. L., Moffitt, T. E., & Silva, P. A. (1989). A prospective replication of the protective effects of IQ in subjects at high risk for juvenile delinquency. *Journal of Clinical and Consulting Psychology, 57*, 719–724.

Williams, J. H. (1994). *Understanding substance use, delinquency involvement, and juvenile justice involvement among African American and European American adolescents*. Unpublished doctoral dissertation, University of Washington, Seattle.

Williams, J. H., Stiffman, A. R., & O'Neal, J. L. (1996). *Environmental and behavioral factors associated with violence among urban African American youths*. Manuscript submitted for publication.

Wilson, J. Q., & Herrnstein, R. J. (1985). *Crime and human nature.* New York: Simon & Schuster.

Wolfgang, M. E. (1983). Delinquency in two birth cohorts. *American Behavioral Scientist, 27*(1), 75–86.

Wolfgang, M. E., Figlio, R. F., & Sellin, T. (1972). *Delinquency in a birth cohort.* Chicago: University of Chicago Press.

Wolfgang, M. E., Thornberry, T. P., & Figlio, R. M. (1987). *From boy to man—from delinquency to crime: Follow up to the Philadelphia birth cohort of 1945.* Chicago: University of Chicago Press.

Yoshikawa, H. (1994). Prevention as cumulative protection: Effects of early family support and education on chronic delinquency and its risks. *Psychological Bulletin, 115,* 28–54.

9

PREVENTING SEXUALLY TRANSMITTED INFECTIONS AMONG ADOLESCENTS

Kathleen A. Rounds

Sexually transmitted infections (STIs), also called sexually transmitted diseases (STDs), are a major health problem for adolescents. Adolescents account for one-quarter of the 12 million new cases of STI diagnosed each year, according to estimates from the American Social Health Association ([ASHA], 1995). Others estimate that at least one in every four adolescents will become infected before graduating from high school (Shafer & Moscicki, 1991). For various biological, developmental, psychological, and social reasons, sexually active adolescents are at higher risk than adults for contracting STIs, and adolescent girls more so than adolescent boys (the anatomy of adolescent girls makes them more susceptible to STIs, less likely to experience symptoms, and more difficult to diagnose). The more severe consequences of STIs for adolescents—again, especially girls, whose fertility, pregnancy, and offspring may be jeopardized—may not become apparent until young adulthood.

This chapter describes the nature of the adolescent STI epidemic; details the risk and protective factors associated with adolescents' risky sexual behavior and examines differences in these factors by age, gender, and race or ethnicity; discusses the assessment of risky behavior; and addresses implications for prevention, early intervention, and treatment of STIs in the adolescent population. For the purposes of this chapter, human immunodeficiency virus (HIV) will be regarded as an STI, because the major route of transmission of HIV for adolescents is through sexual activity.

THE STI EPIDEMIC AMONG ADOLESCENTS

According to Cates and Rauh (1985), it was not until the 1970s that public health and medical clinicians began to understand the true magnitude of STIs among adolescents. They realized then that STIs had reached epidemic levels among adolescents, and the HIV epidemic in the 1980s and 1990s further heightened awareness of the magnitude of the STI problem. As Yarber & Parrillo (1992) stated, STIs "are common infections affecting adolescents" (p. 331). They are common indeed: Among sexually active adolescents, STIs are the most common infections for which adolescents seek health care (Shafer & Moscicki, 1991). The risk of contracting nearly all STIs is greater for sexually active adolescents than for any other age group (Rosenthal, Cohen, & Biro, 1994). In a recent survey of adolescents and adults, three of 10 adolescents noted that they knew another adolescent with an STI (ASHA, 1996a).

Because of the variability in reporting across states and within states, accurate, complete statistics on the incidence and prevalence of STIs among adolescents are difficult to obtain. Syphilis, gonorrhea, and HIV are the only STIs reported by all 50 states to the Centers for Disease Control and Prevention (CDC) (Cates, 1991; Irwin & Millstein, 1986). Common STIs, such as genital herpes and chlamydia, are not tracked systematically in all states. Screening for several STIs varies considerably among states, depending on the availability of laboratory testing facilities and federal and state funding for screening programs (ASHA, 1996b). Another factor that influences the accuracy of STI statistics is the differential reporting between public clinics and private physicians. Prevalence estimates for certain STIs vary widely, depending on the source of data. For example, estimates derived from public clinic data, particularly STI clinics, are affected by selection bias—that is, individuals who tend to have higher rates of STIs, such as homeless youths and prostitutes, are overrepresented in public clinic data (Cates, 1991). Moreover, many cases of STIs are asymptomatic, so many infected adolescents do not seek health care because they are not experiencing symptoms, and those who do have symptoms may not have access to care. Statistics on the number of HIV cases among adolescents illustrates the problem: because most adolescents who contract HIV will not develop symptoms that would lead to testing until young adulthood, the number of adolescents infected with HIV is much higher than reported (DiClemente, 1992; Kelly, Murphy, Sikkema, & Kalichman, 1993).

Multiple syndromes and more than 20 organisms are known to be transmitted sexually. The most common STIs reported among adolescents include two bacterial infections, Neisseria gonorrhea and Chlamydia trachomatis. Syphilis, another bacterial STI, is less common, but it is clearly on the rise in the adolescent population. Viral STIs that this population frequently contracts include genital herpes (herpes simplex virus, or HSV type 2) and genital warts (human papillomavirus). Viral STIs are life-long infections for which there is no known cure (ASHA, 1995; Cates & Rauh, 1985; Shafer & Moscicki, 1991). HIV, although estimated to be less common than other viral STIs among adolescents, obviously has the most serious consequences. Bacterial STIs, if detected, can usually be treated and cured with antibiotics, but the most common of these, gonorrhea and chlamydia, are often asymptomatic and thus go undetected.

Rates for these STIs, which are based on data from large population studies, are reported below. The rates for STIs are much higher for certain subgroups of the adolescent population—youths in the juvenile justice system, adolescents who reside where the STI prevalence is high among the general population, adolescents who exchange sex for drugs or other benefits, adolescents who are runaways or homeless, and youths who live where the prevalence of intravenous drug use is high (Wood & Shoroye, 1993). The highest STI rates during the 1980s were among adolescents who were poor, pregnant, or incarcerated (Morris, Warren, & Aral, 1993). Adolescent girls, particularly young ones, are especially susceptible to infection from some STIs because of cervical ectopy and the immaturity of their urogenital immune system (Cates & Rauh, 1985; CDC, 1994b; Shafer & Moscicki, 1991).

BACTERIAL STIs

Neisseria Gonorrhea

The statistics on gonorrhea for adolescents probably give the best picture of STI trends and patterns in this population (Cates, 1991). The 1993 gonorrhea rate for youths 15 to 19 years old was 742.1 per 100,000 population, with the rate for females

(868.0) higher than that for males (622.7) (CDC, 1994b). Overall rates have declined in the last three years, but they remain higher than for other age groups. In 1992, for youths ages 10 to 14, the gonorrhea rate was higher for females than for males in 49 states (including the District of Columbia). The gonorrhea rate was higher for females 15 to 19 years old than for males in the same age group in 45 states. Adolescent females between the ages of 15 and 19 in fact have the highest rate of gonorrhea among all women (ASHA, 1995).

The national trend appears to be toward a reduction in gonorrhea rates for adolescents: The rate dropped 15 percent from 1982 to 1992 for males and 26 percent for females in the 15- to 19-year-old age group (CDC, 1994b, 1995b). Another troubling trend remains, however: the gap between the rates for white and African American teenagers widened considerably during the 1980s (Cates, 1991).

Chlamydia Trachomatis

Chlamydia is not a reportable disease, it is often asymptomatic, and it may not be diagnosed until a woman experiences fertility problems or an ectopic pregnancy (Newcomer & Baldwin, 1992). Data on adolescent rates of chlamydia are therefore difficult to come by. Nevertheless, the ASHA, which reports that the disease is the fastest-spreading STI in the United States and the cause of at least half of the cases of pelvic inflammatory disease (PID) diagnosed each year, estimates that 29 percent to 30 percent of sexually active teenage girls have chlamydia (ASHA, 1995). Women are disproportionately affected by this STI: the 1992 nationwide rate for females of all ages (270.0 per 100,000) was more than six times higher than the rate for males (43.9 per 100,000) (CDC, 1995b). Large-scale screening projects have demonstrated that adolescent women have higher rates than older women (CDC, 1994b). The national aim stated in *Healthy People 2000— National Health Promotion and Disease Prevention Objectives* (Public Health Service, 1991) is to reduce chlamydia infections to no more than 170 cases per 100,000 people.

Syphilis

Between 1975 and 1987 the prevalence of primary and secondary syphilis doubled among 15- to 19-year-old girls (Shafer & Moscicki, 1991), and rates have been climbing since 1986; 10- to 19-year-olds accounted for 10 percent of the 45,535 cases reported in 1989 (Morris et al., 1993). The rate for white males of all ages decreased during the 1980s, but the rate for African American males has rapidly increased since 1985 (Cates, 1991).

Viral STIs

Herpes Simplex Virus

Herpes simplex virus (HSV) is not a reportable STI and thus exact prevalence rates are not available. Like chlamydia, HSV can be asymptomatic and go undetected. In fact, perhaps two-thirds of the individuals who are infected do not know that they have herpes (ASHA, 1995). Cates (1991) estimated that by the end of adolescence, 4 percent of white youths and 17 percent of African American youths will carry the HSV virus.

Human Papilloma Virus

Human papilloma virus (HPV), which commonly presents as genital warts, concerns public health officials especially because it is associated with cervical cancer (Newcomer & Baldwin, 1992; Shafer & Moscicki, 1991). HPV, too, can be asymptomatic and go undetected. The prevalence of HPV among adolescents is not known precisely, but ASHA (1995) estimates that as many as 30 percent of sexually active adolescents have the virus.

AIDS and HIV

As of 1992, 846 youths between 15 and 19 years of age (588 males and 258 females) had been diagnosed with AIDS. Because the period between HIV infection and clinical diagnosis of AIDS is lengthy—from eight to 10 years—these numbers truly underestimate the cases of HIV infection among adolescents (Chesney, 1994; Strunin, 1994). Even an enormous increase in the number of HIV-infected adolescents would not increase the current number of AIDS diagnoses for adolescents. That increase would most likely show up later as an increase in AIDS diagnoses for individuals 20 to 29 years old (DiClemente, 1992; Strunin, 1994). Seroprevalence studies of HIV would be better indicators of HIV infection in adolescents, but no population-based studies of adolescent HIV seroprevalence exist. The available data are primarily from seroprevalence studies of adolescents entering the Job Corps, the military, homeless shelters, and STI clinics—subpopulations that may be at higher risk of HIV. DiClemente (1992) reviewed these studies and found that, in general, seropositive rates were higher for African American than for Hispanic adolescents and lowest for white youths. Chesney (1994) stressed that seroprevalence data should be examined together with rates for risky sexual behavior and rates for prevalence of other STIs among adolescents. It would then be possible to determine whether rates of HIV infection are disproportionately high among specific adolescent subgroups—for example, sexually active adolescents in communities with high rates of HIV and drug use (Wallace, 1990), adolescents who are incarcerated or otherwise involved in the juvenile justice system (Wood & Shoroye, 1993), and adolescents who exchange sex for drugs or money (Rosenthal et al., 1994).

CONSEQUENCES OF STIs FOR ADOLESCENTS

Adolescents may not experience the consequences of STI infections until young adulthood. HIV infection clearly results in the most severe consequences: chronic illness with bouts of opportunistic infections, disability, and death. The consequences for other STIs include cervical cancer, heart disease, blindness, reproductive problems, and affected offspring (Cates, 1991; Yarber & Parrillo, 1992). For example, untreated gonorrhea and chlamydia in females can lead to pelvic inflammatory disease (PID), which puts women at risk of reproductive loss (through ectopic pregnancy, for example) and infertility. It is estimated that 50 percent to 75 percent of all ectopic pregnancies are related to a history of chalymydia or gonorrhea (Yarber & Parrillo, 1992). Girls ages 15 to 19 have the highest rate of hospitalization for acute and chronic PID among all age groups of women (ASHA, 1995). Investigators estimate that the risk of PID among sexually active 15-year-old females is one in eight (Morris et al., 1993). A more immediate consequence of STIs is that they can facilitate the transmission of HIV (Chesney, 1994;

Grosskurth et al., 1995), just as HIV influences the transmission and course of other STIs (Wasserheit, 1991).

The most severe consequences of some STIs concern their effects on pregnancy and offspring. For example, a major risk for adolescent females with undetected or untreated gonorrhea or chlamydia is PID, which may result in an ectopic pregnancy. If a pregnant adolescent is infected, the STI can be transmitted to the fetus in utero or at birth; in that event, possible consequences include spontaneous abortion or stillbirth, developmental anomalies, prematurity, intrauterine growth retardation, and infections for the neonate such as conjunctivitis and pneumonitis. Pregnancy loss or death of an infant, or having a child with chronic health problems or developmental disabilities, all have profound short- and long-term implications for adolescent girls and their families (Rosenthal et al., 1994).

The literature describing the consequences of STIs focuses almost exclusively on medical and reproductive health issues. Although some researchers have examined the psychosocial consequences of STIs, in particular HSV and HIV, few researchers have focused on these consequences for adolescents in particular (Rosenthal et al., 1994). The stigma associated with having an STI can be damaging. Examining the psychological impact of STIs on adolescent females with a history of infections, Rosenthal and Biro (1991) found that 82 percent of the study respondents reported that receiving an STI diagnosis would be the "worst thing that could happen" or "a major upset."

RISKY SEXUAL BEHAVIOR AMONG ADOLESCENTS

The primary risky sexual behaviors that increase the likelihood of transmitting and contracting STIs include unprotected sex and having multiple sexual partners (concurrent or sequential) (Santelli & Beilenson, 1992; Yarber & Parrillo, 1992). Having multiple partners increases risk because the "number of potentially infectious exposures is greater"; moreover, it indicates the lack of a "selective partner recruitment strategy," which increases the chances of selecting an infected partner (Seidman, Mosher, & Aral, 1994, p. 127). Other factors that increase the risk of STIs for sexually active adolescents— even those who do not necessarily engage in risky behavior—include the immunological and physiological immaturity of the urogenital tract in young adolescents (particularly females), having another STI, and high STI prevalence rates among an adolescent's sexual partners.

As background to this discussion on risky sexual behaviors, it is critical to keep in mind that although early, risky sexual behavior clearly can have negative consequences, adolescent sexual behavior in itself is not necessarily negative and may serve many developmental functions. Jessor (1992) argued that adolescent "risk behaviors" are "functional, purposive, instrumental, and goal-directed," and that "the goals involved are often those that are central in normal adolescent development" (p. 24). For example, by engaging in sex with others, adolescents may seek to enhance their sense of intimacy and connection with others, elevate their status in their peer group, and challenge authority or assert their autonomy. Moreover, adolescents may believe that the initiation of intercourse marks their transition to adulthood.

In 1990 the Centers for Disease Control and Prevention began surveying high school students about health-risk behaviors, including sexual behavior (CDC, 1995a). The CDC's Youth Risk Behavior Surveillance System monitors six categories of health-risk behaviors among adolescents and young adults, one of which is "sexual behaviors." Some Youth Risk Behavior Survey (YRBS) questions specific to sexual behavior include the following: (1) Have you ever had sexual intercourse? (2) During your life, with how many people have you had sexual intercourse? (3) During the past three months, with how many people did you have sexual intercourse? (4) The last time you had sexual intercourse, did you or your partner use a condom? (5) During your life, have you ever injected (shot up) any illegal drug? (CDC, 1995b; Morris et al., 1993). (For more detailed information about this surveillance system, see Kann et al., 1995.)

During the 1980s reported sexual experience among high school students increased significantly. The level of sexual activity remained stable from 1990 to 1993, and the number of high school students who reported using condoms at last intercourse increased (Kann et al., 1995) (Table 9-1). Results from the 1993 survey indicate that 53.0 percent of high school students had had sexual intercourse in their lifetime (55.6 percent males and 50.2 percent females); 37.6 percent were currently sexually active, that is, they had had sexual intercourse during the past three months (37.6 percent males and 37.5 percent females); 18.8 percent had sexual intercourse with four or more people in their lifetime (22.3 percent males and 14.9 percent females); 52.8 percent of sexually active students had used a condom during last sexual intercourse (59.2 percent males and 46.0 percent females); and 1.4 percent reported that they had at some time injected an illegal drug (1.9 percent males and 0.8 percent females) (CDC, 1995a, 1995b; Kann et al., 1995).

African American males and females were significantly more likely than Hispanic and white males and females to have had sexual intercourse (Table 9-2). Current sexual activity was significantly more likely among African American males and females than among Hispanic and white males and females. African American males (58.8 percent) and females (27.2 percent) were significantly more likely to report having had four or more sexual partners in their lifetime than Hispanic males (26.3 percent) and females (11.0 percent) and white males (15.2 percent) and females (13.3 percent). According to these data, males were significantly more likely to have used a condom than females during last intercourse (except in the case of ninth graders). African American and white females (47.8 percent and 46.1 percent, respectively) were more likely to use a condom than Hispanic females (36.9 percent) during last intercourse (Kann et al., 1995).

These data from samples of high school students do not include subpopulations of adolescents who may be engaging in risky sexual behavior at much higher rates, such as adolescents who have dropped out of school or are at risk for dropping out, homeless or runaway youths, or youths who are incarcerated (CDC, 1994a). In a study to examine sexual and drug use behaviors among adolescents at risk of dropping out of school, researchers at the University of Miami School of Medicine surveyed 159 adolescents in a dropout prevention program, Cities in Schools, Incorporated (CIS). They compared their findings with results from the YRBS that had been completed by students in Miami public schools (*n* = 1,602). The CIS students were more likely than the public school respondents to report ever having had sexual intercourse. They also reported more sexual partners than the public school students. More of them had had sex in the past three months, and more had consumed alcohol or used drugs before last sexual intercourse (CDC, 1994c). Findings about incidence may be underreported: the term sexual intercourse may not be understood by respondents to include oral and anal sex, which are practices that could transmit STIs (Morris et al., 1993).

Table 9-1. Percentage of High School Students Reporting Selected Sexual Risk Behaviors, United States, 1990, 1991, and 1993

	1990		1991		1993	
BEHAVIOR	%	95% CI	%	95% CI	%	95% CI
Ever had sexual intercourse	54.2	51.3–57.1	54.1	51.1–57.1	53.0	50.3–55.7
Had sexual intercourse during the three months preceding the survey	39.4	36.7–42.1	37.5	34.8–40.2	37.6	35.6–39.6
Ever had sexual intercourse with four or more partners	19.0	17.0–21.0	18.7	16.8–20.6	18.8	16.8–20.8
Used condoms at last sexual intercourse	NA		46.2	43.1–49.3	52.8	50.1–55.5
Used alcohol or drugs before last sexual intercourse	NA		11.8	10.3–13.3	11.0	10.2–11.8
Used birth control pills at last sexual intercourse	14.6	12.6–16.6	17.8	15.6–20.0	18.4	16.3–20.5*

SOURCE: Centers for Disease Control and Prevention. (1995a). Trends in sexual risk behavior among high school students, United States, 1990, 1991, and 1993. *Morbidity and Mortality Weekly Report, 44*(7), 125.
NOTES: Data are from the Youth Risk Behavior Survey (YRBS); the YRBS was not conducted in 1992. CI = confidence interval; NA = not available (the question was worded differently in 1990).
*$p < .05$.

RISK FACTORS FOR ADOLESCENT INVOLVEMENT IN RISKY SEXUAL BEHAVIOR

In earlier chapters risk factors were said to be influences that increase the probability of onset, digression to a more serious state, or maintenance of a problem condition. For the purposes of this discussion of STIs, the problem condition is defined as engaging in risky sexual behavior that increases the likelihood of contracting an STI. Risk factors associated with adolescents' engagement in risky sexual behaviors are listed in Table 9-3 along two dimensions: proximity to engaging in risky sexual behaviors (proximal and distal) and the system level at which these risk factors occur (biological; psychological, cognitive, and behavioral; family, school, and neighborhhood; and the broader environmental or contextual). These various systems levels all influence adolescent sexual behavior at different developmental stages. The following discussion covers selected risk factors discussed in the empirical literature on adolescent sexuality. The focus is on factors that are associated with adolescents' risky sexual behavior, not on factors that

Table 9-2. Percentage of High School Students Engaging in Sexual Behaviors, by Gender, Race or Ethnicity, and Grade, United States, 1993

CATEGORY	EVER HAD SEXUAL INTERCOURSE			FOUR OR MORE SEX PARTNERS DURING LIFETIME			CONDOM USE DURING LAST SEXUAL INTERCOURSE[a]			CURRENTLY SEXUALLY ACTIVE[b]			BIRTH CONTROL PILL USE DURING LAST SEXUAL INTERCOURSE		
	FEMALE	MALE	TOTAL	FEMALE	MALE	TOTAL	FEMALE	MALE	TOTAL	FEMALE	MALE	TOTAL	FEMALE	MALE	TOTAL
Race or ethnicity															
White, non-Hispanic	47.4	49.3	48.4	13.3	15.2	14.3	46.1	58.5	52.3	35.2	32.9	34.0	24.0	17.1	20.4
Black, non-Hispanic	70.4	89.2	79.7	27.2	58.8	42.7	47.8	63.7	56.5	53.2	65.1	59.1	20.6	10.5	15.1
Hispanic	48.3	63.5	56.0	11.0	26.3	18.6	36.9	55.1	46.1	37.9	40.7	39.4	15.3	9.8	12.4
Grade															
9	31.6	43.5	37.7	6.2	15.4	10.9	59.2	63.1	61.6	22.5	26.8	24.8	11.1	7.5	9.0
10	44.9	47.4	46.1	12.8	18.9	15.9	45.8	63.3	54.7	30.7	29.6	30.1	17.4	10.0	13.7
11	55.1	59.5	57.5	16.3	23.1	19.9	46.1	64.8	55.3	40.9	39.1	40.0	22.2	11.7	16.8
12	66.3	70.2	68.3	23.2	30.7	27.0	41.2	51.5	46.5	53.2	52.7	53.0	29.0	22.7	25.8
Total	50.2	55.6	53.0	15.0	22.3	18.8	46.0	59.2	52.8	37.5	37.5	37.6	22.3	14.7	18.4

Source: Kann, L. et al. (1995). Youth Risk Behavior Surveillance, United States, 1993. *Morbidity and Mortality Weekly Report, 44*(No. SS-1), 47.

[a]Among currently sexually active students.
[b]Sexual intercourse during the three months preceding the survey.

make adolescents more susceptible hosts to infection (being female, for example, or being a young adolescent or having another STI).

BIOLOGICAL FACTORS

Biological theory argues that adrogenic hormones begin to multiply at puberty, thus spurring the disposition for becoming sexually active (Udry, 1988). There is association between the timing of pubertal maturation and initiation of sexual intercourse; adolescents who mature earlier than usual are more likely to initiate sexual intercourse earlier (Irwin & Shafer, 1992), particularly adolescent females. Irwin and Millstein (1986) argued that adolescent girls who physically mature early may also reach some other developmental stages earlier (for example, a desire for independence, more interest in sexual activities), and thus they tend to interact in social networks composed primarily of older adolescents. Involvement in these social networks increases peer pressure on young adolescent girls to be sexually involved with older boys when they are not developmentally mature enough to understand the consequences of sexual activity or to effectively assert their wishes. Early pubertal maturation makes biological, psychological, and social development asynchronous, which may predispose adolescents to engage in risky sexual behaviors (Irwin & Shafer, 1992).

PSYCHOLOGICAL AND BEHAVIORAL FACTORS

Cognitive Development

Practicing safer sex requires that one accept and acknowledge that one is sexually active and vulnerable to STIs, and that one be capable of planning for sex (Pestrak & Martin, 1985). Yet most youths do not attain formal operational thinking—the stage of development in which abstract concepts can be comprehended (and consequences foreseen)—until they are older. Individuals in early and middle adolescence are limited in their ability to translate their knowledge about STI prevention (assuming that they have some knowledge) into actual behavior. They may also construct the "personal fable" that they are immune to STIs (Pestrak & Martin, 1985).

Early Sexual Activity

Early onset of sexual intercourse increases an adolescent's risk for exposure to STIs, because it may be associated with increased opportunity (the span of time spent sexually active could be longer, and the number of partners greater). In addition, young adolescents may be less likely than older adolescents to seek treatment for STI symptoms (Irwin & Shafer, 1992) and, as discussed above, they may be less knowledgeable and less able to negotiate safer sexual practices. In a statewide survey of family planning clients in Pennsylvania (*n* = 4,342), Greenberg, Magder, and Aral (1992) compared women who reported becoming sexually active before 15 years of age with women who became sexually active at 17 years of age or older. The women who were sexually active at an earlier age were twice as likely to report a history of STIs, four times more likely to have had five or more partners in the previous year, and three and a half times more likely to have sex with men who injected drugs or were bisexual or HIV-positive. Using data from the 1988

Table 9-3. Risk Factor Framework for Adolescents' Risky Sexual Behaviors for Sexually Transmitted Infections

SYSTEM LEVEL	PROXIMITY TO ENGAGING IN RISKY SEXUAL BEHAVIORS	
	PREDISPOSING OR DISTAL FACTOR	SITUATIONAL OR PROXIMAL RISK
Broad environmental and contextual conditions	Lack of universal access to health care Lack of emphasis on prevention Societal ambivalence about sexuality Societal attitudes against sexuality education Societal lack of awareness about STIs Lack of economic and educational opportunities for adolescents Media that sexualize women and promote unsafe sexual practices Social and economic policies that destabilize poor communities	Poor access to services for and education about STIs Poor access to medical treatment Increasing social disorganization of poor communities
Family, school, and neighborhood settings	Risky neighborhood environment (violence, substance abuse, poverty) Subculture that promotes multiple partners Poor communication with parents about safer sex practices Older siblings who are sexually active Parental substance abuse Neighborhood and peer norms that accept early sexual activity Lack of effective sexuality education	Ineffective adult supervision Peer pressure Forced sex Environments or activities that provide sexual opportunities Environments or activities where alcohol and drugs are used

Psychological, cognitive, and behavioral factors

Lack of acceptance of one's sexuality
Incomplete cognitive development
Being a consistent oral contraceptive user
Early onset of sexual activity
Inaccurate perception of adult rules and attitudes
Lack of knowledge about sexuality and safer sex practices
Sense of invulnerability
Low self-efficacy about safer sex
Inadequate communications skills
Having been sexually abused

Lack of access to condoms
Inability to say no or to negotiate safer sex
Denial regarding one's own sexual behaviors
Poor impulse control
Inability to use a condom properly
Inaccurate perception of risk
Lack of partner support for use of condoms
Substance abuse

Biological

Early puberty

NOTE: STI = sexually transmitted infection.

National Survey of Family Growth Cycle IV, investigators found that in a sample of 3,378 women of reproductive age, earlier first intercourse predicted multiple recent partners for never-married white and African American females (Seidman et al., 1994).

Many other variables are associated with age at onset of intercourse. Race and gender, for example, are associated with early intitiation of sexual activity. In general, African American males begin sexual activity earlier than Hispanic males, who begin earlier than white males; and males initiate sexual intercourse at an earlier age than females (Irwin & Shafer, 1992; Strunin, 1994). Cates (1991) listed four covariables that were significantly associated with age at onset of intercourse: mother's education, the degree of religious affiliation, age at menarche, and family stability at age 14. Irwin and Shafer (1992) listed other factors reported in the empirical literature: early onset of sexual activity by older siblings, peer behavior, and family structure (adolescents from nonintact families tend to initiate earlier sexual intercourse than adolescents from intact families). The family structure factor may be related to supervision, in that adolescents in single-parent households may have less supervision than those in two-parent households (Irwin & Shafer, 1992). Poor school performance, negative experiences with school, or dropping out of school are also associated with early initiation of sexual intercourse (Santelli & Beilenson, 1992). Research suggests too that there is an association between early sexual activity and drug and alcohol use (Strunin, 1994).

Substance Use

Adolescents may use alcohol and drugs to cope with feelings about their sexuality, or they may use them to feel less inhibited about engaging in sexual activities. In either event, alcohol and drug use reduce the likelihood that adolescents will take precautions to prevent contracting STIs (Hingson, Strunin, Berlin, & Heeren, 1990). In a study examining the association between use of crack-cocaine and risk behaviors for STIs and HIV among African American adolescents, Fullilove and colleagues (1993) found that adolescents who used crack were twice as likely to engage in HIV/STI risk behaviors as nonusers ($p < .001$); similarly, adolescents whose relatives used drugs were twice as likely to engage in risky sexual behavior ($p < .01$) as those who had nonusing relatives. Investigators postulated that the increase in gonorrhea rates among African American adolescent males in urban areas was associated with the onset of crack-cocaine use in those areas (Shafer & Moscicki, 1991). Findings from a study on unprotected sex among 16- to 19-year-old adolescents indicated that, among respondents who used drugs or drank alcohol, 16 percent reported using condoms less often after drinking, and 25 percent reported using condoms less often after using drugs (Hingson et al., 1990).

Sexual Abuse

First, sexually abused adolescents are at risk of STIs transmitted by those who abuse them. According to the 1987 National Survey of Children, 12.7 percent of white women, 9 percent of African American women, 1.9 percent of white men, and 6.1 percent of African American men reported that they had experienced forced sex by age 20 (Emans, Brown, Davis, Felice, & Hein, 1991). Second, adolescents who have been abused are more likely than others to subsequently engage in behaviors that put them at risk of STIs (early sexual activity, multiple partners, and substance use). Springs and

Friedrich (1992) reported that, among adult women, those who had been sexually abused as children had earlier onset of sexual activity, more sexual partners as adolescents, and higher drug abuse prevalence than those who had not been abused. Based on an anonymous self-report survey of 3,448 eighth- and 10th-grade students, researchers found that victims of forced sex (conservatively defined as intercourse) reported significantly higher levels of risky health behaviors and risky attitudes. These adolescents were disproportionately African American females, who were more likely than the other students to reside in single-parent households (Nagy, Adcock, & Nagy, 1994).

INFLUENCE OF FAMILY, SCHOOL, AND NEIGHBORHOOD

Family Dynamics

The research findings on the association between family factors and adolescent sexual behavior are mixed. For example, some studies show that parental attitudes and communication do influence the age of initiation of intercourse. Other studies suggest that they do not; instead, these studies claim that they influence whether or not adolescents use some type of protection or contraceptives (Santelli & Beilenson, 1992).

The extent to which parents play a role in their children's education about sexuality is also unclear. "Whatever parents are doing that they feel qualifies as a discussion, from the perspective of teenagers, especially teenage sons, it simply does not register on the seismic sexual conversation scale" (Kahn, 1994, p. 291). Indeed, adolescents recalled fewer discussions on sexuality with parents than their parents reported having, and adolescent boys had relatively less recall of such conversations than did adolescent girls. In a study of parent–child communication about sexuality in white and African American families, Kahn (1994) found that mothers more often than fathers take responsibility for communicating with adolescents about sexuality. The closeness of the parent–child relationship was the strongest predictor of teenagers' recall of sexually related discussions with their parents. That family communication about sexuality is lacking (or seldom recalled) is supported by findings from a recent survey of STI knowledge among adults and teenagers. Only 12 percent of teenagers reported first learning about STIs from family members; when asked about current sources of information on STIs, 11 percent said family members supplied that information (ASHA, 1996a).

One review of the literature suggests that the most important family factors affecting adolescent sexuality may be parental control of dating (supervision and control over hours, partners, and locations) and overall closeness of family ties (Santelli & Beilenson, 1992). The sexual behavior of older siblings may also influence that of adolescents. Rodgers and Rowe (1988) found, for instance, that when siblings were close in age, the younger child became sexually active at a younger age than did the older sibling; similarly, the younger siblings of sexually active older youths were more likely to be sexually active than those whose older siblings had never had sexual intercourse.

Peer Group Attitudes

Peer groups play a critical role in adolescent development and behavior. As individuals reach middle adolescence, the peer pressure to engage in sex increases (Udry,

1988). For example, sexually inexperienced white females with sexually experienced best friends (of both genders) were almost certain to initiate sexual intercourse sometime during the two years that they were studied by Billy and Udry (1985). In their description of hip-hop culture, McLaurin and Juzang (1993) discussed how the intense emphasis on peer approval, rejection of mainstream norms and values, and encouragement of risky behaviors such as substance abuse and sexual promiscuity put African American inner-city adolescents at high risk of STIs. Many would argue that sexual intercourse for adolescents, particularly young adolescents, is a violation of social norms, but in many adolescent subcultures, early initiation of sexual behavior is the norm. Other authors (Mann, 1994; Pipher, 1994) have addressed the issue of peer pressure on adolescent girls to become sexually active at increasingly younger ages and the difficulty that young adolescent girls have in dealing with this pressure.

Community and Neighborhood

Researchers use the term "ecology of risk" to suggest an association between the likelihood of an individual engaging in a risky behavior when there is a high prevalence of such behavior in his or her environment (Andrews, 1985). Research by Brewster, Billy, and Grady (1993) found that the timing of first intercourse and the use of contraception at that time were shaped by the normative environment and the local opportunity structure. Community social disintegration, low socioeconomic status, and lack of employment opportunities were found to be important influences on adolescent female sexual behavior. This study specifically examined these relationships in the light of pregnancy prevention; however, because unprotected intercourse is the route to both pregnancy and STI transmission, the findings ought to be applicable also to STI prevention. These investigators noted the role of "community religiosity to reduce the risk of first coitus by increasing the psychic costs of early nonmarital intercourse" (Brewster et al., 1993, p. 717).

BROAD ENVIRONMENTAL AND CONTEXTUAL FACTORS

Social and Economic Policy

Ill-conceived social and economic policies can destabilize poor communities, which can lead to increased social disorganization, as evidenced by high rates of STIs, among other things. The highest rates of STIs among adolescents are in urban pockets of poverty, such as those in the District of Columbia (CDC, 1994b; Wood & Shoroye, 1993). Wallace (1990), who studied the impact of urban desertification on sharply rising rates of violent death, substance abuse, low birthweight, and HIV infection in the Bronx, New York, demonstrated how the disintegration and disruption of key social networks (individual, family, and community) "express themselves in exacerbation of a nexus of behavior, including violence, sexuality, substance abuse and general criminality" (p. 811). In the Bronx, as in other urban areas with largely African American populations, government policies have allowed essential community services and housing to disintegrate. The result is the disruption or destruction of social networks. Wallace (1990) argued that rapid urban social decay and the resulting social disintegration were strong cofactors to risky sexual behavior and intravenous drug use in the spread of HIV.

Inadequate Social Response to STIs

Several factors converge to contribute to the epidemic of STIs in the adolescent population: societal lack of awareness of STIs, adolescents' lack of access to health care; and lack of emphasis on prevention of STIs. In 1995 the American Social Health Association conducted a study to find out how much adolescents and adults knew about STIs. The results were not encouraging. Forty-two percent of adolescents and 26 percent of adults could not name an STI other than HIV or AIDS, and only 12 percent of adolescents and 4 percent of adults were aware that an STI infects one in five people in the United States; nearly half of each group dramatically underestimated the prevalence of STIs (other than HIV), responding that only one in 100, or fewer, are infected with STIs (ASHA, 1996a). This lack of awareness by the general population about the prevalence of STIs makes it difficult to institute policies and implement programs that effectively address the problem. The public, which is apparently unaware of the epidemic nature of the problem, is not pressuring policymakers for more funds to address prevention, screening, and treatment of STIs.

One of seven adolescents (ages 10 to 18) lacks health insurance. Many adolescents with private insurance may not be covered for preventive services, such as sexuality counseling and education or reproductive health care, unless they belong to a health maintenance organization (Dougherty, 1993; Klerman, 1992). Legal barriers, such as the requirement that parents consent to or be notified of certain services, further hinder adolescents' access to health care. In addition, few health care professionals are trained specifically to deliver care to adolescents; only 1,400 primary care physicians specialize in adolescent medicine (Dougherty, 1993).

PROTECTIVE FACTORS

Protective factors decrease exposure to risk, buffer the negative effects of risks, mediate the relationship between exposure to risk and negative outcomes, or increase the resilience of an individual (see chapter 2). The discussion of factors that protect adolescents from engaging in risky sexual behavior is very sparse in the empirical literature, which has focused almost exclusively on risk factors. Some protective factors might be thought of as the opposite of risk factors or as at one end of a continuum with risk factors at the other end. Jessor (1992) conceptualized the degree of risk for adolescents as "an outcome of the balance of risk and protection" (p. 32). More research on protective factors is needed to develop effective interventions for adolescents' risky sexual behavior.

RELIGION

Seidman, Mosher, and Aral (1994) and Santelli and Beilenson (1992) cited many studies that found that attending religious services and being affiliated with a religious organization was inversely related to adolescents' risky sexual behaviors, such as initiating sexual intercourse at an early age, having multiple partners, and having sex with a stranger.

Positive Attitudes toward Condom Use

The positive attitudes of an adolescent and his or her partner toward condom use and their belief that condoms are efficacious in preventing STIs may act as a protective factor. A study of 390 sexually active, 12- to 19-year-old female adolescents of predominantly lower and lower-middle SES found that condom use increased as cognitive maturity and positive attitudes about condom use grew (Orr et al., 1992). According to these researchers, salient attitudes included adolescents' perceptions that condom use was accepted among partners and peers and that condoms did not interfere with sexual enjoyment. Hingson et al. (1990) found that respondents who believed that they were susceptible to HIV were 1.8 times more likely to use condoms all the time; if they believed that condoms could prevent HIV, they were 3.1 times more likely to use them. Respondents who believed that condoms did not reduce sexual pleasure and reported that they would not be embarrassed to discuss their use with partners were 3.1 and 2.4 times, respectively, more likely to use them.

Cates (1991) noted that of all the factors associated with adolescent condom use ready availability (that is, actually having condoms in their possession) seemed to be most predictive of use. In the Hingson et al. (1990) study cited above, respondents who carried condoms with them were 2.7 times more likely to use them than respondents who did not carry them.

Summary

The same factors that influence whether or not an adolescent engages in risky sexual behaviors could also be applied to an examination of the consequences of acquiring STIs. Some risk factors—lack of access to medical treatment and lack of knowledge about sexuality and STIs, for example—may put adolescents at risk of STI consequences that are far more serious than they would have been had adolescents recognized symptoms and had access to early, effective treatment. Protective factors, such as open communication with an adult about sexuality, support to seek treatment, and access to culturally and developmentally sensitive health care, may result in less negative, shorter-term consequences.

Consequences and their associated risks also need to be considered in an ecological context. Jessor (1992), in his description of a conceptual framework for adolescent risk behavior, noted that any such framework must adapt as adolescents mature within their ever-changing contextual environment of family, school, community, and the larger society. Others have stressed the need to monitor the salience of particular risk factors to adolescents (and their families) at different developmental stages (Coie et al., 1993). Changes in the larger society may also affect the role that various risk factors play in contributing to risky behavior. For example, media portrayals of sexuality, combined with societal ambivalence about teaching adolescents how to protect themselves, may result in higher numbers of adolescents initiating sexual activity at earlier ages and engaging in risky sexual behavior. Similarly, the lowering age of pubertal development of U.S. adolescents (Udry, 1988) coincides with larger societal changes that result in less parental supervision—more single-parent households and more two-worker, two-parent households—thus increasing the likelihood that young adolescents will engage in risky sexual behavior and putting adolescents at risk of STIs at an increasingly young age.

ASSESSING RISK AND PROTECTIVE FACTORS

Jessor (1992) distinguished between two stages of being at risk. The first stage refers to an adolescent's risk of engaging in the behavior (in this case, risky sexual behavior); the second stage, which applies to adolescents who are already engaging in the behavior, refers to "the degree of risk associated with the engagement in risk behaviors" (p. 30). The focus of assessment is different for each stage.

Assessment of risk for adolescents who are not yet sexually active should focus on the salient risk factors listed in Table 9-3 and on protective factors. For example, the assessment should find out community, peer, and family norms about sexuality; the adolescent's knowledge and attitudes about sexuality; whether the adolescent had ever been sexually abused; at what age older siblings became sexually active; level of religiosity; and the adolescent's intent to initiate sexual intercourse. Risky behavior is often seen in clusters, so it is critical to find out also whether an adolescent is involved in other risky behavior, particularly drug or alcohol use (Irwin & Millstein, 1986; Jessor, 1992).

For adolescents already involved in risky sexual behavior, the assessment should focus on four areas: (1) degree or intensity of involvement (the overall pattern of risky sexual behavior and the degree to which the pattern is established); (2) the number of risky behaviors (multiple partners, frequency of unprotected intercourse, having sex while using substances, for example); (3) age of onset of sexual intercourse, and how long the adolescent has been sexually active; and (4) the degree to which the adolescent engages in protective sexual behaviors (Jessor, 1992). In this type of assessment, the practitioner asks when the adolescent first started having sex, how many partners he or she has had since first initiating sex, if he or she uses condoms and how consistently, and the extent to which he or she uses substances in conjunction with having sex. Protective factors that should be assessed include the adolescent's access to health care, to STI prevention education, and to condoms; the extent to which the adolescent can demonstrate the ability to negotiate safer sex and to use a condom properly and the degree to which he or she has positive attitudes about condom use.

Hingson et al. (1990) also stressed the need in any assessment to recognize the role of the social environment in influencing behavior. That is, not only is risky sexual behavior accepted more in some adolescent social environments than in others, but the risk behaviors produce more adverse outcomes in some social environments, such as those with high STI rates.

The Health Belief Model (Becker, 1974), a framework for explaining and predicting preventive, illness, and sick-role behavior, can be used clinically to assess an adolescent's likelihood of engaging in risk-reduction behaviors specific to STI prevention (Boyer & Kegeles, 1991; Hingson et. al., 1990). Using the Health Belief Model, one would assess the adolescent's perceptions about his or her susceptibility to STIs, the seriousness of contracting an STI, internal and external cues to practicing safer sex (such as having peers who use condoms), self-efficacy for engaging in protective sexual behaviors, and barriers to and benefits of practicing safer sex. The extent to which structural, psychosocial, and other factors modify these perceptions would be examined also.

IMPLICATIONS FOR PREVENTION, EARLY INTERVENTION, AND TREATMENT

Epidemiologists use the term "web of causation" to refer to the complex models that explain causes of chronic diseases (MacMahon, Pugh, & Ipsen, 1960, p. 18). The term could also describe the many factors that might explain or predict the epidemiology of STIs among adolescents. The immediate behavioral cause is well understood (engaging in unprotected sex with an infected partner), but frameworks to explain both the proximal and distal factors associated with engagement in risky sexual behavior are much more complex.

Thus interventions—preventive, early intervention, and treatment—must use a comprehensive approach to address the various factors that contribute to adolescents' risky sexual behavior. Comprehensive approaches include interventions aimed at changing individual adolescent behavior, community norms, organizational behavior (schools and health systems, for example), societal beliefs, and government policies. Effective approaches will require coordinated and integrated efforts among adolescents, "parents, families, schools, religious organizations, health departments, community agencies, and the media" (CDC, 1992, p. 887; Irwin & Shafer, 1992).

Because sexuality and sexual behavior are integral parts of adolescent development, interventions should focus on making sexual behavior and the exploration of one's sexuality less risky. For example, interventions should be designed to help adolescents delay the onset of sexual intercourse, consistently and appropriately use condoms, reduce the number of sexual partners, and avoid having sex while using drugs or alcohol.

To be effective, interventions need to speak to cultural differences in how sexuality is viewed and practiced (Ward & Taylor, 1994). Strunin (1994) emphasized the need to understand the patterns of risk behavior among racial and ethnic minority groups, as well as the diversity of norms, values, and behavioral patterns within groups. Knowing how individuals in various cultural groups interpret information and translate it into behavior is critical to the design of culturally competent interventions. McLaurin and Juzang (1993), who conducted focus groups on HIV education with inner-city African American youths, found that participants wanted concrete messages about skills, ones that fit with their peer culture: "Don't tell us what to do, tell us how to do it, step by step, without losing the approval of our peers" (p. 3). They also noted that urban African American youths are very sophisticated consumers of media programming, whose communication style and beliefs about the role of communication differ markedly from those of the mainstream culture.

PREVENTION

Primary prevention interventions should focus on helping adolescents postpone sexual activity (Greenberg et al., 1992; Irwin & Shafer, 1992) for important biological and developmental reasons. As suggested earlier, because of physical and immunological immaturity, sexually active young adolescent females are at higher risk of contracting STIs and they experience more severe outcomes when they are infected. Second, in terms of cognitive and psychosocial development, young adolescents are much less likely to be able to engage in protective behaviors to reduce the risk of STIs. The Postponing Sexual Involvement Program conducted in the Atlanta school system by Grady Memorial Hospital is an example of a successful program based on a model of social inoculation and social influence; in this program, older adolescents teach younger adolescents (Howard & McCabe, 1990). Results showed that at the completion of eighth grade, students who had not participated in the program were five times more likely than program participants to have begun having sex. Programs such as this one create a social norm among adolescents and their peers that discourages early initiation of sexual intercourse.

Because of the strong association between substance use and the initiation of sexual intercourse (Irwin & Shafer, 1992; Jessor, 1993), one could argue that prevention programs for STIs should also be aimed at delaying the onset of substance use in adolescents. As Jessor (1992) pointed out, these behaviors may be learned at the same time, and combining sexual activity with drug and alcohol use may be a norm among peers; furthermore, some adolescents may not engage in sexual activity unless they are under the influence of alcohol or drugs.

EARLY INTERVENTION

Early intervention programs target adolescents who intend to initiate sexual activity or have just recently done so. These programs aim to provide adolescents with the knowledge, skills, and motivation to develop and consistently engage in safer sexual practices (effectively and consistently using condoms, reducing the number of partners, and refraining from combining sex and drug and alcohol use). Early intervention also includes increasing adolescents' knowledge about STIs, helping them to develop realistic perceptions about their own susceptibility, and teaching them when, how, and where to seek screening and treatment. Chesney (1994) described several risk-reduction interventions that use cognitive–behavioral approaches to target changes in beliefs and attitudes.

Sexuality education for adolescents, in addition to focusing on safer sex, needs to emphasize the context of relationships. Strunin (1994), who conducted focus groups with adolescents, found that most adolescents thought the sexuality education that they had received in school did not "fit the reality of their lives, since it leaves out the feelings, fears and passions, inconvenience, embarrassment, and romance that affect sexual decision making and that occur within a context framed by cultural values and beliefs" (p. 85). In her interviews with adolescents and parents about communication regarding sex, Kahn (1994) found that adolescents saw "their parents, especially their mothers, as playing a very important role in their sexual learning" (p. 305) and wanted more discussion about "dating, love, marriage and divorce, and the parents' own experiences" (p. 306).

To effect and maintain change at the individual level, interventions at the neighborhood, school, and community levels are needed to promote safer sex practices and social norms that discourage risky sexual behavior (Chesney, 1994). Through social marketing, programs can create a social milieu in which risk reduction becomes the norm among groups (Rosenthal et al., 1994).

One of the most effective ways to make reproductive health care accessible to students is through school-based or school-linked health clinics (Cates, 1991). In addition, outreach efforts must be aimed at those 9 million youths between the ages of 14 and 21 who do not attend school, because many in this large group may be at particularly high risk of contracting STIs (Yarber & Parrillo, 1992).

TREATMENT

The goal of treatment interventions is to treat adolescents who have contracted STIs to prevent further morbidity and to change their risky sexual behaviors so that they will not infect others or acquire other STIs. Adolescents with STIs need to have access to health care, seek care promptly, and actively participate in their treatment by adhering to the required regimen. As discussed earlier, several issues make effective treatment challenging: Many STIs are asymptomatic; adolescents lack knowledge about STIs in general and, specifically, about how to recognize symptoms of STIs; access to treatment is barred in several ways (by lack of health insurance and transportation, for example, and by the need for parental consent); and many adolescents find it difficult to adhere to antibiotic or other treatment regimens. The medical aspects of treatment are important, of course, but it is critical also to address the psychosocial effects of having an STI and to examine other risk factors to find out why an individual adolescent may be engaging in risky sexual behavior (Biro & Rosenthal, 1992). In addition to serving the student population in school-based or school-linked clinics, medical and psychosocial treatment interventions need to be designed specifically and located to address the multiple and complex needs of groups of adolescents who are not in school (incarcerated adolescents, runaways, and homeless adolescents, for example) (Rosenthal et al., 1994). To increase the effectiveness of clinical interventions, comprehensive strategies should include training for health and mental health providers in issues related to adolescents and adolescent sexuality (Cates, 1991).

An ecological framework reveals many factors, individual and environmental, that increase the likelihood that adolescents will engage in risky sexual behaviors that increase the chances of contracting an STI. Factors that protect adolescents from engaging in risky sexual behaviors have also been discussed in this chapter, but only briefly because research on protective factors is scanty, not because they are inconsequential. Some of these protective factors are the absence or opposite of particular risk factors; others are at one end of a continuum, with risk factors at the other. Clearly, more needs to be done to identify protective factors, individual and environmental, that decrease the likelihood that adolescents will engage in risky sexual behaviors.

Interventions to reduce the incidence and prevalence of STIs among adolescents will be more effective when they are grounded in an ecological framework. That is, interventions should be designed to simultaneously influence both risk and protective factors at various levels in the ecology. For example, interventions at the individual level often focus on adolescents' acquisition of specific knowledge, attitudes, and behaviors that will help them postpone sexual activity or engage in safer sexual practices. But to initiate and maintain these behaviors, adolescents need considerable support from their peer groups, families, schools, communities, and the larger social system. In many cases, support will not be forthcoming without changes in the adolescent's environment. Thus, interventions also need to target the larger context of adolescent life, and the systems within that context, to meet the ultimate goal of helping adolescents take care of themselves and their peers. Interventions must be aimed in several directions: teaching adults how to communicate effectively and develop caring, supportive relationships with adolescents; ensuring personal and community safety; making health care and prevention programs accessible; and increasing opportunities for adolescents' education, employment, recreation, healthy development, and achievement. All of these interventions give adolescents the message that they are valued and that their health and well-being are important.

REFERENCES

American Social Health Association. (1995). *STD fact sheet.* Research Triangle Park, NC: Author.

American Social Health Association. (1996a). Teenagers know more than adults about STDs, but knowledge among both groups is low. *STD News, 3*(2), 1, 5.

American Social Health Association. (1996b). Decrease in lab testing may mask STD problem. *STD News, 3*(2), 4.

Andrews, H. (1985). The ecology of risk and the geography of intervention: From research to practice for the health and well-being of urban children. *Annals of the Association of American Geographers, 75*, 375–382.

Becker, M. H. (Ed.). (1974). The health belief model and personal health behavior. *Health Education Monographs, 2*, 324–473.

Billy, J. O., & Udry, J. R. (1985). The influence of male and female best friends on adolescent sexual behavior. *Adolescence, 20*, 20–32.

Biro, F. M., & Rosenthal, S. L. (1992). Psychological sequelae of sexually transmitted diseases in adolescents. *Pediatric and Adolescent Gynecology, 19*, 209–218.

Boyer, C. B., & Kegeles, S. M. (1991). AIDS risk and prevention among adolescents. *Social Science and Medicine, 33*, 11–23.

Brewster, K. L., Billy, J.O.G., & Grady, W. R. (1993). Social context and adolescent behavior: The impact of community on the transition to sexual activity. *Social Forces, 71*, 713–740.

Cates, W., Jr. (1991). Teenagers and sexual risk taking: The best of times and the worst of times. *Journal of Adolescent Health, 12*, 84–94.

Cates, W., Jr., & Rauh, J. L. (1985). Adolescents and sexually transmitted diseases: An expanding problem. *Journal of Adolescent Health, 6*, 257–261.

Centers for Disease Control and Prevention. (1992). Sexual behavior among high school students: United States, 1990. *Morbidity and Mortality Weekly Reports, 40*, 885–888.

Centers for Disease Control and Prevention. (1994a). Health risk behaviors among adolescents who do and do not attend school: United States, 1992. *Morbidity and Mortality Weekly Reports, 43*, 129–132.

Centers for Disease Control and Prevention. (1994b). *STD surveillance 1993.* Atlanta: Author.

Centers for Disease Control and Prevention. (1994c). Sexual behaviors and drug use among youth in dropout-prevention programs, Miami, 1994. *Morbidity and Mortality Weekly Reports, 43*, 873–876.

Centers for Disease Control and Prevention. (1995a). Trends in sexual risk behavior among high school students: United States, 1990, 1991, and 1993. *Morbidity and Mortality Weekly Reports, 44* ,124–133.

Centers for Disease Control and Prevention. (1995b). *Adolescent health: State of the nation—pregnancy, sexually transmitted diseases, and related risk behaviors among U.S. adolescents* (Monograph Series No. 2, DHHS Publication No. CDC 099-4630). Atlanta: Public Health Service.

Chesney, M. A. (1994). Prevention of HIV and STD infections. *Preventive Medicine, 23*, 655–660.

Coie, J. D., Watt, N. F., West, S. G., Hawkins, J. D., Asarnow, J. R., Markman, H. J., Ramey, S. L., Shure, M. B., & Long, B. (1993). The science of prevention: A conceptual framework and some directions for a national research program. *American Psychologist, 48*, 1013–1022.

DiClemente, R. J. (1992). Epidemiology of AIDS, HIV prevalence, and HIV incidence among adolescents. *Journal of School Health, 62*, 325–330.

Dougherty, D. M. (1993). Adolescent health reflections on a report to the U.S. Congress. *American Psychologist, 48*, 193–201.

Emans; S. J., Brown, R. T., Davis, A., Felice, M., & Hein, K. (1991). Society for Adolescent Medicine position paper on reproductive health care for adolescents. *Journal of Adolescent Health, 12*, 629–661.

Fullilove, M. T., Golden, E., Fullilove, R. E., III, Lennon, R., Porterfield, D., Schwarcz, S., & Bolan, G. (1993). Crack cocaine use and high-risk behaviors among sexually active black adolescents. *Journal of Adolescent Health, 14*, 295–300.

Greenberg, J., Magder, L., & Aral, S. (1992, November–December). Age at first coitus. *Sexually Transmitted Diseases*, pp. 331–334.

Grosskurth, H., Mosha, F., Todd, J., Mwijarubi, E., Klokke, A., Senkoro, K., Mayaud, P., Changalucha, J., Nicoll, A., ka-Gina, G., Newell, J., Mugeye, K., Mabey, D., & Hayes, R. (1995). Impact of improved treatment of sexually transmitted diseases on HIV infection in rural Tanzania: Randomised controlled trial. *Lancet, 346*(8974), 530–536.

Hingson, R., Strunin, L., Berlin, B., & Heeren, T. (1990). Beliefs about AIDS, use of alcohol, drugs, and unprotected sex among Massachusetts adolescents. *American Journal of Public Health, 80*, 295–300.

Howard, M., & McCabe, J. B. (1990). Helping teenagers postpone sexual involvement. *Family Planning Perspective, 22*, 21–26.

Irwin, C. E., Jr., & Millstein, S. G. (1986). Biopsychosocial correlates of risk-taking behaviors during adolescence: Can the physician intervene? *Journal of Adolescent Health, 7*(6, Suppl.), 82S–96S.

Irwin, C. E., Jr., & Shafer, M. A. (1992). Adolescent sexuality: Negative outcomes of a normative behavior. In D. Rogers & E. Ginsberg (Eds.), *Adolescents at risk: Medical and social perspectives* (pp. 35–79). Boulder, CO: Westview Press.

Jessor, R. (1992). Risk behavior in adolescence: A psychosocial framework for understanding and action. In D. Rogers & E. Ginsberg (Eds.), *Adolescents at risk: Medical and social perspectives* (pp. 19–34). Boulder, CO: Westview Press.

Jessor, R. (1993). Successful adolescent development among youth in high-risk settings. *American Psychologist, 48,* 117–126.

Kahn, J. R. (1994). Speaking across cultures within your own family. In J. M. Irvine (Ed.), *Sexual cultures and the construction of adolescent identities* (pp. 285–309). Philadelphia: Temple University Press.

Kann, L., Warren, C. W., Harris, W. A., Collins, J. L., Douglas, K. A., Collins, M. E., Williams, B. I., Ross, J. G., & Kolbe, L. J. (1995). Youth risk behavior surveillance: United States, 1993. *Morbidity and Mortality Weekly Reports, 44*(No. SS-1).

Kelly, J. A., Murphy, D. A., Sikkema, K. J., & Kalichman, S. C. (1993). Psychological interventions to prevent HIV infection are urgently needed. *American Psychologist, 48,* 1023–1034.

Klerman, L. V. (1992). The influence of economic factors on health-related behaviors in adolescents. In S. C. Millstein, A. C. Petersen, & E. O. Nightingale (Eds.), *Promoting the health of adolescents: A new direction for the 21st century* (pp. 38–57). New York: Oxford University Press.

MacMahon, B., Pugh, T. F., & Ipsen, J. (1960). *Epidemiological methods.* Boston: Little, Brown.

Mann, J. (1994). *The difference: Growing up female in America.* New York: Warner Books.

McLaurin, P., & Juzang, I. (1993). Reaching the hip-hop generation. *Focus: A Guide to AIDS Research and Counseling, 8*(3), 1–4.

Morris, L., Warren, C. W., & Aral, S. O. (1993). Measuring adolescent sexual behaviors and related health outcomes. *Public Health Reports, 108*(Suppl. 1), 31–36.

Nagy, S., Adcock, A. G., & Nagy, M. C. (1994). A comparison of risky health behaviors of sexually active, sexually abused, and abstaining adolescents. *Pediatrics, 93,* 570–575.

Newcomer, S., & Baldwin, W. (1992). Demographics of adolescent sexual behavior, conception, pregnancy, and STDs. *Journal of School Health, 62,* 265–270.

Orr, D. P., Langefeld, C. D., Katz, B. P., Caine, V. A., Dias, P., Blythe, M., & Jones, R. B. (1992). Factors associated with condom use among sexually active female adolescents. *Journal of Pediatrics, 120,* 311–317.

Pestrak, V. A., & Martin, D. (1985). Cognitive development and aspects of adolescent sexuality. *Adolescence, 20,* 981–987.

Pipher, M. (1994). *Reviving Ophelia: Saving the selves of adolescent girls.* New York: Ballantine Books.

Public Health Service. (1991). *Healthy people 2000: National health promotion and disease prevention objectives—full report with commentary* (DHHS Publication No. 91-50212). Washington, DC: U.S. Department of Health and Human Services.

Rodgers, J. L., & Rowe, D. C. (1988). Influence of siblings on adolescent sexual behavior. *Developmental Psychology, 24,* 722–728.

Rosenthal, S. L., & Biro, F. M. (1991). A preliminary investigation of psychological impact of sexually transmitted diseases in adolescent females. *Adolescent and Pediatric Gynecology, 4*, 198–201.

Rosenthal, S. L., Cohen, S. S., & Biro, F. M. (1994). Sexually transmitted diseases: A paradigm for risk-taking teens. In R. J. Simeonsson (Ed.), *Risk resilience and prevention: Promoting the well-being of children* (pp. 239–264). Baltimore: Paul H. Brookes.

Santelli, J. S., & Beilenson, P. (1992). Risk factors for adolescent sexual behavior, fertility, and sexually transmitted diseases. *Journal of School Health, 62*, 271–279.

Seidman, S. N., Mosher, W. D., & Aral, S. O. (1994). Predictors of high-risk behavior in unmarried American women: Adolescent environment as risk factor. *Journal of Adolescent Health, 15*, 126–132.

Shafer, M. B., & Moscicki, A. B. (1991). Sexually transmitted diseases. In W. R. Hendee (Ed.), *The health of adolescents* (pp. 211–249). San Francisco: Jossey-Bass.

Springs, F. E., & Friedrich, W. N. (1992). Health risk behaviors and medical sequelae of childhood sexual abuse. *Mayo Clinic Proceedings, 67*, 527–532.

Strunin, L. (1994). Culture, context, and HIV infection: Research on risk taking among adolescents. In J. M.Irvine (Ed.), *Sexual cultures and the construction of adolescent identities* (pp. 71–87). Philadelphia: Temple University Press.

Udry, J. R. (1988). Biological predispositions and social control in adolescent sexual behavior. *American Sociological Review, 53*, 709–722.

U.S. Congress, Office of Technology Assessment. (1991). *Adolescent health: Vol. 1. Summary and policy options* (OTA-H-464). Washington, DC: U.S. Government Printing Office.

Wallace, R. (1990). Urban desertification, public health and public order: "Planned shrinkage," violent death, substance abuse and AIDS in the Bronx. *Social Science and Medicine, 31*, 801–813.

Ward, J. V., & Taylor, J. M. (1994). Sexuality education for immigrant and minority students: Developing a culturally appropriate curriculum. In J. M. Irvine (Ed.), *Sexual cultures and the construction of adolescent identities* (pp. 51–68). Philadelphia: Temple University Press.

Wasserheit, J. (1991). Epidemiological synergy: Interrelationships between HIV infection and other STDs. In L. C. Chen, J. S. Amor, & S. J. Segal (Eds.), *AIDS and women's reproductive health*. New York: Plenum Press.

Wood, V., & Shoroye, A. (1993). Sexually transmitted disease among adolescents in the juvenile justice system of the District of Columbia. *Journal of the National Medical Association, 85*, 435–439.

Yarber, W. L., & Parrillo, A. V. (1992). Adolescents and sexually transmitted diseases. *Journal of School Health, 62*, 331–338.

10

ADOLESCENT PREGNANCY: MULTISYSTEMIC RISK AND PROTECTIVE FACTORS

Cynthia Franklin, Jacqueline Corcoran, and Susan Ayers-Lopez

In recent years adolescent pregnancy has become a serious social problem and the subject of heated political debate and controversy. The sexuality of adolescents in general has been put on trial, under the guise of welfare reform and expenditure reduction. This chapter discusses current statistics on adolescent pregnancy and nonmarital childbearing and frames these statistics in relationship to the pregnancy and childbearing patterns of women of all ages. Several empirical studies that provide information on both risk and resilience for prevention of adolescent pregnancy and childbearing are highlighted. Findings from these studies help us identify risk factors, as well as protective factors that prevent pregnancy or buffer adolescents against the adverse effects of early childbearing.

NATURE OF THE PROBLEM

One million adolescents in the United States become pregnant each year (Perkins, 1991). The rates of pregnancy, birth, and abortion for U.S. adolescents are significantly higher than for adolescents in other developed countries (McAnarney & Hendee, 1989). Rates of nonmarital pregnancies and births for women of all ages have been on the rise in the past 50 years, but in recent years they have escalated, thus making adolescent pregnancy a social problem. Nonmarital births increased slowly in the years between 1940 and 1960; in the 1970s, however, the number, rate, and ratio of nonmarital childbirths grew significantly, and that increase has continued to the present time (U.S. Department of Health and Human Services, 1995). Births to 15- to 19-year-old youths, for example, rose from one-third of all births in 1970 to one-half of all births in the early 1980s and to two-thirds of all births in 1988 (Chilman, 1989). Data from the U.S. Department of Health and Human Services indicate that between 1940 and 1993, the proportion of all births occurring outside of marriage (nonmarital birth ratio) rose from 38 to 310 per 1,000 births (that is, from 4 percent of all births to 31 percent). This nonmarital birth ratio rose by 4 percent annually during the 1980s and by about 3 percent annually between 1990 and 1993.

Consistent with an ecological and multisystemic perspective, the larger sociocultural and contextual trends of nonmarital childbirths to women of all ages is the frame for the increase in adolescent nonmarital childbirth rates. Several sociodemographic factors have contributed to the prevalence of early nonmarital childbearing, including an expanded adolescent cohort in post-World War II America;

less-strict prohibitions concerning adolescent sexual behavior; an increase in premarital sex among women of all ages, and young women in particular; a decrease in marriage (marriages of younger couples, in particular); a marked increase in cohabitation outside of marriage (Burke, 1991); and decreased adoption rates for unmarried persons.

These factors constitute larger sociological trends that affect marriage and family relationships and childbearing patterns. For example, rates at which couples married after a nonmarital conception of a child dropped from 31 percent to 8 percent from the 1960s to the 1980s (from 33 percent to 23 percent for Hispanic couples and from 61 percent to 34 percent for white couples). Between 1960 and 1973, one child in five children born to unmarried white women was relinquished for adoption. (Formal adoption is rarely chosen by unmarried African American or Hispanic parents.) In the late 1970s one in 10 premarital births resulted in adoption, and in the 1980s only one child in 30 children of premarital conception was adopted. Further documenting the overall change in familial and childbearing patterns is the fact that the abortion rate for adolescents is extremely high—40 percent (Chilman, 1989), a rate that accounts for one-third of all abortions performed in the United States each year (McAnarney & Hendee, 1989).

Despite the increase in nonmarital childbirths over 30 years, recent evidence suggests that the growth in adolescent nonmarital births may be slowing. The Children's Defense Fund, in *State of America's Children Yearbook* (CDF, 1995), reported that the rate dropped 2.3 percent in 1992 from the 1991 rate, the first decrease in five years. Girls ages 15 to 19 gave birth to 505,419 children in 1992, which translates into a childbirth rate of 60.7 births per 1,000 girls. Nearly all of the decline in that birth rate can be attributed to teenagers between the ages of 15 and 17, according to the Centers for Disease Control and Prevention (CDC) (CDF, 1995). The CDC and the Alan Guttmacher Institute (1994) posited that the drop in the adolescent birth rate from 1991 to 1992 corresponded to a decrease in the estimated adolescent pregnancy rate (from 254 to 208 per 1,000 teenage girls ages 15 to 19). The estimated number of adolescents in this age group who had sexual intercourse doubled over this period, leading to the hypothesis that sexually active adolescents are increasingly likely to use contraception.

DESCRIPTION OF RISK AND PROTECTIVE FACTORS

Risk and protective factors, as defined in chapter 2, need further elaboration when applied to the social problem of adolescent pregnancy. The usual definitions of risk and protective factors would imply that adolescents can incur the problem condition of pregnancy and that protective factors can prevent that problem condition. But pregnancy itself is not an illness that can be contracted, nor is bearing a child necessarily a problem condition. Rather, early pregnancy and childbearing can produce adverse consequences, which are intricately intertwined with the social and economic circumstances of many women who are single parents and poor. Nevertheless, certain risk factors are associated with adolescents becoming pregnant, and some protective factors can help adolescents delay pregnancy or avoid unfavorable outcomes if they do choose to bear children.

A vast amount of research has been conducted on adolescent pregnancy. Space limitations preclude a full exploration of all the literature. We therefore rely on reviews of empirical studies to explore the risk factors associated with early sexual relationships and the adverse implications of early childbearing for adolescents' economic future, health, and general well-being, as well as for their children. Few research studies have focused on resilience of adolescents who become pregnant, but some protective factors have emerged from studies on risk, and these will be highlighted. Repucci (1987) noted that social issues that affect children, adolescents, and families—such as adolescent pregnancy—should be viewed from an ecological perspective. We agree. Studies that follow an ecological perspective are given priority in this chapter.

Only studies that have been published since 1980 will be reviewed—the magnitude of social changes in the United States over the past two decades makes earlier studies irrelevant for construction of an ecological perspective. Not all of the research on the effects of risk and protective factors is consistent. This chapter explores differences in results based on ethnicity and gender. Studies that are reviewed fall into the following four types: (1) studies that focus on the adverse personal and social consequences of adolescent pregnancy, as well as negative consequences for the children of adolescents; (2) studies that look specifically at psychological variables associated with the risk of pregnancy; (3) studies that compare and contrast pregnant or parenting adolescents to those who have never been pregnant; and (4) studies that have attempted to build models that predict adolescent pregnancy (See Table 10-1 for risk and protective factors gleaned from these empirical studies).

RISK AND PROTECTIVE FACTORS ASSOCIATED WITH ADOLESCENT CHILDBEARING

In 1994 Northeastern University's Center for Labor Market Studies and the CDC emphasized that many adolescents became pregnant and bore children because they lacked hope and opportunity, a situation caused by living in poverty and consequently failing to develop basic academic skills. Eighty-three percent of adolescents who give birth are from economically disadvantaged households (U.S. Department of Health and Human Services, 1995). Data from the National Longitudinal Survey of Youth indicate that as family income rises, the proportion of adolescents who become teenage mothers declines; one in four poor youths became teenage mothers, compared with one of 10 in the highest income bracket. Three of eight teenagers with the weakest basic academic skills have children, compared with only one of 20 youths with the strongest skills. Socioeconomic status (SES) also accounts for some differences in adolescent fertility-related behavior found among different ethnic groups (see, for example, Bingham, Miller, & Adams, 1990; Furstenberg, Brooks-Gunn, & Morgan, 1987). Poverty and lack of educational achievement, which often go hand in hand, therefore appear to be both major precursors and major consequences of adolescent pregnancy.

RISK AND PROTECTIVE FACTORS IN EDUCATIONAL ACHIEVEMENT

The protective consequences of educational achievement extend from individual and psychosocial factors across family and community (Table 10-1). Conversely, lack of educational achievement or school dropout is definitely a risk factor for adolescents who become pregnant. DeBolt, Pasley, and Kreutzer (1990) reported that 40 percent of female

Table 10-1. Multisystemic Risk and Protective Factors for Adolescent Pregnancy

RISK FACTORS	PROTECTIVE FACTORS
Larger Systems	*Larger Systems*
Poverty/low SES	Adolescent health services (school-based clinics)
Inadequate social welfare, health, and educational system for adolescents	Asset-based welfare system
	Alternative schools and educational programs for pregnant and parenting teens
Family and Community Systems	*Family and Community Systems*
Lack of educational achievement/dropout	High educational achievement and staying in school
Low job skills	Job training and advanced education
Unmarried childbirth/single parent	Marriage/two-earner household
Family structure of parents: single parent, chaotic family, low SES, permissive sexual attitudes	Two-parent family background: parents with higher SES and education
Peers who are sexually active, do not use contraceptives effectively, or have borne a child	Open family communication
	Close to parents, especially mother
Lack of family and community supports	Parental control of dating and supervision
	Religious affiliation and attendance
	Prosocial peers who delay sex or use contraceptives
	Social support from family, friends, and community
	Pregnancy prevention programs
Individual and Psychosocial Systems	*Individual and Psychosocial Systems*
Younger age at pregnancy (14 or younger)	Delaying sex and/or pregnancy to age 18 or older
Substance use and abuse	Normal development, lack of substance use and other behaviors indicative of behavioral disorders
Sexual abuse	
Lack of knowledge or resistance to the use of contraceptives	Effective use of contraceptives
Low motivation toward academic achievement and career orientation	Goal directed, high educational aspiration, and career goals
Hopelessness toward future	Hopeful future goals and plans beyond parenthood
Multiple childbirths	Delaying repeat pregnancy
Biological Influences	*Biological Influences*
Health risks (toxemia, anemia, cephalopelvic disproportion, hypertension)	Older at pregnancy (16 years or older)
Low birthweight of child	Prenatal and perinatal care
Infant mortality	
Deficits to maternal and child nutrition	
Obesity	
Stunted growth of mother	

NOTE: SES = socioeconomic status.

dropouts identified pregnancy or marriage as their central explanation for leaving school. Adolescents who have low academic achievement, low academic ability, and low educational goals are also more likely to experience sexual intercourse at an early age (Perkins, 1991; Santelli & Beilenson, 1992). In a review of studies, Rudd, McKenry, and Nah (1990) found that women who gave birth before the age of 18, compared with those who waited until their 20s to have children, had fewer years of education and were less likely to obtain a high school diploma or continue on to college. These findings held up even after controlling for SES, ethnicity, academic ability, and motivation.

Problematic school experiences also have consequences for adolescent pregnancy: Adolescent females who have a negative school experience are more likely than others to get pregnant, and adolescent males are more likely to impregnate their partners (Hofferth, 1987). One hypothesis for the association between negative school experiences and pregnancy is that students who perform poorly in school may engage in early sexual activity or become pregnant as an alternative to continued involvement in self-devaluing school experiences (Zelnick & Kantner, 1980). Positive school experiences, on the other hand, may act as a protective factor against early sexual experiences and childbearing. But it is difficult to tease out the protective effects of positive school experiences, because those experiences may result from personal, family, or other social resources that themselves protect the adolescent from pregnancy.

Consistent with the problems of multideterminism and reciprocated causation in risk models discussed in chapter 1, it is difficult to know which comes first, adolescent pregnancy or school underachievement, but adolescent pregnancy and parenthood are negatively correlated with educational achievement (Jones, 1991). Of course, lack of education is further correlated with other risk factors, such as family size, divorce, welfare dependence, and use of health services (Moore & Burt, 1982). This leads to the conclusion that pregnancy may not be solely responsible for pregnant adolescents leaving school. In fact, since the late 1950s the number of adolescent mothers finishing high school has increased. Certain subgroups of pregnant or parenting adolescents, such as the economically advantaged and those who were older at first childbearing, account for most of that increase (McCarthy & Radish, 1982).

RISKS TO ECONOMIC SECURITY

Poverty is the crux of many of the concerns about adolescent pregnancy. Associations among childbearing, educational achievement, and income are especially important for contemporary women, because responsibility for the economic security of their families often falls to them, as does the traditional role of caretaker in the family (Scott-Jones & Turner, 1990). Variables in the larger systems shown in Table 10-1, such as low SES and an inadequate social welfare and educational system, put adolescents at risk of pregnancy. At the family and community level, however, higher SES, being reared in a better-educated family, and having access to job training and advanced education—all of which are often associated with higher SES levels—serve as protective factors.

Furstenberg, Brooks-Gunn, and Morgan (1987) described four factors, each of which comes under the umbrella of economic security, that influence the life course of adolescents who become pregnant. The first involves the availability of resources, including informal networks, parental support, and role models; the most salient of these is the presence of educated and economically secure parents. The second factor contributing to outcomes is represented by individual differences in competence (school achievement) and motivation (high educational aspirations); such achievements and aspirations strongly correlate with high SES. Third is participation in social welfare programs supported through a economically secure society that gives generous economic support to its members. Finally, career contingencies, the decisions made during or following the first pregnancy that may have facilitated or constrained events in later life (the pace of additional childbearing and marital decisions, for example), can greatly harm or enhance the resilience of adolescent parents insofar as educational achievement and economic security are concerned.

The long-term economic security of adolescents who become pregnant is at risk. Studies have demonstrated repeatedly that adolescent mothers are less likely to have stable, well-paying jobs than control and comparison groups and thus are more likely to be subject to prolonged dependency on public assistance and social welfare programs (Furstenberg et al., 1987; Harris, 1991; Hofferth, 1987; McAnarney & Hendee, 1989; Rudd et al., 1990; Turner, Grindstaff, & Phillips, 1990). Adolescent mothers also tend to have less job training and poorer wages. Furthermore, they do not have the experience or opportunity to train for and search for higher-paying jobs. Other studies confirm the risks to economic security experienced by women who become adolescent mothers. For example, Furstenberg et al. (1987) reported that, five years after initial assessment, significantly fewer mothers were employed than were their classmates, many of whom were also attending school full-time. The jobs that adolescent mothers did hold were mostly low-skill, low-paying work. Many of the adolescent childbearers were still mired in poverty 17 years after assessment, although their financial situation had improved somewhat over the second segment of the study. As an example, approximately one-quarter of the women had relied on public assistance during the past year as opposed to one-third of the mothers at the five-year follow-up. In addition, of the 70 percent who ever depended on welfare, almost two-thirds no longer received assistance.

These findings indicate that, despite ongoing economic hardships, all may not be gloom and doom for adolescent mothers. Some mothers' situations do improve over time, and some protective and resilient characteristics have been identified in subsequent studies. For example, Harris (1991) focused on welfare dependency when analyzing the longitudinal data from the study by Furstenberg et al. (1987). This study indicated that mothers who relied on welfare while finishing high school were more likely to attain self-sufficiency than mothers who dropped out and entered the labor market, which suggests that becoming pregnant and receiving welfare does not trap a young mother in the welfare system. In fact, entering the welfare system for a time may actually serve as a protective factor and enhance long-term economic security for some women.

One question related to economic security that is often raised is, What keeps women who can work on welfare? Several responses are plausible. First, child-care responsibilities may restrict the number of hours a mother can work. Second, deficiencies in education and family resources often push some mothers into low-paying jobs, and part-time or low-wage employment cannot bring in enough money to sustain a family so that women can leave welfare. As stated before, educational attainment is a protective factor against both pregnancy and its potential long-term negative consequences; moreover, Harris (1991) argued, academic achievement is the best predictor of higher-wage employment and self-sufficiency. The effects of educational deficits are twofold: They increase reliance on welfare, and the duration of welfare dependency is prolonged for single parents who lack the skills necessary to find employment that pays enough to support a family (Rudd et al., 1990).

Other factors, aside from a good education, can promote the resilience of mothers and their ability to exit public assistance through employment. These protective factors include age, previous work experience, and marriage (Table 10-1). These are attributes of both individual and psychosocial and family and community systems. Age, in particular, is a significant factor. Harris (1991) found that the younger the age at pregnancy, the more at risk the mother seemed for a negative sequence of employment and public assistance. Mothers who relied on assistance even while employed were younger at first pregnancy, started welfare at an earlier age, and became employed later than women who left the welfare system. The implications of this research are that younger adolescents who become pregnant are at the highest risk of lifelong problems in establishing economic security for themselves and their children.

Although not a choice or an available option for many adolescent mothers, marriage (or residing with a partner) is a protective factor and an important way in which women exit welfare, particularly African American women (Harris, 1991; Rudd et al., 1990). Rudd and colleagues, for example, argued that marriage protects against adverse financial circumstances. A married woman may be able to exit welfare because she has more opportunities to pursue gainful employment when child-care arrangements are shared or because her partner makes financial contributions to the family (Harris, 1991). Fourteen-year-old mothers who had partners spent less time on welfare because, in general, being part of a two-parent family has a positive association with educational achievement and a negative association with time as a single parent.

Of course, marriage as a route to economic security remains a high-risk endeavor for adolescent childbearers (Furstenberg et al., 1987). For example, young adolescents who postpone marriage are more likely to stay in school after the birth of a child. Moreover, early marriages are likely to break up, which can then lead to economic dependence.

Finally, social interventions such as social welfare programs and school-based pregnancy and parenting programs may serve as protective factors on outcomes for adolescent parents, and they might help prevent pregnancy in the first place (Hechtman, 1989). Furstenberg et al. (1987) found moderate effects on crucial life-course contingencies, such as the decision to graduate from high school and to postpone further childbearing, for those participating in social interventions. When the long-term success of an intervention program was defined in terms of total fertility, educational achievement, social and relationship involvement, fertility control, and an internal locus of control, active participation in the program intervention was associated 20 years later with financial success (Horwitz, Klerman, Kuo, & Jekel, 1991).

To summarize, the economic situation of pregnant adolescents is affected by schooling, marital status, and employment. Educational achievement, which serves as a protective factor against early sexual experiences and childbearing, is influenced by family background, marital status, and educational ability and aspirations. Consistent with a multisystemic perspective, the decisions of adolescent childbearers in one domain tend to affect other areas. For example, adolescents who postpone marriage appear to be more likely to stay in school after childbirth and, in the long run, secure higher-paying employment. Furthermore, adolescent marriages are likely to break up, a fact that contributes to economic dependence for the adolescent mother. The intertwined effects of life decisions are not easy to disentangle.

Implications for the Health of the Adolescent Mother and Child

Adolescent childbearing has often been reported as a risk factor for adverse maternal and child health. Obstetric health risks to the mother include such conditions as toxemia, anemia, cephalopelvic disproportion, and hypertension. Adverse health risks to the child include low birthweight, prematurity, and infant mortality. These conditions are probably overattributed in the early literature to the physiological immaturity of the adolescent. The more likely contributors to poor health outcomes for the adolescent mother and her child are sociodemographic in origin, such as low SES, single status, and poor prenatal care (McAnarney & Hendee, 1989; Stevens-Simon & Beach, 1992; Turner et al., 1990). Hechtman (1989) argued that adolescents younger than 15 might experience perinatal outcomes poorer than for older adolescents, but research is constrained by the small number of such young subjects in most samples. A main confounding variable for this group is lack of prenatal care: Very young teens may conceal their pregnancy, thus forgoing care at this crucial time. Poor perinatal outcomes might be attributed to the competing nutritional needs of the adolescent and her fetus; evidence suggests that females who give birth to a child when they are younger than 16 tend to stop growing. In addition, Black and DeBlassie (1985) reported that the risk of morbidity during or immediately after pregnancy is five times greater for females under the age of 16 than for females who give birth between the ages of 20 and 24. However, neonatal morbidity and mortality differences between adolescent and adult mothers disappear when ethnic and SES factors are held constant (Brooks-Gunn & Furstenberg, 1986).

Research on the relationship between adolescent childbearing and long-term health outcomes is modest and inconclusive. Although direct etiologic pathways have not been demonstrated, adolescent childbearing appears to be related to obesity and hypertension (Stevens-Simon & Beach, 1992). Stevens-Simon and Beach also cited evidence, though inconclusive, that adolescent mothers' lactation might increase their likelihood for bone demineralization. Furthermore, depletion of nutrient reserves could contribute to the greater likelihood of neonatal risk in subsequent pregnancies.

The evidence on whether infants of adolescents suffer from higher mortality rates is mixed. Some reviews suggest that infants of adolescent mothers have a greater mortality rate—as much as two to three times higher than the average (Hechtman, 1990)—in the first 28 days of life (McAnarney & Hendee, 1989) and in the first year of life. Higher postneonatal mortality rates are attributable to such problems as sudden infant death syndrome (six times higher than the average rate), accidents, illnesses, injuries, and infection. In contrast to these reviews, the study by Brooks-Gunn and Furstenberg (1986) found that general health outcomes, including mortality, do not differ for adolescents' infants up to a year old when results are controlled for SES. An exception was accident rates, which tend to be higher in babies of females under 20 years old, even after holding maternal education and parity constant; these data suggest that the supervision patterns of adolescent mothers are deficient.

Evidence seems to indicate that the increased health risks for the adolescent mother and her child may be attributable as much to SES and education levels as to age of childbearing per se. By the same token, females with a lower SES and poor educational achievement are at greater risk of becoming adolescent parents. Hence, the causes and effects of adolescent pregnancy are again intertwined.

PEER RELATIONS AS A RISK FACTOR

Peer relations act as both protective and risk factors for adolescent pregnancy. Despite some deviations in findings, peer relations are believed to significantly influence adolescent sexual behavior. For example, a study of the sexual activity of 1,610 private school adolescents (grades seven to 12) found that the best predictor of sexual intercourse frequency involved differential peer associations, defined as the number of best friends who were sexually active (DiBlassio & Benda, 1990). Twenty-eight percent of the variance in this study was explained by this single variable.

The support for peer relations as a protective and risk factor is strong, but it is difficult to know whether adolescents' sexual behavior is influenced by their sexually active friends or whether they select friends among peers who, like themselves, are sexually active. How can we know which came first? Studies on the effects of peer relations on sexual activity are based on the assumption that peers influence a particular individual's deviant behavior rather than vice versa; yet it is equally plausible that friends are selected on the basis of the individual's own preferences for level of sexual activity. Because of the correlational nature of the studies, causal inference is hard to determine. This is a general weakness in studies on peer relations. Another limitation of the studies is that they are based on perceptions of peer behavior rather than on actual behavior (Hayes, 1987). One exception to this limitation is work by Billy and Urdy (1985), who conducted a longitudinal study of 1,153 junior high school respondents and obtained information from same-sex and opposite-sex friends. The importance of peer relations held up. Findings indicated that adolescents were influenced by close friends of both sexes when it came to sexual activity.

Finally, it should be noted that the influence of peers may not carry the same significance for all relationship patterns. Jorgensen, King, and Torrey (1980) examined relationship satisfaction, interpersonal power, and pregnancy risk. In their study pregnancy risk was determined by frequency of sexual activity and regularity of contraceptive use. Qualities of the dyadic relationship were found to have more influence on behavior than variables for either the peer or family social network. The implication is that the quality of relationships may be the important element influencing an adolescent's decisions, and some peer relationships may have more influence than others.

To summarize, the sexual behavior of adolescents is affected by the sexual behavior of best friends of the same sex (see, for example, DiBlassio & Benda, 1990) and close friends of both sexes (for example, Billy & Urdy, 1985), although the differential effects of opposite-sex friends and romantic partners have not been well distinguished. Evidence is mixed as to whether certain groups—females or males, younger or older adolescents—are more vulnerable to peer influence. Self-selection bias may explain some of the effect of peer sexual status, because adolescents pick their friends, at least in part, based on their friends' behaviors (Hofferth, 1987; Urdy, 1980). On the other hand, peers who delay sex or use contraceptives are likely to serve as an important protective factor by influencing other adolescents to make decisions that will not lead to early childbearing.

FAMILY STRUCTURE AND PATTERNS AS RISK FACTORS

Peers have an important influence, but the family still plays a central role in adolescence (Brown & Mann, 1990). Many studies have examined family factors in relation to sexual activity and adolescent pregnancy. Both structural and functioning factors have been studied, often separately, although it is recognized that these factors have an impact on each other. Examples of family factors that have been addressed include parental permissiveness and control of dating, parents' own dating behavior, family structure, and communication about issues of sexuality. Table 10-1 illustrates how these family factors serve as both protective and risk factors for adolescent pregnancy. A full explication of the family literature in this area is beyond the scope of this chapter, but a few studies that have important implications for dealing with adolescent pregnancy are summarized below.

Many studies report that adolescents from one-parent homes tend to be more sexually active than those from two-parent homes (Dawson, 1986; Flewelling & Bauman, 1990; Flick, 1986; Newcomer & Urdy, 1985; Zelnick, Kantner, & Ford, 1981). Murry (1992), who focused on African American adolescents, found parents' marital status (structure of family) to be a factor in adolescent pregnancy. Hogan and Kitagawa (1985) found that African American children whose parents were unmarried when the adolescents were 11 years of age were 36 percent more likely to become pregnant during adolescence than those from intact families, and earlier research found that African American youths whose SES was above that of most in the study cohort were more likely to become pregnant if they were from single-parent homes. The National Research Council pointed out that in these studies that ethnicity and SES might be confounded (Murry, 1992).

Parental control of dating—that is, their supervision and control over hours, locations, and dating partners—is a strong inhibitor of adolescent sexual activity and pregnancy, even after controlling for other social risk factors (Santelli & Beilensen, 1992). Early dating and frequent dating have been associated with early initiation of sexual intercourse (McAnarney & Schreider, 1984; Shah & Zelnick, 1981). McAnarney and Hendee (1989) reported that adolescents with less parental control and less parental disapproval of problem behaviors were more likely to be sexually active than those whose parents offered consistent guidance. Maternal disapproval of sexual activity, however, may have an effect on child behavior only in the context of a close relationship. Newcomer and Urdy (1985) canvassed actual parental attitudes on sexual behavior rather than adolescents' perception of those attitudes; they discovered that parental attitudes did not have an effect on adolescent sexual behavior. This might mean, as Santelli and Beilensen (1992) suggested, that adolescents' perception of adult rules and attitudes may be more important in influencing behavior than adults' actual attitudes.

Several studies have examined the effects of family communication on sexual activity (Cvetkovich & Grote, 1981; Jorgensen et al., 1980; Kastner, 1984; Newcomer & Urdy, 1985; Shah & Zelnik, 1981). White and DeBlassie (1992) found that adolescents rated their parents highly in terms of influence on sexual opinions, beliefs, and attitudes, but lower than friends, school, and books as sources of sexual information. Almost all respondents preferred that sex education come from parents, but only 15 percent identified parents as a central source of information.

Findings on the influence of adolescent–parent communication in general are mixed (Santelli & Beilensen, 1992). Newcomer and Urdy (1985) got contradictory reports from mothers and their daughters. Mothers stated that their daughters delayed sexual intercourse when communication between them was open, whereas their daughters' reports showed no significant differences between characteristics of parent–child communication and early sexual activity. A central factor that emerged is that, in most families, communication about sexual matters is minimal. Other studies have also indicated that family communication may have little effect on adolescent sexual behavior but some positive influence on contraceptive use (Fox, 1980; Hayes, 1987). Perkins (1991), however, reported that communication with family was not correlated with contraceptive use; other studies (Flaherty & Maracek, 1982; Kastner, 1984) found that if a girl has open communication with her mother and if her mother is a source of birth control information, then the girl tends to be an effective contraceptor.

Yet other studies indicate that the relationship between parental communication and sexual behavior is conditional. Moore, Peterson, and Furstenberg (1986) found that parent–child communication about sex education may delay sexual activity only when families hold traditional values about sexuality. Gender can also make a difference. Paternal communication produces one result for girls and another for boys: With daughters positive paternal communication appears to inhibit sexual activity, but with sons it is associated with greater sexual activity. Kahn, Smith, and Roberts (1984) argued that fathers often hold and convey different behavioral standards for sons and daughters. In general, mother–daughter communication appears to be more important (Fox & Inazu, 1980; Inazu & Fox, 1980), with positive relationships linked to delays in sexual activity, better contraceptive use, and fewer partners. But overall, the research suggests that communication with parents is only weakly associated with adolescent sexual behavior. The closeness of relationships between adolescents and their parents and the presence of structured, consistent rules about dating appear to be much more influential than parent–child communication per se (Santelli & Beilenson, 1992).

In sum, family structure and processes do appear to be related to adolescent pregnancy. Single-parent families have a higher incidence of adolescent pregnancy, but because poverty is associated with family structure, it is not clear whether this elevated risk is caused by family structure or by the effects of poverty. Adolescents from chaotic families with permissive attitudes toward premarital sex are also at risk for early sexual activity, as are those from excessively rigid, overbearing families. Another variable related to family processes is active religious affiliation; although participation in a religion appears to serve a protective function against sexual activity, it is a risk factor for ineffective contraceptive use (Studer & Thornton, 1987; Thornton & Camburn, 1989). Apparently, a curvilinear relationship might be present: Moderate levels of supervision and control may help delay sexual activity, and extreme control or extreme permissiveness may be related to early sexual activity and ineffective contraceptive use (Santelli & Beilenson, 1992). Clearly, consistent and reasonable parental supervision, rule setting, and discipline serve as protective factors against early childbearing.

SOCIAL SUPPORT AS A PROTECTIVE FACTOR

Social support serves as a protective factor for both pregnant and parenting adolescents (Table 10-1). Social support may reduce stress by altering appraisals of stressors, by changing coping patterns, or by affecting self-perceptions (Barrera, 1986; Turner et al., 1990). Reviews on social support suggest that it is not a singular construct (Barrera, 1986; Cohen & Wills, 1985; Streeter & Franklin, 1992; Turner et al., 1990). Cohen and Wills argued that social support has four distinct elements: esteem or emotional support (feeling valued and accepted by others), social companionship (time spent in leisure and recreational activities with others), informational support (assistance in defining, giving meaning to, and coping with stressful events); and instrumental support (the receipt of needed services and financial and material resources). Oakley (1985) found that psychosocial assets, such as social support, mediate stress and other complicating factors associated with adolescent pregnancy. Colletta and Gregg (1981) conducted a study of 65 African American parents ages 14 to 19 to discover the situational and individual factors that mediated their stress. A positive relationship was found between amount of perceived social support and frequency of appropriate maternal interactions. Central in importance was emotional support, particularly when it involved the mother's family of origin.

The quality and character of support appears to be more important than the number of sources of support, whether friends, siblings, parents, or others. Barth and Schinke (1983) studied 52 pregnant or parenting adolescents (ages 14 to 19) from school-based parent programs in urban, suburban, and semirural areas, representing an ethnic mix of African American and white youths. Results indicated that those with adequate support experienced less distress. Schilmoeller, Baranowski, and Higgins (1991) used a longitudinal design that compared adolescent and older mothers on size and quality of social networks and perception of support at one month, six months, and 12 months postpartum to determine the effect of social support on maternal adjustment and behavior. No significant differences emerged between the two groups on size and quality of social networks, although adults scored significantly higher on perceived family support. For both adolescent and adult mothers, quality of interaction and perceived family support—not size of social support systems—was significantly associated with adjustment, and effects were most pronounced for the adolescent group.

Giblin, Poland, and Sachs (1987) studied social support as a multidimensional construct made up of perceptions of and satisfaction with network members, as well as with "social services as sources of instrumental and/or tangible assistance, information, empathy and understanding" (p. 273). Results indicated that satisfaction was related to emotional support from peers and siblings, health-seeking information from the adolescent's mother, and adolescents' assessment of support. Satisfaction was measured by self-report and was derived from an a priori grouping of related questionnaire items that were analyzed through factor analysis. In contrast, tangible assistance (housing, health care, child care, social services) was unrelated to satisfaction with pregnancy and prenatal care, but it was related to postpartum clinic attendance. This study suggests that the benefits of tangible assistance may be specific (clinic attendance, for example), whereas emotional support may be related to more global states of well-being. To summarize, social support from peers and family appears to serve a protective and buffering function for pregnant or parenting adolescents.

RISKS ASSOCIATED WITH PSYCHOLOGICAL AND DEVELOPMENTAL FACTORS

Although most studies on adolescent pregnancy focus on social variables, psychological variables such as developmental status, psychological states (self-esteem, depression), and social psychological factors (sexual abuse, substance abuse) have also been studied. The lack of research on psychological variables may in part result from the difficulties of measuring these variables. In addition, psychological variables may be linked to other salient individual and psychosocial variables such as age, physical maturity, and developmental level (Santelli & Beilensen, 1992).

Adolescent Development

The close tie between the pubertal hormones that determine development and the social interpretation of physical maturity complicates the separation of biological and social effects in understanding adolescent pregnancy. A decade ago, the social interpretation of physical maturity held sway: In that explanation for adolescent pregnancy, the developing adolescent is perceived as a potential sexual partner and begins to be treated as such (Santelli & Beilensen, 1992). However, Santelli and Beilensen cited evidence for the direct effect of hormones on sexual behavior. In females, androgen- and estrogen-mediated development independently influence initiation of sexual activity. Relatedly, physically immature females appear to be less prone to the influence of their friends' sexual behavior. For males, androgen-mediated development affects sexual behavior, with the free testosterone index (FTI) being the central determinant of sexual motivation (libido). Indeed, when holding FTI constant, no independent effect of physical development or age is demonstrated. Evidence is suggestive that a model involving the social interpretation of development may be more salient for females, although biosocial models that combine the biological and the social may be most predictive of sexual involvement for both boys and girls (Santelli & Beilensen, 1992; Smith, Urdy, & Morris, 1985).

In a recent meta-analysis of studies of adolescent pregnancy prevention outcomes, Franklin, Grant, Corcoran, O'Dell, and Bultman (1995) found adolescent development and age to have salient effects. Results indicated that older adolescents (ages 15 to 19 years) perform better on contraceptive use measures than girls 14 and younger, and that older adolescents are less likely to get pregnant. These findings are consistent with previous research revealing that older female adolescents are more likely to use contraceptives effectively than are younger ones (Alan Guttmacher Institute, 1994). The Alan Guttmacher Institute reported that younger females rely more on less effective methods of contraception such as condoms and withdrawal, and that young adolescents are more likely to use contraception in an inconsistent manner.

These findings may be related to cognitive development (Franklin, 1987). In the stage of concrete thinking, a child can represent cognitively only what exists in reality, which means that hypothetical events are not represented mentally. Hence, the challenge for younger adolescents: To use contraceptive methods effectively, they must plan ahead for sexual behavior, control impulses, seek out the necessary information, and then apply what they have learned to their own behavior. Involved in this sequence are not only innate cognitive developmental processes, but also formal operational thought, which is the ability to hypothesize behavioral consequences, to evaluate consequences, and to follow through on the pattern of behaviors that are involved in producing the desired outcome. Environmental factors, such as cultural differences, schooling, and individual experiences, may also influence the development of formal operations.

Psychological Variable: Self-Esteem

Out of all the research conducted on psychological states, the effect of self-esteem on adolescent sexual behavior has perhaps been the most studied. In general, the research on the connection of self-esteem to fertility-related behavior is mixed (Dryfoos, 1990; Hofferth, 1987; Miller & Moore, 1990). In a review of the effect of self-esteem, Santelli and Beilensen (1992) reported different findings for males and females, although these findings tend to be inconsistent across the literature. Although some research indicates that sexually experienced girls may suffer from lower self-esteem (Orr et al., 1989, as cited in Santelli & Beilensen, 1992), others have found no relationship (Hofferth, 1987, for example). Longitudinal work in this area (Vernon, Green, & Frothingham, 1983) has also shown that adolescent girls who became pregnant did not have lower self-esteem than their nonpregnant counterparts. For males, Orr et al. (cited in Santelli & Beilensen, 1992) discovered no association between self-esteem and sexual behavior; other studies have indicated higher self-esteem for sexually active males (see Santelli & Beilensen, 1992). However, causal order could be at play, in that sexual activity may improve self-esteem for young men.

Other research suggests that the connection between self-esteem and sexual activity may be indirect and mediated by other variables. For instance, Miller, Christensen, and Olson (1987) found that self-esteem was related to sexual activity only as mediated by attitudes toward sexual activity. That is, if adolescents felt that engaging in premarital sexual activity was wrong, they experienced low self-esteem; conversely, if they felt sexual intercourse was right, they experienced high self-esteem if they were sexually active.

Social Psychological Variable: Substance Use

The studies involving substance use have focused mainly on its relation to sexual activity rather than to contraceptive use or pregnancy (an exception is Yamaguchi & Kandel, 1987) and have tended to identify substance use as a risk factor for early sexual behavior (Zabin, Hardy, Smith, & Hirsch, 1986). However, the causal order of relationships is not clear. For example, Elliott and Morse (1989), in an analysis of longitudinal national survey data, discovered that substance use preceded sexual activity, whereas other studies (Mott & Haurin, 1988; Rosenbaum & Kandel, 1990) have found the influence of substance use and sexual activity to be reciprocal. Rodgers and Rowe (1990) argued that a single "deviance trait" may underlie both adolescent sexual behavior and behaviors such as drug and alcohol use. What is clear is that a significant relationship between substance use and sexual activity has been found. Future studies should examine more closely the ways in which substance use might be a risk factor affecting contraceptive use and pregnancy.

Social Psychological Variable: Sexual Abuse

As a result of sexual assaults ranging from intimidation to rape, many female adolescents are forced prematurely into sexual activity (Alan Guttmacher Institute, 1994; Laumann, Gagnon, Michaels, & Michaels, 1994; Moore, Nord, & Peterson, 1989). Approximately 50 percent to 75 percent of females whose first sexual experience happened before age 14 or 15 were forced into sexual relationships. Interventions need to target the vulnerability and inculpability of adolescents, especially younger females, in relationship to coercive sexual activity and sexual abuse. Making available training in self-defense, assertiveness, and empowerment strategies, as well as providing safe environments and education on how to avoid involuntary sexual activity, may be important protective factors for younger female adolescents.

SUMMARY

In sum, psychological and developmental tasks complicate issues associated with adolescent pregnancy, and more attention needs to be given to the attendant psychological and developmental variables. Complicated developmental and behavioral disorders can lead to early sexual behavior. This is evidenced in both substance use and sexual abuse. Sexual abuse, in particular, is a risk factor that accounts for the sexual activity of a large percentage of younger adolescents. Although lack of self-esteem is often described as a cause, it does not appear to be nearly as important as other developmental and behavioral processes in explaining early sexual activity, inconsistent contraceptive use, and pregnancy.

ASSESSMENT MEASURES

This section briefly describes examples of measures available: two used to assess family relationships, one social support measure, and one measure that assesses global characteristics in relationship to the behavioral functioning of adolescents. These four measures may be used by practitioners to assess risk and protective factors in adolescents. See Card (1993) for a more comprehensive review of adolescent sexuality and pregnancy measures.

FAMILY RELATIONSHIPS

The Family Adaptability and Cohesion Scale III (FACES III) is a 20-item, normative-based, paper-and-pencil self-report inventory that uses the circumplex model. It was developed by Olson and colleagues at the University of Minnesota, Department of Family Social Science (1985). The circumplex model is a circular matrix that classifies family functioning along three major dimensions, family cohesion (bonding), family adaptability (change), and communication. The FACES III measures only the first two dimensions. The third dimension, communication, can be assessed with another inventory developed by the authors, the Parent and Adolescent Communication Form. Cohesion and adaptability dimensions each have a four-point continuum ranging from low cohesion (disengaged) to high cohesion (enmeshed) and from low adaptability (rigid) to high adaptability (chaotic). The FACES III has been used in studies on adolescent pregnancy (Romig & Bakken, 1990; Barnett, Papini, & Gbur, 1991), but different researchers have gotten different answers about the families of pregnant or parenting adolescents. Romig and Bakken (1990) found that pregnant adolescents were more likely to have families who were extremely rigid and less flexible than those of other groups. Barnett and colleagues (1991), however, found that pregnant teenagers reported their families to be high in flexibility, and nonpregnant adolescents had families with higher cohesion.

FACES III is reported to have good face, content, concurrent, and discriminant validity. Internal consistency reliability for each of the scales is fair to good, with Cronbach's alphas of .62 for adaptability and .77 for cohesion. Test–retest reliability based on a four-week interval was good, with alphas of .80 for adaptability and .83 for cohesion (Olson, Poertner, & Lavee, 1985). Test–retest reliability based on a four-week interval was good, with alphas of .80 for adaptability and .83 for cohesion (Olson, Poertner, & Lavee, 1985). Construct validity was originally reported by the authors to be good, but this assertion has recently been challenged (Green, Harris, Forte, & Robinson, 1991). In response to criticisms concerning the validity of the FACES III measure, Olson and colleagues reconceptualized the circumplex model as a three-dimensional circumplex model, which converts the curvilinear model to a linear model that measures cohesion and flexibility as linear dimensions ranging from high to low on a nine-point continuum. Franklin and Streeter (1993) presented a more detailed description of the 3-D circumplex model and how it differed from the curvilinear model. Olson (1991) argued that when used in conjunction with the 3-D model, the FACES III provides a valid assessment of family functioning. However, Franklin and Streeter (1993) found that the 3-D formulation did not fully correct the problems with construct validity. The general curvilinear hypothesis, however, has been confirmed using data from families in neurotic and schizophrenic groups. The clinical rating scale version of the measure has also consistently confirmed the curvilinear hypothesis. Olson and colleagues are further refining the instrument, and FACES IV will be available soon.

The Family Environment Scales (FES) evolved from research on social climates; that is, the unique personality or attributes of social environments (Moos, 1989). The FES is a 90-item, true–false, self-report measure that assesses whole family functioning; it is compatible with social- and ecological-systems theory. It has 10 subscales that assess three construct dimensions: relationships, personal growth, and systems maintenance (organizational structure) of the family. The subscales for the dimensions are as follows: for the relationship dimension, cohesion, expressiveness, and conflict; for personal growth, independence, achievement orientation, intellectual cultural orientation, active recreational orientation, and moral religious emphasis; and for systems maintenance, organization and control. The FES has been widely used in both clinical research and practice and has been demonstrated to be an effective outcome measure.

The FES has excellent psychometric characteristics. The 10 subscales have demonstrated adequate internal consistency reliability ranging from .61 to .78. Test–retest reliability coefficients range from .68 to .86. The FES was constructed using factor analysis, and the construct validity of the measure has been examined in more than 200 studies. One limitation of this measure, however, is that it has not been widely normed on low-SES families. See Grotevant and Carlson (1989) for a more detailed exploration of the psychometric studies on the FES.

The FES offers a more global assessment of family functioning than the FACES III described above. The first construct dimension of relationships, comprising cohesion, conflict, and expressiveness, has been used as a unitary measure of family support. As such, it could be used to work with adolescents at risk for pregnancy, because adolescents' perceptions of family support are important protective factors. (See Jordan and Franklin, 1995, for reviews of other measures of family functioning that may be helpful in assessing family risk and protective factors associated with adolescent pregnancy.)

SOCIAL SUPPORT AND BEHAVIORAL FUNCTIONING

The Social Support Behaviors (SSB) instrument was developed by Vaux (1988) to measure five types of social support: emotional, socializing, practical assistance, financial assistance, and advice and guidance. The SSB is a 45-item, paper-and-pencil, self-report measure that asks adolescents to indicate, on the basis of past experience, how likely a friend or a family member is to perform a supportive behavior. Because social support has been found to be a protective factor for adolescents who are pregnant or parenting, it seems particularly important to know what types of supportive behavior (for example, emotional support versus financial assistance) an adolescent might receive from family and friends. The SSB was developed along with two other instruments for measuring social support, the Social Support Resources and the Social Support Appraisal Scale (Vaux, 1988). The three measures examine social support from different angles.

Several studies show the SSB to have good psychometric characteristics. Internal consistency was tested on several samples of college students and found to be good, with alphas of .85. There is also evidence for the content, concurrent, predictive, and construct validity of the measure. Factor analysis supported the measure's factor structure. (See Streeter & Franklin, 1992, for a review of eight social support measures that may be used in clinical practice.)

The Hilson Adolescent Profile (HAP) is a standardized behavioral assessment instrument developed specifically for troubled youth. It was designed to screen for the presence and extent of adolescent behavior patterns and problems. In short, the purpose of the HAP is to help mental health practitioners, school personnel, and professionals in the juvenile justice system identify adolescents at risk. The HAP is a 310-item, true–false, self-report instrument. A shorter version of the measure is currently being developed. Scoring is based on a *t* score distribution with a mean of 50 and a standard deviation of 10 (Inwald, Brobst, & Morrissey, 1987).

The HAP contains 16 subscales that fall along the four construct dimensions of validity measure, "acting out" behaviors, interpersonal adjustment measures, and internalized conflict measures. The subscales are as follows: for validity measure, guarded responses; for acting out behaviors, alcohol use, drug use, educational adjustment difficulties, law violations, frustration tolerance, antisocial risk taking, and rigidity/obsessiveness; for interpersonal adjustment measures, interpersonal/ assertiveness difficulties, home life conflicts, and social sexual adjustment; for internalized conflict measures, health concerns, anxiety-phobic avoidance, depression/ suicidal potential, suspicious temperament, and unusual responses. Several of these subscales have relevance for assessing risk and protective factors associated with adolescent pregnancy. For example, the alcohol and drug use subscales help clinicians identify youths with substance abuse problems, the home life conflict subscale has items that screen for sexual abuse, and the educational adjustment subscale identifies youths with school and academic achievement problems that may serve as a risk factor for early childbearing.

The HAP has been shown to have good internal construct validity and external criterion-related validity. It has also been shown to have fair to good internal consistency reliability, with KR20 coefficients ranging from .67 to .90. Most scales show reliability coefficients of .80 or better. Preliminary data on test–retest reliability showed Pearson correlation coefficients between the HAP scales at two time periods ranged from .76 to .998, with 11 of the 16 scales having correlations of .95 or greater (Inwald, Brobst, & Morrissey, 1987).

Implications for Prevention, Intervention, and Treatment

Several risk and protective factors for adolescent pregnancy have been identified, and they are all closely intertwined. Multiple interventions should therefore be considered (U.S. Department of Health and Human Services, 1995).

Family Life and Sex Education

Research suggests that the most effective family life and sex education programs combine the teaching of abstinence or delay of early sex with information about contraception. However, even these programs have had only modest success. Programs that are more comprehensive and combine such activities as role playing and life skills training may have better outcomes. Developmentally appropriate programs from elementary through high school are needed. This is especially the case for younger adolescents (age 14 and younger), who face increased risks because their cognitive development is insufficient to the task of managing sexual behavior and contraceptive use.

Programs should be offered in settings other than schools for several reasons. For one, schools are often constrained from offering programs with sufficiently comprehensive content. Second, teenagers who attend school services risk stigma and embarrassment. Moreover, some adolescents do not attend conventional schools. In a meta-analysis, Franklin et al. (1995) found community-based pregnancy prevention programs to be more effective than school-based programs.

Programs to Improve Educational and Occupational Options

Because educational and occupational programs focus on several risk factors and are aimed at enhancing job skills, occupational prospects, and income, their potential benefits are large. These types of programs appear to increase motivation and skills. Alternative schools that have been demonstrated to be effective in dropout retrieval should be replicated (Franklin, 1992). In addition, programs that assure advanced education and job training, and the accumulation of resources such as asset-based welfare programs, may be a promising method for helping pregnant or parenting adolescents overcome educational and employment problems.

Increased Funding for Contraceptive Services

The U.S. Department of Health and Human Services (1995) reported that of all unmarried females ages 15 to 44 nationwide, "Less than one in ten are sexually active, do not want to become pregnant, and yet do not use contraception. However, these women account for about half of all unintended pregnancies in the United States" (p. 2). Although lack of motivation, concern over side effects, or not knowing how to use contraceptive methods account for some of this paradox, inability to pay for contraception can be a major problem. Effective contraceptive use would mitigate several risk factors associated with early sexual activity. Although the major federal source of funding for pregnancy prevention is Title X of the Public Health Services Act (P.L. 99-272), the money may not be enough to meet the need.

REMOVAL OF BARRIERS TO ADOPTION AND OTHER FAMILY LIFE OPTIONS

Larger systems interventions should focus on the removal of the financial, legal, and policy barriers to adoption, abortion, or marriage that serve to increase the number of nonmarital childbirths. In particular, it is not easy for adolescents to seek adoption or abortion as alternatives to pregnancy. Marriage is also a difficult option for younger adolescents, who need parental consent to marry. In general, adolescents in this society have a hard time finding jobs that can support them and a new family, which may act as another deterrent to marriage. Restructuring policies around family life options for adolescents may assist them in taking greater responsibility for pregnancy and childbirth.

COMMUNITY AWARENESS AND MEDIA INTERVENTION

Information campaigns are needed to help communities foster awareness about adolescent sexual activity, substance abuse, and sexual abuse, as well as other risk factors associated with adolescent pregnancy. The media could be used to portray positive role models and offer information about the risks of unprotected sex and the costs of nonmarital parenthood.

STRENGTHENING FAMILIES

A major point of intervention involves policy and practices designed to preserve and strengthen families. This would have multiple benefits for at-risk adolescents, because having unmarried parents has been shown to be linked to early initiation of sexual behavior. Enhanced family relationships may positively influence teenagers' sexual behavior. More efforts could be targeted at involving members of the extended kin network, who could pass their knowledge about child-rearing practices to both mothers and fathers, to help them develop the skills to influence adolescents. Approaches to preventing child abuse would also benefit teenagers at risk of sexual abuse and early sexual involvement.

DEVELOPMENT OF PEER LEADERSHIP

Because peers so strongly influence the sexual choices of adolescents, schools and community agencies might focus efforts on developing programs run by prosocial youths. Young people might then be influenced to delay initiation of sexual activity and to practice effective contraception if they are sexually active. For example, peer leaders could serve as instructors and leaders for sex education groups. Older adolescents could serve as mentors to younger adolescents and support them in choices to delay sexual activity or to use contraceptives.

CHILD SUPPORT ENFORCEMENT AND CHANGES IN PUBLIC POLICIES

Fathers who do not marry the mothers of their children suffer few of the disadvantages of child rearing. Strong enforcement of child support laws may encourage these men to marry the mothers or to prevent pregnancy in the first place (U.S. Department of Health and Human Services, 1995). Marriage penalties in government programs and in the tax code bear rethinking, as do proposed cutbacks on the earned income tax credit. Government policies need to be assessed to find out how they affect both marital and fertility behavior.

SOCIAL SUPPORT PROGRAMS

Schools, churches, and community agencies should consider orchestrating social support programs for pregnant teens and operating prosocial, antipregnancy programs for youths at risk of early childbearing. Such programs may focus on educational interventions, skills training, and mentoring of youths. Communities may implement a norm of "no early pregnancy" if parents, community leaders, and youth leaders work together to this end. Career development programs may be especially helpful in motivating youths to commit themselves to this type of community norm.

HEALTH-RELATED SERVICES AND PROGRAMS

Franklin et al. (1995) found that community-based clinic services were more effective in increasing contraceptive use and reducing the rate of adolescent pregnancy than were other sex education programs. Increasing funding for a full spectrum of community health and substance abuse services may reduce risk and serve as a protective factor both for adolescent pregnancy and for health outcomes for teenage mothers and their children.

REFERENCES

Alan Guttmacher Institute. (1994). *Sex and America's teenagers.* New York: Author.

Barnett, J. K., Papini, D. R., & Gbur, E. (1991). Familial correlates of sexually active pregnant and nonpregnant adolescents. *Adolescence, 26,* 457–472.

Barrera, M. (1986). Distinctions between social support concepts, measures, and models. *American Journal of Community Psychology, 14,* 413–445.

Barth , R. P., & Schinke, S. P. (1983). Coping with daily strain among pregnant and parenting adolescents. *Journal of Social Service Research, 7*(2), 51–63.

Billy, J., & Urdy, J. R. (1985). The influence of male and female best friends on adolescent sexual behavior. *Adolescence, 20,* 21–32.

Bingham, C. R., Miller, B. C., & Adams, G. R. (1990). Correlates of age at first intercourse in a national sample of young women. *Journal of Adolescent Research, 5,* 18–33.

Black, C., & DeBlassie, E. R. (1985). Adolescent pregnancy, Contributing factors: Consequences, treatment, and plausible solutions. *Adolescence, 20*, 281–290.

Brooks-Gunn, J., & Furstenberg, F. F. (1986). The children of adolescent mothers: Physical, academic, and psychological outcomes. *Developmental Review, 6*, 224–251.

Brown, J. E., & Mann, L. (1990). The relationship between family structure and process variables and adolescent decision making. *Journal of Adolescence, 13*, 25–37.

Burke, P. J. (1991). Methodological issues for adolescent pregnancy research. *Journal of Pediatric Nursing, 6*, 30–37.

Card, J. J. (Ed.). (1993). *Handbook of adolescent sexuality and pregnancy: Research and evaluation instruments.* Newbury Park, CA: Sage Publications.

Children's Defense Fund. (1995). *The state of America's children yearbook.* Washington, DC: Author.

Chilman, C. S. (1989). Some major issues regarding adolescent sexuality and childbearing in the United States. *Journal of Social Work and Human Sexuality, 8*, 3–25.

Cohen, S., & Wills, T. A. (1985). Stress, social support, and the buffering hypothesis. *Psychological Bulletin, 98*, 310–357.

Colletta, N. D., & Gregg, C. H. (1981). Adolescent mothers' vulnerability to stress. *Journal of Nervous and Mental Disorders, 169*, 50–54.

Cvetkovich, G., & Grote, B. (1981). Psychosocial maturity and teenage contraceptive use: An investigation of decision making and communication skills. *Population and Environment, 4*, 211–226.

Dawson, D. A. (1986). The effects of sex education on adolescent behavior. *Family Planning Perspectives, 18*, 162–184.

DeBolt, M. E., Pasley, B. K., & Kreutzer, J. (1990). Factors affecting the probability of school dropout: A study of pregnant and parenting adolescent females. *Journal of Adolescent Research, 5*, 190–205.

DiBlassio, F. A., & Benda, B. B. (1990). Adolescent sexual behavior: Multivariate analysis of a social learning model. *Journal of Adolescent Research, 5*, 449–466.

Dryfoos, J. (1990). *Adolescents at risk: Prevalence and prevention.* New York: Oxford University Press.

Elliott, D. S., & Morse, B. J. (1989). Delinquency and drug use as risk factors in teenage sexual activity. *Youth & Society, 21*, 32–60.

Flaherty, E., & Maracek, J. (1982). *Psychological factors associated with fertility regulation among adolescents* (Final report to the National Institute of Child Health and Human Development). Philadelphia: Philadelphia Health Management Corporation.

Flewelling, R. L., & Bauman, K. E. (1990). Family structure as a predictor of initial substance use and sexual intercourse in early adolescence. *Journal of Marriage and the Family, 52*, 171–180.

Flick, L. (1986). Paths to adolescent parenthood: Implications for prevention. *Public Health Reports, 101*, 132–146.

Fox, G. L. (1980). The mother–adolescent daughter relationship as a sexual socialization structure: A research review. *Family Relations, 29,* 21–28.

Fox, G. L., & Inazu, J. K. (1980). Patterns and outcomes of mother–daughter communication about sexuality. *Journal of Social Issues, 36,* 7–29.

Franklin, C. (1992). Alternative school programs for at-risk youth. *Social Work in Education, 14,* 239–251.

Franklin, C., Grant, D., Corcoran, J., O'Dell, P., & Bultman, L. (1995). *Effectiveness of teen pregnancy prevention programs: A meta-analysis.* Unpublished manuscript, University of Texas, School of Social Work, Austin.

Franklin, C., & Streeter, C. L. (1993). Validity of the 3-D circumplex family assessment model. *Research on Social Work Practice, 3,* 258–275.

Franklin, D. L. (1987). Black adolescent pregnancy: A literature review. *Child and Family Youth Services, 9,* 15–39.

Furstenberg, F. F., Brooks-Gunn, J., & Morgan, S. P. (1987). *Adolescent mothers in later life.* Cambridge, England: Cambridge University Press.

Giblin, P. T., Poland, M. L., & Sachs, B. A. (1987). Effects of social supports on attitudes and health behaviors of pregnant adolescents. *Journal of Adolescent Health Care, 8,* 273–279.

Green, R. G., Harris, R. N., Forte, J. A., & Robinson, M. (1991). Evaluating FACES III and the circumplex model: 2,440 families. *Family Process, 30,* 55–73.

Grotevant, H. D., & Carlson, C. I. (1989). *Family assessment: A guide to methods and measures.* New York: Guilford Press.

Harris, K. M. (1991). Teenage mothers and welfare dependency: Working off welfare. *Journal of Family Issues, 12,* 492–518.

Hayes, C. (Ed.). (1987). *Risking the future: Adolescent sexuality, pregnancy, and childbearing* (Vol. 1). Washington, DC: National Academy Press.

Hechtman, L. (1989). Teenage mothers and their children: Risks and problems: A review. *Canadian Journal of Psychiatry, 34,* 569–575.

Hofferth, S. L. (1987). Social and economic consequences of teenage childbearing. In S. L. Hofferth & C. D. Hayes (Eds.), *Risking the future* (pp. 123–144). Washington, DC: National Academy Press.

Hogan, D., & Kitagawa, E. (1985). The impact of social status, family structure, and neighborhood on the fertility of black adolescents. *American Journal of Sociology, 90,* 825–855.

Horwitz, S. M., Klerman, L. V., Kuo, H. S., & Jekel, J. F. (1991). School-age mothers: Predictors of long-term educational and economic outcomes. *Pediatrics, 87,* 862–868.

Inazu, I., & Fox, J. (1980). Maternal influence on the sexual behaviors of teenage daughters. *Journal of Family Issues, 1,* 81–99.

Inwald, R. E., Brobst, K. E., & Morrissey, R. F. (1987). *Hilson Adolescent Profile.* Kew Gardens, NY: Hilson Research.

Jones, L. C. (1991). Community-based tertiary prevention with the adolescent parent and child. In S. S. Humenick, N. N. Wilkerson, & N. W. Paul (Eds.), *Adolescent pregnancy: Nursing perspectives on prevention* (pp. 235–249). White Plains, NY: March of Dimes Birth Defects Foundation.

Jordan, C., & Franklin, C. (1995). *Clinical assessment for social workers: Quantitative and qualitative methods.* Chicago: Lyceum/Nelson Hall.

Jorgensen, S., King, S., & Torrey, B. (1980). Dyadic and social influences on adolescent exposure to pregnancy risk. *Journal of Marriage and the Family, 42,* 141–155.

Kahn, J. R., Smith, K., & Roberts, E. (1984). *Familial communication and adolescent sexual behavior* (Final report to the Office of Adolescent Pregnancy Program). Cambridge, MA: American Institutes for Research.

Kastner, L. (1984). Ecological factors predicting adolescent contraceptive use: Implications for intervention. *Journal of Adolescent Health Care, 5,* 79–84.

Laumann, E. O., Gagnon, J. H., Michaels, R. T., & Michaels, S. (1994). *The social organization of sexuality: Sexual practices in the United States.* Chicago: University of Chicago Press.

McAnarney, E. R., & Hendee, W. R. (1989). Adolescent pregnancy and its consequences. *JAMA, 262,* 74–77.

McAnarney, E. R., & Schreider, C. (1984). *Identifying social and psychological antecedents of adolescent pregnancy: The contribution of research to concepts of prevention.* New York: William T. Grant Foundation.

McCarthy, J., & Radish, E. S. (1982). Education and childbearing among teenagers. *Family Planning Perspectives, 14,* 154.

Miller, B. C., Christensen, R., & Olson, T. D. (1987). Self-esteem in relation to adolescent sexual attitudes and behavior. *Youth & Society, 18,* 93–111.

Miller, B. C., & Moore, K. A. (1990). Adolescent sexual behavior, pregnancy, and parenting: Research through the 1980s. *Journal of Marriage and the Family, 52,* 1025–1044.

Moore, K., & Burt, M. R. (1982). *Private crisis, public cost: Policy perspectives on teenage childbearing.* Washington, DC: Urban Institute Press.

Moore, K. A., Nord, C. W., & Peterson, J. L. (1989). Non-voluntary sexual activity among adolescents. *Family Planning Perspectives, 21,* 110–114.

Moore, K., Peterson, J., & Furstenberg, F. (1986). Parental attitudes and the occurrence of early sexual activity. *Journal of Marriage and the Family, 49,* 235–240.

Moos, R. H. (1989). *Family Environment Scale (FES) dimensions and subscales.* Palo Alto, CA: Consulting Psychologists Press.

Mott, F. L., & Haurin, R. J. (1988). Linkages between sexual activity and alcohol and drug use among American adolescents. *Family Planning Perspectives, 20,* 128–136.

Murry, V. (1992). Incidence of first pregnancy among black adolescent females over three decades. *Youth & Society, 23,* 478–506.

Newcomer, S., & Urdy, J. (1985). Parent–child communication and adolescent sexual behavior. *Family Planning Perspectives, 17,* 169–174.

Oakley, A. (1985). Social support and the outcome in pregnancy: The soft way to increase birth weight? *Social Science and Medicine, 21,* 1259–1268.

Olson, D. H. (1991). Commentary: Three-dimensional (3D) circumplex model and revised scoring of FACES III. *Family Process, 30,* 74–79.

Olson, D. H., Poertner, J., & Lavee, Y. (1985). *FACES III.* St. Paul, MN: University of Minnesota, Department of Family Social Science.

Perkins, J. L. (1991). Primary prevention of adolescent pregnancy. In *Birth Defects* (Original Article Series 0.27) (No. 1, pp. 9–28).

Public Health Services Act, Title X, P.L. 99-272, 42 U.S.C.A. §10003(a) (1986).

Repucci, N. D. (1987). Prevention and ecology: Teen-age pregnancy, child sexual abuse, and organized youth sports. *American Journal of Community Psychology, 15,* 1–22.

Rodgers, J. L., & Rowe, D. C. (1990). Adolescent sexual activity and mildly deviant behavior: Sibling and friendship effects. *Journal of Family Issues, 11,* 274–293.

Romig, C. A., & Bakken, L. (1990). Teens at risk for pregnancy: The role of ego development and family processes. *Journal of Adolescence, 13,* 195–199.

Rosenbaum, E., & Kandel, D. B. (1990). Early onset of adolescent sexual behavior and drug involvement. *Journal of Marriage and the Family, 52,* 783–798.

Rudd, N. M., McKenry, P. C., & Nah, M. (1990). Welfare receipt among black and white adolescent mothers: A longitudinal perspective. *Journal of Family Issues, 11,* 334–352.

Santelli, J. S., & Beilensen, P. (1992). Risk factors for adolescent sexual behavior, fertility, and sexually transmitted diseases. *Journal of School Health, 62,* 271–279.

Schilmoeller, G. L., Baranowski, M. D., & Higgins, B. S. (1991). Long-term support and personal adjustment of adolescent and older mothers. *Adolescence, 26,* 787–797.

Scott-Jones, D., & Turner, S. L. (1990). The impact of adolescent childbearing on educational attainment and income of black females. *Youth & Society, 22,* 35–53.

Shah, F., & Zelnick, M. (1981). Parent and peer influence on sexual behavior, contraceptive use, and pregnancy experience of young women. *Journal of Marriage and the Family, 43,* 339–348.

Smith, E. A., Urdy, J. R., & Morris, N. M. (1985). Pubertal development and friends: A biosocial explanation of adolescent sexual behavior. *Journal of Health and Social Behavior, 26,* 183–192.

Stevens-Simon, C., & Beach, R. K. (1992). School-based prenatal and postpartum care: Strategies for meeting the medical and educational needs of pregnant and parenting students. *Journal of School Health, 62,* 304–309.

Streeter, C. L., & Franklin, C. (1992). Social support and psychoeducational interventions with middle-class dropout youth. *Child and Adolescent Social Work, 9,* 131–135.

Studer, M., & Thornton, A. (1987). Adolescent religiosity and contraceptive use. *Journal of Marriage and the Family, 49,* 117–128.

Thornton, A. D., & Camburn, D. (1989). Religious participation and adolescent sexual behavior. *Journal of Marriage and the Family, 51,* 641–653.

Turner, R. J., Grindstaff, C. F., & Phillips, N. (1990). Social support and outcome in teenage pregnancy. *Journal of Health and Social Behavior, 31*, 43–57.

Urdy, J. R. (1980). Biological predisposition and social control in adolescent sexual behavior. *American Sociological Review, 53*, 709–722.

U.S. Department of Health and Human Services. (1995). *Executive summary: Report to Congress on out-of-wedlock childbearing.* (DHHS Publication No. 95-1257-1). Washington, DC: U.S. Government Printing Office.

Vaux, A. (1988). *Social support: Theory, research, and intervention.* New York: Praeger.

Vernon, M., Green, J. A., & Frothingham, T. E. (1983). Teenage pregnancy: A prospective study of self-esteem and sociodemographic factors. *Pediatrics, 72*, 632–635.

White, S. B., & DeBlassie, R. R. (1992). Adolescent sexual behavior. *Adolescence, 27*, 183–191.

Yamaguchi, K., & Kandel, D. (1987). Drug use and other determinants of premarital pregnancy and its outcome: A dynamic analysis of competing life events. *Journal of Marriage and the Family, 49*, 257–270.

Zabin, L. S., Hardy, J. B., Smith, E. A., & Hirsch, M. B. (1986). Substance use and its relation to sexual activity among inner-city adolescents. *Journal of Adolescent Health Care, 7*, 320–331.

Zelnick, M., & Kantner, J. S. (1980). Sexual activity, contraceptive use, and pregnancy among metropolitan-area teenagers: 1971–1979. *Family Planning Perspectives, 12*, 230–237.

Zelnick, M., Kantner, J., & Ford, K. (1981). *Sex and pregnancy in adolescents.* Beverly Hills, CA: Sage Publications.

11

CHILDHOOD DEPRESSION: A RISK FACTOR PERSPECTIVE

M. Carlean Gilbert

Sad affect, withdrawal, sleep disorders, appetite disturbances, hyperactivity, aggressiveness, somatic complaints, school underachievement or failure, and difficulties in peer and family relationships are among the symptoms of children at risk of depression. Because parents, teachers, and practitioners tend to be more responsive to behavioral manifestations such as hyperactivity, teasing, and losing control, they may fail to recognize that interpersonal difficulties and less disruptive behaviors such as social isolation also can be indicators of childhood depression. Diminished energy, for example, can be hidden under bursts of hypomanic excitement (Lieberman, 1979).

For decades researchers and practitioners have puzzled over depression in children. Can children be depressed? If the answer is yes, are their symptoms identical to those of adults and thus diagnosable by the same criteria? Is childhood depression part of a more complex mental disorder yet unidentified? Do children have prodromal depressions that are harbingers of adult mood disorders? What are the risk and protective factors associated with childhood mood disorders? This chapter examines the nature of childhood depression, identifies risk and protective factors associated with it, reviews assessment techniques, and discusses implications for prevention, early intervention, and treatment of childhood depression.

Like research on other disorders in health and mental health, research regarding the assessment, diagnosis, and treatment of children with depression has lagged behind research on adults. Several factors account for this delay. First, more adults suffer from depression, and thus the scope of the problem and its impact on resources are greater for adults than for children. Second, the long-held belief that children do not suffer from depression has been a significant barrier to the designation of research funds for the diagnosis and treatment of childhood depression. Third, disparate views about diagnostic categories and assessment measures have rendered findings of many studies incomparable.

CONTROVERSY OVER CHILDHOOD DEPRESSION

Early attempts to understand depression, particularly in children, were sparse. Freud attempted to explain normal and abnormal melancholia, or depression, in "Mourning

The author thanks N. Shannon Buckner, Sally W. Logan, and Bindu J. Rao, research assistants, Graduate School of Social Work, University of North Carolina at Chapel Hill, for their able assistance in the preparation of this chapter.

and Melancholia" (1917/1957). His psychodynamic explanation of depression was based on the assumption that people with depression respond to psychological loss by turning anger inward. In 1946, Spitz coined the term "anaclitic depression" to describe the weight loss, psychomotor retardation, withdrawal, and sleep disturbances of infants and children who had been institutionalized (Spitz, 1946). Relatedly, the stages of protest, despair, and detachment secondary to maternal deprivation, especially during hospitalization, were later developed by Bowlby (1960), who employed the term "mourning."

In the 1950s and 1960s, the view that children suffer from depression was challenged by a new group of psychoanalytic theorists (Mahler, 1961; Rie, 1966; Rochlin, 1959). This community of analysts asserted that before adolescence, children had neither a stable concept of self nor an internalized superego, both of which were necessary for punitiveness. They concluded that children lacked the personality structure to experience the conflicts between ego and superego that resulted in depression. This highly influential psychoanalytic stance caused many to reject the concept of childhood depression (Carlson & Garber, 1986).

At the same time, however, the concept of "masked" depression in children was advanced by Toolan (1962). He argued that before mid-adolescence, childhood depression is disguised by behavioral problems such as runaway episodes, temper tantrums, academic failure, boredom, and fatigue (Toolan, 1974). Delinquency and criminal behavior also were considered indicators of underlying depression (Chwast, 1974). The usefulness of this concept was later challenged, because the symptoms that allegedly masked depression spanned almost the entire range of childhood mental disorders. Criteria for differentiating between depression and masking disorders were never adequately established (Carlson & Cantwell, 1979; Carlson & Garber, 1986). Subsequently, support for the concept of masked depression diminished (Hynd & Hooper, 1992).

Since the 1970s, however, attempts to classify, assess, and treat childhood depression have multiplied (Hammen & Rudolph, 1996; Kazdin, 1990; Kovacs et al., 1984a; Rutter, 1986). In 1973 Weinberg, Rutman, Sullivan, Penick, and Dietz proposed diagnostic criteria based on the assumption that children manifested depression much as adults did. Acknowledging the ecology of childhood, they argued that a child's decreased academic performance and interest in school were equivalent to an adult's diminished work performance and interest in work. At about the same time, the Feighner Criteria (Feighner et al., 1972) and Research Diagnostic Criteria (Spitzer, Endicott, & Robins, 1978) were developed by researchers studying depression. These three sets of criteria are precise and exclusive. Consequently, they tend to identify fewer cases of "true" childhood depression than do clinically oriented diagnostic criteria such as those presented in the *Diagnostic and Statistical Manual of Mental Disorder—Third Edition* (DSM-III) (Newman & Garfinkel, 1992) and later editions. Conflicting classificatory criteria continue to complicate the study of childhood depression and render research findings incommensurable. Still emerging, a valid and reliable classification system is a prerequisite for studies of prevalence, development of assessment instruments, and measurement of intervention outcomes.

THE NATURE OF DEPRESSION IN CHILDREN

Current thinking accepts that children experience depression; childhood depression can be classified; other mood disorders of childhood exist in addition to depression.

Although this chapter focuses on depression, these other mood disorders are of great importance; they include bipolar (manic–depressive) disorders, mood disorders attributable to a medical condition, and substance-induced mood disorders. Discussion of depression remains challenging, for the term "depression" is employed in both the popular and professional literature. Distinctions must be made among depression as a sign (for example, one's observation of a child's psychomotor agitation), as a symptom (for example, a child's self-report of feeling grouchy), or as a syndrome (for example, a constellation of signs and symptoms that meet specific diagnostic criteria such as those in the *Diagnostic and Statistical Manual of Mental Disorders—Fourth Edition* (DSM-IV) (American Psychiatric Association [APA], 1994; Hammen & Rudolph, 1996; Kaplan, Sadock, & Grebb, 1994).

The DSM-IV and earlier versions have been widely used in the United States to define and diagnose childhood depression. The DSM-IV today identifies depression as one of four major categories of mood disorders. Subgroups of depression are major depressive disorder (MDD), which is acute, and dysthymic disorder (DD), which is milder but chronic. Although many researchers and practitioners continue to question the application of adult criteria to depression in children, the same diagnostic criteria are used for both populations (APA, 1994; Hammen & Rudolph, 1996; Rutter, 1986; Ryan et al., 1987). The use of these criteria probably excludes some cases of childhood depression by failing to incorporate the age-related influences of cognitive, emotional, behavioral, and social development on symptom expression (Cicchetti & Schneider-Rosen, 1986; Hammen & Rudolph, 1996; Kazdin, 1988).

The criteria for MDD are either (1) a depressed or, for children, irritable mood, or (2) a diminished interest or pleasure in activities. Children must also demonstrate four or more of the following symptoms:

- significant weight increase or loss or failure to make expected developmental gains
- almost daily sleep disturbance
- almost daily psychomotor agitation or retardation
- almost daily loss of energy or fatigue
- feelings of worthlessness or inappropriate guilt
- diminished ability to think or concentrate
- recurrent thoughts of death.

Symptoms must coexist for two weeks and produce significant functional changes (APA, 1994; Kaplan et al., 1994). Sadness, appetite loss, sleep disturbance, and fatigue are the most common symptoms in children under six years old (Kashani & Carlson, 1987). Prepubertal children often exhibit sad affect, exaggerated somatic complaints, psychomotor agitation, separation anxiety, fears, hallucinations, irritability, uncooperativeness, and disinterest (Kashani, Holcomb, & Orvaschel, 1986; Ryan et al., 1987). Adolescents experience a loss of interest in activities, feelings of hopelessness, hypersomnia, weight changes, illicit use of substances, and suicidal ideation and attempts (Ryan et al., 1987). The reported mean duration of an MDD episode is approximately 25 weeks (Keller et al., 1988; Lewinsohn, Clarke, Seeley, & Rohde, 1994).

Criteria for DD in children require a depressed or irritable mood most of the day, for most days, and for longer than one year. Children must also have three of the following symptoms: sleep disturbances, low energy or fatigue, loss of interest in activities, hopelessness or pessimism, social withdrawal, feelings of guilt, low self-esteem, appetite changes, and poor mentation (concentration, memory, and problem solving). In clinical populations DD can last a long time, with a reported median duration of 3.5 years (APA, 1994; Kaplan, Sadock, & Grebb, 1994; Kovacs et al., 1984a).

PREVALENCE OF DEPRESSION IN CHILDREN

Collapsing data from eight epidemiological surveys of children that were completed between 1987 and 1993, Hammen and Rudolph (1996) found overall rates for MDD to be between 6 percent and 8 percent. Rates of depression increase with age. For preschool children, rates are low; they range from 0.9 percent in a clinic sample (Kashani & Carlson, 1987) to 0.3 percent in community samples (Kaplan et al., 1994). Between 2.0 percent and 3.0 percent of 6- to 11-year-old youths are reported to have MDD. And between 5.0 percent and 8.0 percent of adolescents are reported to have MDD (Cohen et al., 1993); DD is less common (3.3 percent) than MDD in teenagers (Kaplan et al., 1994). Birth-cohort studies provide some evidence that prevalence rates of depression are increasing (Hammen & Rudolph, 1996).

Gender Differences

The prevalence of depression appears to vary by gender; however, gender-related patterns are far from clear. Findings of gender-related differences in prevalence rates are controversial. Some studies of prepubertal children found that boys and girls have equal rates of depression (Fleming, Offord, & Boyle, 1989), whereas others found that boys have higher rates of depression (Costello et al., 1988). In their recent review of studies of prevalence rates for adolescents, Hammen and Rudolph (1996) reported that adolescent girls are more frequently depressed than boys. However, in one middle-school sample MDD rates were 9 percent in males and 5 percent in females, and the DD rates were 8 percent and 9 percent, respectively. The unusually high rates of male depression in this study may arise from biases in measuring depression on the basis of maternal reports (Garrison, Addy, Jackson, McKeown, & Waller, 1992). The lifetime risk for MDD is known to vary from 10 percent to 25 percent for women and from 5 percent to 9 percent for men (Kaplan et al., 1994).

Relationship of Suicide to Depression

Suicide and suicide attempts are not only diagnostic criteria and outcomes of depressive disorders but also risk factors for future episodes of depression. Overall prevalence rates for suicide increase with age. Under the age of 14, the frequency of suicide is low, approximately one per 100,000 children in the United States. Between the ages of 15 and 19, the rates climb to 13.6 per 100,000 for boys and 3.6 per 100,000 for girls (Kaplan et al., 1994).

Suicidal ideation and attempts are higher among children with depression than among children in the general population. In a recent study of 187 children ages six to 18 who were recruited from a psychiatric clinic and met criteria for MDD, 67 percent of the children reported suicidal ideation (Ryan et al., 1987). Moreover, prepubertal and adolescent children reported similar levels of seriousness of suicidal ideation and intent. Twenty-five percent of the prepubertal children and 34 percent of the teenagers had attempted suicide; the lethality of the method used in suicide attempts, however, was significantly higher for teenagers. In addition, the rates of suicide ideation, intent, lethality, and attempt were significantly higher for adolescents whose MDD had been present over two years than for those with shorter episodes of MDD.

SUMMARY

Recent attempts to estimate the prevalence of childhood depression are compromised by classification differences that fail to distinguish between the symptoms and the disorders themselves, the wide variation in assessment methods (for example, self-reports, structured or semistructured interviews, and epidemiological surveys), and clinic versus community samples. Different sources and methods produce very different estimates of the severity, duration, and frequency of depression (Hammen & Rudolph, 1996). Thus, pending findings from large epidemiological studies of childhood depression (with representative national samples), caution is warranted in discussing the precise extent and seriousness of this disorder in childhood. It is clear, however, that many children experience depression, and many become so seriously ill that they injure themselves.

RISK FACTORS FOR CHILDHOOD DEPRESSION

The ecological perspective is based on a conceptualization of interactions that continuously inform and bind person and environment (Germain & Gitterman, 1995). Coupled with a strengths perspective (see chapter 13), ecological theory emphasizes coping with stress, adapting to adversity, and modifying hostile conditions in the environment. To assess the "goodness-of-fit" between person and environment, one must examine the risk and protective factors that affect the onset, severity, and duration of childhood problems such as depression. These factors may be classified as broad environmental conditions; family, school, and neighborhood conditions; and individual biopsychosocial characteristics.

BROAD ENVIRONMENTAL RISK FACTORS

Findings on poverty as a risk factor for childhood depression are equivocal. Most studies fail to find significant correlations between socioeconomic status (SES) and depression (APA, 1994; Kaplan et al., 1994). However, many children live with parents who have depressive symptomatology that is associated with poverty. Epidemiological studies have found modest correlations between depressive symptoms (but not an Axis I diagnosis of depression) and lower SES (Hammen & Rudolph, 1996; Mrazek & Haggerty, 1994). In particular, divorced single women with minor children and low income appear to experience more depression than either divorced single mothers with high incomes or divorced remarried mothers (Garvin, Kalter, & Hansell, 1993). The combination of having a single parent and low income may elevate the risk of depression for some children.

FAMILY, SCHOOL, AND NEIGHBORHOOD RISK FACTORS

Family Relationships

A growing body of research suggests that some family interactions increase the risk for the maintenance, if not development, of childhood depression. Various studies suggest that the emotional climate in families with depressed children is less cohesive, less emotionally expressive, more hostile, more critical, less accepting, more conflictual, and more disorganized than in families without depressed members (DuRant, Cadenhead, Pendergrast, Slavens, & Linder, 1994; Hammen & Rudolph, 1996). It appears that the social, economic, and psychological strains associated with families of divorce have a cumulative negative effect that contributes to increased childhood depression (Wallerstein & Kelly, 1980). But although these findings are intriguing, much research is needed to differentiate the family conditions that cause depression in children from those that may result from depression in children.

Parental Depression

Prevalence rates of adult depression suggest that many children spend their formative years with a caregiver, more often a mother, who is depressed. Women are twice as likely as men to suffer from MDD. The average age of onset is the mid-20s, when many parents have children. Untreated episodes can last from six months to 13 months, whereas a treated episode typically lasts three months (APA, 1994; Kaplan et al., 1994).

Mothers and fathers suffering from MDD may be especially challenged to fulfill parental roles, because they are withdrawn, irritable, preoccupied, fatigued, and disorganized. As caregivers for infants and toddlers, when a reciprocal relationship is necessary for attachment (Bowlby, 1980), they may have difficulty bonding, responding to infants' cues, and protecting young children from accidents and trauma. Recently psychiatrist Daniel Stern contended that the strongest influence on emotional development is "attunement," which is parental mirroring of a child's emotional expressions (Begley, 1996). When the child's emotion is "played back" repeatedly, Stern argues, the electrical and chemical signals that created it are positively reinforced. If emotions are ignored or punished, these circuits are thought to atrophy. Much of this critical "wiring" appears to occur between 10 and 18 months of age (Begley, 1996). Depressed parents of older children may be unable to act playful, help with homework, assist with grooming, or maintain a home where playmates are welcome—all factors that may promote academic achievement and social development.

It should be no surprise, then, that parental depression is often found to be linked to symptoms of childhood depression. Of nine preschoolers diagnosed with MDD, for example, mothers of six were found to be depressed (Kashani & Carlson, 1987). In their review of the literature, Hammen and Rudolph (1996) found that infants and toddlers of depressed mothers had symptoms of depression, such as negative facial expressions, decreased verbalizations, decreased playfulness, increased inhibition, and anxiety with peers. In one prospective study, negative affective quality and low task involvement of mothers predicted later child affective disorder (Burge & Hammen, 1991). Thus, parental depression appears to be a major risk factor for childhood depression; however, the mechanisms that place children at risk are not fully delineated and most likely involve both biological and social processes.

Child Abuse and Neglect

Young children with MDD are often found to have a history of child abuse and neglect (Kaplan et al., 1994). In a study of nine preschool children with MDD, a history of physical abuse and neglect was found in each child (Kashani & Carlson, 1987). In a larger study, depression was correlated with severity of corporal punishment among 225 African American adolescents (DuRant et al., 1994). Such findings are particularly alarming because the numbers of physically abused and neglected children in the United States have risen dramatically ("More Children," 1996).

School-Related Problems

Researchers generally find that interpersonal problems with teachers and peers are developmental risk factors for depression (Hammen & Rudolph, 1996). But, because many of the studies are cross-sectional, it is unclear whether interpersonal difficulties lead to depression or vice versa.

Neighborhood Violence

The few studies that have examined the association between depression and neighborhoods, particularly violent ones, indicate that an unsafe neighborhood can be a risk factor for childhood depression. Among 221 urban African American children ages seven to 18, being the victim of violence was associated with symptoms of depression (Fitzpatrick, 1993). Depression was significantly correlated with witnessing or participating in violent activity in a sample of 225 African American youths, ages 11 to 19, who lived in or around urban housing projects (DuRant et al., 1994; DuRant, Getts, Cadenhead, Emans, & Woods, 1995).

INDIVIDUAL BIOPSYCHOSOCIAL RISK FACTORS

Academic Performance

Difficulties with academic performance often plague children with depression. But, as with other school-related problems, whether these difficulties are antecedents, concomitants, or consequences of depression disorder is unclear. Academic performance and grades often are negatively affected by childhood depression, but findings suggest that these declines are secondary to anhedonia and difficulties with concentration, not the result of intellectual impairment (Kovacs & Goldston, 1991).

Neurobiological Vulnerabilities

Neurotransmitters, the chemicals that carry impulses between neurons (nerve cells), have been strongly implicated in the etiology of depression. In this regard, the two most studied neurotransmitters are norepinephrine (NE) and serotonin (5-HT). Following its release from the axon terminal of one neuron, NE crosses a minute pathway called the synaptic cleft and is received by the dendrites of an adjacent neuron. This process generates an electrical impulse. The transmitting neuron has NE receptor sites that indicate when NE production should stop. Some of the unused NE is then reabsorbed by the first neuron, and the rest is metabolized. When a child is depressed, NE is not well regulated. The receptors become either oversensitized or undersensitized and, as levels of NE fluctuate, respond too much or perhaps not at all. Both excesses and deficiencies in NE breakdown products, which can be detected in urine, are associated with symptoms of depression (Bentley & Walsh, 1996; Grinspoon & Bakalar, 1995; Kazdin, 1988; Riddle & Cho, 1989). Unusually high levels of 5-HT, which is thought to affect mood and bodily functions such as sleep, appetite, sexual behavior, and circadian rhythms, have been found in many depressed patients. However, the explanation for the correlation between low 5-HT and depression is elusive (Bentley & Walsh, 1996; Grinspoon & Bakalar, 1995). The intricate pathways of these billions of neurons and their relationships to depression remain the focus of much research.

Neuroendocrine dysfunctions also are implicated in the etiology of depression. Disturbances along the hypothalamic–pituitary–adrenal axis, where cortisol is produced, are associated with depression. Hypersecretion of cortisol and disruption in its 24-hour cycle are found in a substantial number of adults with MDD (Grinspoon & Bakalar, 1995). This phenomenon of high blood levels of cortisol in depressed adults is less well studied in children. Compared with control groups, neither prepubertal children (Puig-Antich et al., 1989) nor adolescents with MDD (Dahl et al., 1989) have demonstrated significant differences in hypersecretion. However, Dahl and colleagues found that one suicidal teenager had significantly elevated cortisol levels at the onset of sleep. Clearly, more research is needed.

Disturbances along the hypothalamic–pituitary–thyroid (HPT) axis have also been reported as risk factors for depression. The thyroid gland produces hormones that control the basal metabolic rate of the body; abnormally low levels of thyroid hormones result in fatigue, listlessness, and other symptoms of depression. Between 25 percent and 70 percent of people suffering from MDD have a poor response to an experimental injection of thyroid-releasing hormone (TRH), which normally is secreted by the hypothalamus to stimulate the pituitary gland to produce thyroid-stimulating hormone (TSH). The TSH in turn promotes the release of thyroid hormones (Grinspoon & Bakalar, 1995). When a person has a blunted, delayed response to the injection of TRH, it suggests a dysfunction at the hypothalamic level. Whether the disturbances on the HPT axis precede, accompany, or follow depressive illness is a subject of disagreement.

Research on neurotransmitters and neuroendocrine systems, which are highly interdependent, has contributed greatly to understanding the neurobiological characteristics of depression. Additional areas of research include studies of the relationship of depression to sleep disorders and growth hormone. Also important, there is considerable "chicken or egg" controversy over findings, for it is not clear whether depression causes changes in a child's neurobiology or whether changes in a child's neurobiology cause depression.

Genetic Factors

Few studies of children have been conducted, but studies with adult probands suggest that vulnerability to depression runs in families. Gershon, Targum, Kessler, Mazure, and Bunney (1977) found the heritability of an affective disorder in monozygotic twins to be about 65 percent. Using two sources to acquire a sample of more than 15,000 adult twins and their relatives, Kendler et al. (1994) found a correlation of depressive symptoms in 30 percent to 37 percent of monozygotic twins. The concordance among dizygotic twins was half that for monozygotic twins, strongly suggesting a genetic effect.

Although genetic studies consistently show familial trends toward depression, especially MDD, neither a single gene, a constellation of genes, or a genetic marker correlated with depression has been identified. Moreover, although genetic vulnerability is extremely important, its course appears to be influenced by environmental factors. The diathesis-stress model posits that although the origins of depression may be attributable to genetics, the course of the disorder is affected by the interplay among biological and environmental factors such as stress and social support (Bentley & Walsh, 1996; Hammen & Rudolph, 1996; Lazarus & Folkman, 1984).

Comorbidity with Other Childhood Mental Disorders

Although it is debatable whether other mental disorders precede, coexist with, or follow childhood depression, their co-occurrence is not. A review of six epidemiological studies indicated that the existence of childhood depression increases the likelihood of other disorders by 20-fold (Angold & Costello, 1993). Whether comorbidity is the result of overlapping risk factors, a distinct syndrome, or the creation of risk factors by an initial disorder is a focus of investigation (Caron & Rutter, 1991). Anxiety disorders are the most prevalent comorbid conditions with childhood depression (Kovacs et al., 1984a; Ollendick & Yule, 1990). In her review, Kovacs (1990) concluded that 30 percent to 75 percent of depressed children experienced a coexisting anxiety disorder. Later, Kovacs, Paulauskas, Gatsonis, and Richards (1988b) reported that in two-thirds of children with MDD, symptoms of anxiety disorder preceded those of depression by more than two months. Moreover, the anxiety disorder tended to persist after recovery from MDD.

Depression also co-occurs frequently with conduct disorder. Conduct disorder was present in 38 percent of prepubertal children and 25 percent of adolescents with MDD according to Ryan et al. (1987). Puig-Antich (1982) found that approximately one-third of prepubertal males with MDD also met criteria for conduct disorder. That conduct disorder symptoms sometimes decrease when children receive antidepressants caused Kovacs, Gatsonis, Paulauskas, and Richards (1988a) to ask whether a single disorder may underlie both conditions. They reported that 23 percent of latency-aged children had both MDD and conduct disorder; the estimated risk of having both increased to 36 percent by age 19. Like anxiety disorders, conduct disorder commonly preceded depression (Puig-Antich, 1982; Sack, Beiser, Phillips, & Baker-Brown, 1993) and remained after recovery from depression (Kovacs et al., 1988b).

Having DD increases the risk of having initial, repeated, or more severe MDD; having MDD once also increases risk for more, or more severe, episodes. Sequentially sampling from a clinic-based population of eight- to 13-year-old children, Kovacs et al. (1984b) found that 50 percent of children with dysthymia later developed MDD. The median time for the onset of MDD was 3.3 years after the diagnosis of DD. The cohort of children with MDD had a cumulative 26 percent risk of a second episode within a year and a 72 percent risk within five years. Although DD is not considered a prodrome to MDD, it is thought to increase a child's vulnerability to it. Overall studies found that 24 percent to 76 percent of children with DD eventually develop MDD.

This pattern of MDD superimposed on DD is sometimes described as "double depression" (APA, 1994; Keller et al., 1988; Kovacs, Akiskal, Gatsonis, & Parrone, 1994).

Mental disorders reviewed in earlier chapters also co-occur with depression. Studies with clinical populations of youths who abuse substances (see chapter 7) have found comorbid rates of depression ranging from 16 percent to 50 percent; community samples have found adolescent users of illicit drugs to have more depressed mood than nonusers (Buckstein, 1995). Dysthymic disorder preceded substance abuse with a majority of hospitalized teenagers, and thus may be a risk factor for substance abuse (Hovens, Cantwell, & Kiriakos, 1994). Comorbidity rates between depression and attention-deficit hyperactivity disorder (ADHD) (see chapter 5) have ranged from chance levels to 70 percent. Some controversial findings suggest that subgroups of children with ADHD have coexisting MDD or DD. Furthermore, conduct disorder co-occurs frequently with both depression and ADHD, which suggests possible linkages among them (Biederman, Newcorn, & Sprich, 1991; Fleming & Offord, 1990; Hinshaw, 1994). The identification of comorbid disorders thus "unmasks" childhood depression, heightening awareness of risk factors that may exponentially increase a child's biopsychosocial vulnerability to multiple disorders.

Comorbidity with Chronic Illness

Somatic presentations in children have long been considered manifestations of depression in children, presumably because children lack cognitive and verbal skills to communicate their emotional pain. A met-analysis of 60 studies found that 9 percent to 14 percent of children with a chronic medical condition have an increased risk of symptoms of depression (Bennett, 1994). Bennett reported that children with asthma, sickle-cell disease (SCD), and recurrent abdominal pain appeared to be at greater risk of depression than children with other medical conditions, but studies are equivocal. Children with asthma were rated significantly higher on measures of depression by their parents, but self-reports were not statistically significant when compared with those of healthy children and those with diabetes or cancer (Padur et al., 1995). Children with SCD had higher scores on the Depression Rating Scale–Revised than a healthy control group; however, clinical interviews with a child psychiatrist found fewer subjects with SCD to be depressed (Yang, Cepeda, Price, Shah, & Mankad, 1994). Generally, children with chronic illnesses appear to internalize their responses to their illnesses more than they externalize, but the precise relationship between chronic illness and depression is poorly understood (Bennett, 1994). Kashani, Cantwell, Shekim, and Reid (1982) reported that children with depression and somatic complaints did not have conduct disorder and, conversely, children with depression and conduct disorder rarely manifested somatic complaints, perhaps because children with physical limitations tend to internalize responses.

Cognitive Styles

Several cognitive styles of perceiving the world are correlated with depression. The influential "learned helplessness" model (Seligman, 1975), which posited that depression results from uncontrollable and aversive events, was reformulated to a causal attribution model (Abramson, Seligman, & Teasdale, 1978). This revision introduced the concept of attributional style, the way in which one perceives events and interprets outcomes. A depressive attributional style is the tendency to expect negative outcomes and to attribute them to the combination of three factors: individual internal attributes, global and largely uncontrollable forces, and the stability of hostile attributes over time (Alloy, Peterson, Abramson, & Seligman, 1984). Positive outcomes, in contrast, are attributed to external, specific, and unstable factors. A number of cross-sectional and longitudinal studies have linked children's depression with a depressive attributional style (Hammen & Rudolph, 1996).

Cognitive models of depression, notably those of Beck, emphasize three aspects of cognitive functioning: negative core beliefs (that is, fundamental beliefs about oneself), negative intermediate beliefs (that is, one's basic assumptions, attitudes, and rules), and negative automatic thoughts (that is, one's distorted interpretations of situations and events) (Beck, Rush, Shaw, & Emery, 1979; Beck, 1995). Negative perceptions of self, the world, and the future constitute the "negative cognitive triad," a distorted style of thinking that appears to be highly correlated with depression.

PROTECTIVE FACTORS IN CHILDHOOD DEPRESSION

Like risks, protective factors are distinguished as broad environmental factors; characteristics of family, school, and neighborhood; and individual attributes. Unfortunately, this is an area of developing knowledge, and information on protective factors for childhood depression is limited.

FAMILY

A few studies have found that increased SES and familial support decrease the risk of childhood depression. Parental education, employment, and health appear to protect children who live in poor, high-crime, urban neighborhoods from depression (DuRant et al., 1994; DuRant et al., 1995). DuRant et al. compared African American adolescents who reported lower levels of hopelessness, higher scores on purpose in life, and greater belief that they would be alive at age 25 with depressed and hopeless teenagers. Teenagers who lived in households headed by people with higher education reported fewer feelings of depression and hopelessness. Parental employment was correlated with higher scores on purpose in life. In turn, these more optimistic adolescents were less likely to engage in violent behavior, which, as discussed earlier, has been reported as a risk factor for depression. One study showed that support from a male partner significantly decreased depression in African American adolescent new mothers (Thompson & Peebles-Wilkins, 1992). Another study found that social support from an infant's grandmother or father was associated with significantly lower rates of depression among pregnant and postpartum African American teenagers (Barnet, Joffe, Duggan, Wilson, & Repke, 1996). In contrast to families in which a single parent had bipolar disorder, two-parent families in which the ill parent received medications and outpatient psychotherapy had a comparatively lower incidence of depression in offspring (LaRoche, 1986).

PARENTS' TREATMENT FOR DEPRESSION

Children appear to be protected from depression when, as LaRoche (1986) noted, parents with mood disorders receive adequate treatment and subsequently fulfill parental and other roles. A meta-analysis of the use of cognitive therapy with adults suffering from MDD demonstrates its efficacy (Dobson, 1989). In addition, psychopharmacological treatment is widely viewed as effective in shortening the duration of illness, lessening the severity of symptoms, and preventing relapse in adults with severe MDD. Since the 1950s, two classes of medications have been standard treatment for depressive disorders. Tricyclic antidepressants (TCAs) such as imipramine (Tofranil), amitriptyline (Elavil), desipramine (Norpramin), and doxepin (Sinequan) block the reabsorption of NE by receptors and thus enhance its effects. Clinical trials report that between 65 percent and 85 percent of people with depression improve on TCAs, in contrast to 20 percent to 40 percent of control groups taking a placebo (Grinspoon & Bakalar, 1995). Monoamine oxidase inhibitors (MAOIs) constitute the other traditional class of antidepressant medications. MAOIs such as phenelzine (Nardil) or isocarboxazid (Marplan) block the actions of an enzyme that results in the breakdown of dopamine, NE, and 5-HT (Gelenberg, Bassuk, & Schoonover, 1991; Grinspoon & Bakalar, 1995). Serotonin-reuptake inhibitors (SSRIs) constitute the newest class of antidepressants, which include fluoxetine (Prozac), sertraline (Zoloft), paroxetine (Paxil), and fluvoxamine (Luvox). Introduced in the 1980s, the SSRIs generally have fewer side effects than other antidepressants because they target specific neurotransmitters and are safer in overdose (Bentley & Walsh, 1996). Clinical trials have established the efficacy of TCAs, MAOIs, and SSRIs in adults, where choice of a particular medication generally is based on minimization of negative side effects.

A variety of therapies—psychopharmacological and psychotherapeutic approaches based on cognitive, interpersonal, couples, family, and group interventions—may reduce adult depression. Although these interventions are largely untested on children, their effectiveness with adults suggests that treatment of parental depression may alter and perhaps even "untrigger" biological and social risk factors for their children.

RISK AND PROTECTIVE FACTORS BY AGE, GENDER, AND RACE OR ETHNICITY

AGE

Studies over the past decade indicate that early onset is a risk factor for increased duration of depressive illness. Onset of MDD in younger school-aged children, particularly in children under 11 years of age, is significantly associated with slower recovery (Kovacs et al., 1984a). In 14- to 18-year-old high school students, early onset—defined as prior to 15.5 years of age—has been reported to be correlated also with increased duration and suicidal ideation (Lewinsohn et al., 1994). One study found that rates for the onset of depression after exposure to violence were significantly higher in younger children, ages seven to 10, than in older children, ages 11 to 19 (Fitzpatrick, 1993).

GENDER

The lifetime prevalence for depression is significantly higher for females than for males. Once MDD occurs, females are almost twice as likely to develop a second MDD episode as males (29 percent compared with 16 percent); however, the mean time to recurrence, 28.4 months for females and 21.1 months for males, does not appear to differ significantly (Lewinsohn et al., 1994). Female gender was found to predict early-onset MDD and to be correlated with higher rates of depressive disorder in 14- to 15-year-old adolescents (Rutter, Graham, Chadwick, & Yule, 1976).

Compared with males, females appear to be more susceptible to depressive reactions. Decreased self-esteem and stressful events are more highly correlated with depression in ninth- through 12th-grade girls than in boys (Allgood-Merten, Lewinsohn, & Hops, 1990). Among pregnant teenagers, nearly half (42 percent) have reported depressive symptoms. In addition, one-third report depressive symptoms at two and four months postpartum (Barnet et al., 1996). These rates are higher than the overall rate for postpartum depression, excluding the short-lived "baby blues" of new mothers reported by O'Hara and Zekowski (1988).

Violence, too, appears to affect boys and girls differently. In a study that examined the combined effects of exposure to violence and low income, females, ages seven to 19, had a statistically significant increase in symptoms of depression compared with males exposed to similar conditions (Fitzpatrick, 1993).

ETHNICITY, RACE, AND CULTURE

The study of depression among youths of color is much neglected by researchers, and there is considerable controversy about the impact of language, cultural values, and norms on diagnostic methods and findings. In one epidemiological study, Roberts and Chen (1995) found that Mexican American middle school students reported significantly more depression than their white counterparts. Mexican American females experienced the highest rate of depressive symptoms. Mexican American students also reported significantly more suicide ideation. Researchers found the strongest associations with depression to be loneliness and limited ability to speak English, suggesting that the concomitants of minority ethnic status—not ethnic status per se—increase the risk for depression.

Too few studies have examined childhood depression among African American children, and the results to date are equivocal. Sampling 550 suburban middle school children, researchers found higher rates of depression among African American children in grade seven; later sampling the same students in grade nine, they reported that only African American females showed a greater prevalence rate over white students (Garrison, Jackson, Marsteller, McKeown, & Addy, 1990). No difference in prevalence rates of depression between African American and white participants was found in a clinical sample of 300 children ages seven to 11 (Costello et al., 1988), nor in a longitudinal study of 1,004 young adults (24.7 years of age) who were depressed nine years earlier (Kandel & Davies, 1986).

Racial and ethnic influences may contribute to differences in the severity of depressive symptoms reported by sexually abused girls. In a study of 134 females ages six to 18, the 38 Latina girls of primarily Mexican American origin who experienced penetration tended to be more depressed than African American or white females who experienced penetration and Latina females who had not experienced penetration. The importance of chastity and virginity in the Hispanic or Latino culture may account for the increased level of distress and contribute to depressive symptoms (Mennen, 1995).

ASSESSMENT OF CHILDHOOD DEPRESSION

As suggested by the risk factors, assessment of childhood depression must use complementary types of evaluative methods, screen for comorbid disorders, and evaluate the social context. A comprehensive assessment should include a physical examination by a child neurologist or psychiatrist; review of educational and medical records; administration of a battery of psychological tests; observation in multiple settings; and reports from parents, teachers, coaches, guidance counselors, friends, clergy, and significant others. To provide a thorough assessment, two sources of information from children, family members, and significant others are recommended: self-reports and structured or semistructured interviews. Because perceptions of informants may be discordant, no source can be regarded as singularly valid. A triangulation of data is needed to increase the likelihood of making an accurate diagnosis and developing a comprehensive treatment plan.

Child's Self-Report

The majority of measures used to assess childhood depression are self-report assessments. Self-reports are especially important to the assessment of depression because many of the key criteria—sadness, guilt, and worthlessness—are based on subjective feelings. The number of measures has increased greatly in the past 15 years, and they vary in their goals (for example, clinical diagnosis versus assessment of symptom severity) (Kazdin, 1988; Mash & Terdal, 1988). Self-report assessments generally take the form of structured or semistructured clinical interviews and paper-and-pencil tests. Diagnostic interviews provide broad indicators for the presence or absence of disorders. Interviews require considerable time, however, and careful staff training. Paper-and-pencil instruments are useful measures of symptom severity, but they are inadequately discriminatory for making a diagnosis.

Diagnostic Interview Schedule for Children (DISC-C).

The DISC-C and its parent version (DISC-P) are structured interviews that are particularly useful in assessing depression. The DISC-C can be administered to six- to 18-year-olds by lay interviewers who have completed two or three days of training. Completed in 40 to 60 minutes, the DISC-C explores the onset, duration, and severity of depressive and other symptoms. On the basis of DSM-related criteria, it provides scores in 27 symptom areas, including affective and conduct disorders (Costello, 1991; Costello, Edelbrock, & Costello, 1985; Costello, Edelbrock, Dulcan, Kalas, & Klaric, 1984; Shaffer et al., 1993).

Schedule for Affective Disorders and Schizophrenia for School-Age Children (K-SADS)

The K-SADS is a widely used semistructured interview that is given individually to parents and to children ages six to 17 (Puig-Antich et al., 1978). Designed for compatibility with recent editions of the DSM, the K-SADS is often used to identify children with affective disorders. Because there is considerable latitude in adapting questions and probes to the respondent, it must be administered by a trained practitioner. The first part of the interview is unstructured, and the informant identifies a wide range of symptoms; the second part of the interview is structured and elicits information on onset, severity, and duration of identified symptoms (Costello, 1991; Kazdin, 1988).

Interview Schedule for Children (ISC)

Another widely used semistructured interview is the ISC, which is liked for its flowing design, severity rating scales, flexibility, and usefulness in research on childhood depression. It was developed for children ages eight to 17, and it is administered to both them and their parents (Kovacs, 1984b). The ISC specifically assesses depressive, conduct, and other comorbid disorders, and interviewers who use it must be knowledgeable about DSM-related criteria and have advanced clinical skills (Costello, 1991; Kazdin, 1988).

Children's Depression Inventory (CDI)

The CDI is a frequently used and well-researched measure of depression in children between the ages of seven and 17 (Kovacs, 1984a; Kovacs & Beck, 1977). The CDI includes 27 items that measure cognitive, affective, and behavioral signs of depression. Reviewing several studies using the CDI, Kazdin (1988) concluded that it has high internal consistency and moderate test–retest reliability. It is correlated in expected directions with self-esteem, negative cognitions, hopelessness, and other constructs. The CDI was designed to measure severity; it does not always discriminate depression from other disorders.

Person-In-Environment (PIE)

Because childhood depression is influenced by a variety of risk factors, it is important to evaluate the broader social context. The PIE system is designed to help practitioners describe, classify, and code the social functioning of adults with minor children (Karls & Wandrei, 1994a, 1994b). Funded in 1981 by a grant from the National Association of Social Workers, PIE is structured to examine four factors, namely, social functioning, environmental conditions, mental health, and physical health. It thus incorporates systems and ecological theories. A portion of PIE, the Coping Index, is designed to assist workers in rating the social functioning of clients. This section of PIE involves assessing protective resources such as ego strength, insight, intellectual abilities, problem-solving skills, capacity to act independently, and role functioning. Although PIE is designed only for adult clients, it may be used in a systematic examination of the contextual elements of family life (Karls & Wandrei, 1994a, 1994b).

Implications for Prevention, Early Intervention, and Treatment of Childhood Depression

Childhood depression is explained—at least in part—by biological factors that may be influenced by contextual risks. Clearly, then, the enhancement of protective factors holds enormous potential as a strategy for both prevention and intervention. Individual, family, neighborhood, school, health, and environmental risk factors must be addressed to reduce the severity and duration of childhood depression. Although they may have little or no effect on middle-income children, environmental conditions may cause and exacerbate depression in low-income children or children of color. Some children of color have special problems. They may lack the language skills that are prerequisite for academic and social success in English-speaking settings and that promote resilience among at-risk children. Others may find that access to adequate health and mental health care is limited or that service providers are insensitive to cultural differences that affect depression. Parental depression is a risk factor for childhood depression, but adult depression can be treated if mental health services are available. Thus, the degree to which a community is successful in developing accessible mental health services may be viewed as a protective factor for childhood depression.

PREVENTION AND EARLY INTERVENTION

Community settings and schools can provide primary prevention at three levels: universal, selected, or indicated (Bucy, 1994). Universal programs are offered to all children in an effort to develop awareness of feelings and to build social skills in managing anger, sadness, and other affect. An example is Developing Understanding of Self and Others (DUSO) by Dinkmeyer (cited in Bucy, 1994), a program that uses activities such as storytelling, puppetry, and role plays to improve self-esteem and positive self-images among school-aged children. Selected programs target children who are members of a group considered to be at risk of internalizing disorders such as depression. The Children of Divorce Intervention Program (CODIP) by Alpert-Gillis, Pedro-Carroll, and Cowen (cited in Bucy, 1994) attempts to increase children's self-awareness about divorce, to develop a mutually supportive network, to increase problem-solving abilities, and to highlight positive qualities in themselves and their families. Similar programs have been developed for youths who are exposed to violence, who are pregnant, or who experience significant losses and, as a result, may be at risk of depression. Indicated primary prevention is designed to help children who are at risk because of particular individual characteristics that are linked with depression. The evidence for increased comorbidity of depression with conduct disorder, ADHD, anxiety disorders, substance-abuse disorders, and possibly some chronic illnesses requires that practitioners screen for underlying depression when these other disorders evoke their attention.

TREATMENT

Treatment of Parental Depression

Studies indicate that parents with mood disorders are at risk for impaired role functioning as partners, parents, and employees. However, mounting evidence demonstrates that psychopharmacological, cognitive–behavioral, and interpersonal therapies can reduce the severity, duration, and frequency of depression in adults. It follows that appropriate treatment of parental depression will enhance role functioning. Treated parents are likely to be more capable of promoting resilience in their children and of protecting them from psychosocial stressors that may trigger childhood depression.

Medication for Children

Findings on the effectiveness of medications for childhood depression are limited and equivocal. Although the efficacy of antidepressant medications with adults is well established, there are few reports of use of antidepressants in treating childhood depression. Fluoxetine (Prozac) has been used with some success in teenagers with MDD (Kaplan et al.,1994). However, because of their potentially serious side effects—cardiac arrhythmia, blood pressure changes, seizures, toxicity, coma, and death—many psychotropic medications have not been approved by the Food and Drug Administration for use with children (Gelenberg, Bassuk, & Schoonover, 1991; Kaplan et al., 1994). Caution is warranted.

Treatment Groups for Children and Adolescents

Because depression has only recently been recognized as a serious disorder in childhood, few empirical studies with adequate samples have examined treatment outcomes for children. Some studies indicate that cognitive–behavioral group treatment reduces symptoms of depression in adolescents. And implicating again the importance of parental functioning, Lewinsohn and colleagues (cited in Craighead, Curry, & McMillan, 1994) reported that therapeutic gains were greater when treatment groups included both adolescents and parents, as opposed to teenagers only.

Future Research

It is critical to develop longitudinal research to further examine the individual, family, school, and other risk and protective factors that contribute to childhood depression. Prevention trials based on an improved understanding of risk and resilience are needed. For example, if children with conduct disorders were routinely evaluated and subsequently treated for early symptoms of depression, would depression be reduced in frequency, severity, and duration? Studies must examine transactional models of interpersonal functioning among children with depression and family members, who may themselves be suffering from depression, which further complicates the research. Culturally sensitive interventions must be provided for African American, Hispanic, American Indian, and other children of diverse ethnicities whose rates of depression may be adversely affected by environmental conditions and limited access to services. Finally, also needed are studies to develop effective psychological and pharmacological treatments for children.

Conclusion

So to ask again the question raised by psychoanalytic theorists from an earlier era: Do children experience depression? Clearly, yes. Moreover, etiological models of childhood depression suggest that the origins of depression are biopsychosocial. Although there is strong evidence for neurobiological contributors to childhood depression, the impact of psychosocial factors remains an essential part of the etiology. And the directionality of the biological and psychosocial conditions that appear to cause depression is unclear. Are biological factors triggered by social and other factors, or are psychosocial risks the direct manifestation of neurobiological conditions? The studies reviewed here summarize significant gains in the knowledge base regarding childhood depression, but far deeper examinations of the factors that produce and protect against childhood depression are needed.

REFERENCES

Abramson, L. Y., Seligman, M. E., & Teasdale, J. D. (1978). Learned helplessness in humans: Critique and reformulation. *Journal of Abnormal Psychology, 87,* 49–74.

Allgood-Merten, B., Lewinsohn, P., & Hops, H. (1990). Sex differences and adolescent depression. *Journal of Abnormal Psychology, 99,* 55–63.

Alloy, L. B., Peterson, C., Abramson, L. Y., & Seligman, M. E. (1984). Attributional style and the generality of learned helplessness. *Journal of Personality and Social Psychology, 46,* 681–687.

American Psychiatric Association. (1994). *Diagnostic and statistical manual of mental disorders* (4th ed.). Washington, DC: Author.

Angold, A., & Costello, E. (1993). Depressive comorbidity in children and adolescents: Empirical, theoretical, and methodological issues. *American Journal of Psychiatry, 150,* 1779–1791.

Barnet, B., Joffe, A., Duggan, A. K., Wilson, M. D., & Repke, J. T. (1996). Depressive symptoms, stress, and social support in pregnant and postpartum adolescents. *Archives of Pediatrics & Adolescent Medicine, 150,* 64–69.

Beck, A. T., Rush, A. J., Shaw, B. F., & Emery, G. (1979). *Cognitive theory of depression.* New York: Guilford Press.

Beck, J. S. (1995). *Cognitive therapy: Basics and beyond.* New York: Guilford Press.

Begley, S. (1996, February 19). Your child's brain. *Newsweek,* pp. 54–61.

Bennett, D. S. (1994). Depression among children with chronic medical problems: A meta-analysis. *Journal of Pediatric Psychology, 19*(2), 149–169.

Bentley, K. J., & Walsh, J. (1996). *The social worker and psychotropic medication.* Pacific Grove, CA: Brooks/Cole.

Biederman, J., Newcorn, J., & Sprich, S. (1991). Comorbidity of attention deficit hyperactivity disorder with conduct, depressive, anxiety, and other disorders. *American Journal of Psychiatry, 148,* 564–577.

Bowlby, J. (1960). Grief and mourning in infancy and early childhood. *Psychoanalytic Study of the Child, 15,* 9–52.

Bowlby, J. (1980). *Attachment and loss: Loss, sadness, and depression* (Vol. 3). New York: Basic Books.

Buckstein, O. G. (1995). *Adolescent substance abuse: Assessment, prevention, and treatment.* New York: John Wiley & Sons.

Bucy, J. E. (1994). Internalizing affective disorders. In R. J. Simeonsson (Ed.), *Risk, resilience, and prevention: Promoting the well-being of all children* (pp. 219–238). Baltimore: Paul H. Brookes.

Burge, D., & Hammen, C. (1991). Maternal communication: Predictors of outcome at follow-up in a sample of children at high and low risk for depression. *Journal of Abnormal Psychology, 100,* 174–180.

Carlson, G. A., & Cantwell, D. P. (1979). Unmasking masked depression in children and adolescents. *American Journal of Psychiatry, 137,* 445–449.

Carlson, G. A., & Garber, J. (1986). Developmental issues in the classification of depression in children. In M. Rutter, C. E. Izard, & P. B. Read (Eds.), *Depression in young people* (pp. 399–434). New York: Guilford Press.

Caron, C., & Rutter, M. (1991). Comorbidity in child psychopathology: Concepts, issues and research strategies. *Journal of Child Psychology and Psychiatry, 32,* 1063–1080.

Chwast, J. (1974). Delinquency and criminal behavior as depressive equivalents in adolescents. In S. Lesse (Ed.), *Masked depression* (pp. 219–235). New York: Jason Aronson.

Cicchetti, D., & Schneider-Rosen, K. (1986). An organizational approach to childhood depression. In M. Rutter, C. E. Izard, & P. B. Read (Eds.), *Depression in young people* (pp. 71–134). New York: Guilford Press.

Cohen, P., Cohen, J., Kasen, S., Velez, C. N., Hartmark, C., Johnson, J., Rojas, M., Brook, J., & Streuning, E. L. (1993). An epidemiological study of disorders in late childhood and adolescence: I. Age and gender-specific prevalence. *Journal of Child Psychology and Psychiatry, 34,* 851–867.

Costello, A. J. (1991). Structured interviewing. In M. Lewis (Ed.), *Child and adolescent psychiatry: A comprehensive textbook* (pp. 463–472). Baltimore: Williams & Wilkins.

Costello, A. J., Edelbrock, C. S., & Costello, E. J. (1985). Validity of the NIMH Diagnostic Interview Schedule for Children: A comparison between psychiatric and pediatric referrals. *Journal of Abnormal Child Psychiatry, 13,* 579–595.

Costello, E. J., Costello, A. J., Edelbrock, C., Burns, B. J., Dulcan, M. K., Brent, D., & Janiszewski, S. (1988). Psychiatric disorders in pediatric primary care. *Archives of General Psychiatry, 45,* 1107–1116.

Costello, A. J., Edelbrock, C., Dulcan, M. K., Kalas, R., & Klaric, S. H. (1984). *Development and testing of the NIMH Diagnostic Interview Schedule for Children in a client population* (Contract No. RFP-DB-81-0027). Rockville, MD: National Institute of Mental Health, Center for Epidemiological Studies.

Craighead, W. E., Curry, J. F., & McMillan, D. K. (1994). Childhood and adolescent depression. In L. W. Craighead, W. E. Craighead, A. E. Kazdin, & M. J. Mahoney (Eds.), *Cognitive and behavioral interventions: An empirical approach to mental health problems* (pp. 301–312). Boston: Allyn & Bacon.

Dahl, R., Puig-Antich, J., Ryan, N., Nelson, B., Novacenko, H., Twomey, J., Williamson, D., Goetz, R., & Ambrosini, P. J. (1989). Cortisol secretion in adolescents with major depressive disorder. *Acta Psychiatrica Scandanavia, 80,* 18–26.

Dobson, K. S. (1989). A meta-analysis of the efficacy of cognitive therapy for depression. *Journal of Consulting and Clinical Psychology, 57*, 414–419.

DuRant, R. H., Cadenhead, C., Pendergrast, R. A., Slavens, G., & Linder, C. W. (1994). Factors associated with the use of violence among urban black adolescents. *American Journal of Public Health, 84*, 612–617.

DuRant, R. H., Getts, A., Cadenhead, C., Emans, S. J., & Woods, E. R. (1995). Exposure to violence and victimization and depression, hopelessness, and purpose in life among adolescents living in and around public housing. *Developmental and Behavioral Pediatrics, 16(9)*, 233–237.

Feighner, J., Robins, E., Guze, S. B., Woodruff, R. A., Winokur, G., & Munoz, R. (1972). Diagnostic criteria for use in psychiatric research. *Archives of General Psychiatry, 26*, 57–63.

Fitzpatrick, K. M. (1993). Exposure to violence and presence of depression among low-income, African-American youth. *Journal of Consulting and Clinical Psychology, 61*, 528–531.

Fleming, J. E., & Offord, D. R. (1990). Epidemiology of childhood depressive disorders: A critical review. *Journal of the American Academy of Child and Adolescent Psychiatry, 29*, 571–580.

Fleming, J. E., Offord, D. R., & Boyle, M. H. (1989). The Ontario Child Health Study: Prevalence of childhood and adolescent depression in the community. *British Journal of Psychiatry, 155*, 647–654.

Freud, S. (1957). Mourning and melancholia. In J. Strachey (Ed. and Trans.), *The standard edition of the complete psychological works of Sigmund Freud* (Vol. 19, pp. 243–250). London: Hogarth Press. (Original work published 1917)

Garrison, C. Z., Addy, C. L., Jackson, K. L., McKeown, R. E., & Waller, J. L. (1992). Major depressive disorder and dysthymia in young adolescents. *American Journal of Epidemiology, 135*, 792–802.

Garrison, C. Z., Jackson, K. L., Marsteller, F., McKeown, R., & Addy, C. (1990). A longitudinal study of depressive symptomatology in young adolescents. *Journal of the American Academy of Child and Adolescent Psychiatry, 29*, 581–585.

Garvin, V., Kalter, N., & Hansell, J. (1993). Divorced women: Individual differences in stressors, mediating factors, and adjustment outcome. *American Journal of Orthopsychiatry, 63*, 232–240.

Gelenberg, A. J., Bassuk, E. L., & Schoonover, S. C. (1991). Depression. In A. J. Gelenberg, E. L. Bassuk, & S. C. Schoonover (Eds.), *The practitioner's guide to psychoactive drugs* (3rd ed., pp. 23–89). New York: Plenum Medical Books.

Germain, C. B., & Gitterman, A. (1995). Ecological perspective. In R. L. Edwards (Ed.-in-Chief), *Encyclopedia of social work* (19th ed., Vol. 1, pp. 816–824). Washington, DC: NASW Press.

Gershon, E. S., Targum, S. D., Kessler, L. R., Mazure, C. M., & Bunney, W. E., Jr. (1977). Genetic studies and biological strategies in the affective disorders. *Progress in Medical Genetics, 2(3)*, 101–164.

Grinspoon, L., & Bakalar, J. B. (1995). *Depression and other mood disorders* (Mental Health Review No. 4). Boston: President and Fellows of Harvard College.

Hammen, C., & Rudolph, K. D. (1996). Childhood depression. In E. J. Mash & R. A. Barkley (Eds.), *Child psychopathology* (pp. 153–195). New York: Guilford Press.

Hinshaw, S. P. (1994). *Attention deficits and hyperactivity in children.* Thousand Oaks, CA: Sage Publications.

Hovens, J. G., Cantwell, D. P., & Kiriakos, R. (1994). Psychiatric comorbidity in hospitalized adolescent substance abusers. *Journal of the American Academy of Child and Adolescent Psychiatry, 33,* 476–483.

Hynd, G. W., & Hooper, S. R. (1992). *Neurological basis of childhood psychopathology.* Newbury Park, CA: Sage Publications.

Kandel, D. B., & Davies, M. (1986). Adult sequelae of adolescent depressive symptoms. *Archives of General Psychiatry, 4,* 255–262.

Kaplan, H. I., Sadock, B. J., & Grebb, J. A. (1994). *Kaplan and Sadock's synopsis of psychiatry: Behavioral sciences, clinical psychiatry* (7th ed.). Baltimore: Williams & Wilkins.

Karls, J. M., & Wandrei, K. E. (Eds.). (1994a). *Person-in-environment system: The PIE classification system for social functioning problems.* Washington, DC: NASW Press.

Karls, J. M., & Wandrei, K. E. (1994b). *PIE manual: Person-in-environment system: The PIE classification system for social functioning problems.* Washington, DC: NASW Press.

Kashani, J. H., Cantwell, D. P., Shekim, W. O., & Reid, J. C. (1982). Major depressive disorder in children admitted to an inpatient community mental health center. *American Journal of Psychiatry, 139,* 671–672.

Kashani, J. H., & Carlson, G. A. (1987). Seriously depressed preschoolers. *American Journal of Psychiatry, 144,* 348–350.

Kashani, J. H., Holcomb, W. R., & Orvaschel, H. (1986). Depression and depressive symptoms in preschool children from the general population. *American Journal of Psychiatry, 143,* 1138–1143.

Kazdin, A. E. (1988). Childhood depression. In E. J. Mash & L. G. Terdal (Eds.), *Behavioral assessment of childhood disorders* (2nd ed., pp. 157–195). New York: Guilford Press.

Kazdin, A. E. (1990). Childhood depression. *Journal of Child Psychology and Psychiatry and Allied Disciplines, 31*(1), 121–160.

Keller, M. B., Beardslee, W., Lavori, P. W., Wunder, J., Dorer, D. L., & Samuelson, H. (1988). Course of major depression in non-referred adolescents: A retrospective study. *Journal of Affective Disorders, 15,* 235–243.

Kendler, K. S., Walters, E. E., Truett, K. R., Heath, A. C., Neale, M. C., Martin, N. G., & Eaves, L. J. (1994). Sources of individual differences in depressive symptoms: Analysis of two samples of twins and their families. *American Journal of Psychiatry, 151,* 1605–1614.

Kovacs, M. (1984a). The Children's Depression Inventory (CDI). *Psychopharmacology Bulletin, 21,* 995–998.

Kovacs, M. (1984b). The Interview Schedule for Children (ISC). *Psychopharmacology Bulletin, 21,* 991–994.

Kovacs, M. (1990). Comorbid anxiety disorders in childhood-onset depressions. In J. D. Maser & C. R. Cloninger (Eds.), *Comorbidity of mood and anxiety disorders* (pp. 272–281). Washington, DC: American Psychiatric Press.

Kovacs, M., Akiskal, H. S., Gatsonis, C., & Parrone, P. L. (1994). Childhood-onset dysthymic disorder: Clinical features and prospective naturalistic outcome. *Archives of General Psychiatry 51*, 365–374.

Kovacs, M., & Beck, A. T. (1977). The wish to die and the wish to live in attempted suicides. *Journal of Clinical Psychology, 33*, 361–365.

Kovacs, M., Feinberg, T. L., Crouse-Novak, M. A., Paulauskas, S. L., & Finkelstein, R. (1984a). Depressive disorders in childhood: I. A longitudinal prospective study of characteristics and recovery. *Archives of General Psychiatry, 41*, 229–237.

Kovacs, M., Feinberg, T. L., Crouse-Novak, M., Paulauskas, S. L., Pollock, M., & Finkelstein, R. (1984b). Depressive disorders in childhood: II. A longitudinal study of the risk for a subsequent major depression. *Archives of General Psychiatry, 41*, 643–649.

Kovacs, M., Gatsonis, C., Paulauskas, C., & Richards, C. (1988a). Depressive disorders in children: IV. A longitudinal study of co-morbidity with and risk for anxiety disorders. *Archives of General Psychiatry, 46*, 776–782.

Kovacs, M., & Goldston, D. (1991). Cognitive and social cognitive development of depressed children and adolescents. *Journal of the American Academy of Child and Adolescent Psychiatry, 30*, 388–392.

Kovacs, M., Paulauskas, S., Gatsonis, C., & Richards, C. (1988b). Depressive disorders in childhood: III. Longitudinal study of comorbidity with and risk for conduct disorders. *Journal of Affective Disorders, 15*, 205–217.

LaRoche, C. (1986). Prevention in high risk children of depressed parents. *Canadian Journal of Psychiatry, 31*, 161–165.

Lazarus, R. S., & Folkman, S. (1984). *Stress, appraisal, and coping.* New York: Springer.

Lewinsohn, P. M., Clarke, G. N., Seeley, J. R. , & Rohde, P. (1994). Major depression in community adolescents: Age at onset, episode duration, and time to recurrence. *Journal of the American Academy of Child and Adolescent Psychiatry, 38*, 809–818.

Mahler, M. (1961). On sadness and grief in infancy and childhood: Loss and restoration of the symbiotic love object. *Psychoanalytic Study of the Child, 16*, 332–351.

Mash, E. J., & Terdal, L. G. (1988). Behavioral assessment of child and family disturbance. In E. J. Mash & L. G. Terdal (Eds.), *Behavioral assessment of childhood disorders* (2nd ed., pp. 3–65). New York: Guilford Press.

Mennen, F. E. (1995). The relationship of race/ethnicity to symptoms in childhood sexual abuse. *Child Abuse & Neglect, 19*, 115–124.

More children being abused and neglected, U.S. says. (1996, September 19). *News & Observer* [Raleigh, NC], p. 13A.

Mrazek, P. J., & Haggerty, R. J. (Eds.). (1994). *Reducing risks for mental disorders: Frontiers for preventive intervention research* (pp. 127–214). Washington, DC: National Academy Press.

Newman, J. P., & Garfinkel, B. D. (1992). Major depression in childhood and adolescence. In S. R. Hooper, G. W. Hynd, & R. W. Mattison (Eds.), *Child psychopathology: Diagnostic criteria and clinical assessment* (pp. 65–105). Hillsdale, NJ: Lawrence Erlbaum.

O'Hara, M. W., & Zekowski, E. M. (1988). Postpartum depression: A comprehensive review. In R. Kumar & I. F. Brockington (Eds.), *Motherhood and mental illness: 2. Caregivers and consequences* (pp. 17–63). London: Wright.

Ollendick, T. H., & Yule, W. (1990). Depression in British and American children and its relation to anxiety and fear. *Journal of Consulting and Clinical Psychology, 58*, 126–129.

Padur, J. S., Rapoff, M. A., Houston, B. K., Barnard, M., Danovsky, M., Olson, N. Y., Moore, W. V., Vats, T. S., & Lieberman, B. (1995). Psychosocial adjustment and the role of functional status for children with asthma. *Journal of Asthma, 32*, 345–353.

Puig-Antich, J. (1982). Major depression and conduct disorder in prepuberty. *Journal of the American Academy of Child and Adolescent Psychiatry, 21*, 118–128.

Puig-Antich, J., Blau, S., Marx, N., Greenhill, L. L., & Chambers, W. (1978). Prepubertal major depressive disorders: A pilot study. *Journal of the American Academy of Child Psychiatry, 17*, 695–707.

Puig-Antich, J., Dahl, R., Ryan, N., Novancenko, H., Goetz, D., Goetz, R., Twomey, J., & Klepper, T. (1989). Cortisol secretion in prepubertal children with major depressive disorder. *Archives of General Psychiatry, 46*, 801–809.

Riddle, M. A., & Cho, S. C. (1989). Biological aspects of adolescent depression. In G. R. Adams, R. Montemayor, & T. P. Gullotta (Eds.), *Biology of adolescent behavior and development* (pp. 223–246). Newbury Park, CA: Sage Publications.

Rie, H. E. (1966). Depression in childhood: A survey of some pertinent contributions. *Journal of the American Academy of Child Psychiatry, 5*, 653–685.

Roberts, R. E., & Chen, Y. W. (1995). Depressive symptoms and suicidal ideation among Mexican-origin and Anglo adolescents. *Journal of the American Academy of Child and Adolescent Psychiatry, 34*, 81–90.

Rochlin, G. (1959). The loss complex. *Journal of the American Psychoanalytic Association, 7*, 299–316.

Rutter, M. (1986). The developmental psychopathology of depression: Issues and perspectives. In M. Rutter, C. E. Izard, & P. B. Read (Eds.), *Depression in young people* (pp. 3–30). New York: Guilford Press.

Rutter, M., Graham, P., Chadwick, O., & Yule, W. (1976). Adolescent turmoil: Fact or fiction? *Journal of Child Psychology and Psychiatry, 17*, 35–56.

Ryan, N. D., Puig-Antich, J., Ambrosini, P., Rabinovich, H., Robinson, D., Nelson, B., Iyengar, S., & Twomey, J. (1987). The clinical picture of major depression in children and adolescents. *Archives of General Psychiatry, 44*, 854–861.

Sack, W. H., Beiser, M., Phillips, N., & Baker-Brown. (1993). Co-morbid symptoms of depression and conduct disorder in first nations children: Some findings from the Flower of Two Soils Project. *Culture, Medicine and Psychiatry, 16*, 471–486.

Seligman, M. E. (1975). *Helplessness: On depression, development and death.* San Francisco: W. H. Freeman.

Shaffer, D., Schwab-Stone, M., Fisher, P., Cohen, P., Piacentini, J., Davies, M., Conners, C. K., & Regier, D. (1993). The Diagnostic Interview Schedule for Children–Revised Version (DISC-R): I. Preparation, field testing, interrater reliability, and acceptability. *Journal of the American Academy of Child and Adolescent Psychiatry, 32,* 643–650.

Spitz, R. A. (1946). Anaclitic depression. *Psychoanalytic Study of the Child, 2,* 313–342.

Spitzer, R. L., Endicott, J., & Robins, E. (1978). Research Diagnostic Criteria: Rationale and reliability. *Archives of General Psychiatry, 35,* 773–782.

Thompson, M. S., & Peebles-Wilkins, W. (1992). The impact of formal, informal, and societal support networks on the psychological well-being of black adolescent mothers. *Social Work, 37,* 322–328.

Toolan, J. M. (1962). Depression in children and adolescents. *American Journal of Orthopsychiatry, 32,* 404–415.

Toolan, J. M. (1974). Masked depression in children and adolescents. In S. Lesse (Ed.), *Masked depression* (pp. 141–164). New York: Jason Aronson.

Wallerstein, J. S., & Kelly, J. B. (1983). *Surviving the breakup.* New York: Basic Books.

Weinberg, W. A., Rutman, J., Sullivan, L., Pencik, E. C., & Dietz, S. G. (1973). Depression in children referred to an educational diagnostic center. *Journal of Pediatrics, 83,* 1065–1072.

Yang, Y. M., Cepeda, M., Price, C., Shah, A., & Mankad, V. (1994). Depression in children and adolescents with sickle-cell disease. *Archives of Pediatric and Adolescent Medicine, 148,* 457–469.

12

PROMOTING THE DEVELOPMENT OF YOUNG CHILDREN WITH DISABILITIES

Irene Nathan Zipper and Rune J. Simeonsson

C hildren with disabilities face unique challenges. Lack of agreement about definitions of disability, difficulties in assessment, inadequate resources, and limited information about effective interventions, coupled with negative societal attitudes toward those who are different, all contribute to the challenges they face. Although development is inevitably affected, the extent and nature of disabilities' effects on children are highly variable. The development of all children is dependent on complex transactions involving the child, the family, and the community. If children with disabilities are to attain their optimal development, it is critically important to identify those factors that may facilitate or impede development in each of these contexts.

The scope and severity of disabilities vary substantially, as do the definitions of disability (Simeonsson, Edmondson, Smith, Carnahan, & Bucy, 1995). In infancy and early childhood, definitions of disability typically reflect developmental delay, identified through functional assessment. For school-aged children, disability is generally defined in categorical terms such as mental retardation, learning disability, and motor impairment. With the transition to adulthood, the term "developmental disability" indicates a variety of conditions associated with mental retardation, autism, cerebral palsy, and seizure disorders, among others. These differences in terminology result, to some extent, from lack of conceptual clarity about the nature of disability, complicated by the individual and variable rate at which children develop. Agreed on definitions of disability are needed to guide effective intervention and development of criteria for determining eligibility for services.

The multiple factors salient in children's postnatal development include their unique characteristics and qualities, as well as the context within which they develop. Such factors as infant adaptive skills and behavioral processes, infant social performance, availability and use of resources, and relationships between families and service providers are key to further understanding the issues (Guralnick & Bennett, 1987; Kopp & Kaler, 1989). The purpose of this chapter is twofold: to identify and define the factors that place children with atypical development at risk of more severe disabilities and their secondary effects and to examine the factors that protect them against these possibilities.

ISSUES CONCERNING DISABILITY IN YOUNG CHILDREN

It is hard to know the actual prevalence of childhood disabilities, because no single classification system has been adopted and inconsistent data collection procedures make the aggregation of data difficult (Aron, Loprest, & Steuerle, 1996). Yet the figures that are available suggest that at least 6.1 percent of the U.S. population under 18 years of age have a disability (U.S. Department of Education, 1996). Furthermore, the complexity of the problems caused by disabilities is often underestimated, because traditional categorical definitions suggest that disabilities are relatively unidimensional constructs. In fact, the child with impairments in one domain may well exhibit delays in other domains, so a broad evaluation of functioning may be more useful in assessing risk and protective factors for purposes of intervention planning. These impairments account for only about 42 percent of the conditions causing disability, however; the other 58 percent of impairments among children are accounted for by diseases and disorders not addressed in this chapter. (Information on the prevalence of impairments associated with disability in children under age 18 is presented in Table 12-1.)

Approaches to serving children with disabilities and their families have changed dramatically in recent decades. Medical and technological advances have meant that babies born with complex anomalies or prematurely at low birthweight are more likely to survive; these infants are frequently at risk for disabilities that become apparent only as they mature. At the same time, changing attitudes toward people with disabilities have contributed to the movement toward deinstitutionalization, with the result that children who have disabilities are likely to live with their families and participate in community activities. Consequently, the need for community-based resources and services has increased, along with public awareness of the pertinent issues. Eligibility

Table 12-1. Impairments Causing Disability in Children under Age 18, by Condition

CONDITION	PREVALENCE (IN 1,000s)	%
Visual impairment	83	1.7
Hearing impairment	190	3.8
Speech impairment	335	6.7
Learning disabilities	167	3.4
Mental retardation/Down syndrome	786	15.8
Absence of loss	18	0.4
Paralysis	140	2.8
(cerebral palsy)	99	2.0
Deformities	134	2.7
(Spina bifida)	17	0.3
Orthopedic impairment	144	2.9
Other and ill-defined impairments	69	1.4
Impairment	2,069	41.6
All diseases or disorders	2,906	58.4
All conditions	4,974	100.0

SOURCE: U.S. Department of Education, National Institute on Disability and Rehabilitation Research. (1996). *Disabilities among children* (Disability Statistics Abstract No. 15, p. 3). Washington, DC: Author.

for intervention services is determined through an assessment process, and it is important that such an assessment be accurate and reliable.

ISSUES IN IDENTIFICATION

Limitations of Assessment

Accurate diagnosis of developmental disability in young children is a challenge. In young children, delayed development in one or more of the major domains of functioning generally serves as a marker for later developmental disability, but assessment findings obtained in infancy are only weakly predictive of developmental status in later childhood. This apparent inconsistency results both from the dynamic nature of early development and from the difficulty of trying to precisely assess the functioning of young children.

Variable Rate of Development

The infant and preschool years account for dramatic accomplishments, as evidenced by the remarkable transition from a newborn with primitive sensory and motor behavior to a young child with significant competencies in social and communicative interaction, motor control, and cognitive readiness for academic skills. The rate at which children develop in the domains of cognitive, communicative, motor, social, and behavioral functioning is enormously variable, and even more so for children with neurological complications or deficits in visual, motor, and auditory functioning, who may acquire developmental skills at a pace and in a sequence different from the typical pattern. Such variability suggests the need for caution in the diagnosis of disability in very young children—particularly in light of the lowered expectations and stigmatization that frequently accompany diagnosis. Because none of the general developmental instruments has been standardized on a population with disabilities, their usefulness for assessing children with disabilities is limited (Farran, 1990). These difficulties in assessing children with significant deficits largely account for the paucity of information about typical development among children with perceptual and motor impairments.

Unknown Etiologies

Developmental disabilities manifest themselves as mental retardation, motor and sensory impairment, and learning and behavioral difficulties. Mental retardation may be categorized as congenital in nature or as an acquired condition (Alexander, 1992), and the same categorization may be applied to developmental disability in general. Etiologies include genetic and prenatal conditions as well as postnatal factors. Biological etiologies, in particular, are being increasingly identified in biomedical and genetic research, but the explanation for functional delays in development remains unknown for most children. For example, there are more than 350 known causes of mental retardation, yet those causes do not account for many cases of mental retardation. For many of these children with unexplained developmental disability, it is likely that delays are acquired. Acquired conditions may result from risk factors first evident during the postnatal period. These risk factors include respiratory disorders, infections, accidents, exposure to environmental contaminants, and nutritional deficiencies (Kopp & Kaler, 1989). Whether the etiologies are congenital or acquired, developmental disability reflects the ongoing interaction of congenital and environmental factors.

Even when disability results from an identified congenital condition, the identification of the disabling condition does not, by itself, provide adequate information about the child's functioning or prognosis. The extent to which a disability affects a child's development is a function of several factors—the nature of the condition, its severity, the context within which the child develops, and the interrelationship of all these contribute to developmental outcome and to the challenges and limitations faced by children with disabilities (see, for example, Guralnick & Bennett, 1987; Sameroff & Fiese, 1990). Furthermore, it is becoming increasingly apparent that developmental delays do not exist in isolation; rather, a delay in one domain of functioning frequently co-occurs with difficulties in functioning in other domains. Definitions of disability need to reflect all of this variability accurately.

For example, the term "developmental delay"—as opposed to developmental disability—recognizes the plasticity of development in infants and young children and signals the potential for protection against more severe difficulty. This terminology reflects the fact that many specific conditions are difficult to diagnose at young ages (Simeonsson, 1991a, 1991b) and avoids the additional risks that identification as a class member may impose on the child (stigmatization and lowered expectations, for example). Postponing the diagnostic label allows time to enhance the salience of factors that protect the child against more severe manifestations of an existing condition. Eligibility criteria for early intervention services in most states thus call for the determination of functional developmental delay in one or more domains of development; a categorical diagnosis that might suggest the likelihood of developmental disability in the future need not be established.

Although some delays in development are readily explained by obvious physical disability, the explanation for delays in other domains may be less apparent. Even children born without obvious congenital anomalies may gradually manifest developmental disabilities if their environment is inadequate. Moreover, existing developmental delays and deviations may be exacerbated by such an environment, as proposed in the transactional model of mediated effects (Sameroff & Chandler, 1975). The transactions that account for development are complex, but it is possible to identify some of the specific factors that may increase or reduce risk for adaptation and developmental progress.

AN ECOLOGICAL FRAMEWORK OF CHILDHOOD DISABILITY

An ecological perspective views the child in the context of the family, and the family in the context of the community and the wider society (Bronfenbrenner, 1979). Consistent with this view, one must look beyond the child to identify risk and protective factors for children with developmental disabilities. It is now widely acknowledged that children's development is influenced by their interactions with their environment (see, for example, Hartup, 1989; Landesman & Ramey, 1989; Resnick et al., 1992; Sameroff & Fiese, 1990), but the complex interaction of biological and environmental factors makes it difficult to discern cause from effect in these interactions (Sameroff & Chandler, 1975). Nonetheless, it is clear that conditions both within the child and in the environment can place a child at risk of more pronounced developmental disability; likewise, some individual and environmental factors can protect the child against more severe manifestations of an existing impairment.

Educational programs set up to provide "normalizing" experiences for children with disabilities illustrate the complexity of transactions between child and environment. Legislative mandates require that children with disabilities be educated within the "least restrictive environment" appropriate (Wang, 1989), so that they can be protected from the negative effects of isolation and can learn to cope with the realities of their impairment, among other goals. The extent to which children with disabilities can benefit from such programs, however, may depend as much on conditions within the environment as on those within the child. Such programs constitute a protective factor for children with disabilities when the school system is committed to such placements, as evidenced by, for example, giving priority to placing children with skilled, enthusiastic teachers; allowing for gradual transition into the classroom; and maintaining relatively small class sizes. The child's temperament and readiness to interact with other children may protect the child against social difficulties. Moreover, in such a setting a child may acquire other individual, unique coping strategies—protective factors—that facilitate development in various domains. No single factor can protect the child from further disability, but in transaction all can help promote the child's development.

Because development is dynamic and variable, all children encounter factors that jeopardize aspects of their functioning and factors that facilitate development along typical trajectories. For infants, a caregiving environment that elicits and reinforces early communication, provides opportunities for object manipulation and play, and contributes to an awareness of cause and effect is crucial for fostering development. For toddlers and preschool children, socialization experiences in the form of small group activities, opportunities for incidental learning, and exposure to readiness skills are key elements for developmental mastery. The same factors that are salient for typically developing children are salient for those with disabilities. However, children whose effective functioning is challenged by impairment can develop secondary conditions or more severe forms of disability. The extent to which they are able to avoid these possibilities depends on a number of complex and interrelated factors. We need to identify those factors that place a child at risk and those that contribute to the child's resilience, so that interventions may promote children's optimal development by preventing disability or ameliorating its effects.

RISK AND PROTECTIVE FACTORS RELEVANT TO CHILDREN WITH DISABILITIES

Longitudinal research on the development of young children with disabilities is sparse (Shonkoff, Hauser-Cram, Krauss, & Upshur, 1992), thus the empirical foundation for a discussion of risk and protection for children with disabilities is limited. Some of the factors that we know are likely to influence children's development are described below. Each risk factor increases the odds that the development of a child with disabilities will be jeopardized. When risk factors cluster, as they often do, their additive effects place the child's development in even greater jeopardy and the likelihood of negative outcomes increases (Dunst, 1993; Schorr, 1988).

SPECIFIC DISABILITY

Children born with congenital anomalies are at risk of secondary conditions that vary according to the nature and severity of the primary impairment. An event or a sequence of events that could harm the brain—premature birth at low birthweight, perinatal asphyxia, infection or trauma of the central nervous system, for example—place children at biological risk (Bennett, 1987). In a year-long study of 190 infants and toddlers who were receiving early intervention services, Shonkoff and colleagues (1992) found that children with seizure disorders or relatively severe psychomotor impairments were slower than other children in the sample to develop in cognitive and social domains. The authors noted that psychomotor development in the first two years of life is relatively predictable regardless of the child's environment. Is the delayed development of children with seizure disorders influenced by the condition itself, or is it a secondary condition resulting from the effects of medications used to control seizures? The answer is unknown, but the question illustrates the difficulty of identifying the differential effects of disabilities and their secondary conditions.

RELATIONSHIP WITH THE PRIMARY CAREGIVER

Some risk factors can be either exacerbated or ameliorated by their interactions with environmental conditions. For example, a premature, low-birthweight infant in a neonatal intensive care unit (NICU) is likely to be at risk of a variety of developmental disabilities. The situation could be exacerbated, as McFadyen (1994) observed, if the emotional state of the infant's parents—which may include confusion, anxiety, and helplessness—makes it hard for them to relate to their baby. Parents under such stress may distance themselves from their baby, thereby limiting the kinds of interactions that promote optimal development. One study of 50 couples with children in NICUs found that mothers reported greater levels of emotional disturbance than fathers (Affleck, Tennen, & Rowe, 1990).

Ramey and colleagues have hypothesized that the behavioral interactions between infants and adults are the most important influence on cognitive development (Ramey et al., 1992; Ramey, Bryant, Sparling, & Wasik, 1984). Children subject to grossly pathological care involving disregard for their basic emotional needs are at risk of developing serious mental disorders that may be associated with developmental delay, among other difficulties (American Psychiatric Association, 1994). A parent's mental illness, conditions of extreme poverty, and frequent changes in primary caregiver are among the factors associated with such inadequate care. On the other hand, a strong, consistent relationship between the primary caregiver and the child may well provide the most important protection against the development of more severe disability. Although the mechanism by which this takes place is not well understood, Hartup (1989) has hypothesized that mothers who have good relationships with their children may be more likely to engage them and support them in solving problems, and children in these relationships may be more open to maternal assistance and more likely to use their mothers as a stable emotional base from which to explore the wider world. The child's efforts to explore and interact with the environment may be particularly critical for development when a disabling condition limits or modifies the way in which he or she incorporates newly learned information. Thus, a strong and secure attachment between the child who has a developmental disability and the child's primary caregiver may moderate the effects of disability to some degree and provide important protection for the child.

PARENTAL SUBSTANCE ABUSE

A fair amount of research on prenatal effects of parental substance abuse has been conducted (see, for example, Edmondson, 1994), but less is known about longer-term effects on postnatal development. Fetal alcohol syndrome is covered even in the popular literature, and its effects on children after birth have been described extensively. Parental substance abuse by itself places the child's development at risk, because abusing parents frequently have accompanying physical, psychological, and social problems that may render them incapable of meeting the child's needs. Because information about the effects of parental drug use on children has come primarily from families involved with the public service system, most information is based on a biased sample. It is likely, however, that these children face inconsistent caregiving, untrained caregivers, and poor attachment (Vincent, Poulsen, Cole, Woodruff, & Griffith, 1991), which put them at increased risk. It also seems likely that the extent of that risk depends on duration of use, the nature of the substance, and the likelihood of polydrug use.

POVERTY

Poverty itself, with its attendant conditions, places children at significant risk of developmental delay and disability (Farran, 1990; Kamerman & Kahn, 1995); moreover, risk factors for many conditions occur far more frequently among children living in poverty (Schorr, 1988). Poor nutrition, medical complications of pregnancy, lack of access to medical care, and inadequate housing all arise from low socioeconomic status (SES) (Bryant & Ramey, 1987). Each of these conditions increases the likelihood that the child's needs will go unmet; their cumulative effects make it very difficult to provide an environment in which the child can thrive. Furthermore, living under adverse conditions, including poverty, directly influences the relationships between children and their primary caregivers. The stress that results from such conditions may make it impossible for parents to engage in the positive, nurturant interactions that facilitate children's optimal development. Although it is difficult to establish the differential effects of the conditions attendant with poverty on the functioning of the family and the development of the child, it is obvious that poverty constitutes a significant risk factor for both congenital and acquired developmental disability.

SECONDARY CONDITIONS

Children are vulnerable to secondary effects of their disabilities. These secondary conditions may be physical, social, or psychological (Lollar, 1994). For example, difficulties in peer interactions may result from a sense of self that is grounded in difference, from limitations on the ability to participate in certain activities, from the unrealistic or inappropriate expectations of others, and from lack of information or understanding on the part of peers about the effects of a child's disability and its implications. The likelihood that children with developmental delays and disabilities will develop positive social behaviors is increased when they are included in normal daily activities as much as possible. In addition to facilitating their interaction with typically developing peers, their inclusion offers the opportunity to increase public sensitivity to the challenges they face and to enhance recognition of their potential contributions.

ADEQUACY OF RESOURCES AVAILABLE TO THE FAMILY

Parents who have access to financial and other resources and to information to support them in raising their child are far more likely to be able to provide an environment in which the child's development will be optimized. Dunst, Leet, and Trivette (1988) found that the adequacy of resources available to the child's mother was closely correlated with both her sense of well-being and an avowed commitment to carrying out professionally prescribed educational and therapeutic interventions with the child. Their findings suggest that when resources are inadequate, families are less likely to be able to participate actively in intervention activities that might promote the child's development. Adequate resources therefore constitute a protective factor for the child.

PARENTS' SENSE OF EFFICACY

The beliefs and values of the child's primary caregivers play a subtle but critical role in the child's development. Parents who believe in their own efficacy expect to be able to positively influence their child's development, even if the process is slow and tentative. These parents are more likely to refuse to accept results of a diagnostic assessment with which they disagree and to insist on validation of the original findings in an effort to get accurate information about the child's condition and prognosis. The relationships that they develop and maintain with service providers reflect their own decision-making authority vis-à-vis their child, and they take an active role in the planning and implementation of services. Thus, parents who believe in their own ability to shape their circumstances may provide critical protection against the development of more severe disability.

HOW FACTORS PROVIDE RISK PROTECTION

Not surprisingly, some of the same factors that place a child at risk of compromised development may serve to protect the child against further disability when they are present in their positive form. As an example, a family living in poverty with a child with a developmental delay might benefit from information about promoting the child's development, as well as from such resources as housing assistance, food stamps, and consistency in medical care. When the family's access to needed services and resources is impeded by such bureaucratic barriers as long waiting lists, complicated eligibility criteria, and documentation requirements, the likelihood that the child's development will be further compromised is increased. Conversely, a well-coordinated, culturally competent service system that responds to the needs of children and families by providing information about services and convenient access to resources can do much to support the family in protecting the child against further disability. It is important to recognize, however, that mere absence of risk factors does not necessarily lead to optimal development. Optimal development is more likely to occur in the presence of multiple opportunity factors, Dunst (1993) hypothesized, just as the likelihood of negative outcomes increases when multiple risk factors are present.

Despite the fact that families with children with disabilities face special challenges, it is important to recognize that they are not necessarily subject to severe distress. In their study of 190 infants and their families, Shonkoff and colleagues (1992) found that a child's condition did not necessarily lead to maladaptive family functioning. In fact, the mothers reported no greater stress as parents than did mothers of typically developing children. It is likely, however, that parents who are themselves very young, who do not have access to adequate resources, and who have little support from family and friends will have difficulty when faced with the additional challenges involved in raising a child with disabilities.

DIFFERENCES IN RISK AND PROTECTIVE FACTORS AMONG CHILDREN WITH DISABILITIES

Comprehensive information about developmental disability among infants and toddlers is hard to gather, because methods of identifying children with disabilities are inconsistent and criteria for eligibility for early intervention services vary. However, the 1986 amendments to the Education of the Handicapped Act (P.L. 99-457) later incorporated into the Individuals with Disabilities Education Act ([IDEA], P.L. 101-476, 1990) require that states establish a system for identifying infants and toddlers who are eligible for services, as well as a system for compiling data on early intervention programs. The legislation thus provides a unique opportunity to establish a national database for learning the incidence and prevalence of developmental disability among infants and toddlers in this country (Kopp & Kaler, 1989). These data should lead to a greater level of understanding of the factors that contribute to risk and resilience in young children with disabilities. The data would also be extremely useful for comparing the effectiveness of ongoing early intervention efforts.

Information about children receiving special education services includes rates of service use, although a disproportionately high rate of placement of students of color in special education programs has been noted, suggesting that placement in special education is not dependent on disability status alone (Harry, 1992). (Table 12-2 indicates numbers and percentages of children, by race, ethnicity, and poverty status, who needed and received special education in 1992. According to these data, children living below the poverty line were more likely to receive special education than others.)

POVERTY

There is general agreement that children living in poverty are at significant risk of various developmental difficulties. In this country, 26 percent of all children under six years old live in poverty (Knitzer & Aber, 1995). The youngest children are

Table 12-2. Number and Percentage of Children Ages Five to 17 Needing and Receiving Special Education, by Race or Ethnicity and Poverty Status, 1992

	TOTAL		RECEIVES SPECIAL EDUCATION SERVICES		NEEDS BUT DOES NOT RECEIVE SPECIAL EDUCATION SERVICES	
	N	%	n	%	n	%
All children, ages 5–17	46,828	100.0	1,484	3.2	245	0.5
Race or ethnicity						
White (non-Hispanic)	31,041	100.0	1,054	3.4	155	0.5
Black (non-Hispanic)	7,160	100.0	257	3.6	51	0.7
Hispanic (any race)	4,529	100.0	100	2.2	16[a]	0.4
Economic status						
Above poverty line	34,907	00.0	969	2.8	152	0.4
Below poverty line	8,047	100.0	416	5.2	77	1.0

SOURCE: U.S. Department of Education, National Institute of Disability and Rehabilitation Research. (1996). *Disabilities among children* (Disability Statistics Abstract No. 15, p. 3). Washington, DC: Author.
NOTE: Numbers in thousands.
[a]Estimate has low statistical reliability: Standard error exceeds 30 percent of estimate.

disproportionately represented in these statistics—more than 20 percent of all poor children in 1990 were under three years of age (Kamerman & Kahn, 1995). Given the influence of the child's earliest years on later development, these data suggest that a substantial number of children in this country are at risk of developmental delay or disability. This critical risk factor varies across racial and ethnic lines: 52 percent of African American children, 42 percent of Hispanic children, and 15 percent of white children under age two were living in poverty in 1990 (Kamerman & Kahn, 1995).

RACE AND ETHNICITY

Relatively little is known about the relationship between developmental delay and race or ethnicity, although some studies have focused on the relationships among race or ethnicity, parental attitudes, and involvement with the human services system. For example, in a study examining how 60 African American, Hispanic, and white mothers reacted to having a child with mental retardation, Mary (1990) found no significant differences in reports of negative feelings. However, Mary also found that Hispanic mothers reported a greater sense of self-sacrifice and were more likely to say they experienced loneliness. Such findings suggest that race and ethnicity may affect children indirectly through their parents' beliefs, values, and support.

Participation in educational and other services also appears to be related to race or ethnicity. Research findings indicate that parents of color want to be involved actively in their children's education, but they tend to be less involved in special education programs (Chavkin & Garza-Lubeck, 1990; Harry, 1992). In a study of more than 500 families with young children with special needs, Sontag and Schacht (1994) found that American Indian and Hispanic parents reported a greater need for information about services than did white parents, and white parents were more likely to report that they helped make decisions about their children's programs and that they coordinated their services for their children. These differences suggest that some families are not gaining information and access to resources through collaborative relationships with service providers.

TYPE OF DISABILITY

Although there is little empirical information about the differential effect of children's disabilities on their families, Shonkoff and colleagues (1992) found that parents of children with motor impairments reported greater stress than parents of children with other disabilities. Moreover, parents of children with motor impairments reported decreasing social support over time, presumably because the nature of their children's condition made it difficult for them to participate in routine school and community activities. Such findings suggest that children with motor impairments may be at increased risk for difficulties resulting from parental stress and isolation.

AGE OF CHILD

The nature of child development suggests that risk factors vary by age, and there is some evidence of this for children with disabilities (Coie et al., 1993; Kamerman & Kahn, 1995). Between the ages of four and seven years, measures of a child's development may, by themselves, predict later disability. For children under the age of one, however, efforts to predict developmental disability must focus on factors in the environment as well as on the child (Kochanek, Kabacoff, & Lipsitt, 1990).

GENDER

Evidence from longitudinal studies carried out by Werner and colleagues in Kauai indicate that the factors that promote resilience may vary by gender (Werner, 1990). These studies do not specifically focus on developmental disability, yet their findings have implications for understanding protective factors for children with disabilities. Resilient girls in the Kauai sample seemed to come from households that provided consistent emotional support for the child and emphasized risk taking and independence. Resilient boys, on the other hand, were from homes in which emotional expressiveness was encouraged, where greater structure and supervision were provided, and a male role model was available for the child (Werner, 1990).

ASSESSING RISK AND RESILIENCE

Research in the field of developmental disabilities has focused on risk. Knowledge of the factors that place a child at risk of developmental disability has therefore been growing, but understanding of the factors that protect children against disability is far more limited. Working within the transactional model, assessment of risk and protective factors should encompass the child, the family, and the broader environment. Meisels and Wasik (1992) have described the use of multiple risk indexes, constructed around biological, caregiving, and behavioral risk conditions. Defining and measuring opportunity factors may constitute another area for further exploration (see, for example, Dunst, 1993). The development of indices to profile the specific risk and protection factors affecting individual children would be helpful in tailoring services to enhance the resilience and promote the development of children in a wide range of community settings.

An important implication of an ecological framework is that families should be directly involved in the process of assessing the child's development and relevant risk and protective factors. The significant role that families can play in assessment has been recognized by Bloch and Seitz (1989) and has emerged as a major trend in intervention efforts for infants and young children in the context of effective partnerships between parents and professionals (Stonestreet, Johnson, & Acton, 1991). Even when the opportunity for participation is provided, the level of family involvement may vary substantially as a function of family preference and availability, as well as the nature and focus of the assessment.

The emphasis on involvement of families and other caregivers in the assessment process coincides with a growing interest in functional assessment, which emphasizes documentation of functional ability. These converging trends promote a more comprehensive approach to assessment of risk and protective factors, one in which the perspectives and experiences of families complement those of evaluation specialists. With information gathered through questionnaires, and observations by families and service providers, and interactions between parents and professionals, risk as well as protective factors can be identified. Data obtained in this manner can include documentation of child characteristics, such as the nature and severity of the disability (Bailey, Simeonsson, Buysse, & Smith, 1993). Together with information about the child's behavioral style or temperament (Huntington & Simeonsson, 1993), these data provide initial information about the additional demands placed on the family by the child's condition. Further assessment of factors that affect the child's development involves learning about the family's needs and concerns (Bailey, Blasco, & Simeonsson, 1992) and about their expectations (Simeonsson et al., 1995). Their expectations are particularly important, because these are grounded in the context of the family's resources, as described by Dunst, Trivette, and Deal (1988). With this information, the likelihood that services will be provided in a manner consistent with family priorities is increased.

The data derived through these means can be used to help determine eligibility or plan interventions at the level of individuals or populations. A good example of such integration of data is a report by Sinclair (1993) that described children with special needs in Head Start programs. Child characteristics, medical and developmental history, family background, and behavioral and academic functioning served as the basis for profiling children. Cluster analysis of the profiles yielded three distinct groups of children who were certified as having special needs. The clusters were defined by different combinations of risk and protective factors in terms of family context, developmental and medical history, and current functioning. The differentiation of these groups along these variables was paralleled by differential rates of recommendation for special education placement in kindergarten. Such approaches are useful for applying knowledge of risk and protective factors to prevention efforts.

Identifying and defining individual and contextual factors that promote resilience constitute emerging areas of inquiry—information about the factors that enhance resilience in young children with disabilities is still limited. Additional studies are needed about the protective factors that characterize the child, the child's immediate environment, and the broader environment within which the family functions. More needs to be learned about the factors that place children at risk for disability, about their differential effect on development, and about their complex interactive effects. The information gained from these studies should guide early intervention efforts that focus on the development of protective factors and enhance their salience.

IMPLICATIONS FOR PREVENTION AND EARLY INTERVENTION

Efforts to reduce risk and enhance resilience in young children with disabilities must include programs that address the context for children's development as well as the children directly. To be effective, a prevention agenda must be broad-based and include an array of programs to support families (Chamberlin, 1994). Secondary prevention programs, ranging from hospital-based stimulation programs for low-birthweight infants born prematurely to home-based parent support efforts, have been assigned increasing priority in the past two decades. These programs targeted at infants and toddlers and their families provide critical protection against further developmental delay or disability.

A prevention agenda has been formalized in the past decade through federal legislation for the states (Florian, 1995), radically altering the broad context for the development of young children with disabilities. The policies and procedures developed to carry out this governmental mandate should play an important role in increasing the resilience of young children and protecting them against some of the effects of developmental disability. Part H of the Individuals with Disabilities Education Act, which applies to children under the age of three, provides financial assistance to the states for developing comprehensive, coordinated service systems for eligible infants and toddlers. Part H is intended to enhance the development of infants and toddlers with disabilities by providing support to their families, both directly and indirectly. It gives the strongest legislative direction to date for family-centered services, promoting active participation on the part of parents and authorizing them to make decisions about early intervention services for their children (Zipper, Weil, & Rounds, 1993). Its specific mandates define how services are provided at the local level. The legislation outlines a process for the development of an "individualized family service plan," as a means by which the family's concerns, resources, and priorities guide service planning and service provision. By assuring that services address parents' priorities, Part H focuses on enhancing the family's ability to foster the child's optimal development.

A further provision of Part H is intended to promote an effective and consistent relationship between the family and the service system. Eligible infants and toddlers and their families are assigned a service coordinator, who acts as a liaison between the family and the service system by facilitating their access to resources and services and ensuring that services are coordinated. Service coordination has been conceptualized as a means of reducing family stress, mobilizing resources, and linking clients to needed services (Dunst & Trivette, 1988; Singer et al., 1993; U.S. General Accounting Office, 1992). The service coordinator's role is to ensure the family's access to resources and services, to monitor the provision of services, to facilitate collaboration, and to evaluate service effectiveness. Thus, the service coordinator can act as an advocate within the service system to ensure that appropriate services are provided as effectively as possible (Zipper et al., 1993). In addition, the service coordinator may be instrumental in linking the family to available advocacy organizations, which can play an important role by telling families about relevant policies and regulations and other issues and by linking them with other families with similar concerns. In facilitating access to such resources, the service coordinator promotes resilience in the family and the child.

The guidelines for eligibility for early intervention services under Part H are established by the states themselves, 10 of which have opted to include children who are at risk of developing disabilities among those eligible for early intervention. Their decision to do so reflects the recognition that services provided to children during their very early years may help to reduce the likelihood of disability among older children. It is likely that states with a more limited definition of eligibility simply feared that the price tag would be too high (Carolina Policy Studies Program, 1993). One idea being discussed in the reauthorization process for Part H is differentiated services for children who do not have documented disabilities but are still at risk. The level of service for these children could involve tracking the child's development and providing service coordination; all the processes and services to which eligible children with a disability are currently entitled would not have to be provided (personal communication, J. Hurth, associate director, National Early Childhood Technical Assistance System, University of North Carolina, Chapel Hill, June 20, 1996). States that have so far not opted to serve children at risk might decide to do so under such an arrangement.

These legislative mandates have a direct effect on children and families through community-based services. Because opportunities for children with disabilities are enhanced when they are able to develop in an environment that is as normal as possible, the community context is critical for the development of circumstances and characteristics that protect the child from the negative effects of disability. Inclusion of children in normalized environments protects against isolation from typically developing peers and from a self-image grounded in difference. To this end, the provisions of IDEA reflect a commitment to promote protective factors in the community. The mandate that children be served in the "least restrictive environment" feasible is intended to normalize the educational process for children with disabilities and to protect them against the effects of segregation from their peers.

Legislation protecting the civil rights of individuals with disabilities should go far toward increasing public sensitivity to the needs of individuals with disabilities, thereby increasing the likelihood that they will be active participants in the community. The Americans with Disabilities Act of 1990 (P.L. 101-336) prohibits discrimination against individuals with disabilities. P.L. 94-142, the Education for All Handicapped Children Act of 1975 (renamed the Individuals with Disabilities Education Act in 1990), ensures that school-aged children with disabling conditions have access to a free and appropriate public education in the least restrictive environment feasible. Through P.L. 99-457, this access was extended to children three years of age and older, with inducements for states to develop appropriate services for eligible infants and toddlers and their families, as described above.

These legislative efforts have been key to increasing public sensitivity to the rights and needs of young children with disabilities, and they have created a climate conducive to development of services and programs to protect children against further disability. As an example, programs that provide factual information to typically developing young children about their peers with disabilities (see, for example, Heekin & Mengel, 1983) can increase the likelihood of positive outcomes resulting from the inclusion of children with disabilities in normal activities. Such programs can increase children's awareness and understanding of the issues surrounding the challenges posed by disabling conditions.

Notwithstanding these advances, further efforts are needed to increase public knowledge about the nature of developmental disabilities and the factors that protect children and adults from their effects. The public needs to know much more about the factors that increase the likelihood of giving birth to a child with a developmental disability, the importance of prenatal care, the ways in which optimal development in infancy is promoted, and the rights of children with disabilities and their families, among others.

The mandate to provide community-based services for children with disabilities implies a greater level of public responsibility for the well-being of children with disabilities and for their families. Weiss (1990) argued that nurturing children is the joint and interdependent responsibility of the family, the state, the volunteer community, and the private sector. Efforts to create the conditions under which parents are able to protect their children against developmental delay, then, must be comprehensive and integrated. Perhaps most basic is addressing the poverty that limits the ability of parents to provide adequately for their children (Farran, 1990; Knitzer & Aber, 1995; Schorr, 1988). It seems obvious that parents need access to medical care, appropriate housing, and adequate nutrition for their child and themselves, if they are to promote their child's optimal development. Programs must be readily accessible, with services provided in the context of collaboration among families, schools, medical services, and other agencies. At present, far too many children are growing up under conditions of poverty that place them at great risk of serious problems, including developmental disability.

All parents benefit from understanding their child's development and from access to supportive services. Families of children with disabilities, however, require additional community resources and supports to promote their children's optimal development (Rounds, Zipper, & Green, in press). Services to benefit young children with disabilities should focus on the needs of the entire family. Parents need specific information about the child's condition and prognosis and about services that may be available. Because caring for the child may require considerable time and attention, the child and the family will benefit from individualized services, including medical and respite care. Service providers must be prepared to address the family's concerns and priorities, and they need to recognize that parents are the ones who know the most about their child (Seitz & Provence, 1990). When service providers respect the family's unique perspective, they are better able to support the family in promoting the child's development.

Positive relationships between families and service providers that are grounded in such mutual respect are key to effective services. Parents are far more likely to respond to service providers who are culturally competent—that is, who respect the values and beliefs of the family and can help family members build on those values to protect their child against more severe disability. It follows that programs that emphasize cultural competence will be more effective in their efforts to engage family members (McGonigel, 1991). To this end, policies should support the recruitment and hiring of professionals from diverse cultural and ethnic backgrounds, and they should offer opportunities for staff development aimed at promoting cultural competence (Lynch & Hanson, 1992). Service providers also need adequate preparation to engage in meaningful collaboration with both parents and service providers; and they need skills in planning and effecting change at community and population levels (Simeonsson & Thomas, 1994; Zipper et al., 1993). To implement these changes, a corresponding shift is needed in the preparation of early intervention service providers, with greater emphasis on cultural competence, collaboration, and respect for the family's decision-making role.

The effectiveness of early intervention programs may be greatly enhanced by operation within a well-integrated service system. The complex needs of children with disabilities and their families may involve multiple service providers operating in different agencies. The services they provide are frequently fragmented and uncoordinated, creating additional stress for family members as they attempt to negotiate an increasingly complicated service system. Frequent changes in personnel, agency, and service setting—which can lead to service gaps and inconsistencies—threaten the child's optimal development (Dokecki & Heflinger, 1989). A coherent, well-integrated service system that allows for close collaboration among service providers can facilitate continuity of services for the child and family. The service coordinator mandated under Part H of IDEA may protect against some of the inconsistent policies and procedures that may result from categorically organized services. The nature of the service coordinator's position suggests that a particular responsibility of the role is to identify and work toward eliminating service gaps (Council for Exceptional Children, 1993).

Parents of all young children, particularly those with disabilities, benefit from increased support in carrying out their caregiving responsibilities. Kamerman and Kahn (1995) have suggested a policy strategy that includes paid leaves for parents. Extended parental leave when a child is born and for a few months afterward would allow parents to be available to their young children when the protection they provide has the greatest effect on the child's future. The Family and Medical Leave Act of 1993 (P.L. 103-3) established the right to parental leave under certain conditions, but the actual effect of this legislation is limited. Although it calls for protection of the employee's employment and benefit rights, the act does not apply to all employees, and it does not provide for payment for employees on leave.

The critical effect of the environment during the first year of life suggests that children's resilience may be enhanced by efforts that begin even before the child is conceived; the focus of these efforts should be providing young adults with information about risk and protective factors for optimal development. Prevention of disability in infants and young children with delayed development and in those who are at risk should focus on promoting positive, nurturing experiences by parents and other primary caregivers. Such efforts can be productively approached within a framework that encompasses the factors associated with increased risk and those that offer opportunities for promoting development.

REFERENCES

Affleck, G., Tennen, H., & Rowe, J. (1990). Mothers, fathers, and the crisis of newborn intensive care. *Infant Mental Health Journal, 11*(1), 12–25.

Alexander, D. F. (1992). Prevention of disabilities: Priorities and research directions. In T. Thompson & S. C. Hupp (Eds.), *Saving children at risk: Poverty and disabilities* (pp. 13–27). Newbury Park, CA: Sage Publications.

American Psychiatric Association. (1994). *Diagnostic and statistical manual of mental disorders* (4th ed.). Washington, DC: Author.

Americans with Disabilities Act of 1990, P.L. 101-336, 104 Stat. 327.

Aron, L. Y., Loprest, P. J., & Steuerle, C. E. (1996). *Serving children with disabilities: A systematic look at the programs*. Washington, DC: Urban Institute Press.

Bailey, D. B., Blasco, P. B., & Simeonsson, R. J. (1992). Needs expressed by mothers and fathers of young children with disabilities. *American Journal of Mental Retardation, 97*(1), 1–10.

Bailey, D. B., Simeonsson, R. J., Buysse, V., & Smith, T. M. (1993). Reliability of an index of child characteristics. *Developmental Medicine and Child Neurology, 35*, 806–815.

Bennett, F. C. (1987). The effectiveness of early intervention for infants at increased biological risk. In M. J. Guralnick & F. C. Bennett (Eds.), *The effectiveness of early intervention for at-risk and handicapped children* (pp. 79–112). Orlando, FL: Academic Press.

Bloch, J., & Seitz, M. (1989). Parents as assessors of children: A collaborative approach to helping. *Social Work in Education, 11*, 226–244.

Bronfenbrenner, U. (1979). *The ecology of human development*. Cambridge, MA: Harvard University Press.

Bryant, D. M., & Ramey, C. T. (1987). An analysis of the effectiveness of early intervention programs for environmentally at-risk children. In M. J. Guralnick & F. C. Bennett (Eds.), *The effectiveness of early intervention for at-risk and handicapped children* (pp. 33–78). Orlando, FL: Academic Press.

Carolina Policy Studies Program. (1993). *The study of federal policy implementation: Infants/toddlers with disabilities and their families*. Chapel Hill: University of North Carolina.

Chamberlin, R. W. (1994). Primary prevention: The missing piece in child development legislation. In R. J. Simeonsson (Ed.), *Risk, resilience, and prevention: Promoting the well-being of all children* (pp. 33–52). Baltimore: Paul H. Brookes.

Chavkin, N. F., & Garza-Lubeck, M. (1990). Multicultural approaches to parent involvement: Research and practice. *Social Work in Education, 13*, 22–33.

Coie, J. D., Watt, N. F., West, S. T., Hawkins, J. D., Asarnow, J. R., Markman, H. J., Ramey, S. L., Shure, M. B., & Long, B. (1993). The science of prevention: A conceptual framework and some directions for a national research program. *American Psychologist, 48*, 1013–1022.

Council for Exceptional Children. (1993). *DEC position on early intervention services for children, birth to age eight*. Pittsburgh: Author, Division for Early Childhood.

Dokecki, P. R., & Heflinger, C. A. (1989). Strengthening families of young children with handicapping conditions: Mapping backward from the "street level." In S. J. Meisels & J. P. Shonkoff (Eds.), *Handbook of early childhood intervention* (pp. 59–84). Cambridge, England: Cambridge University Press.

Dunst, C. J. (1993). Implications of risk and opportunity factors for assessment and intervention practices. *Topics in Early Childhood Special Education, 13*(2), 143–153.

Dunst, C. J., Leet, H. E., & Trivette, C. M. (1988). Family resources, personal well-being, and early intervention. *Journal of Special Education, 22*(1), 108–116.

Dunst, C. J., & Trivette, C. M. (1988). An enablement and empowerment perspective of case management. *Topics in Early Childhood Special Education, 8*(4), 87–102.

Dunst, C. J., Trivette, C. M., & Deal, A. (1988). *Enabling and empowering families: Principles and guidelines for practice.* Cambridge, MA: Brookline Books.

Edmondson, R. (1994). Drug use and pregnancy. In R. J. Simeonsson (Ed.), *Risk, resilience, and prevention: Promoting the well-being of all children* (pp. 151–168). Baltimore: Paul H. Brookes.

Education for All Handicapped Children Act of 1975, P.L. 94-142, 89 Stat. 873.

Education of the Handicapped Act Amendments of 1986, P.L. 99-457, 100 Stat. 1145.

Family and Medical Leave Act of 1993, P.L. 103-3, 107 Stat. 6.

Farran, D. (1990). Effects of intervention with disadvantaged and disabled children: A decade review. In S. J. Meisels & J. P. Shonkoff (Eds.), *Handbook of early childhood intervention* (pp. 501–539). Cambridge, England: Cambridge University Press.

Florian, L. (1995). Part H early intervention programs: Legislative history and intent of the law. *Journal of Early Intervention, 15*, 247–262.

Guralnick, M. J., & Bennett, F. C. (1987). Early intervention for at-risk and handicapped children: Current and future perspectives. In M. J. Guralnick & F. C. Bennett (Eds.), *The effectiveness of early intervention for at-risk and handicapped children* (pp. 365–382). Orlando, FL: Academic Press.

Harry, B. (1992). *Cultural diversity, families, and the special education system.* New York: Teachers College Press.

Hartup, W. W. (1989). Social relationships and their developmental significance. *American Psychologist, 44*, 120–126.

Heekin, M. D., & Mengel, P. N. (1983). *New friends: Mainstreaming activities to help young children understand and accept individual differences.* Chapel Hill, NC: Chapel Hill Training-Outreach Project.

Huntington, G. S., & Simeonsson, R. J. (1993). Temperament and adaptation in young handicapped children. *Infant Mental Health Journal, 14*(1), 49–60.

Individuals with Disabilities Education Act, P.L. 101-476, 104 Stat. 1142 (1990).

Kamerman, S. B., & Kahn, A. J. (1995). *Starting right: How America neglects its youngest children and what we can do about it.* New York: Oxford University Press.

Knitzer, J., & Aber, J. L. (1995). Young children in poverty: Facing the facts. *American Journal of Orthopsychiatry, 65*, 174–176.

Kochanek, T. T., Kabacoff, R. I., & Lipsitt, L. P. (1990). Early identification of developmentally delayed and at-risk preschool children. *Exceptional Children, 56*, 528–538.

Kopp, C. B., & Kaler, S. R. (1989). Risk in infancy: Origins and implications. *American Psychologist, 44*, 224–230.

Landesman, S., & Ramey, C. (1989). Developmental psychology and mental retardation: Integrating scientific principles with treatment practice. *American Psychologist, 44*, 409–415.

Lollar, D. J. (Ed.). (1994). *Preventing secondary conditions associated with spina bifida or cerebral palsy: Proceedings and recommendations of a symposium.* Washington, DC: Spina Bifida Association of America.

Lynch, E. W., & Hanson, M. J. (1992). Steps in the right direction: Implications for interventionists. In E. W. Lynch & M. J. Hanson (Eds.), *Developing cross-cultural competence: A guide for working with young children and their families* (pp. 353–370). Baltimore: Paul H. Brookes.

Mary, N. L. (1990). Reactions of black, Hispanic, and white mothers to having a child with handicaps. *Mental Retardation, 28*(1), 1–5.

McFadyen, A. (1994). *Special care babies and their developing relationships.* London: Routledge.

McGonigel, M. J. (1991). Philosophy and conceptual framework. In M. J. McGonigel, R. K. Kaufmann, & B. H. Johnson (Eds.), *Guidelines and recommended practices for the individualized family service plan* (2nd ed., pp. 7–14). Bethesda, MD: Association for the Care of Children's Health.

Meisels, S. J. (1992). Early intervention: A matter of control. *Zero to Three, 12*(3), 1–6.

Meisels, S. J., & Wasik, B. H. (1990). Who should be served? Identifying children in need of early intervention. In S. J. Meisels & J. P. Shonkoff (Eds.), *Handbook of early childhood intervention* (pp. 605–632). Cambridge, England: Cambridge University Press.

Ramey, C. T., Bryant, D. M., Sparling, J. J., & Wasik, B. (1984). A biosocial systems perspective on environmental interventions for low birth weight infants. *Clinical Obstetrical Gynecology, 27,* 672–692.

Ramey, C. T., Bryant, D. M., Wasik, B. H., Sparling, J. J., Fendt, K. H., & LaVange, L. M. (1992). Infant health and development program for low birth weight, premature infants: Program elements, family participation, and child intelligence. *Pediatrics, 89,* 454–465.

Resnick, M. B., Roth, J., Ariet, M., Carter, R. L., Emerson, J. C., Hendrickson, J. M., Packer, A. B., Larsen, J. J., Wolking, W. D., Lucas, M., Schenck, B. J., Fearnside, B., & Bucciarelli, R. L. (1992). Educational outcome of neonatal intensive care graduates. *Pediatrics, 89,* 373–378.

Rounds, K., Zipper, I. N., & Green, T. P. (in press). Social work practice in early intervention: Child service coordination in a rural health department. In T. S. Kerson (Ed.), *Social work in health settings: Practice in context* (2nd ed.). New York: Haworth Press.

Sameroff, A. J., & Chandler, M. J. (1975). Reproductive risk and the continuum of caretaking casualty. In F. D. Horowitz (Ed.), *Review of child development research* (Vol. 4, pp. 182–244). Chicago: University of Chicago Press.

Sameroff, A. J., & Fiese, B. H. (1990). Transactional regulation and early intervention. In S. J. Meisels & J. P. Shonkoff (Eds.), *Handbook of early childhood intervention* (pp. 119–149). Cambridge, England: Cambridge University Press.

Schorr, L. B. (1988). *Within our reach: Breaking the cycle of disadvantage.* New York: Doubleday.

Seitz, V., & Provence, S. (1990). Caregiver-focused models of early intervention. In S. J. Meisels & J. P. Shonkoff (Eds.), *Handbook of early childhood intervention* (pp. 400–427). Cambridge, England: Cambridge University Press.

Shonkoff, J. P., Hauser-Cram, P., Krauss, M. W., & Upshur, C. C. (1992). Development of infants with disabilities and their families. *Monographs of the Society for Research in Child Development, 57*(6, Serial No. 230).

Simeonsson, R. J. (1991a). Early intervention eligibility: A prevention perspective. *Infants and Young Children, 3*(4), 48–55.

Simeonsson, R. J. (1991b). Early prevention of childhood disability in developing countries. *International Journal of Rehabilitation Research, 14*, 1–12.

Simeonsson, R. J., Edmondson, R., Smith, T., Carnahan, S., & Bucy, J. E. (1995). Family involvement in multidisciplinary team evaluation: Professional and parent perspectives. *Child Care, Health, and Development, 21*(3), 199–215.

Simeonsson, R. J., & Thomas, D. (1994). Promoting children's well-being: Priorities and principles. In R. J. Simeonsson (Ed.), *Risk, resilience, and prevention: Promoting the well-being of all children* (pp. 321–343). Baltimore: Paul H. Brookes.

Sinclair, E. (1993). Early identification of preschoolers with special needs in Head Start. *Topics in Early Childhood Special Education, 13*(2), 184–201.

Singer, G.H.S., Irvin, L. K., Irvine, B., Hawkins, N. E., Hegreness, J., & Jackson, R. (1993). Helping families adapt positively to disability: Overcoming demoralization through community supports. In G.H.S. Singer & L. E. Powers (Eds.), *Families, disability, and empowerment* (pp. 67–83). Baltimore: Paul H. Brookes.

Sontag, J. C., & Schacht, R. (1994). An ethnic comparison of parent participation and information needs in early intervention. *Exceptional Children, 60*, 422–433.

Stonestreet, R. H., Johnson, R. G., & Acton, S. J. (1991). Guidelines for real partnerships with parents. *Infant–Toddler Intervention: The Transdisciplinary Journal, 1*(1), 37–46.

U.S. Department of Education, National Institute on Disability and Rehabilitation Research. (1996). Disabilities among children (Disability Statistics Abstract No. 15). Washington, DC: Author.

U.S. General Accounting Office. (1992). *Integrating human services: Linking at-risk families with services more successful than system reform efforts.* Washington, DC: Author.

Vincent, L. J., Poulsen, M. K., Cole, C. K., Woodruff, G., & Griffith, D. R. (1991). *Born substance exposed, educationally vulnerable.* Reston, VA: Council for Exceptional Children.

Wang, M. C. (1989). Implementing the state of the art and integration mandates of P.L. 94-142. In J. J. Gallagher, P. L. Trohanis, & R. M. Clifford (Eds.), *Policy implementation and P.L. 99-457: Planning for young children with special needs* (pp. 33–58). Baltimore: Paul H. Brookes.

Weiss, H. B. (1990). Beyond parens patriae: Building policies and programs to care for our own and others' children. *Children and Youth Services Review, 12*, 269–284.

Werner, E. E. (1990). Protective factors and individual resilience. In S. J. Meisels & J. P. Shonkoff (Eds.), *Handbook of early childhood intervention* (pp. 97–116). Cambridge, England: Cambridge University Press.

Zipper, I. N., Weil, M., & Rounds, K. (1993). *Service coordination for early intervention: Parents and professionals*. Cambridge, MA: Brookline Books.

13

Toward a Resilience-Based Model of Practice

Mark W. Fraser and Maeda J. Galinsky

S ocial work and other helping professions have embraced ecological and systems theories as inclusive frames of reference for education and practice. Because they constantly remind us that behavior is shaped by both individual and environmental factors, these theories provide important points of reference for understanding the experience of childhood. A person exists in an environment, and it is the interplay of individual characteristics with contextual influences that ultimately yields human behavior (Germain, 1991).

But although they lay an essential groundwork for understanding human behavior, ecological and systems theories are insufficiently specific for practice. They lack detail in articulating adequately explicit information on which to conduct case assessments and develop intervention plans. Theories and frames of reference that provide more specific knowledge about childhood depression, delinquency, teenage pregnancy, and other problems are needed to guide action.

A Risk and Resilience Perspective

This book has traced the elements of an emerging risk and resilience perspective, one that holds the potential to provide social work and other professions with an improved frame of reference for the design of child and family services. The book defines risk factors as any influences that increase the probability of onset, digression to a more serious state, or the maintenance of a problem condition. It defines protective factors as both the internal and external forces that help children resist or ameliorate risk. And the authors in this book have defined resilience as adaptive behavior that produces positive social and health outcomes arising from the interplay of risk and protective factors.

On the basis of these concepts, the risk and resilience perspective has two essential elements. First, it consists of a growing body of knowledge of individual and environmental markers that appear to underlie many childhood social and health problems. In aggregate, these markers, correlates, and possibly causes can be thought of as elements of a common or cross-cutting model for risk and protective factors for a variety of childhood disorders. Shown in Table 13-1, they can be classified ecologically as (1) broad environmental conditions; (2) family, school, and neighborhood conditions; and (3) individual, psychosocial, and biological conditions. Common risk and protective factors, as they were described in chapter 2, are given for each of the three system levels.

Second, building on these common factors, the risk and resilience perspective recognizes that some risk factors contribute uniquely to particular problems and that some protective factors provide safeguards against particular problems. Thus, to better

Table 13-1. Common and Problem-Specific Risk and Protective Factors for Sexually Transmitted Infections: An Ecological and Multisystems Perspective

SYSTEM	RISK FACTORS	PROTECTIVE FACTORS
Broad environmental conditions	*Common Risk Factors* Few opportunities for education and employment Racial discrimination and injustice Poverty/low SES *Problem-Specific Risk Factors* Norms favoring early sexual activity Lack of community awareness of STDs Lack of access to health care	*Common Protective Factors* Many opportunities for education, employment, growth, and achievement *Problem-Specific Protective Factors* High community religiosity Access to culturally and developmentally sensitive health care
Family, school, and neighborhood conditions	*Common Risk Factors* Child maltreatment Interparental conflict Parental psychopathology Poor parenting *Problem-Specific Risk Factors* Sexual abuse Sexually active older sibling Sexually active peers	*Common Protective Factors* Social support Presence of caring and supportive adult Positive parent–child relationship Effective parenting *Problem-Specific Protective Factors* Parental supervision of dating Peer or partner support of use of condoms
Individual, psycho-social, and biological factors	*Common Risk Factors* Gender Biomedical conditions and problems *Problem-Specific Risk Factors* Early puberty Inability to hypothesize distal consequences Early initiation of sexual activity Substance use	*Common Protective Factors* "Easy" temperament as an infant High self-esteem and self-efficacy Competence in normative roles High intelligence *Problem-Specific Protective Factors* Formal operational thinking Positive attitudes toward use of condoms

NOTES: SES = socioeconomic status; STI = sexually transmitted infection. Each of the problem-specific risk and protective factors is adapted from chapter 9 and focuses on STIs. Common factors remain the same for different types of problems, but the content of problem-specific factors changes. See chapters 4 through 12 for summaries of problem-specific content.

understand a particular childhood problem, one needs not only to consider common risk and protective mechanisms, but also to develop a list of problem-specific risk and protective factors. Chapters 4 through 12 presented the disorder-specific risk conditions that combine with common risk conditions to give rise to childhood problems. These chapters also introduced and began discussion of the disorder-specific protective conditions associated with resistance to and amelioration of those problems.

In Table 13-1, problem-specific risk and protective factors are shown for sexually transmitted infections (STIs), the topic of chapter 9. As can be seen in Table 13-1, STIs are clearly affected by a combination of common and STI-specific risk and protective factors. It is also evident that there is overlap between the common and specific factors. For example, poor parenting is a common risk factor that is related to many of the problem-specific risk and protective factors—sexual abuse, early initiation of sexual activity, poor supervision of dating, and substance abuse. The problem-specific risk and protective factors, however, provide significantly more information about the etiology of the problem. In addition, compared with the common factors, the problem-specific factors provide more precise clues for the design of intervention and prevention programs.

MULTIDETERMINISM

This risk and resilience perspective is based on the idea that childhood problems are multidetermined. That is, they develop as a result of many causes, whether at the level of the individual, the family or community, or the broader environment. For example, some children may have a genetic predisposition to a problem such as attention-deficit hyperactivity disorder, yet familial and environmental conditions, as well as other individual factors, strongly affect whether and how the disorder is manifest. Most childhood problems have multiple individual and contextual determinants. This concept is central to resilience-based practice.

RECIPROCATED CAUSE

Furthermore, many relationships are thought to be reciprocal. Although individual, family, school, neighborhood, and environmental factors clearly influence behavior, the causal order and relative strength of each in producing life course outcomes are often unclear. Consider the problem condition of delinquency. Delinquency may be strongly influenced by the neighborhood rate of violence, but the rate of neighborhood violence is often linked to major risk factors such as association with delinquent peers, parental criminality, poor supervision by parents, and even school risk conditions. Factors at the individual, family, school, and neighborhood levels are intertwined. Which comes first? And what is the strength of competing contextual and other influences? Because delinquency occurs across neighborhoods with different levels of violence, and because children may be exposed to a variety of neighborhood, school, and other systems-level effects, the causal order of relationship is difficult to untangle. Given the complexity of relationships, some scholars are beginning to argue that many relationships are best characterized as reciprocal (see, for example, Thornberry, Lizotte, Krohn, Farnsworth, & Jang, 1991).

Because child development is enormously complicated, no single theory is likely to account fully for the many different factors that affect substance abuse, mood disorders, truancy, academic failure, and other childhood problems. The factors that may trigger or untrigger a condition such as conduct disorder do not appear to operate equivalently at all points in a child's development. And they may vary by gender and by race or ethnicity. In the absence of dramatic new discoveries in cognitive, labeling, psychoanalytic, social control, social learning, structural opportunity, and other theories often applied to the problems of childhood, the risk and resilience perspective provides a mechanism for beginning to organize the multitude of factors that affect children and, as described below, for improving the precision of social programs.

TOWARD A THEORY OF RESILIENCE-BASED PRACTICE

Problems develop through etiologic chains that often have roots in early childhood. These risk chains are multisystemic in nature; that is, they incorporate individual, familial, and extrafamilial conditions that increase the odds of negative life course outcomes for children. In a growing number of studies, combinations of risk factors have been shown to function as precursors of many different kinds of problems and disorders in childhood (for reviews, see chapters 4 through 12; Coie et al., 1993; Mrazek & Haggerty, 1994; Simeonsson, 1994).

In addition, recent studies of vulnerability to risk show that the influence of risk factors is often moderated, if not mediated, by protective factors (Garmezy, 1993a, 1993b, 1994; Werner & Smith, 1992). Although we know far less about protective factors, they also appear to be subject to classification as individual, familial, and extrafamilial factors. Children who deal effectively with risk are usually found to have benefited from one or more protective conditions, whether personal traits, family strengths, or environmental resources. Their resilience in the face of adversity results from the competing pushes and pulls of risk and protective factors.

Two Strategies for Resilience-Based Practice

In our view, the risk and resilience perspective offers an important clue for answering the question of how to make profound differences in the lives of children who are at risk of ADHD, delinquency, mental disorders, pregnancy, STDs, and other problems. To make a difference, we must adopt and simultaneously implement two strategies. First, risk must be reduced. Risk factors should guide intervention efforts, and the goal of intervention should be to reduce the effect of specifically targeted risk factors significantly.

Second, protective factors must be strengthened. Because some risk factors can be changed quickly, the protective mechanisms that operate for children who are in high-risk circumstances but who do not manifest problems must be understood and used to construct interventions. Interventions that strengthen protective factors and concomitantly reduce the effects of risk factors form the basis of a resilience orientation in practice. From an understanding of etiologic chains, intervention should mitigate risk, enhance protection, and promote resilience.

Identifying Local Risk and Protective Chains

Because environmental resources, local traditions, and cultural practices of communities vary widely across the country, no single risk chain for a childhood condition is likely to apply to all children. Furthermore, each risk chain may differentially apply to children, depending on how groupings of personal characteristics, such as race or ethnicity, gender, and age, are approached in each community. Thus, specific risk and protective factors, as they occur in specific communities, must be identified for specific childhood conditions. As shown throughout the book, cross-cutting information on risk and, to a lesser degree, on protection is beginning to emerge from longitudinal studies in the United States and other countries. If we adopt an ecological perspective, we implicitly adopt the idea that the local environment significantly influences behavior, and knowledge of environmental conditions must be incorporated into intervention planning. Building on knowledge of common risk and protective factors and findings from studies of problem-specific risk and protective factors, then, intervention must begin with an understanding of local risk and protective conditions. Risk and resilience must be placed in the context of culture, tradition, community values, and community responses to diversity.

To set a risk and resilience strategy into operation, local epidemiological knowledge must be combined with knowledge of the comparative effectiveness of change strategies (see, for example, Hawkins, Catalano, & Associates, 1992). Conceptually, a resilience-based intervention is founded on the specification of risk and protective chains for a presenting problem. These chains should link common and problem-specific knowledge and should accurately reflect community conditions, values, practices, and beliefs.

Fitting Change Strategies to Keystone Risk Factors

Because risks vary in influence and because we often cannot mount change strategies that affect all risk conditions, "keystone" risk factors must be identified and used as the basis for devising interventive strategies. *Keystone risks* are those conditions and social processes that are thought to be predominant in etiologic chains (Loeber & Stouthamer-Loeber, 1996). Much delinquency, for example, never progresses beyond a first offense. It makes little sense, some scholars have argued, to intervene if a large number of children will desist without intervention. On the other hand, we know that some first offenders do not desist and in fact go on to engage in behaviors that endanger others. Consequently, the challenge we face is to identify the risk factors that distinguish those who will desist from those who will escalate their delinquent involvement. Then we must note which of these risk factors are most critical for producing different outcomes. Keystone risks are those conditions or processes that make a child most vulnerable to problems and that, if left unattended, will cause problems to remain or worsen. On balance, then, keystone risks are markers for intervention.[1]

The development of etiologic chains and the designation of keystone influences enables practitioners and program planners to identify appropriate interventive goals. Most goals will focus on reducing risk and strengthening protective factors. Keystone risk factors must be matched to interventive strategies with the capacity to produce change that will reduce the influence of a risk factor or a set of risk factors. Strategies should be developed also to strengthen protective processes. To develop such strategies

---

[1] Keystone protective factors also may exist, but, because so little is known about protective mechanisms, it makes sense for interventions to seek to strengthen all protective factors and processes. As knowledge about protective factors increases, it may be possible to identify keystone protective factors that warrant special attention.

for reducing risk and promoting resilience, one needs to know which interventions work and which do not. Fortunately, there is a rich and growing multidisciplinary literature on the effectiveness of interventions. This literature should be used in planning, developing, and carrying out interventions. Interventive knowledge and research are the bases for defining substantive service activities related to intervention goals, both for reducing risk and for strengthening protective processes.

A risk and resilience perspective therefore requires:

- basic knowledge of risk and protection
- specific knowledge of risk and protective factors for specific problems or disorders
- knowledge of risk and protective factors in the local community
- specification of keystone risk factors
- knowledge of interventive research so that effective change strategies can be used to reduce the influence of keystone risks
- knowledge of interventive research so that effective change strategies can be used to strengthen protective mechanisms.

IMPLICATIONS OF RESILIENCE-BASED PRACTICE

This risk and resilience perspective conjoins practice and research. The practitioner must have skills both in mapping etiologic chains and in employing multicomponent change strategies. Use of this perspective requires skills in conducting community and individual assessments and in developing a hierarchy of change strategies that address the keystone factors affecting children in a community.

Multisystemic Assessment and Intervention

What is evident from the research is that intervention to address risk and protective factors must be multisystemic (see, for example, Henggeler & Borduin, 1990). No childhood problem exists in isolation at any one systemic level. Individual, group, family, community, and societal levels must be included in any program to approach the variety of childhood problems described in chapters 4 through 12. The overwhelming evidence presented in these chapters indicates that a multiplicity of factors, from the individual and family through neighborhood and societal levels, affects resilience and life course outcomes.

Even when a program is initiated at the individual or family level, community and societal factors should be part of the assessment and intervention strategy. Although it may not be possible to intervene actively at all levels, it is still essential to estimate the effect of an intervention at each level of risk and protection. Similarly, no policy or community action strategy can be considered fully developed if its designers fail to assess the potential effect on individuals, families, and schools. From a resilience perspective, risk and protective factors at all levels need to be identified and considered in assessment, intervention, and evaluation.

Each chapter in this book has included a discussion on risk assessment, often with reviews of case and community assessment instruments. Because assessment of risk factors and the identification of keystone risks are essential for promoting resilience, we argue that they are essential too for improving practice effectiveness. Separating factors that warrant intervention from those that do not is a major challenge for social workers who seek to design more effective services. Continuing refinements in clinical assessment tools are beginning to be helpful in this endeavor.

Practitioners as a Source of Information

If services for children and families are to adopt a resilience basis, ways must be found to build on the practice wisdom of the many practitioners who already employ ecological strategies. We need to discover what skilled practitioners look for in individual, family, and extrafamilial circumstances; what they consider to be the most important variables; how they put the various pieces of information together for an assessment and plan of action; and what they believe to be essential elements of intervention. Although they may not articulate their practice in the same terms that we have used here, many practitioners operate from a risk and resilience perspective. They are a rich source of information for the study of risk and protective factors, for the development of assessment instruments, and for the design of intervention strategies.

A STRENGTHS PERSPECTIVE

Resilience-based practice is communitywide practice, building on and extending the strengths perspective in social work, psychology, education, and other fields (Chapin, 1995; Saleebey, 1992; Saleebey, 1996; Weick, Rapp, Sullivan, & Kisthardt, 1989). In chapters 4 through 12, protective factors were described for many childhood conditions; one may think of these protective factors and processes as strengths. A resilience perspective ensures that the strengths of individuals, families, and communities are assessed and used in ways that prevent problems and ameliorate existing difficulties. Of course, risk as well as protective factors must be systematically included in change efforts. But many experts argue that traditional practice has focused excessively on deficits, dysfunctions, and pathology. We argue that practice should devote equal, if not more, energy to the development of strengths.

The study of protective factors among children who face high risks but avoid negative outcomes is a distinguishing feature of resilience-based practice. Knowledge of the way protective mechanisms operate is required for designing intervention strategies for those children whose exposure to risk factors has already placed them in jeopardy. Moreover, it is essential in designing prevention strategies for children who are likely to be exposed to risk in the future.[2]

Empowerment

The resilience and strengths perspectives are closely linked also to empowerment. The concept of empowerment has been used by theorists and practitioners in a variety of ways (Gutierrez, 1990). We use the broadest meaning of

---

[2] A word of caution is in order, however. Because protective factors have been studied primarily in the context of the resilient—those who have avoided or minimized the negative consequences of risk factors—we need to examine whether strengthening the same protective factors will operate in the same way for children who are not successful in initially avoiding negative outcomes.

empowerment, which, according to Gutierrez (1990), "includes combining a sense of personal control with the ability to affect the behavior of others, a focus on enhancing existing strengths in individuals or communities, a goal of establishing equity in the distribution of resources, an ecological (rather than individual) form of analysis for understanding individual and community phenomena, and a belief that power is not a scarce commodity but rather one that can be generated" (p. 150). Empowerment denotes a partnership between the practitioner and the client or consumer. It involves the development and use of the capacities of the individual, family, organization, and community. Drawing on these capacities helps the consumer of services fully realize his or her own abilities and goals (Cowger, 1994; Gutierrez, 1990; Gutierrez, GlenMaye, & DeLois, 1995; Simon, 1994).

Our focus on the local community as a starting point for intervention is rooted in this concept of empowerment. Community stakeholders—representing the diversity of peoples and organizations in the community—must be involved in the planning and specification of local risk and protective processes. This is a central element of resilience-focused practice. It holds the potential to alter through community action the contextual as well as individual influences that affect children.

Discrimination and Empowerment

As we have seen throughout this book, risk and protective factors related to specific childhood problems often differ according to race and ethnicity. Children from African American, Hispanic, and other racial and ethnic backgrounds are subject to the direct and indirect effects of discrimination, compounding and exacerbating their risk for many kinds of problems. The empowerment process is one means by which discrimination can be addressed for children at risk. It includes involvement of respected members of the community in the identification of local risk and protective factors, among which are those related to discrimination and combatting discrimination. It also emphasizes attention to the strengths of local community beliefs, traditions, and practices. It invites members of the local community to focus on their strengths and to devise solutions to their own problems. And it encourages communities to acquire power to act in their own behalf and to affect broader environmental conditions (Gutierrez, 1990; Gutierrez & Ortega, 1991). Successful intervention from a resilience perspective relies on recognition of diversity and on empowerment.

CAN RESILIENCE-BASED PRACTICE MAKE MEANINGFUL DIFFERENCES?

Although it is increasingly clear that the presence of adversity in a child's environment does not always lead to negative outcomes, it is still clearer that the presence of multiple risks in a child's environment is a marker for negative outcomes. We should incorporate this knowledge in the design of public programs and policies. If a program or policy successfully reduces those risks, then the odds of making meaningful differences in the lives of children will go up. Knowledge of risk factors has already been used in public health to implement programs of prevention. For example, this approach gave rise to effective prevention programs that warned people about the spread of AIDS. Can this approach be used in such fields as delinquency, where parents, professionals, and others care deeply about halting the escalating rates of youth violence? Can it be used to develop early intervention programs in child welfare, where services focus on investigation and substitute care, rather than on early intervention and prevention? More generally, can knowledge of risk and protective factors be built into programs of intervention on a policy level, on a community level, on a family level, and on an individual level to make positive changes for children who are already deeply involved in chains of disadvantage and problem behavior?

Recent progress in our understanding of human behavior holds out promise that we can make meaningful differences. This progress, described throughout this book, is beginning to be realized in many fields. The elements of a resilience-based practice strategy are taking shape. These elements connect community practice with strategies often associated with work with individuals, families, and groups. They

- educate community stakeholders on recent research on common and problem-specific risk and protective factors for various childhood problems
- empower community stakeholders to identify a comprehensive range of local risk and protective factors
- employ systematic methods for the assessment of risk and protective factors
- identify keystone risk factors
- select intervention strategies to reduce keystone risk factors and strengthen protective factors.

Although this new resilience-based perspective on behavior and health is beginning to work its way into the curricula of professional schools and into the strategic planning of state and local agencies where services are developed and implemented, progress is slow. The application of knowledge on risk and resilience to policy and practice must become a higher priority.

CONCLUSION

Children are placed at risk by many individual and environmental conditions, so the processes that are likely to improve their status must involve many different systems. Change strategies should be multisystemic and combine community practice with organizational, group, family, and individual interventions. They must build on emerging knowledge of risk and resilience to identify local risk and protective factors through a process that involves the community. They require specification of protective mechanisms that appear to help children prevail over adversity. They require that children or groups of children with many risks be identified and comprehensive strategies be developed to reduce those risks. And, whether at the community or the individual level, they require matching risk profiles with effective change strategies that capitalize on and strengthen protective mechanisms. Such ecologically based interventions and public policies, which buffer risk and build resilience, offer new promise for millions of children and their families across the country.

REFERENCES

Chapin, R. K. (1995). Social policy development: The strengths perspective. *Social Work, 40,* 506–514.

Coie, J. D., Watt, N. F., West, S. G., Hawkins, J. D., Asarnow, J. R., Markman, H. J., Ramey, S. L., Shure, M. B., & Long, B. (1993). The science of prevention: A conceptual framework and some directions for a national research program. *American Psychologist, 48,* 1013–1022.

Cowger, C. D. (1994). Assessing client strengths: Clinical assessment for client empowerment. *Social Work, 39,* 262–268.

Garmezy, N. (1993a). Children in poverty: Resilience despite risk. *Psychiatry, 56,* 127–136.

Garmezy, N. (1993b). Vulnerability and resilience. In D. C. Funder, R. D. Parke, C. Tomlinson-Keasey, & K. Widaman (Eds.), *Studying lives through time* (pp. 377–398). Washington, DC: American Psychological Association.

Garmezy, N. (1994). Reflections and commentary on risk, resilience, and development. In R. J. Haggerty, L. R. Sherrod, N. Garmezy, & M. Rutter (Eds.), *Stress, risk and resilience in children and adolescents: Processes, mechanisms and interventions* (pp. 1–18). New York: Cambridge University Press.

Germain, C. B. (1991). *Human behavior in the social environment: An ecological view.* New York: Columbia University Press.

Gutierrez, L. M. (1990). Working with women of color: An empowerment perspective. *Social Work, 35,* 149–154.

Gutierrez, L., GlenMaye, L., & DeLois, K. (1995). The organizational context of empowerment practice: Implications for social work administration. *Social Work, 40,* 249–258.

Gutierrez, L., & Ortega, R. (1991). Developing methods to empower Latinos: The importance of groups. *Social Work with Groups, 14*(2), 23–44.

Hawkins, J. D., Catalano, R. F., Jr., & Associates. (1992). *Communities that care.* San Francisco: Jossey-Bass.

Henggeler, S. W., & Borduin, C. M. (1990). *Family therapy and beyond: A multisystemic approach to treating the behavior problems of children and adolescents.* Pacific Grove, CA: Brooks/Cole.

Loeber, R., & Stouthamer-Loeber, M. (1996). The development of offending. *Criminal Justice and Behavior, 23*(1), 12–24.

Mrazek, P. J., & Haggerty, R. J. (Eds.). (1994). *Reducing risks for mental disorders: Frontiers for preventive intervention research.* Washington, DC: National Academy Press.

Saleebey, D. (Ed). (1992). *The strengths perspective in social work practice: Power in the people.* White Plains, NY: Longman.

Saleebey, D. (1996). The strengths perspective in social work practice: Extensions and cautions. *Social Work, 41,* 296–305.

Simeonsson, R. J. (Ed.) (1994). *Risk, resilience, and prevention: Promoting the well-being of all children.* Baltimore: Paul H. Brookes.

Simon, B. L. (1994). *The empowerment tradition in American social work: A history.* New York: Columbia University Press.

Thornberry, T. P., Lizotte, A. J., Krohn, M. D., Farnsworth, M., & Jang, S. J. (1991). Testing interactional theory: An examination of reciprocal causal relationships among family, school, and delinquency. *Journal of Criminal Law and Criminology, 82*(1), 3–35.

Weick, A., Rapp, C., Sullivan, W. P., & Kisthardt, W. (1989). A strengths perspective for social work practice. *Social Work, 34,* 350–354.

Werner, E. E., & Smith, R. S. (1992). *Overcoming the odds: High risk children from birth to adulthood.* Ithaca, NY: Cornell University Press.

INDEX

A

Abortion, 196, 213
Abuse. *See* Child maltreatment; Child sexual abuse; Family violence
Academic performance, 7
    ADHD effects, 76–77
    ADHD interventions, 87–88
    ADHD protective factors, 81–82
    adolescent pregnancy interventions, 212
    adolescent pregnancy, sexual behavior and, 197–199
    adolescent substance use risk, 123
    common risk factors, 20
    conduct disorder risk factors, 148
    cumulation of stress, 12
    depression and, 226
    dropout rates, 95–96
    economic outcomes for adolescent mothers, 199–200
    individual consequences of school failure, 95, 96
    marginal students, 96–97
    as protective factor, 199, 200–201
    protective factors for success in, 101
    racial or ethnic trends, 98, 100
    risk factors, 11, 98–100
    social consequences, 95, 96
    student typology, 97–98
ADHD. *See* Attention deficit hyperactivity disorder
Adolescent pregnancy, 7
    abortion rates, 196
    ADHD risk, 81
    adoption and, 213
    age-related outcomes, 201
    alcohol and substance abuse and, 208
    child support issues, 214
    community-level intervention, 213
    conceptualization of risk and protective factors, 196–197
    consequences of sexually transmitted infection in, 174–175
    contraception use, 196, 207, 212–213
    data sources, 197

    dating behaviors and, 204
    developmental risk factors, 206–207
    educational achievement and, 197–199
    epidemiological research methodology, 40
    family structure and functioning and, 203–205, 209–210
    health outcomes, 202
    individual economic outcomes related to, 199–202
    interventions, 212–214
    marital status and, 195, 196, 201
    media programs for prevention, 213
    peer leadership intervention, 213
    peer relations as risk factor, 203
    prenatal care, 202
    preventive interventions, 201
    psychological factors in risk and protection, 206
    risk assessment, 209–211
    self-esteem as risk mediator, 207–208
    sexual abuse and, 208
    social support as protective factor, 205–206
    social support interventions, 214
    social support risk assessment, 210–211
    socioeconomic risk factors, 197–199
    sociological trends and, 195–196
    statistics, 195
    trends, 195, 196
Adolescent Problem Situation Inventory, 131
Age-related variables
    adolescent alcohol and drug use, 126–127
    adolescent pregnancy outcomes, 201
    cessation of delinquent acts, 145
    developmental disabilities, 254
    exit from public assistance, 201
    onset of delinquency, 144–145
    onset of depression, 231
    onset of sexual activity and risk of STIs, 179–182
    victims of child maltreatment, 52
Aggressive behavior
    and conduct disorder risk, 145–146

About the Editor

Mark W. Fraser, MSW, PhD, holds the John A. Tate Distinguished Professorship for Children in Need at the School of Social Work, University of North Carolina, Chapel Hill, where he is the principal investigator of the Carolina Children's Initiative, an early intervention program for high-risk elementary schoolchildren and their families. He has written numerous articles and chapters on children's services, family-centered intervention, delinquency, and research methods. He is the coauthor of two books, *Families in Crisis* (with P. Pecora and D. Haapala, 1991) and *Evaluating Family-Based Services* (with P. Pecora, K. Nelson, J. McCroskey, and W. Meezan, 1995).

About the Contributors

Michael W. Arthur, PhD, received his degree in community psychology from the University of Virginia in 1990. His current research interests explore community interventions to prevent adolescent antisocial behavior and to promote social competency, prevention research methodology, and prevention needs-assessment methods. Current publications include chapters in *Handbook of Antisocial Behavior* (1997) and *Building a Safer Society: Strategic Approaches to Crime Prevention* (1995). Dr. Arthur is a research assistant professor, University of Washington, School of Social Work, and a researcher at the Social Development Research Group, Seattle, Washington.

Charles D. Ayers, MSW, is a faculty member and PhD candidate at the School of Social Work, University of Washington. He is also the Social Work Discipline Head at the Division of Adolescent Medicine, Center on Human Development and Disabilities. His current research explores the identification of risk and protective factors relating to problem behavior and effective prevention programs, including adventure-based social work/therapy. His most recent publications have appeared in *Journal of Primary Prevention* and *Social Work Research*.

Susan Ayers-Lopez, MEd, is a research associate at the University of Texas at Austin, Center for Social Work Research. Ms. Ayers-Lopez has conducted research in numerous areas related to the welfare of children and families. Her research interests include adoption, child protective services, and adolescent pregnancy prevention.

Gary L. Bowen, MSW, PhD, is Kenan Distinguished Professor of Social Work at the University of North Carolina at Chapel Hill. He also holds a joint appointment in the Department of Communication Studies. His current research examines how aspects of the social environment influence the ability of adolescents to succeed at school. He is the author of *Navigating the Marital Journey* (1994) and coeditor of *The Organization Family* and *The Work and Family Interface: Towards a Contextual Effects* (1995).

Jacqueline Corcoran, PhD, is assistant professor at the University of Texas at Arlington, School of Social Work, where she teaches courses in human behavior and practice methods. Dr. Corcoran's practice and research interests include family therapy and adolescent pregnancy prevention. She maintains a part-time clinical practice.

S. Rachel Dedmon, MSSW, PhD, is an associate professor in the School of Social Work, University of North Carolina at Chapel Hill, where she teaches and offers continuing education in child and adult mental disorders and ethical decision making. Her recent publications have focused on case management, appearing as chapters in *Case Management for Children's Mental Health* (1994) and *From Case Management to Service Coordination for Children with Emotional, Behavioral, or Mental Disorders* (1995).

Cynthia Franklin, PhD, is an associate professor at the University of Texas at Austin, School of Social Work, where she teaches courses on clinical practice and research. Dr. Franklin has written many publications on clinical assessment, practice theories, and child and family practice, including several studies on school social work practice and adolescent pregnancy prevention. She is coauthor (with Dr. Catheleen Jordan) of two books, *Clinical Assessment for Social Workers: Quantitative and Qualitative Methods* (1995) and *Family Practice: Brief, Constructive and Systemic Methods* (in press). Dr. Franklin maintains a part-time clinical practice specializing in marriage and family therapy.

Maeda J. Galinsky, MSW, PhD, is Kenan Distinguished Professor at the School of Social Work, University of North Carolina at Chapel Hill. Her research interests center on the analysis and evaluation of social interventions, particularly group services. Her recent publications focus on social support groups, multicultural groups, and telephone conference-call and computer-assisted (technology-based) groups. She has served on various editorial boards, including those for *Social Work Research & Abstracts*, *Small Group Research*, *American Journal of Orthopsychiatry*, and *Social Work with Groups*.

M. Carlean Gilbert, MSW, DSW, is an assistant professor in the Graduate School of Social Work, University of North Carolina at Chapel Hill. She teaches courses in health and mental health practice and has contributed to several textbooks and journals. Her recent publications, focusing on chronic health and mental health conditions of children and families, have appeared in *Child & Adolescent Social Work Journal*.

Jeffrey M. Jenson, MSW, PhD, is associate professor and associate director of the School of Social Work, University of Iowa, Iowa City. Dr. Jenson's interests include the etiology, prevention, and treatment of adolescent substance abuse; juvenile delinquency; juvenile justice policy; and social work education. He has been involved in research, program design, and evaluation in the areas of child welfare, delinquency, and drug abuse for the past 14 years. His current studies are analyzing racial and ethnic disproportionality and recidivism in the juvenile justice system. Recent publications appear in *Research on Social Work Practice*, *American Journal of Drug and Alcohol Abuse*, and *Social Work Research*.

Laura D. Kirby, MSW, MPH, is a recent graduate of the Schools of Social Work and Public Health, University of North Carolina at Chapel Hill. During graduate school, Ms. Kirby worked as a research assistant for a longitudinal study on child abuse and neglect and an evaluation of a large-scale family support program. She plans to work in the field of early intervention.

James K. Nash, MSW, is a doctoral student in the School of Social Work, University of North Carolina at Chapel Hill. After receiving his MSW in 1990, he worked for four years as a mental health case manager with children and adolescents displaying aggressive behavior. His research activities include the design and evaluation of early intervention programs for children. He is especially interested in mentoring interventions as a prevention and treatment strategy.

Jack M. Richman, MSW, PhD, is an associate professor of social work, University of North Carolina at Chapel Hill. In addition to teaching, he is involved in research and practice with individuals, families, and groups. His current areas of research examine adolescents and school success; evaluating, monitoring, and planning the best practice interventions with clients; and assessing and using the social support process and networks as an intervention strategy. He is the author and coauthor of many professional articles and book chapters.

Kathleen A. Rounds, MSW, PhD, MPH, is associate professor at the School of Social Work, University of North Carolina at Chapel Hill. Her research interests include the evaluation of support services for people with HIV and treatment interventions for pregnant and postpartum women who use drugs and alcohol. Her practice interests focus on social work in medical care and community and public health settings. Recent publications have appeared in *Families in Society, Social Work with Groups*, and *Research on Social Work Practice*.

Rune J. Simeonsson, MSPH, PhD, is a professor of education and psychology at the University of North Carolina at Chapel Hill, with teaching responsibilities in the school psychology and special education graduate programs. His major teaching and research focuses are childhood disability, developmental assessment, and quality of life. Recent publications include *Risk, Resilience, and Prevention: Promoting the Well-Being of All Children* (1994) and *Psychological and Developmental Assessment of Special Children* (1986).

Barbara Thomlison, MSW, PhD, is a professor of social work at the University of Calgary, Alberta, Canada. She has worked in the areas of child welfare, family services, and mental health. Her current research examines the process and methods of family reconciliation for older children in care. She is the author or coauthor of four books and 13 book chapters; she has also written numerous articles and made international presentations on the subject of child and family initiatives.

James Herbert Williams, PhD, received his degree in social welfare from the University of Washington, School of Social Work, in 1994. His current research explores racial differences in risk and protective factors for childhood and adolescent antisocial behavior, race disproportionality and disparities in juvenile justice, and the relationship of family management and structure to antisocial behavior for African American youths. Recent publications have appeared in *Social Work Research* and the *Journal of Gay and Lesbian Social Services*. He is an assistant professor at the George Warren Brown School of Social Work, Washington University, St. Louis.

Irene Nathan Zipper, MSW, PhD, is clinical assistant professor at the School of Social Work, University of North Carolina at Chapel Hill. Her major teaching and research interests are in the areas of childhood disability, children's mental health, service coordination and case management, and service integration. She edited (with M. Weil) *Case Management for Children's Mental Health: A Training Curriculum for Child-Serving Agencies* (1994) and has written several book chapters on coordination of services for children and their families.

RISK AND RESILIENCE IN CHILDHOOD: AN ECOLOGICAL PERSPECTIVE

Cover design by The Watermark Design Office

Composed by Patricia D. Wolf, Wolf Publications, Inc., in Garamond and Bauer Bodini

Printed by Boyd Printing Company on 60# Windsor Offset

INFORMATION ON CHILDREN & FAMILIES FROM THE NASW PRESS

Risk and Resilience in Childhood, *Mark W. Fraser, Editor.* How is it that some children face enormous odds but prevail over adversity to become successful? How can you develop practice models that foster resilience and build exciting new knowledge about risk and protection in childhood? You'll find answers to these questions and more in *Risk and Resilience in Childhood,* a unique text that introduces and explores the concepts of protection and resilience in the face of adversity.
ISBN: 0-87101-274-X. Item #274X. $35.95

Painful Passages: *Working with Children with Learning Disabilities, by Elizabeth Dane.* Children with learning disabilities often find the passage from youth to adulthood painful and perplexing. These children require understanding, knowledge, and skilled intervention to facilitate the growing process. *Painful Passages* helps social workers, as well as administrators, educators, and parents, respond creatively and effectively to those needs.
ISBN: 0-87101-175-1. Item #1751. $24.95

Caring Families: *Supports and Interventions, by Deborah S. Bass.* Advances in medical technology enable the ill or disabled family member to live longer, and changes in the economic structure of the family often take the caregiver away from the home and into the workplace. *Caring Families* identifies the stress factors and rewards that affect families and presents techniques to help the professional support them.
ISBN: 0-87101-185-9. Item #1859. $23.95

Helping Vulnerable Youths: *Runaway and Homeless Adolescents in the United States, Deborah S. Bass, Principal Investigator.* The book presents the results of an intensive, year-long investigation undertaken by NASW, with support from the Family and Youth Services Bureau, U.S. Department of Health and Human Services.
ISBN: 0-87101-221-9. Item #2219. $18.95

Research on Children, *Shirley Buttrick, Editor.* This special issue of *Social Work Research* focuses on child welfare, child mental health, and family preservation.
ISBN: 0-87101-223-5. Item #2235. $14.95

(Order form on reverse side)

ORDER FORM

Title	Item #	Price	Total
___ Risk and Resilience in Childhood	Item 274X	$35.95	_____
___ Painful Passages	Item 1751	$24.95	_____
___ Caring Families	Item 1859	$23.95	_____
___ Helping Vulnerable Youths	Item 2219	$18.95	_____
___ Research on Children	Item 2235	$14.95	_____
		Subtotal	_____
	+ 10% postage and handling		_____
		Total	_____

❐ I've enclosed my check or money order for $ _____.

❐ Please charge my   ❐ NASW Visa*   ❐ Other Visa   ❐ MasterCard

_____   _____

Credit Card Number   Expiration Date

Signature _____

Use of this card generates funds in support of the social work profession.

Name_____

Address _____

City _____ State/Province _____

Country _____ Zip _____

Phone _____   _____

NASW Member # (if applicable)

(Please make checks payable to NASW Press. Prices are subject to change.)

NASW PRESS

NASW Press
P.O. Box 431
Annapolis JCT, MD 20701
USA

Credit card orders call
1-800-227-3590
(In the Metro Wash., DC, area, call 301-317-8688)
Or fax your order to 301-206-7989
Or e-mail nasw@pmds.com

Visit our Web site at http://www.naswpress.org   RRBI97